The English Gardener
by William Cobbett

THE
ENGLISH GARDENER;

OR,

A TREATISE

On the Situation, Soil, Enclosing and Laying-Out of Kitchen Gardens; *on the* Making and Managing of Hot-Beds and Green-Houses ; and on the Propagation and Cultivation of all sorts of Kitchen-Garden Plants, and of Fruit-Trees whether of the Garden or the Orchard.

And also

On the Formation of Shrubberies and Flower-Gardens ; and on the Propagation and Cultivation of the several sorts of Shrubs and Flowers ; concluding with

A Kalendar,

Giving Instructions relative to the Sowings, Plantings, Prunings, and other labours, to be performed in the Gardens, in each Month of the Year.

BY WILLIAM COBBETT.

" I went by the field of the slothful, and by the vineyard of the man void
" of understanding : and, lo! it was all grown over with thorns, and nettles
" covered the face thereof, and the stone-wall thereof was broken down.
" Then I saw and considered it well : I looked upon it, and received in-
" struction."—Proverbs : Chap. XXIV. Ver. 30.

PRINTED BY B. BENSLEY, ANDOVER,

AND

PUBLISHED BY THE AUTHOR, 183, FLEET STREET, LONDON;
AND SOLD BY ALL BOOKSELLERS.

1829.

CONTENTS.

CHAPTER I.

On the arrangement of the divers matters contained in the subsequent Chapters, and on the method which ought to be pursued in the studying of these matters.

CHAPTER II.

On the Situation, Form and Extent, Enclosing, and Laying-out, of Kitchen-gardens.

CHAPTER III.

On the making and managing of Hot-beds and Green-houses.

CHAPTER IV.

On Propagation and Cultivation in general.

CHAPTER V.

Kitchen-garden Plants, arranged in Alphabetical order, with Directions relative to the Propagation and Cultivation of each sort.

CHAPTER VI.

Fruits. — Propagation, Planting, and Training and Pruning, whether wall-trees, espaliers, or standards, with an Alphabetical List of the several Fruits, and with observations on the Diseases of Fruit-trees.

CHAPTER VII.

The formation of Shrubberies, with a List of Shrubs, and instructions as to the Propagation and Cultivation of each sort; the formation of Flower-gardens, with a List of Flowers, and directions for the Propagation and Cultivation of each sort: a List of Shrubs and Flowers, classed according to their proper uses, or, situations, in the Shrubbery or Flower-garden. Annexed is a Kalendar of the principal sowings, and other work, to be done in each month of the year; and an Index.

THE

ENGLISH GARDENER.

———◆———

CHAPTER I.

On the arrangement of the divers matters contained in the subsequent Chapters, and on the method which ought to be pursued in the studying of those matters.

———

1. BEFORE we begin to study the contents of any book ; that is to say, before we begin to endeavour to obtain a thorough knowledge of those contents, we ought, if possible, to get a clear and neat view of the outline of those contents, and of the purposes to which they are intended to become applicable. To insist, as some authors have done, on the *utility* of a knowledge of the means to obtain garden-plants, fruits, and flowers, would be useless. It is notorious that it is useful to have these things ; and, therefore, all that we have to do, is, to obtain a knowledge of the means of obtaining them in the greatest perfection, and with the least proportionate quantity of

expense or trouble; and also, with the least risk of experiencing a disappointment of our hopes.

2. There must be, of necessity, numerous divisions of the matter, where subjects so numerous are to be treated of : and it is of great advantage to take a view of these several divisions before we enter upon the treatise. And, therefore, in this chapter, I shall endeavour to give the reader this view; so that he will see, not only what he is going to read about; but also the order in which the matter is intended to be brought before him. The SECOND Chapter of the work will describe that which I deem to be the proper *Situation* of a garden ; next, it will treat of the *Soil,* its nature, its preparation, and the general mode of manuring it, and of making provision of manure : next, of the *Form* of the Kitchen-Garden, and also of the extent necessary under different circumstances : next, of the manner of *Enclosing* the Garden, and of the Walls and other Fences applicable to the purpose. The Situation having been fixed on, the Soil prepared, the Form determined on, and the enclosures made, the next thing that will be presented to the reader will be the manner of laying out the ground within the enclosure, whether into plats, borders, or otherwise.

3. The THIRD Chapter will form a sort of Episode, disconnected with the general course of the work. It will treat of the managing of Hot-beds and Greenhouses; that is to say, it will treat of the management of things which are to be produced by artificial heat; and that are cultivated by rules exclusively adapted to this species of gardening. I shall not treat of *Hot-*

houses; the management of those being a science of itself, having nothing to do with gardening in general, and of use to comparatively very few persons. My object will be to make a book of general utility ; to do this, moderate bulk and moderate price are requisites ; and, to have these, the management of hot-houses must be necessarily excluded.

4. The FOURTH Chapter will treat of Propagation and Cultivation in general. First, of the sort of the seed, and of the methods of procuring true seed, and of ascertaining whether it be sound : next, of the manner of harvesting and of preserving seeds : next, of the manner of sowing seeds : next, of transplanting plants : next, of the after cultivation, until the plant be fit for the uses for which it is intended.

5. After these general observations on propagation and cultivation, there will follow, in Chapter V. a complete list, in alphabetical order, of all kitchen-garden plants, including pot-herbs, with particular instructions relative to each plant ; so that, these instructions, together with the reader's previous knowledge respecting propagation and cultivation in general, will leave nothing that will be unknown to him with regard to the kitchen-garden plants and pot-herbs.

6. Next; in Chapter VI. will come the important subject of *Fruits*. This Chapter will treat of the manner of propagating, rearing up, planting, pruning, and cultivating fruit-trees ; whether wall-trees, espaliers, or standards, and whether for the garden or the orchard ;

B 2

also of those plants of inferior size which bring us goose-berries, currants, raspberries, and strawberries. After the instructions which will be given under these heads, and which will include observations on the diseases of fruit trees, and on the manner of curing those diseases, and of protecting the trees against the depredations of birds, vermin, and insects, will come an alphabetical list of fruits, noticing, under each name, any thing peculiar and necessary to be known, respecting the management of the tree or plant.

7. The SEVENTH, and last Chapter, will treat of the formation of Shrubberies and Flower-gardens; will point out the proper shrubs suited to the several possible situations, and the several Flowers desirable to have as ornaments, together with the manner of placing them in the shrubberies or flower-gardens. Under the head of Shrubberies, there will be an alphabetical list of shrubs, with instructions against each relative to its propagation, pruning, and cultivation. The same will follow in the case of Flower-gardens; so that, here also, with the general instructions taken into view, the reader will possess all the information necessary relative to these matters.

8. Having thus obtained a knowledge with respect to what is to be done relative to every plant and tree known in the gardens, the work will conclude with the Kalendar, described in the title-page; a very convenient thing, even for gardeners themselves; and much more convenient for those whose pursuits in life necessarily render it impossible that the garden should be an object of their constant attention. Something depends upon the

situation, and also upon the nature of the ground : for, in some ground, you may safely sow a fortnight earlier ; and, in other ground, a fortnight later, than the fit season for sowing in the general run of ground. Nevertheless, this Kalendar is of great use in all cases ; because, without it, many pieces of necessary work would be wholly omitted. The performance of them would be put off to a season so late, that to perform them would be of no use at all.

9. In the writing of this book, I shall proceed upon the principle, or, rather, the admitted assumption, that the reader is wholly unacquainted with all the matters of which it will treat. On the same principle I have proceeded, in my three grammars ; in my Cottage Economy ; in my Woodlands ; and in every work in which I have attempted to *teach* any thing. Experience has taught me the necessity of proceeding in this way; for, when I have had to apply to books to be my teachers, I have invariably found that the authors proceed upon the notion that the reader only wanted *a little* teaching ; that he understood a great part of the subject, and only wanted information relative to that part which the author happened to think of the greatest importance. By looking on the reader as knowing nothing at all about the matter, the author is led to tell all that he knows. This can do gardeners, and gentlemen who have studied something of gardening, no harm ; while it must be good, and even necessary, to those who have never had an opportunity of paying close attention to the matter. I make no apology for the minuteness with which I shall give my instructions ; for my business is *to teach* that which I know ;

and those who want no teaching, do not want my book. My opinion is, that any man who is so disposed, may become a good gardener by strictly attending to this work. If I knew of any other work so likely to effect this purpose, I should not undertake this. It is useless to know how to write, unless, by the use of that talent, we communicate something useful to others. The reason why books on gardening are read in general with so little benefit, is this ; that they are put together by men (generally speaking, observe,) who, though they understand how to do the thing themselves, and though they very sincerely wish to teach others, are unable to convey their instructions in language easily to be understood ; and easily it must be, to be attended with success ; for, the moment the reader comes to what he cannot understand, he begins to be weary ; and, the third or fourth occurrence of this sort, makes him lay down the book. If he ever take it up again, it is from sheer necessity : and, instead of delight, disgust is likely to be the end of the attempt.

10. The far greater part of persons who possess gardens, and who occasionally partake in the management of them, really know very little about the matter. They possess no *principles* relating to the art : they do things pretty well, because they have seen them done before ; but, for want of proceeding upon principle ; that is to say, for the want of knowing the reasons for doing the several things that are done in the garden, they are always in a state of uncertainty : they know nothing of the causes, and, therefore, are always rather guessing at, than relying upon, the effects. I shall endeavour, in

every case, to give a good reason for that which I recommend; and, when once the learner knows the reason for that which he does, he may be said to have learnt it, and not before.   Lord Bacon is well known to have taken great delight in horticulture as well as in agriculture; and Mr. Tull, in his famous work on the Horse-hoeing husbandry, relates, that his Lordship, who had made a vast collection of books on these subjects, had them, one day, all collected together, omitting not one; had the pile carried into the court yard, and there set *on fire;* saying, " In all these books I find *no principles;* they " can, therefore, be of no use to any man; he must get " principles for himself, or he must go on till the ele- " ments have instructed him; and, in either case, he can " stand in no need of books like these."

11. As to the manner of studying this book of mine, I would advise the reader to begin by reading it all through, *from the beginning to the end;* and not to stop here or there, to learn one part of it at a time.   If he were to do this three times over, it would only require the time frequently devoted to three or four volumes of a miserable novel.   This would give him an enlarged general view of the whole matter; and he might then apply himself to any particular part of which he might more immediately stand in need of knowledge in detail. This is not a work of that kind which would require to be transcribed to be firmly fixed in the mind: three careful readings from the beginning to the end might suffice, until the reader came to put the instructions in practice; and then he would go into the detail, being particularly attentive not to omit any part of that which

the book recommended him to do; for, a part omitted, may, and frequently does, render all that is done of no use. MR. TULL very justly complained that those who condemned his scheme (and it is curious that VOLTAIRE was one of these), and asserted that they had *tried* it and found it to fail; always omitted some one thing, which omission rendered the other operations abortive. MR. TULL said, " Their great error is in the mis-use of the word IT: " they say they have tried IT: they have tried something, " to be sure; but they have not tried my scheme." VOLTAIRE, in one of his letters (I forget to whom), says, as nearly as I can recollect the words, " J'ai *essayé* le " fameux système de Monsieur Tull de l'Angletèrre, et, " je vous avoue que je *le* trouve *abominable*." *   He goes on, however, to show most satisfactorily, that it was not the system of Mr. Tull that he had tried; for he says, " Les intervalles, ou les espaces entre les sillons, furent, " dès le mois de Mai, remplis de mauvaises herbes, qui " ont bientôt étouffé le blé." †   So that, he had *tried it* after the manner of those whom MR. TULL had complained of in England; that is to say, he had made the ridges, sowed the rows of wheat, all in very exact proportions as to distance and every thing else; but he had not ploughed or horse-hoed the intervals; whereas that operation was the very soul of the system.

12. Thus it is with but too many persons, who complain of having failed, though, as they allege, they have

---

* I have tried the famous system of MR. TULL of England, and I confess to you that I find it to be abominable.

† The intervals, or the spaces, between the ridges, were, from the month of May, full of weeds, which quickly smothered the wheat.

pursued the instructions given them. They do not pursue those instructions *except in part:* therefore, I beg leave to caution the reader against falling into this error ; a caution particularly necessary to those who leave the performance to others : it is useless to see a part done, if you neglect to see the other parts done : with this caution, as necessary as any that I can possibly give, I conclude this introductory chapter.

CHAPTER II.

On the Situation, Soil, Form and Extent, Enclosing, and Laying-out, of Kitchen-Gardens.

SITUATION.

13. IF one could have what one wished, in point of situation, from the wall on the north side of the garden, after a little flat of about a rod wide, one would have a gentle slope towards the south, about thirty feet in width. The remainder of the ground, to the wall on the south side of the garden, one would have on a true level. The gentle slope contributes to early production ; and though it is attended with the inconvenience of washing, from heavy rains, that inconvenience is much more than made up for by the advantage attending the circumstance of earliness. I recollect the ancient kitchen-garden, which had been that of the monks, at Waverley Abbey. It lay full to the south, of course ; it had a high hill to the back of it, and that hill covered with pretty lofty trees. The wall, on this north side of the garden, was from twelve to fourteen feet high, built partly of flints, and partly of the sand stone, which is found in abundance in the neighbourhood, and it was about three feet through, even at the top. The ground of which the garden con-sisted had been the sloping foot of a hill, taking in a part of the meadow that came after the hill, and lay between it and the river Wey. A flat of about twenty

feet wide had been made on the side of the hill, and, at the back of this flat, the wall was erected. After the flat, towards the south, began the slope; at the end of the slope began the level ground, which grew more and more moist as it approached the river. At the foot of the garden, there ran a rivulet, coming from a fish-pond, and at a little distance from that, emptying itself into the river. The hill itself was a bed of sand; therefore, the flat, at the back of which the north wall stood; that is to say, the wall on the north side of the garden; this flat must have been *made* ground. The slope must have been partly made, otherwise it would have been too sandy.

14. This was the finest situation for a kitchen-garden that I ever saw. It was wholly torn to pieces about fifty years ago; the wall pulled down; the garden made into a sort of lawn, and the lower part of it, when I saw the spot about three years ago, a coarse, rushey meadow, all the drains which formerly took away the oozings from the hill, having been choaked up or broken up; and that spot, where the earliest birds used to sing, and where prodigious quantities of the finest fruits used to be borne, was become just as sterile, and as ill-looking a piece of ground, short of a mere common or neglected field, as I ever set my eyes on. That very spot where I had seen bushels of haut-boy strawberries, such as I have never seen from that day to this; that very spot, the precise locality of which, it took me (so disfigured was the place!) the better part of an hour to ascertain, was actually part of a sort of swampy meadow, producing sedgy grass and rushes. This most secluded and beau-

tiful spot was given away by the ruthless tyrant, Henry
the Eighth, to one of the basest and greediest of his
cormorant courtiers, Sir William Fitzwilliams; it
became afterwards, according to Grose, the property of
the family of Orby Hunter; from that family it passed
into the hands of a Sir Robert Rich, much about fifty
years ago. The monastery had been founded by Giffard,
Bishop of Winchester, who brought to inhabit it the
first community of Cistercian monks that were settled in
England. He endowed the convent at his own expense;
gave it the manor and estate, and gave it also the great
tythes of the parish of Farnham, in which it lies. A
lofty sand-hill sheltered it to the north; others, in the
form of a crescent sheltered it to the east. It was well
sheltered to the west; open only to the south, and a
little to the south-west. A valley let in the river Wey at
one end of this secluded spot, and let it out at the other
end. Close under the high hill on the north side, a good
mansion-house had been built by the proprietors who
succeeded the monks; and these proprietors, though they
had embellished the place with serpentine walks and
shrubberies, had had the good taste to leave the ancient
gardens, the grange, and as much of the old walls of the
convent as was standing; and, upon the whole, it was
one of the most beautiful and interesting spots in the
world. Sir Robert Rich tore every thing to atoms,
except the remaining walls of the convent itself. He
even removed the high hill at the back of the valley;
actually carried it away in carts and wheel-barrows;
built up a new-fashioned mansion-house with grey bricks,
made the place look as bare as possible; and, in defiance

of nature, and of all the hoar of antiquity, made it very little better than the vulgar box of a cockney.

15. I must be excused for breaking out into these complaints. It was the spot where I first began to learn to work, or, rather, where I first began to eat fine fruit, in a garden ; and, though I have now seen and observed upon as many fine gardens as any man in England, I have never seen a garden equal to that of WAVERLEY. Ten families, large as they might be, including troops of servants (who are no churls in this way), could not have consumed the fruit produced in that garden. The peaches, nectarines, apricots, fine plums, never failed ; and, if the workmen had not lent a hand, a fourth part of the produce never could have been got rid of. SIR ROBERT RICH built another kitchen-garden, and did not spare expense ; but he stuck the walls up in a field, un-sheltered by hills and trees ; and though it was twice the size of the monks' garden, I dare say it has never yielded a tenth part of the produce.

16. It is not every where that spots like this are to be found ; and we must take the best that we can get, never forgetting, however, that it is most miserable taste to seek to poke away the kitchen-garden, in order to get it out of sight. If well managed, nothing is more beautiful than the kitchen-garden : the earliest blossoms come there : we shall in vain seek for flowering shrubs in March, and early in April, to equal the peaches, nectarines, apricots, and plums ; late in April, we shall find nothing to equal the pear and the cherry ; and, in May, the dwarf, or

espalier, apple-trees, are just so many immense garlands of carnations. The walks are unshaded : they are not greasy or covered with moss, in the spring of the year, like those in the shrubberies : to watch the progress of the crops is by no means unentertaining to any rational creature ; and the kitchen-garden gives you all this long before the ornamental part of the garden affords you any thing worth looking at. Therefore, I see no reason for placing the kitchen-garden in some out-of-the-way place, at a distance from the mansion-house, as if it were a mere necessary evil, and unworthy of being viewed by the owner. In the time of fruiting, where shall we find any thing much more beautiful to behold than a tree loaded with cherries, peaches, or apricots, but particularly the two latter ? It is curious enough, that people decorate their chimney-pieces with imitations of these beautiful fruits, while they seem to think nothing at all of the originals hanging upon the tree, with all the elegant accompaniments of flourishing branches, buds, and leaves.

17. We must take, as I said before, the best ground that we have ; and, for my part, I would take it almost any where, except in the front of a mansion-house. It must absolutely be open to the south : well-sheltered, if it can be, from the north and from the east ; but open to the south it must be, or you can have neither fine wall-fruit, nor early crops of garden-plants. If you can have the slope, such as I have described it to have been at Waverley, it is easy to make a flat before the face of the wall, on the north side of the garden : but, to have the whole of a garden upon a slope is by no means desirable ; for, however gentle the slope may be, the water will run

off; and, in certain cases, it is absolutely necessary that the water should not run away; but have time to soak gently into the ground. I have had great opportunity of acquiring knowledge in this respect. Part of my ground at Kensington forms a very gentle slope. The soil of this slope is as good, both at top and bottom, as any ground in the world; but I have always perceived, that seeds never rise there with the same alacrity and the same vigour that they do upon the level part, though there the soil is much inferior. This is particularly the case with regard to strawberries, which will grow, blow like a garland, and even bear pretty numerously, on the side of a bank where scarcely any moisture can lodge; but which I have never seen produce large and fine fruit except upon the level. The same may be said of almost every garden plant and tree; and, therefore, if I could avoid it, I would always have some part of a garden not upon the slope. Slopes are excellent for early broccoli, early cabbages, winter spinage, onions to stand the winter, artichokes to come early, early peas, early beans, and various other things; but there ought to be some part of the garden upon a true level; for, when the month of June comes, that is the part of the garden which will be flourishing.

18. As to shelter, hills, buildings, lofty trees, all serve for the purpose; but the lofty trees ought not to stand too near. They ought not to shade by any means; and none of their leaves ought to drop into the garden. Leaves from such trees, blown into the garden by high winds, are merely a temporary inconvenience; but shade would do injury, though, perhaps, if not too deep, coun-

terbalanced by the warmth and the shelter that the trees would afford.

19. Before I quit this subject of *Situation*, I cannot refrain from attempting to describe one kitchen-garden in England, to behold which is well worth the trouble and expense of a long journey, to any person who has a taste in this way : I mean that of MR. HENRY DRUMMOND, at ALDBURY, in the county of Surrey. This garden is, in my opinion, nearly perfection, as far as relates to situation, and form. It is an oblong square ; the wall, on the north side, is close under a hill ; that hill is crowned with trees which do not shade the garden. There is a flat, or terrace, in the front of this wall. This terrace consists, first of a border for the fruit trees to grow in, next of a broad and beautiful gravel walk, then, if I recollect rightly, of a strip of short grass. About the middle of the length, there is a large basin supplied with water from a spring coming out of the hill, and always kept full. The terrace is supported, on the south side of it, by a wall that rises no higher than the top of the earth of the terrace. Then comes another flat, running all the way along ; this flat is a broad walk, shaded completely by two rows of yew trees, the boughs of which form an arch over it : so that, here, in this kitchen-garden, there are walks for summer as well as for winter : on the gravel walk you are in the sun, sheltered from every wind ; and, in the yew-tree walk, you are completely shaded from the sun in the hottest day in summer. From the yew-tree walk the ground slopes gently down towards the brook which runs from Sheer through Aldbury, down to Chilworth ; where, after supplying the

paper-mills and powder-mills, it falls into the river Wey. The two end walls of the garden have plantations of trees at the back of them ; so that, except that here is no ground, except the terrace, which is not upon the slope, this garden, which is said to have been laid out by SIR PHILIP EVELYN for some member of the family of HOWARD, is every thing that one could wish. The mansion-house stands at a little distance opposite the garden, on the other side of the brook ; and, though all the grounds round about are very pretty, this kitchen-garden constitutes the great beauty of the place. Here, too, though EVELYN *might* have *revived*, this charming spot was chosen, the garden was *made*, and the cloyster of yew-trees planted, by the *monks* of the Priory of St. Austin, founded here in the reign of Richard I., and the estates of which Priory were given by the bloody 'yrant to SIR ANTHONY BROWN.

SOIL.

20. THE plants and trees which grow in a garden, prefer, like most others, the best soil that is to be found ; and the best is, good fat loam at the top, with a bottom that suffers the wet gently to escape. But, we must take that which we happen to have, avoiding, if we possibly can, a stiff clay or a gravel, not only as a top-soil, but as a bottom-soil also, unless at a very great distance. Oak trees love clay, and the finest of that sort of timber grows on such land ; but, no trees that grow in a garden love clay, and they are still less fond of gravel, which always burns in summer time, and which sucks up the manure, and carries it away out of the reach of the roots of the

plants. Chalk, if it be too near to the top, is not good; but it is better than clay or gravel; and by the means of trenching, of which I shall presently speak, chalky soil may make a very good garden; for chalk never burns in summer, and is never wet in winter; that is to say, it never causes stagnant water. It absorbs it, and retains it, until drawn upwards by the summer sun. And hence it is that the chalky downs are fresh and green, while even the meadows in the valleys are burned up so as to be perfectly brown. No tree rejects chalk; chalk is not apt to produce canker in trees; and, upon the whole, it is not a bad soil even for a garden, while, if it have a tolerable depth of earth on the top of it, it is, taking all things together, the pasturage, the sound roads, the easy cultivation in all weathers, the healthiness which it invariably gives to cattle of all sorts, the very best land in the world for a farm; and I, who have, perhaps, seen as many farms and home-steds as any man in England, and in as many different situations, never saw such fine, such beautiful, such generally productive, such neat and really rich farms, as in countries consisting entirely of chalk, excepting the mere bottoms of the valleys along which run the brooks and the rivers, and here, too, are the finest of all the watered meadows that I ever saw.

21. I am by no means, therefore, afraid of chalk, especially as houses are seldom built, and kitchen-gardens seldom wanted on chalk *hills*. In chalky countries, kitchen-gardens are generally wanted on the sides of such hills, where there is generally considerable depth of soil above the chalk; in which case there can seldom be better soil for a kitchen-garden, if the proper preparations

be made; and of those preparations I am now about to speak.

22. Having fixed upon the spot for the garden, the next thing is to prepare the ground. I shall suppose it to be part of a field, or of a coppice: in the former case, there must be ploughing and harrowing to destroy the roots of all weeds most effectually: in the latter, complete grubbing, so as to leave no roots of timber-trees or underwood in the ground; and then must come an operation absolutely indispensible to the making of a good garden; that is to say, *trenching* to the depth of two feet at the least; and, as asparagus, and some other things, send their roots down to a much greater depth than two feet, the whole ought to be trenched to the depth of three feet, with a spit of digging at the bottom of each trench, which would move the ground to the depth of three feet nine inches, or thereabouts.

23. According to the common manner of trenching, the top-soil would be turned down to the bottom of the trench, and the bottom soil brought up to the top; so that, you have at the top, if the land be chalky, a bed of sheer chalk; if clayey, a bed of clay, and so on; and, in the very best of land, you bring up to the top, matter which has never seen the sun, and which, in spite of every thing that you can do in the way of tillage as well as in the way of manure, will require many years before it will become ground fit to bear crops in the manner that it ought to bear them. I have taken away, sometimes, a bank which separated two fields: I have dug, manured, and done every thing in my power to enrich

the land on which the bank stood; but have never, in any instance, been able to make it, even at the end of several years, equal to the land adjoining it. The truth is, this ground had been so long out of the reach of the influence of the elements, the sun, the frosts, the snows, the air, the rains and the dews, that it was not fit for performing that which earth will not perform without the assistance of these elements.

24. Therefore, in the work of trenching, *the top soil must be kept at the top.* This is to be done with the greatest facility imaginable, and with comparatively very little additional expense. Having, in THE WOODLANDS, given full directions for the performing of this work, I have here little more to do than to repeat that which I have said there, accompanying my instructions with an explanatory plate. This I may lawfully do, it being only purloining from myself; this method never having been pointed out by any other writer on the subject, as far as I have observed; nor have I perceived that even the thought ever entered the mind of any other man. Yet the reader will perceive, that, without pursuing this method, it would be impossible to make a good garden in some kinds of soil.

25. The piece of ground that I propose to be made into a garden, will be, from outside to outside, ten rods wide and fifteen rods long. This piece of ground ought to be marked into *strips*, or *lifts*, each a rod wide, in the manner described in the opposite page. This division into narrow strips takes place, because the earth which comes out of the first trench must go to fill up the last trench; and, therefore, in this case, there would be

a b c d	B	D	F	H	K	M	O	Q	S
A	C	E	G	I	L	N	P	R	T

pretty nearly a hundred cart-loads of earth to be carted, or wheeled, from one end of the piece to the other : whereas, by proceeding in the way of strips, you fill up the trench with hardly any wheeling at all. The ground being laid out in strips, you begin at a, and take off all the top earth of a cross strip two feet wide ; and you wheel that earth to the end of the further strip at S. The little cross strip a is marked out by straining a line across the great strip, and making a chop with the spade. When you have taken away the top earth of a, mark out the cross strip b, and wheel away its top earth also to the same place as before, laying this top earth altogether in one round snug heap, just without the limits of the ground at S. You have now got the top earth away from the two first trenches a and b. You next take out the bottom earth of the trench a, down to the depth of three feet, and you wheel that away and put it into a round and snug heap, distinct from the other heap, at the end of the further strip at S. You have now the trench a quite empty down to three feet deep : you then move the earth with a spade, or other tool, to the depth of nine inches at the bottom of the trench a : then you take the bottom earth of the trench b, and keep putting it into the trench a, until you have gone to the depth of three feet ; then you dig or move the earth nine inches deep again at the bottom of the trench b : then you take the top earth from the trench c, and lay it upon the top of the trench a. The trench b remains empty all this time, and you have to toss the top earth of c across the trench b in order to place it upon the top of the trench a. The trench a is now finished : it has got the top earth of c on its top, and all its contents have been completely moved to the depth of three feet nine inches. You next take the bottom earth of c and turn it into the trench b; and when you have moved or dug the bottom of c in the same manner as you did that of a and b, you take the top earth of the trench d and put it upon the top of the trench b; and thus you go on till you arrive at A. When you arrive at A, you will find yourself with an empty trench at the end, and with a trench with no top earth upon it, next to that at the end. You, therefore, now begin the second strip at C: you take the top earth of the first two feet wide and put it upon top of the trench next to the end one of the last strip: you then take the bottom earth of the first two feet wide in this second strip and put it into the bottom of your last trench at A; you then take the top earth of the second trench at C and put it on the last trench at A. Thus the whole of the first strip is completed; and you have again, as you had at a and b, an empty trench at the end, and the trench next to it with the top earth taken off. You then proceed with the rest of this strip as you did with that of the other, until you come to B, when you turn in at D, and do just the same as you did at C. You then go on to E, when you get there you turn in again at G, and thus you proceed till you come to S, when you will find yourself with the last trench completely empty, and with the next to the last wanting the top earth. These are both ready for you. You take the heap of bottom earth, which came out of a, and put it into your empty trench; then you take the heap of top earth, which was wheeled from a and b, and lay it on upon the two last trenches; and thus all the ground will have been completely moved to three feet nine inches deep, every part of it will have changed its place;

and you will find it to stand a foot or fifteen inches higher than the ground in the neighbourhood of it. Great care should be taken to lay the strips out by straight lines. The best way is to divide each end of the piece into rods by sticking up sticks; and then to mark out the lines from one end of the piece to the other. If only very common care be taken, it is next to impossible not to have straight lines. Equal care should be taken that the trenches themselves be of equal width, and that the lines which mark them out be true and parallel; but this is so easy a matter, a matter that it would be a shame, indeed, for any one to pretend difficulty in the performance of it.

26. I have now to speak on the subject of manures as adapted to a garden. Different plants require different sorts of manure, and different quantities. It is certainly true that *dung* is not the best sort of manure for a garden : it may be mixed with other matter, and, if very well rotted, and almost in an earthy state, it may not be amiss; but, if otherwise used, it certainly makes the garden vegetables coarse and gross compared to what they are when raised with the aid of ashes, lime, chalk, rags, salt, and composts. Besides, dung creates innumerable weeds : it brings the seeds of the weeds along with it into the garden, unless it have first been worked in a hot-bed, the heat of which destroys the vegetative quality of the seeds.

27. A great deal more is done by the fermentation of manures than people generally imagine : the shovellings of grass and turf from the sides of roads; weeds or roots of weeds raked off from a field; these laid in a great heap and

turned frequently during the year, having ashes (of wood) lime, rags, salt in a small proportion, mixed with the, rest of the heap, make excellent manure. Provision of manure like this ought to be made, one heap being always ready to succeed another. As to salt, however, which is now so easy to be obtained, and which is, perhaps, the cheapest manure of all, care must be taken that the proportion of it be not too great. About thirty bushels, perhaps, would be enough for the whole extent of the garden at one time; and the best way would be, at the outset, to put this thirty bushels into a heap of stuff consisting of about a hundred cart-loads, mix the whole well together by turning it several times, and manure the ground all over before the planting or sowing is begun. Afterwards new heaps would be formed, and the same proportion of salt might be used. Any other general manuring might not be wanted : the hot-beds would produce a great deal; and even with this hot-bed dung, some salt might be mixed ; not, however, with a view of destroying worms, as some people imagine it to do; for it will destroy worms only when it is used in sufficient quantities to destroy plants, which it will do most effectually and most speedily, if, in its unmixed state, it come at their roots. I shall, hereafter, have to speak about manuring for different plants ; and having made these general observations on the subject, I now proceed to speak of the form and extent of the garden.

FORM AND EXTENT OF THE GARDEN.

28. It is desirable to have as much wall facing the south as you possibly can Have, without incurring inconveniences which would attend a long narrow slip. At least, it is desirable to have a good portion of wall facing in that direction. If the garden be already formed, you must keep what you have got; but if you have to choose, it ought to be more extensive from east to west than from north to south: an oblong square is the proper form; and it very conveniently happens that the proportions ought to be much about those of one of the sides of this book, when neatly bound and lying upon the table, which is five in length, and three in breadth; that is to say, a piece of ground to resemble it in form, would contain five feet in length for every three feet in breadth. I am about to recommend a garden to be walled in, in the first place, and then surrounded with a hedge. The dimensions within the walls I recommend to be (casting away a trifling fraction) two hundred and fifteen feet long, and one hundred and thirty-two feet wide; that is to say, thirteen rods long, at sixteen feet and a half to the rod, and eight rods wide, the area being one hundred and four square rods; sixteen rods short of three quarters of an acre.

29. The walls (of the construction of which I shall speak presently) would be half thrown away in point of horticultural utility, unless there were a piece of garden ground all round them on the outside, and that piece of garden ground protected by an effectual fence. Of this

fence, I shall also presently speak ; but, to conclude the subject of dimensions, the piece of ground between the wall and the outer fence, ought to be a clear rod wide, which would add forty-two rods of ground to the hundred and four enclosed within the walls, making, in the whole, of garden ground, a hundred and fifty-six square rods, being fourteen square rods short of a statute acre. I know that some noblemen and gentlemen find twice or three times this quantity of land insufficient for supplying their houses, though in each house there is but one family ; but, if these noblemen and gentlemen were first to take a look, at any time of the year, at a market garden in the parish of Fulham, and then go immediately and take a look over their own gardens ; they would clearly perceive the cause of the insufficiency of their own. In the former, they would see that there was not a single square yard of ground tenanted by weeds, cabbage-stumps, or plants of lettuce, and other things, suffered to stand and go uselessly to seed ; and, in the latter, they would find all these in great abundance, and large spaces of ground left, apparently as if of no use at all. The quantity of kitchen vegetables which a hundred and forty-six rods of ground is capable of producing in the course of a year, would astonish any man not accustomed to observe and to calculate upon the subject. Many a gardener, with a smaller quantity of land, sends a hundred cart-loads of produce to the market in the course of a year, exclusive of plums, cherries, currants, gooseberries, raspberries, and strawberries. To speak of cabbages, for instance, a square rod of ground will contain about a hundred ; and when are a hundred cabbages to be eaten in almost any family ? Six square rods of winter spinage are more than sufficient to afford a constant supply for even the largest of families. Peas and beans require room; but they are not long upon the ground, and other crops are coming on between them. In short, long experience and observation has convinced me that a large garden is of very little use; and that, while it requires a great deal more labour than a small one to keep it in any thing like good order, it is never made to produce so much. The manure has to be scattered over a larger space; the idle ground is by no means idle in producing mischief: the weeds that are suffered to remain on it produce and nourish and breed up innumerable families of snails and slugs, wood-lice, grubs, and all those things which destroy crops. The weeds, when dug in, generate these mischievous vermin, and furnish them with food at the same time. The grass that is turned in breeds the wireworm; so that, the idle ground not only does no good, but produces a great deal of mischief, while the extent of the garden is really a valid pretence for the employment of a great number of hands.

ENCLOSING.

30. UNDER this head we are first to speak of the walls, which ought to be twelve feet high, two feet thick to the surface of the ground, and nine inches from the ground to the top, with a jam coming out six inches from the wall on the outside; and these jams ought not to be more than eight or ten feet apart. This would give a wall quite smooth in the inside of the garden; and, on

the outside, there would be space for a good large wall-tree between every two jams. The top, or coping, of the wall, ought to consist of semicircular bricks, which should be put on in the firmest and best manner, and the joints well grouted or cemented. When I come to speak of the manner of preserving the blossoms and young fruit of wall trees from the effects of frost and other severe weather, I shall have to say something more about the construction of a particular part of the wall : at present it will be sufficient to add, that it ought to be made of good, solid, smoothly-finished and well-burned bricks ; that the mortar ought to be of the best ; that the joints ought to be uniform in size and well filled with mortar : and that the wall ought to be erected, not later than the month of June, in order for it to become thoroughly dry in every part before the arrival of frost. In making the foundation, great care must be taken to go lower down than the depth of the trenching, in order to come at the solid and immoveable earth.

31. As was observed before, the use of one half of this wall, for horticultural purposes, would be lost, unless wall-trees could be placed on both sides of it ; and wall-trees cannot be placed on the outside, with any chance of utility, unless there be an *effectual fence* to protect the trees on that wall. I knew an old gentleman, one of whose garden walls separated the garden from a meadow, which was unprotected except by a common hedge. Those persons of the village who were fond of wall-fruit, who had none of their own, and who were young enough to climb walls, used to leave him a very undue proportion of his fruit, and that not of the best quality. He, there-

fore, separated a strip of the meadow from the rest by a little fence, very convenient for getting over; turned this strip, which lay along against the wall, into kitchen-garden ground, planted excellent fruit-trees against the wall, trained them and cultivated them properly; and thus, by furnishing his juvenile neighbours with onions for their bread and cheese, as well as fruit for their dessert, ever after he kept the produce of the inside of the garden for himself, generally observing (as he once particularly did to me) that he was not so unreasonable as to expect to have any of the produce of the exterior garden.

32. But there is no necessity for making these sort of diversions, if you can, with the greatest ease imaginable, effectually protect the fortress against every species of attack. This protection is to be obtained by a hedge made of hawthorn, black thorn; or, still better, with honey locust, the thorns of the latter being just so many needles of about an inch and a half, or two inches long, only stouter than a needle and less brittle. The space between the wall and the hedge ought to be a clear rod, allowing, besides, three feet for the hedge. This hedge ought to be planted in the following manner. The plants being first sown in beds, and then put into a nursery, ought to be taken thence when their stems are about the thickness of the point of your fore-finger. They ought to be as equal as possible in point of size; because, if one be weaker than the rest, they subdue it; there comes a low place in the hedge; that low place becomes a gap; and a hedge with a gap in it, is, in fact, no fence at all, any more than a wall with an open door in it is a pro-

tection to a house. Having got the plants ready; or, rather, *before* they be taken up out of the ground, you prepare the place to receive them.' You make a ditch six feet wide, at the top, and two and a half wide at the bottom. I suppose the ground to be trenched to the width of eighteen feet from the wall. You take all the good earth from the top of the place that is to be the ditch, and lay it upon the trenched ground to the extent of two feet wide, which will make a very good and deep bed of earth for the plants which are to form the hedge to grow in. Then the ditch ought to be dug out to the depth of three feet, and shovelled out very clean and smooth at the bottom. This bottom earth of the ditch must be carried away; for it would not do to throw it up into the border. If it be convenient, the slope of the bank ought to be covered with turf, well beaten on, and in the autumn; because, if put on in the spring, the grass would be likely to die. If not convenient to get turf, this slope ought to be thickly sown with grass seeds from a hay-loft; and, in both cases, this slope of the bank ought to be hung very regularly with dead bushes, fastened to the bank by little pegs. This bank and ditch alone, if the bushes were well hung and fastened on, would be no bad protection : few boys, or young fellows, would venture, particularly by night, to take a jump over a ditch of six feet, with about two feet of elevation on the bank ; but the hedge, in addition to this ditch and bank, renders the storming literally impossible, except with the assistance of facines and scaling ladders, which are munitions that the besiegers of gardens are very seldom provided with. To return now to the planting of the hedge, I entirely disapprove of great numbers of plants employed for this purpose. If the plants stand too close to each other, they never can be strong : they never get stout stems : the hedge is weak at bottom ; and the hedge can never be what it would be if fewer and stronger plants were put in. The time of planting is any where between September and April. The plants, when taken up, should have all the fibres taken from their roots with a sharp knife, and their main roots shortened to the length of about six inches ; then they should be planted with great care, the earth put in very finely about the roots, and, every plant fastened well in the ground by the foot. The earth should be then made smooth after the treading, and the plants immediately cut down to within a foot of the ground. The distance that the plants should stand from each other ought to be about fifteen inches, and the row of plants ought to stand at about a foot from the edge of the bank. The plants should be kept perfectly clear from weeds all the summer, which is very easily effected by two or three hoeings. If plants be plentiful, and you desire to have an extraordinarily thick hedge, put in two rows of plants, one row eighteen inches from the other, and the plants of one row placed opposite the middle of the intervals in the other row. The plants will make long and strong shoots the first summer. The next spring cut them down to within an inch of the ground. Go over them in June, when they will have made considerable shoots, and cut off all the shoots close to the stem, except the two strongest of each plant. Let them go on through another year, and these two shoots will then be about five feet high. Then, in winter, take one of the shoots of each plant, and *plash* it close to the bottom; that is to say, bend it down longwise the hedge, and give it a cut on the upper side about two inches from the stem; cut off the top of it so as to leave the remainder a foot long; bend it down to the ground, making it lie as close as possible to the stems of the neighbouring plant, and fasten it to the ground with two pegs. When you have done this all the way along, there will be one plash for every interval between the stems of the plants. When this is done, cut down the upright shoots, which you have not plashed down, to within four inches of the bottom; or, rather, to within an inch or so of that part of the stem out of which the plashed shoot issues. The next October, that is to say, at the end of the fourth summer, you will have a complete, efficient, and beautiful fence. This fence will want topping and clipping, in order to keep it of uniform height, and smooth on the sides. You may let it go to what height you please; but, in order to have a hedge thick at the bottom, you must trim the hedge in such a way as for the outsides of the bottom of it not to be *dripped* by the upper parts of the hedge. This is a very important matter; for, if the bottom of the hedge be hollow, holes are easily made in it, and it soon becomes no fence at all.

33. If the hedge be made of honey locusts, two rows of plants are better than one, the distances being the same as before-mentioned. These do not do so well for *plashing* as the hawthorn or black thorn; but they send out numerous side-shoots, and these very strong. These locusts should not be cut down till the end of the autumn after planting; or they may be cut down the next spring, and close to the ground. Each will then send up three

or four stout shoots. When these have grown through the summer, take out any little weak shoots, close to the stem, and cut down the stout ones within three or four inches of the ground. Out of these stems will come such quantities of shoots, that the fence will be complete in a very short time, and will only want trimming and clipping. The whole of the space between the two rows will be filled up by the side shoots ; and the hedge will be quite impassible by any animal bigger, at any rate, than a rat or a cat ; and, besides all the rest, the foliage is so very fine, that even as an ornament, it would be desirable to have it as a hedge.

34. With regard to the height of this hedge, it might be six or seven feet ; but not higher; for, if too high, it would keep the sun from part of the wall on the south side of the garden. If higher, it would give more shelter, indeed ; but then this benefit would be over-balanced by the injury done in the way of shade. By the means of a hedge of this sort, you not only secure the use of the outsides of your walls ; but you obtain security for the produce of the inside. For gardeners may scold as long and as vehemently as they please, and law-makers may enact as long as they please, mankind will never look upon taking fruit in an orchard, or a garden, as *felony*, nor even as a *serious trespass*. Besides, there are such things as *boys*, and every considerate man will recollect, that he himself was once a boy. So that, if you have a mind to have for your own exclusive use what you grow in your garden, you must do one of two things ; resort to terrors and punishments, that will make you detested by your neighbours, or provide an insurmountable fence.

This prevents *temptation*, in all cases dangerous, and particularly in that of forbidden fruit. Resolve, therefore, to share the produce of your garden with the boys of the whole neighbourhood ; or, to keep it for your own use by a fence that they cannot get through, over, or under. Six feet is no great height ; but in the way of *fence*, four feet of good thorn-hedge will keep the boldest boy from trees loaded with fine ripe peaches ; and, if it will do *that*, nothing further need be said in its praise ! The height is nothing ; but, unless the assailant have wings, he must be content with feasting his eyes ; for, if he attempt to *climb*, he receives the penalty upon the spot ; and he retreats as the fox did from the grapes, only with pain of body in addition to that of a disappointed longing. I really (recollecting former times) feel some remorse in thus plotting against the poor fellows ; but the worst of it is, they will not be content with fair play : they will have the *earliest* in the season, and the *best*, as long as the season lasts ; and, therefore, I must, however reluctantly, shut them out altogether.

85. By the time that the wall-trees begin to produce any thing of a crop, the hedge will become an effectual fence : the latter will go on providing protection as the trees go on in making provision for fruit. The ditch and the bank should be attended to during this time. If the earth moulder down, it should be put up again : any holes or washings that appear in the bank should be regularly stopped, and the earth carefully replaced every autumn : the prunings and clippings should be regularly and carefully performed, once every winter, and once every summer, about the middle of the month of July.

This summer clipping must be earlier or later, according to the season, or to the climate : but it should take place just before the starting of the *Midsummer shoot.* All trees shoot twice in the year : the shoot that comes out in the spring ends about Midsummer, and then begins another shoot that comes out of the end of it; which is about one third and sometimes about one half, smaller than the spring shoot, and the pruning or clipping should take place just before this new shoot comes out : this operation causes many new and small shoots to come forth, and gives the hedge a very beautiful appearance ; and also makes it much thicker than it otherwise would be. The seed of the black thorn is a little sloe, and not easily to be obtained in any quantity : its leaf is not so beautiful as that of the hawthorn ; but its wood is stronger, and its thorns a great deal more formidable. A holly hedge only requires more patience ; and we should recollect that it is *evergeen.:* and as effectual, in a fence, as either of our thorns ; for its leaves are so full of sharp prickles, that no boy will face a holly hedge of any degree of thickness. To have such a hedge, you must gather the berries in autumn, keep them in damp sand for a year ; then sow them in November, and, when they come up in the spring, keep the bed carefully weeded, not only then, but all through the summer ; let them stand in this bed another summer ; then transplant them in rows in a nursery of rich ground ; there let them stand for two or three years ; then plant them for the hedge at the same distances, and in the same manner, as directed for the honey locusts ; then, when they have stood a year thus, cut them down nearly close to the ground, which will bring three or four shoots out of each plant ;

and, with a little topping and side-pruning, carefully performed, they will, in about five years after being planted, form a very beautiful and effectual fence. Neither of the thorns is raised much more quickly; and certainly there is no comparison for such a purpose between an evergreen and a deciduous tree. And, there is this further advantage with regard to the holly, that it will flourish in any soil, from the dryest and most arid bank, to the wettest and sourest clay; and as to duration, as a plant, nothing but the yew-tree equals the holly.

LAYING-OUT.

35. HAVING now given instructions relative to the Situation, the Soil, Form, and Extent, and the Enclosing of the garden, there remains to speak, in this Chapter, only of the laying of it out into plats, borders, paths, and walks. A judicious distribution of the ground is a great matter; for, if any part of it be awkward to get at, great additional labour is occasioned; and, if there be not the proper quantity of paths and walks, there must be great trampling of the ground, and very great inconveniences of various sorts. The outer garden, that is to say, the garden between the hedge and the wall, will not require much attention in the making of paths: the whole of it will be land pretty constantly under cultivation, to within about four or five feet of the wall; and a path there, that is to say, at that distance from the wall, trodden out upon the common ground, and just sufficient to pass along for the purpose of managing the trees which are against the wall, will be sufficient.

36. But, with regard to the garden itself, where the width is considerable, great care must be taken that every part of the ground can be come at without inconvenience ; that there be borders sufficiently wide for the roots of the wall-trees to extend themselves in ; and that the several plats of ground be easily come at for the purpose of manuring, and for all other purposes. I subjoin a plan, which I deem the most proper for a garden of the extent that I have recommended. I shall first give the plan on the opposite page ; and, when I have subjoined the explanations of the plan, I shall proceed to make some remarks on it.

EXPLANATIONS OF THE PLAN.

1. The whole length, from outside to outside, from East to West, is 247½ feet, or 15 rod.

2. The whole width, from North to South, is 165 feet, or 10 rod.

3. The outside line represents the place for the hedge.

4. The double line represents the place for the wall.

5. The walks are described by dotting, and all, except the middle walk, are four feet wide.

6. The walk which goes all along the garden from East to West is six feet wide.

7. *a* A door-way through the hedge, 3 feet wide.

8. *b* a door-way in the wall, 3 feet wide, and 4 feet from the corner of the wall.

9. *c, c, c, c,* is the outer garden, a clear rod wide, between the wall and the hedge.

10. *d* is the Hot-bed ground, 58½ feet from East to West, and 63 feet from North to South.

11. *e e e* is a border, 10 feet wide, under the inside of the wall.

12. *f* is a plat of ground, 50½ feet from East to West, and 49 feet from North to South.

13. *g, h, i, k,* are plats of ground, each of which has 67 feet from East to West, and 49 feet from North to South.

14. *m* is a door-way in the wall, 3 feet wide, and 4 feet from the corner of the wall.

15. *n* is a border, 4 feet under the inside of the West wall.

16. *p* is a door-way in the Western hedge of the Hot-bed ground.

17. *q* is a door-way in the Southern hedge of the Hot-bed ground.

18. *r* The tool-house.

19. The letter N points out the *North side* of the garden ; the letter E the *East side*, and the other letters the South and the West sides.

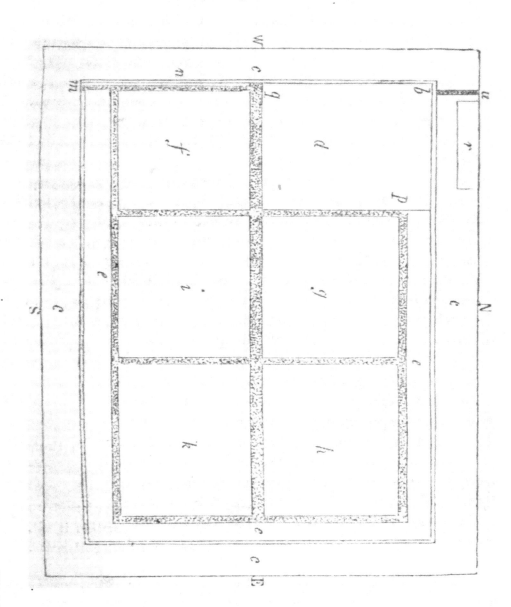

38. It will be seen, that I make but one entrance into the garden, as at *a*; because this entrance, which is a door-way in a hedge, is a somewhat difficult affair: hedges cannot be joined to wood work, as brick work can. There must be posts and a door-frame: and, if great pains be not taken, there will soon be a gap where these join the hedge. This will be the weak part of the fortification. There must be a bridge over the ditch; and that which serves the garrison equally serves the besieger; therefore, this door ought to be well guarded on the top and on the sides by stout pieces of wood projecting in every direction from the top and sides of the door, and well guarded with tenter-hooks. Prevention is better than cure: "lead us not into temptation," is the most sensible of all possible prayers: you inflict no hardship by removing temptation; but you inflict great hardship in the pursuit of compensation or punishment: let the whole neighbourhood be convinced that forcible entry into the garden is not to be accomplished without infinite difficulty: and that is a great deal better than all the steel-traps, spring guns, and penal laws in the world. It is better to have sentry-boxes and sentinels in them than to resort to the steel-trap and spring-gun system; and, for my own part, mortified as I should be at spoliations committed in the garden, I would submit to them, and even to the destruction of the garden itself, rather than disgrace my premises by such terrific threats.

39. The door-way at *a* lets you into a short path to another door-way in the wall at *b*. Through these door-ways the materials naturally go for the making of hot-beds; and, therefore, the hot-bed ground, *d*, is the first

part of the walled garden into which you enter. I will, before I go further, give a particular description of this hot-bed ground, which is by no means an unimportant part of the concern. It is fifty-eight feet and a half from east to west, and sixty-three feet from north to south. A door goes out of it at *q*, another door at *p*. These doorways lead to the several parts of the garden, and are convenient outlets for all purposes, whatsoever. There is, you will perceive, the wall on the north side of this hot-bed ground, and the wall on the west side. The other two sides should be bounded by a *hedge* ; and that hedge should be of *yew*. The fences to hot-bed grounds are frequently made of reed, which are very good for the purpose of shelter ; but which are dead-looking things at the best. The fences to such places are sometimes made of hornbeam ; but this sort of hedge loses its leaves in the winter, and is of little use precisely at the season when it is most wanted. The yew is evergreen. It is by no means difficult to make grow ; it does not grow slowly ; it is clipped into any form that you please ; regularly clipped, it remains in the same form for ever ; it is as close at the bottom as in the middle of its height ; it has all the regularity of a wall itself ; and, in such a case, it is a great deal better than a wall, because it occasions no recoiling or reverberation of the wind. The height of the hedge should not much exceed six feet, for then it would shade part of the beds ; and it is hardly necessary to say, that it should be kept regularly clipped twice in the year, in the same manner as is directed for the hawthorn hedge. There should not only be doorways at *p* and *q*, but doors also ; otherwise the wind would sweep in, and, in part, defeat the object of the hedge. Hardly any family can want a greater space than this for the raising of things for which hot-beds are necessary; and, if the space were found to be larger than was wanted, this would be a very good place for the depositing of a heap of compost, or any other thing which is unsightly, and which, if not somewhat hidden, would disfigure the garden.

40. The borders *e* are, as has been seen in the explanations, ten feet wide; and the earth in them ought to have a little declivity from the wall: it may be very trifling, but it ought to be a little. As to the plats *f, g, h, i, k,* they are for the growth of garden-plants in general; and the parts of them best suited for different plants at different seasons of the year, will be spoken of under the heads of the particular plants. The paths and walks ought to be of gravel, if possible; for, whatever expense this may be attended with in certain cases, there are hardly any other means of having dry paths and walks in winter. Grass is very bad, for it must not only be walked upon, but frequently wheeled upon with barrows heavily laden, and especially in winter-time; and this soon makes them a mass of dirt and of ugliness. But, you cannot have gravel-walks or paths, to be kept in any thing like order, unless you make them well in the first place, and protect them against the falling down of earth upon them for ever afterwards. Therefore, when you have laid out the garden by lines and stumps, the place or places for the walks and paths, should be dug out to the depth of all the *top-soil,* which ought to be thrown over the adjoining ground on both sides, and made perfectly level at the bottom. Then

there should be a bed of brick-bats, or of large flint, or of other stones ; and upon the top of that bed, about six inches of clean gravel.

41. The next thing is to make efficient provision for preventing the earth from the borders and plats, which ought to be about four inches higher than the tops of the walks, from tumbling into the walks when digging, hoeing, and other operations take place ; but especially digging ; for it is impossible to dig the ground close to a walk which has not a sufficient protection, without bringing dirt upon the walk : all the shovelling in the world will not get it off again clean, unless you go down so deep as to take up part of the gravel with the dirt ; so that, your walk must soon become a dirty-looking affair, in which weeds and grass will be everlastingly coming : or you must take away, little by little, the gravel, by shovelling, till you have flung it pretty nearly all upon the borders and plats, and thereby not only destroyed your walk, but injured your cultivated land. To prevent these very great troubles and injuries, you must resolve to have an efficient protection for the walk ; and this, I venture to assert, is to be obtained by no other means than by the use of BOX. Many contrivances have been resorted to for the purpose of avoiding this pretty little tree, which, like all other really valuable things, requires some little time; some little patience, and great attention, after you have got it. In the end, indeed, it is a great deal cheaper than any thing else ; but it requires some attention and patience at first, and regular clipping every year twice. I have seen, and have had, as an *edging* (which ramparts of this sort are called), a little

flowering plant called thrift : I have seen strawberries thickly planted for this purpose : I have seen daisies, and various other things, made use of as edgings : but, all these herbaceous things ramble very quickly over the ground; extend their creepers over the walk, as well as over the adjoining ground; and, instead of being content to occupy the space of three inches wide, to which it is vainly hoped their moderation will confine them, they encroach to the extent of a foot the first summer; and, if left alone for only a couple of years, they will cover the whole of a walk six feet wide, harbouring all sorts of reptiles, making the walk pretty nearly as dirty as if it did not consist of gravel. I have sometimes seen narrow edgings of grass, which, perhaps, are the worst of all. Make such an edging, of four inches wide, in the autumn, and it will be sixteen inches wide before the next autumn, unless you pare down the edges of it three or four times. This must be done by a line; and even then, some dirt must be cut from the edging, to come into the walk : this is, in fact, a rampart of dirt itself. It must be mowed not less than ten times during the summer, or it is ugly beyond description; besides bringing you an abundant crop of seeds to be scattered over the walk, and over the adjoining ground. Of all edgings, therefore, this is the least efficient for the purpose, and by far the most expensive.

42. The box is at once the most efficient of all possible things, and the prettiest plant that can possibly be conceived : the colour of its leaf; the form of its leaf; its docility as to height, width, and shape; the compactness of its little branches; its great durability as a plant : its

thriving in all sorts of soils, and in all sorts of aspects ; its freshness under the hottest sun, and its defiance of all shade and all drip : these are beauties and qualities, which, for ages upon ages, have marked it out as the chosen plant for this very important purpose.

43. The box, to all its other excellent qualities, adds that of facility of propagation. You take up the plants, when they are from three to six inches high, when they have great numbers of shoots coming from the same stem ; you strip these shoots off, put them into the ground, to about the depth of two inches, or a little more ; fasten them well there, first with the hand, and then with the foot ; clip them along at the top to within about two inches of the ground, and you have a box edging at once. You must, indeed, purchase the plants, if you have not taken care to raise them before-hand ; and, as to thrift, strawberries, daisies, or grass edgings, there are generally cart-loads of them to be thrown away, or to be dug from a common. I should suppose, however, that ten pounds' worth of box, bought at the nurseries, would be sufficient for the whole garden ; and, then, with common care, you have neat and efficient edgings for a life-time.

44. To plant the box, some care must be taken. The edging ought to be planted as soon as the gravel walks are formed. The box ought to be placed perpendicularly, and in a very straight line, close to the gravel ; and with no earth at all between it and the gravel. It ought to stand, when planted and cut off, about four inches high ; and the earth in the borders or plats ought to be

pushed back a little, and kept back for the first year, to prevent it from being washed back over the walks. When the edging arrive at its proper height, it will stand about seven inches high, on the gravel side, and will be about three inches higher than the earth in the border, and will act like a little wall to keep the earth out of the walks; which, to say nothing of the difference in the look, it will do as effectually as brick, or boards, or any thing else, however solid. The edging ought to be clipped in the winter, or very early in the spring, on both the sides and at top; a line ought to be used to regulate the movements of the sheers: it ought to be clipped again, in the same manner, just about Midsummer; and, if there be a more neat and beautiful thing than this in the world, all that I can say, is, that I never saw that thing.

45. There is yet one thing to notice in this laying-out of the garden; namely, that there must be a *shed* to serve as a place for depositing tools, flower-pots, and the like; and also, for the gardeners to retire to in case of rain, and to do works there when they cannot do work out of doors. This is a very necessary part of the garden premises, and ought to be sufficiently spacious not only for the purposes just mentioned, but for the hanging up of seeds to dry, and for various other purposes. This shed ought to stand also as near to the hot-bed ground as convenient, and yet it is too dissightly to be in the inside of the garden. A shed about forty feet long, and about seven feet wide, might suffice for this purpose; and it might stand very conveniently, as at *r* in the outer garden, on the east side of the entrance at *a*, the back of the

building being high enough to allow the eves of the roof to be six feet from the ground; and the back being towards the *hedge*, and not towards the wall. As to *water*, I have not pointed out any particular place in the garden for a well or other means of obtaining water. It will be seen, by-and-by, that I am of opinion that a great deal of time and labour bestowed upon watering are, in general, so much time and labour thrown away, and to effect injury instead of good. Nevertheless, there are many cases in which watering by hand is absolutely necessary : in hot-beds, for instance ; in the case of plants in pots ; in the case of things which can be shaded during the day ; in the case of cauliflowers, which grow so much larger and finer when dishes are made round them and plenty of water given. Therefore, there must be water used in a garden of this extent ; and to bring it from any considerable distance would be a thing extremely inconvenient and attended with great expense. If running water can be brought through a part of the garden, that is the desirable thing ; and, when we see the great number of situations where this might be done at a mere trifling expense, we are astonished at the small number of instances in which it has ever been attempted. There is scarcely an instance, where we find a mansion-house of any considerable size, where a river, a brook, or a spring, might not be made to furnish a run of water for the garden. Above ground or under ground, until it came to the wall, where an arch and a grating might be made to let it in, a channel to conduct it across, and another arch and grating to let it out again. Running water, besides the prettiness of it, would give banks or edges for the growth of several things which delight in it : strawberries, raspberries, quince-trees, and almost every sort of tree. But, supposing it to be impossible to have the water in this way, the usual resource of a well must be resorted to. From this well, the water would be raised by a pump pouring the water into a large cistern, made of brick and well cemented, the walls rising about two feet above the ground, which cistern should be kept always pretty nearly full, in order for the water to get softened by the air, and to be more fit for the uses of the garden. There will be plenty of room for this pump and cistern in the hot-bed ground, at the south-east corner ; and, from this spot, it could be carried or wheeled to all parts of the garden. No great pains need be taken with regard to the making of the cistern, so that it were well cemented : the brick-work should be nine inches thick, and the form should be circular, otherwise the sides might fall in.

46. In conclusion of these instructions, as to the laying-out of the garden, I ought to observe that the narrow border at *n*, which is four feet wide between the wall and the path, is necessary, because the path is to be at four feet distance from the wall, in order that the doorway in the wall on the south side may not be close to the corner, which would lessen the strength of the wall. In the work of laying-out, great care ought to be taken with regard to straightness and distances, and particularly as to the squareness of every part. To make lines perpendicular, and perfectly so, is, indeed, no difficult matter, when one knows how to do it ; but one must know how to do it, before one can do it at all. If the *gardener* understand this much of geometry, he will do it without any difficulty ; but, if he only pretend to under-

stand the matter, and begin to walk backward and forward, stretching out lines and cocking his eye, make no bones with him; send for a bricklayer, and see the stumps driven into the ground yourself. The four outside lines being laid down with perfect truth, it must be a bungling fellow, indeed, that cannot do the rest; but if they be only a little *askew*, you have a botch in your eye for the rest of your life, and a botch of your own making too. Gardeners seldom want for confidence in their own abilities; and, in many cases, it requires time and some experience of their doings, to ascertain whether they know their business or do not; especially when in pretensions they are so bold, and the result is at a considerable distance, and clouded with so many intervening circumstances; but this affair of raising perpendiculars upon a given line, is a thing settled in a moment: you have nothing to do but to say to the gardener, " Come, let us see how you do it." He has but one way in which he can do it; and, if he do not immediately begin to work in that way, pack him off to get a bricklayer, even a botch in which trade will perform the work to the truth of a hair.

CHAPTER III.

On the making and managing of Hot-beds and Green-houses.

48. I OBSERVED before, that it did not accord with my
plan to treat of *Hot-houses,* which, as I then observed,
was a branch wholly distinct from gardening in general,
and applicable to the circumstances of comparatively very
few persons; and that, therefore, to enter on such a
treatise, would be of little use to the public in general,
while it would injuriously augment the bulk of my work.
Hot-beds are, however, of a different character: they
may be made an amusement, and are even things of real
utility, to a very considerable number of persons: to all,
in short, who have gardens, and who have the stable-
dung of two or three horses, or even of one horse, at
their command, or who can procure such materials (as is
the case in the neighbourhood of great towns), at a
reasonable rate. A green-house, upon a small scale, or
adapted to the particular circumstances of the proprietor,
is within the reach of a very considerable part of the
community; and, therefore, without, however, consider-
ing it as an essential object, or one worthy of very great
attention, I shall give my opinions upon that species of
gardening also.

49. Hot-beds are used either for raising such things as
are not to be raised during the winter or the spring with-

out such assistance, or for the raising of such things as are not to be had at all in our climate, without artificial heat of some kind. Before we speak of the form and dimensions of a hot-bed, it will be best, perhaps, to describe the *frame*, which is to go upon it ; because the reasons for the directions for the making of the bed will then the more manifestly appear. A *frame* consists of four pieces of wood ; and, let us suppose it to be twelve feet long, and four feet wide. Frames are sometimes of greater and sometimes of less dimensions ; but for the sake of illustration, let us take a frame of this size. There must be one board or two boards joined together, to make the back, twelve feet in length, and eighteen inches wide ; one board, to make the front, twelve feet in length, and nine inches wide. One board at each end, to be joined on to the ends of the front and the back ; eighteen inches at the back, and nine inches at the front. These boards being well dove-tailed together at the four corners, and being about two inches thick, form the frame. Upon this frame, glazed sashes are put, which are called *lights*, and which rest upon the back and front and ends of the frame, and also upon bars put across and fastened into the sides of the frame, in such a way as to form resting-places for the sides of the lights. This is quite enough of description ; because the carpenters know how to make these things ; and all that I have to do in this place, is, so to designate them that the reader may know what I am talking about.

50. Having the intention to make a hot-bed, you must first see that you have a sufficiency of materials. You take the stable dung, carry it into the hot-bed ground

(letter *d* in the plan of the garden), and there put it into a conical heap. If you have not enough of dung from the stable-door, some from cow-stalls, sheep-yards, and even long stuff from pig-beds or pig-styes, half-stained litter; or any thing of a grassey kind, and not entirely dry, will lend you assistance ; but, let it be understood, that the best of all possible materials for the making of hot-beds is dung from the stable of corn-fed horses ; and the next best comes from a sheep-yard, or from stalls where ewes and sucking lambs have been kept. Wheat-straw is by far the best straw to have been used as litter, when the dung is wanted for hot-beds. Bearing in mind that this is the best sort of materials, you must take what you have ; and, if it be of an inferior quality, there must, at any rate, be a greater quantity of it. Having collected your materials together in the hot-bed ground, you next shake them up well together into a heap, in a flattish conical form. It is not sufficient merely to put the dung up together in this form : it must be taken a prongful at a time, and shaken entirely straw from straw, and mixed, long with short, duly and truly through every part of the heap, from the bottom to the top. When thus shaken up, the short stuff on the ground where the dung was tossed down out of the wheel-barrow, ought to be shovelled up very clean, and flung over the heap. If the dung be good, you will see it begin to smoke the next day. It should lie only two days and a half, or three days, before it be moved again. It should now be turned over very truly, well shaken to pieces again, and another conical heap formed of it, care being taken to put the outsides of the first heap towards the inside of the second heap. In two or three days more, it will have

heated again sufficiently; and then it should be turned
once more, especially if there be a great proportion of
long litter in it. If the dung be very dry, and the
weather be dry also, and especially if it have a large portion of long littery stuff in it, it should be watered with a
watering-pot, when it is first mixed up, a watering being
given all over the heap at every foot of height that the
heap rises to. This is necessary to cause that fermentation
without which there cannot be a hot-bed; but, generally
speaking, this is not necessary, for dung is seldom flung
out with so large a portion of clean straw, as to prevent
it from heating when thrown up in a heap.

51. It is as well to consider it to be a general rule,
scarcely ever to be departed from, that the dung should
ferment three several times during the space of nine
days, before it be put into a hot-bed. Unless this be the
case, the heat of the bed (unless the dung be very short
at the beginning) will not be lasting, and will never be
regular; nor will the bed be solid and uniform. It will
sink more in some places than in others, and will be
hotter in some places than in others; therefore, it is
useless to be impatient, since the thing cannot be done
well without this previous preparation.

52. The dung being duly prepared, you make the bed
in the following manner, having first made the ground
on which it is to stand, *perfectly level.* If the general
surface of the ground round about be on the slope, you
must take care so to change the situation of that part of
the ground on which the bed is to stand, as to make
that part perfectly level. It is not sufficient that you

have the top of the bed level. The bottom must be level also, or else the sinking on one side or at one end, will be greater than on the other side, or at the other end ; the frame will stand unevenly ; the slope of the lights will be too steep, or not steep enough ; the bed will sometimes crack ; the water will run off and not sink into the earth ; and, in short, without a perfect level whereon to place the bed, the inconveniences are endless.

53. Having got the level spot, you are to make a bed as nearly as possible of the dimensions of the frame ; and the best possible way is to take the frame itself, put it upon the ground where you intend the bed shall stand, put up a straight piece of wood on the outside of each corner of the frame; while it is standing upon the ground ; then take the frame away ; then put a thin board edgeways upon the ground on the back, and on the front, and at the two ends, which board ought to come on the *outsides* of the four stakes, and to be held up by four pegs. You have then a true guide for making the bottom of the bed ; and you begin by putting a little of the longest of the dung just at the bottom. Then you go on shaking the dung into this sort of box, dividing straw from straw, and mixing long and short duly together, in the same manner as was before directed in the case of the conical heaps, and taking care to keep beating the dung down with the prong in every part of the bed. When you have shaken on dung to the thickness of four or five inches, beat all over again, and so on at every four or five inches deep, until the work be finished. When you get to the top of the boards, you

will proceed very well without any; but you must be very careful to keep the outsides and ends perfectly upright; for this purpose, great care must be taken that the stakes at the four corners of the bed be placed perpendicularly. Strain the line now-and-then from stake to stake, and that will be your guide. Particular care must be taken to keep the *edges* of the bed well-beaten as you proceed; for, if you fail to do this, they will sink more than the middle will sink; and then there will be a crack in the earth in the middle of the bed. As you proceed, the perpendicular sides and ends ought to be well beaten also; and, when the work is finished, it ought to be a building as smooth and as upright as a wall, being perfectly level at the top, and, of course, of uniform height in all its parts.

54. When the bed is completed, put on the frame immediately. If the foregoing instructions have been observed, the bed will be about an inch longer, and an inch wider than the frame. It should not be more, on any account; especially if it be intended to receive those *linings* of which I shall have to speak hereafter. After putting on the frame, put on the lights; and, as you will not push the lights down in order to give air, you will find that the heat of the bed will begin to rise in the course of twelve hours, or thereabouts. As soon as the heat begins to rise, there should be some air given to the bed by pushing the lights, or some of them, down four or five inches from the back, or drawing them up four or five inches from the front; for, *stench* is not good, whether before, or after, plants be put into the bed. In about three days, the bed will be in full heat. Some

persons recommend to put a sharp-pointed stick down a
foot, or a foot and a half into the bed, to ascertain the
degree of the heat. Your finger is a great deal better
than a stick : whatever heat there is must discover itself
at the top of the bed, and there it is that your finger,
well poked down into the centre of the bed, will enable
you to judge of this matter a great deal better than any
thing else. It is a very delicate matter : it is one of the
things that demands the greatest possible attention ; for,
the heat of dung, though it will not probably come to a
blaze, in any case, as a hay-rick sometimes will, it will
burn as completely as fire ; and, if the earth be put on
too soon, it will burn the earth into a sort of cinder, in
which nothing will ever grow until that earth has been
for some time exposed to the atmosphere. You must,
therefore, be very careful to ascertain that the burning
powers of the bed are passed, before you put on the
earth. The rule for arriving at a certainty of this knowledge is this : the next morning after you have made the
bed, poke your fore-finger well down into the centre of
the top of it ; and continue to do the same every morning and every evening, or more frequently. You will
find the heat increase, till (if the bed be a strong one)
the heat be too great for you to endure your finger in it
for a moment : soon after this, you will find the heat
begin to decline ; and, as soon as you can bear your
finger in it without any inconvenience, you may put on
the earth all over the bed to about six inches depth,
which earth ought not to be as dry as dust ; but ought,
at the same time, not to be wet.

55. Thus is the bed ready for the receiving of seeds or

plants : thus is the hot-bed made : these are the general instructions for the making of hot-beds, which are to be of different heights, of different strength, and managed subsequently in a different manner, according with the nature of the different plants to be cultivated in them, and according to the season of the year, when the sowing, planting, and cultivation is to take place. Cucumbers and melons, are, in England, the principal things for the rearing of which hot-beds are usually made : there are, however, several other things which are forced forward by the means of hot-beds ; and, in the treating of cucumbers and melons, and of those other sorts of garden plants which are raised in hot-beds, I shall, under the names of these several plants, in the alphabetical list, give direction for the management of the hot-beds in which they are placed. A hot-bed for the purpose of getting early radishes, is a very different thing from a hot-bed adapted to the raising of melons and cucumbers ; and, therefore, no general directions for the management of the beds can be complete : the heat which is absolutely necessary to bring cucumbers to perfection, would totally destroy radish plants, or, at least, prevent them from ever producing a radish fit to be eaten ; but, as to the manner of making beds, it is the same in all cases; and of that manner, I think I have here given directions sufficient for any person, even though he had never seen a hot-bed in his life. I will just add, that the quantity of materials may be augmented by using a great plenty of straw as litter, instead of being sparing of straw ; and that, if you have the making of hot-beds in your eye, it is good, during the fall and the early part of the winter, while the materials are creating, to let the dung from the stable be flung rather widely about; and not into heaps, in which it would heat, and exhaust itself before-hand.

56. As to the making of green-houses, I shall think of nothing more than a place to preserve tender plants from the frost in the winter, and to have hardy flowers during a season of the year when there are no flowers abroad. It is necessary, in order to make a green-house an agreeable thing, that it should be very near to the dwelling-house. It is intended for the pleasure, for the rational amusement and occupation of persons who would otherwise be employed in things irrational; if not in things mischievous. To have it at a distance from the house would be to render it nearly useless; for, to take a pretty long tramp in the dirt or wet, or snow, to get at a sight of the plants, would be, nine times out of ten, not performed; and the pain would, in most instances, exceed the pleasure. A green-house should, therefore, be erected against the dwelling-house. The south side of the house would be the best for the green-house; but any aspect, to the south of due east and due west may do tolerably well; and a door into it, and a window, or windows looking into it, from any room of the house, in which people frequently sit, makes the thing extremely beautiful and agreeable. It must be glass on the top, at the end most distant from the house, and in the front from about three feet high. There should be an outer door for the ingress and egress of the gardener, and a little flue running round for the purpose of obtaining heat sufficient for the keeping of a heat to between forty and fifty degrees of Fahrenheit's thermometer. Stages, shelves,

and other things necessary for arranging the plants upon, would be erected according to the taste of the owner, and the purposes in view. Besides the plants usually kept in green-houses, such as geraniums, heaths, and the like, I should choose to have bulbous-rooted plants of various sorts, even the most common, not excluding snow-drops and crocuses. Primroses and violets (the common single sorts, for the others have no smell), cowslips and daisies; some dwarf roses; and thus a very beautiful flower-garden would be to be seen in the month of February, or still more early. Green-house plants are always set out of doors in the summer, when they are generally very much eclipsed in beauty by plants of a hardy and more vigorous description. If there be no green-house, these plants are taken into the house, shut up in a small space, very frequently in the shade, and always from strong light, especially early in the morning; which greatly injures, and, sometimes, totally destroys, them; besides, they really give no pleasure, except in winter; for, as was observed before, after the month of May comes, they are far surpassed in beauty by the shrubberies and the parterre.

57. Nor is such a place without its real use, for, few persons will deny that fruit is of use; none will deny that fine grapes are amongst the best of fruit; we all know that these are not to be had in England, in the general run of years, without the assistance of glass; and the green-house, in which the shade of the grapes would do no injury to the plants, because these would be out in the open air, except at the time when there would be little of leaf upon the vines, is as complete a thing for a

grapery as if made for that sole purpose ; for, if the heat of from forty to fifty degrees would bring the vines to bear at a time, or, rather, to send out their leaves at a time inconvenient for the plants, you have nothing to do but to take the vine branches out of the house, and keep them there until such time that they might be put in again without their leaves producing an inconvenient shade over the plants, previous to the time of these latter being moved out into the open air.

58. As the green-house would have given you a beautiful flower-garden and shrubbery during the winter, making the part of the house to which it is attached the pleasantest place in the world, so, in summer, what can be imagined more beautiful than bunches of grapes hanging down, surrounded by elegant leaves, and proceeding on each grape from the size of a pin's head to the size of a plum ? How the vines are to be planted, trained and pruned ; and how the several plants suited to a green-house are to be propagated, reared and managed ; will be spoken of under the head of Vines, and under those of the several plants and flowers ; but I cannot conclude this Chapter without observing, that it is the *moral* effects naturally attending a green-house, that I set the most value upon. I will not, with LORD BACON, praise pursuits like these, because " God Almighty first planted a garden ;" nor with COWLEY, because " a Garden is like Heaven ;" nor with ADDISON, because a " Garden was the habitation of our first parents before their fall ;" all which is rather far-fetched, and puts one in mind of the dispute between the gardeners and the tailors, as to the antiquity of their respective callings ; the former con-

tending that the planting of the garden took place before the sewing of the fig-leaves together ; and the latter contending, that there was no gardening at all till Adam was expelled, and compelled to work ; but, that the sewing was a real and bonâ fide act of tailoring. This, to be sure, is vulgar and grovelling work ; but, who can blame such persons when they have LORD BACON to furnish them with a precedent ?   I like, a great deal better than these writers, SIR WILLIAM TEMPLE, who, while he was a man of the soundest judgment, employed in some of the greatest concerns of his country, so ardently and yet so rationally and unaffectedly praises the pursuits of gardening, in which he delighted from his youth to his old age ; and of his taste in which he gave such delightful proofs in those gardens and grounds at Moor Park in Surrey, beneath the turf of one spot of which he caused, by his will, his heart to be buried, and which spot, together with all the rest of the beautiful arrangement, has been torn about and disfigured within the last fifty years by a succession of wine-merchants, spirit-merchants, West Indians, and God knows what besides : I like a great deal better the sentiments of this really wise and excellent man ; but I look still further as to effects. There must be amusements in every family.   Children observe and follow their parents in almost every thing. How much better, during a long and dreary winter, for daughters, and even sons, to assist, or attend, their mother, in a green-house, than to be seated with her at cards, or, in the blubberings over a stupid novel, or at any other amusement that can possibly be conceived ! How much more innocent, more pleasant, more free from temptation to evil, this amusement, than any other !

How much more instructive, too! "Bend the twig when young :" but, here, there needs no force ; nay, not even persuasion. The thing is so pleasant in itself ; it so naturally meets the wishes ; that the taste is fixed at once, and it remains, to the exclusion of cards and dice, to the end of life. Indeed, gardening in general is favourable to the well-being of man. As the taste for it decreases in any country, vicious amusements and vicious habits are sure to increase. Towns are preferred to the country ; and the time is spent in something or other that conduces to vice and misery. Gardening is a source of much greater profit than is generally imagined ; but, merely as an amusement, or recreation, it is a thing of very great value : it is a pursuit not only compatible with, but favourable to, the study of any art or science : it is conducive to health, by means of the irresistible temptation which it offers to early rising ; to the stirring abroad upon one's legs ; for a man may really ride till he cannot walk, sit till he cannot stand, and lie abed till he cannot get up. It tends to turn the minds of youth from amusements and attachments of a frivolous or vicious nature : it is a taste which is indulged at home : it tends to make home pleasant, and to endear us to the spot on which it is our lot to live : and, as to the *expenses* attending it, what are all these expenses, compared with those of the short, the unsatisfactory, the injurious enjoyments of the card-table, and the rest of those amusements or pastimes which are sought for in the town ?

CHAPTER IV.

On Propagation and Cultivation in general.

———————

59. IN order to have good products, we must be careful and diligent in the propagation and cultivation of the several plants ; for, though nature does much, she will not do all. He who trusts to chance for a crop, deserves none, and he generally has what he deserves.

60. The propagation of plants is the *bringing of them forth,* or the *increasing and multiplying* of them. This is effected in several different ways : by *seed,* by *suckers,* by *offsets,* by *layers,* by *cuttings.* But, bear in mind, that *all* plants from the radish to the oak, *may* be propagated by the means of *seed ;* while there are many plants which can be propagated by *no other means ;* and, of these the radish and the oak are two. Let me just qualify here, by observing, that I enter not into the deep question (which so many have puzzled their heads with) of *equivocal generation.* I confine myself to things of which we have a certain knowledge.

61. With regard to propagation by means *other* than that of seed, I shall speak of it fully enough under the names of the several plants, which are, as to the way of propagating them, to be considered as exceptions to the general rule. Therefore, I shall, in the present Chapter, treat of propagation by *seed* only.

62. Cultivation must, of course, differ, in some respects, to suit itself to certain differences in the plants to be cultivated ; but, there are some principles and rules, which apply to the cultivation of all plants ; and it is of these only that I propose to speak in the present Chapter.

63. It is quite useless, indeed it is grossly absurd, to prepare land and to incur trouble and expense, without duly, and even *very carefully,* attending to the *seed* that we are going to sow. The *sort,* the *genuineness,* the *soundness,* are all matters to be attended to, if we mean to avoid mortification and loss. Therefore, the first thing is the

SORT OF SEED.

64. We should make *sure* here ; for, what a loss to have *late* cabbages instead of *early* ones ! As to beans, peas, and many other things, there cannot easily be mistake or deception. But, as to cabbages, cauliflowers, radishes, lettuces, onions, leeks, and numerous others, the eye is no guide at all. If, therefore, you do not *save your own seed* (of the manner of doing which I shall speak by and by), you ought to be very careful as to whom you purchase of ; and, though the seller be a person of perfect probity, he may be deceived himself. If you do not save your own seed, which, as will be seen, cannot always be done with safety ; all you can do, is, to take every precaution in your power when you purchase. Be very particular, very full and clear, in the order you give for seed. Know the seedsman well, if possible. Speak to him yourself on the subject, if you can ; and, in short, take every precaution in your power, in order to avoid

the mortifications like those of having one sort of cabbage when you expected another, and of having rape when you expected turnips or ruta baga.

TRUE   SEED.

65. But, besides the *kind*, there is the *genuineness* to be considered.   For instance, you want *sugar-loaf cabbage*. The seed you sow may be *cabbage :* it may, too, be *sugar-loaf*, or more that than any thing else : but, still, it may not be *true to its kind*.   It may have become degenerate ; it may have become *mixed*, or *crossed*, in generating.   And thus, the plants may very much disappoint you.   *True seed* is a great thing ; for, not only the time of the crop coming in ; but the quantity and quality of it greatly depend upon the *trueness* of the seed.   You will have *plants* to be sure ; that is to say, you will have *something* grow ; but you will not, if the seed be not *true*, have the thing you want.

66. To *insure* truth in seed, you must, if you purchase, take all the precautions recommended as to *sort of seed*. It will be seen presently, that, to save true seed yourself, is by no means an easy matter. And, therefore, you must sometimes purchase.   Find a seedsman that does not deceive you, and stick to him.   But, observe, that no seedsman *can* always be sure.   He cannot raise *all* his seeds himself.   He must trust to others.   Of course, he may, himself, be deceived. Some kinds of seed will keep good many years ; and, therefore, when you find that

you have got some *very true* seed of any sort, get some more of it ; get as much as will last you for the number of years that such seed will keep ; and, to know how many years the seeds of garden plants will keep, see paragraph 150.

SOUNDNESS OF SEED.

67. SEED may be of the right *sort ;* it may be *true* to its sort ; and yet, if it be *unsound*, it will not grow, and, of course, is a great deal worse than useless, because the sowing of it occasions loss of time, loss of cost of seed, loss of use of land, and loss of labour, to say nothing about the disappointment and mortification. Here, again, if you purchase, you must rely on the seedsman ; and, therefore, all the aforementioned precautions are necessary as to this point also. In this case (especially if the sowing be extensive) the injury may be very great ; and, there is no *redress.* If a man sell you *one sort of seed for another ;* or, if he sell you *untrue seed ;* the *law* will give you redress to the full extent of the injury proved ; and the *proof* can be produced. But, if the seed does *not come up,* what *proof* have you ? You may prove the *sowing ;* but, who is to *prove,* that the seed was not *chilled* or *scorched,* in the ground ? That it was not eaten by insects there ? That it was not destroyed in *coming up,* or in *germinating ?*

68. There are, however, means of ascertaining, whether seed be *sound,* or not, before you sow it in the ground. I

know of no seed, which, if sound and really good, will not *sink in water*. The unsoundness of seed arises from several causes. *Unripeness, blight, mouldiness*, and *age*, are the most frequent of these causes. The two first, if excessive, prevent the seed from ever having the germinating quality in them. Mouldiness arises from the seed being kept in a *damp place,* or from its *having heated.* When dried again it becomes light. *Age* will cause the germinating quality to evaporate; though, where there is a great proportion of *oil* in the seed, this quality will remain in it for many years, as will be seen by-and-by.

69. The way to *try* seed is this. Put a small quantity of it in *luke-warm* warm, and let the water be four or five inches deep. A mug, or basin, will do, but a large tumbler *glass* is best; for then you can *see* the bottom as well as top. Some seeds, such as those of cabbage, radish, and turnip, will, if good, go to the bottom at once. Cucumber, melon, lettuce, endive, and many others, require a few minutes. Parsnip and carrot, and all the *winged* seeds, require to be worked by your fingers in a little water, and well *wetted*, before you put them into the glass; and the carrot should be *rubbed,* so as to get off part of the *hairs,* which would otherwise act, as the feathers do as to a duck. The seed of beet and mangel wurzel are in a *case* or *shell.* The rough things that we sow are not the *seeds,* but the cases in which the seeds are contained, each case containing from *one* to *five* seeds. Therefore the trial by water is not, as to these two seeds, *conclusive,* though if the seed be very good; if there be four or five in a case, shell and all will sink in water, after being in the glass an hour. And, as it is a

matter of such great importance, that every seed should grow in a case where the plants stand so far apart ; as *gaps* in rows of beet and mangel wurzel are so very injurious, the best way is to reject all seed that will not sink, case and all, after being put into warm water, and remaining there an hour.

70. But, seeds of all sorts are, sometimes, if not always, part sound and part unsound ; and, as the former is not to be rejected on account of the latter, the *proportion* of each should be ascertained, if a separation be not made. Count, then, a hundred seeds, taken promiscuously, and put them into water as before directed. If fifty sink and fifty swim, half your seed is bad, and half good ; and so, in proportion, as to other numbers of sinkers and swimmers. There *may* be plants, the sound seeds of which will *not sink;* but I *know of none.* If it be found in any instance, they would, I think, be found in those of the tulip-tree, the ash, the birch, and the parsnip, all of which are furnished with so large a portion of wing. Yet all these, if *sound,* will sink, if put into *warm* water, with the wet worked a little into the wings first.

71. There is, however, another way of ascertaining this important fact, the soundness, or unsoundness of seed ; and that is, by *sowing them.* If you have a *hot-bed* (or, if not, how easy to make one for a hand-glass ?), put a hundred seeds, taken as before directed, sow them in a flower-pot, and plunge the pot in the earth, under the glass, in the hot-bed, or hand-glass. The climate, under the glass, is *warm ;* and a very few days will tell you what

proportion of your seed is sound.   But there is this to be said; that, with strong heat under, and with such complete protection above, seeds may *come up* that would not come up in the *open ground*.   There may be enough of the germinating principle to cause vegetation in a hotbed, and not enough to cause it in the open air and cold ground.   Therefore I incline to the opinion that we should try seeds as our ancestors tried Witches; not by fire, but by water; and that, following up their practice, we should reprobate and destroy all that do not *readily* sink.

SAVING AND PRESERVING SEED.

72. THIS is a most important branch of the Gardener's business.   There are rules applicable to particular plants. Those will be given in their proper places.   It is my business here to speak of such as are applicable to *all* plants.

73. First, as to the *saving* of seed, the *truest* plants should be selected; that is to say, such as are of the most perfect *shape* and quality.   In the Cabbage we seek small stem, well-formed loaf, few spare, or loose, leaves; in the turnip, large bulb, small neck, slender-stalked leaves, solid flesh, or pulp; in the radish, high colour (if red or scarlet), small neck, few and short leaves, and long top.   The marks of perfection are well known, and none but perfect plants should be saved for seed.   The case is somewhat different as to plants, which are some male and

others female, but, these present exceptions to be noticed under the names of such plants.

74. Of plants, the early coming of which is a circumstance of importance, the very earliest should be chosen for seed; for, they will almost always be found to include the highest degree of perfection in other respects. They should have great pains taken with them; the soil and situation should be good; and they should be carefully cultivated, during the time that they are carrying on their seed to perfection.

75. But, effectual means must be taken to prevent a *mixing* of the sorts, or, to speak in the language of farmers, a *crossing of the breeds.* There can be no cross between the *sheep and the dog :* but there can be between the *dog and the wolf;* and, we daily see it, between the *greyhound and the hound;* each valuable when *true* to his kind; and a cross between the two, fit for nothing but the *rope :* a word which, on this occasion, I use, in preference to that of *halter,* out of respect for the modern laws and usages of my country.

76. There can be no cross between a *cabbage and a carrot;* but there can be, between a *cabbage and a turnip;* between a *cabbage and a cauliflower* nothing is more common; and, as to the different sorts of cabbages, they will produce crosses, presenting twenty, and perhaps a thousand, degrees, from the Early York to the Savoy. Turnips will mix with radishes and ruta-baga; all these with rape; the result will mix with cabbages and cauliflowers; so that, if nothing were done to preserve plants true to

their kind, our gardens would soon present us with little besides mere herbage.

77. As to the *causes*, I will not here dive into them. Suffice it, that we know, that sorts will mix, when seed-plants of the same *tribe* stand *near* each other; and we may easily suppose, that this may probably take place though the plants stand at a considerable distance apart, since I have, in the case of my Indian corn, given proof of mixture, when the plants were *three hundred yards* from each other. What must be the consequence, then, of saving seed from cucumbers, melons, pumpkins, squashes, and gourds, all growing in the same garden at the same time? To save the seed of *two sorts* of any tribe, in the same garden, *in the same year*, ought not to be attempted; and this it is, that makes it difficult for any *one man* to raise all sorts of seeds good and *true*.

78. However, *some* may be saved by every one who has a garden; and when raised, they ought to be carefully *preserved*. They are best preserved *in the pod*, or on the *stalks*. Seeds of many sorts will be perfectly good to the age of eight or ten years, if kept in the pod or on the stalks, which seeds, if threshed, will be good for little at the end of three years or less. However, to keep seeds, without threshing them out, is seldom convenient, often impracticable, and always exposes them to injury from mice and rats, and from various other enemies, of which, however, the greatest is *carelessness*. Therefore, the best-way is, except for things that are very curious, and that lie in a small compass, to thresh out all seeds.

79. They should stand till *perfectly ripe*, if possible. They should be cut, or pulled, or gathered, when it is dry ; and, they should, if possible, be dry as dry can be, before they are threshed out. If, when threshed, any *moisture* remain about them, they should be placed in the sun ; or, near a fire in a dry room ; and, when quite dry, should be put into bags, and hung up against a very dry wall, or dry boards, where they will by no accident *get damp*. The best place is some room, or place, where there is, occasionally at least, a *fire* kept in winter.

80. Thus preserved, kept from *open air* and from *damp*, the seeds of *vegetables* will keep sound and good for sowing for the number of years stated in the following list ; to which the reader will particularly attend. Some of the seeds in this list will keep, sometimes, a year longer, if very well saved and very well preserved, and especially if closely kept from exposure to the open air. But, to *lose a crop* from unsoundness of seed is a sad thing, and, it is indeed, negligence wholly inexcusable to sow seed of the soundness of which we are not *certain*.

	YEARS			YEARS
Artichoke	3	Lettuce		3
Asparagus	4	Mangel Wurzel		10
Balm	2	Marjoram		4
Basil	2	Marigold		3
Bean	1	Melon		10
Bean (Kidney)	1	Mint		4
Beet	10	Mustard		4
Borage	4	Nasturtium		2
Broccoli	4	Onion		2
Burnet	6	Parsley		6
Cabbage	4	Parsnip		1
Calabash	7	Pea		1
Cale	4	Pennyroyal		2
Cale (Sea)	3	Potato		3
Camomile	2	Pumpkin		10
Capsicum	2	Purslane		2
Caraway	4	Radish		2
Carrot	1	Rampion		2
Cauliflower	4	Rape		4
Celery	10	Rhubarb		1
Chervil	6	Rosemary		3
Cives	3	Rue		3
Corn	3	Ruta-Baga		4
Corn-Salad	2	Salsify		2
Coriander	3	Samphire		3
Cress	2	Savory		2
Cucumber	10	Scorzenera		2
Dandelion	10	Shalot		4
Dock	1	Skirret		4
Endive	4	Sorrel		7
Fennel	5	Spinage		4
Garlick	3	Squash		10
Gourd	10	Tansy		3
Hop	2	Tarragon		4
Horse-Radish	4	Thyme		2
Hyssop	6	Tomatum		2
Jerusalem Artichoke	3	Turnip		4
Lavender	2	Wormwood		2
Leek	2			

81. Notwithstanding this list, I always sow *new* seed in preference to *old*, if, in *all* other respects, I know the new to be equal to the old. And, as 'to the notion, that seeds can be the *better* for being old, even more than a *year* old, I hold it to be monstrously absurd : and this opinion I give as the result of long experience, most attentive observation, and numerous experiments made for the express purpose of ascertaining the fact.

82. Yet, it is a received opinion, a thing taken for granted, an axiom in horticulture, that *melon* seed is the *better* for being *old*. MR. MARSHALL says, that it ought to be "*about four years old*, though some prefer it *much older*." And he afterwards observes, that " if new seed only *can be had*, it " should be carried a week or two in the *breeches-pocket*, " to dry away some of the more *watery* particles ! " If *age* be a recommendation in rules as well as in melon-seed, this rule has it ; for, English authors published it, and French authors *laughed at it*, more than a *century past !*

83. Those who can afford to have melons raised in their gardens, can afford to keep a *conjuror* to raise them ; and a conjuror will hardly condescend to follow *common sense* in his practice. This would be lowering the profession in the eyes of the vulgar ; and, which would be very dangerous, in the eyes of his employer. However, a great deal of this *stuff* is traditionary ; and how are we to find the conscience to blame a gardener for errors inculcated by gentlemen of erudition !

84. I cannot dismiss this part of my subject without once more cautioning the reader against the danger of *unripe* seed.   In cases where winter overtakes you before your seed be quite ripe, the best way is to pull up the plants and hang them by the heels in a *dry airy* place, till all green depart from the stalks, and until they be quite dry, and wholly rid of juice. Even in hot weather, when the seed would drop out, if the plants were left standing, pull, or cut the plants, and lay them on a cloth in the sun, till the seed be all ready to fall out; for, if *forced* from the *pod*, the seed is never so good. Seeds will grow if gathered when they are *green* as grass, and afterwards dried in the sun; but they do not produce plants like those coming from *ripe seed*. I tried, some years ago, fifty grains of wheat, gathered green, against fifty gathered ripe. Not only were the *plants* of the former feeble, when compared with the latter; not only was the produce of the former two-thirds less than that of the latter; but even the quality of the grain was not half so good. Many of the ears had *smut*, which was not the case with those that came from the ripened seed, though the land and the cultivation were, in both cases, the same.

SOWING.

85. THE first thing, relating to *sowing*, is, the preparation of the ground. It may be more or less *fine*, according to the sort of seed to be sown. Peas and beans do not, of course, require the earth so fine as small seeds. But, still, the finer the better for *every thing*; for, it

is best if the seed be actually *pressed* by the earth in every part; and many seeds, if not all, are best situated when the earth is *trodden down* upon them.

86. Of course the ground should be *good*, either in itself, or made good by manure of some sort. But, in *all cases*, the ground should be *fresh;* that is to say, it should be *dug* just before the act of sowing, in order that the seeds may have the full benefit of the *fermentation*, that takes place upon every moving of the earth.

87. Never sow when the ground is *wet;* nor, indeed, if it can be avoided, perform any other act with, or on, the ground of a garden. If you dig ground in wet weather, you make a sort of *mortar* of it: it *binds* when the sun or wind dries it. The fermentation does not take place: and it becomes unfavourable to vegetation, especially if the ground be, in the smallest degree, stiff in its nature. It is even desirable, that wet should not come for some days after ground has been moved; for, if the wet come before the ground be *dry at top*, the earth will *run together*, and will become bound at top. Sow, therefore, if possible, in dry weather, but in freshly-moved ground.

88. The *season* for sowing will, of course, find a place under the names of the respective plants; and, I do hope, that it is unnecessary for me to say, that sowing according to the *Moon* is wholly absurd and ridiculous; and that it arose solely out of the circumstance, that our forefathers, who could not read, had neither Almanack nor Calendar to guide them, and who counted by Moons

and Festivals, instead of by Months, and days of Months.

89. As to the *act of sowing*, the distances and depths differ with different plants, and these will, of course, be pointed out under the names of those different plants ; but, one thing is common to all seeds ; and that is, that they should be sown in *rows* or *drills;* for, unless they be sown in this way, all is *uncertainty*. The distribution of the seed is unequal ; the covering is of unequal depth ; and, when the plants come up in company with the weeds, the difficulty of ridding the ground of the latter, without destroying the former, is very great indeed, and attended with *ten times* the labour. Plants, in their earliest state, generally require to be *thinned ;* which cannot be done with regularity, unless they stand in rows ; and, as to every future operation, how easy is the labour in the one case, and how hard in the other ! It is of great advantage to almost all plants, to move the ground somewhat deep while they are growing ; but, how is this to be done, unless they stand in rows ? If they be dispersed promiscuously over the ground, to perform this operation is next to impossible.

90. The great obstacle to the following of a method so obviously advantageous, is, the *trouble*. To draw lines for peas and beans is not deemed troublesome ; but, to do this for radishes, onions, carrots, lettuces, beds of cabbages, and other small seeds, is regarded as *tedious*. When we consider the *saving of trouble afterwards*, this trouble is really nothing, even if the drills were drawn one at a time by a line or rule ; but, this need not be

the case; for, a very cheap and simple tool does the business with as much quickness as sowing at random.

91. Suppose there be a bed of *onions* to be sown. I make my drills in this way. I have what I call a *Driller*, which is a *rake* six feet long in the head. This head is made of oak, 2 inches by 2½; and has *teeth* in it at *eight inches* asunder, each tooth being about six inches long, and an inch in diameter at the head, and is pointed a little at the end that meets the ground. This gives *nine* teeth, there being four inches over at each end of the head. In this head, there is a handle fixed of about six feet long. When my ground is prepared, raked nice and smooth, and cleaned from stones and clods, I begin at the left hand end of the bed, and draw across it *nine rows at once*. I then proceed, taking care to keep the left hand tooth of the Driller in the right hand drill that has just been made; so that now I make but *eight new drills*, because (for a guide) the left hand tooth goes this time in the drill, which was before made by the right hand tooth. Thus, at every draw, I make *eight drills*. And, in this way, a pretty long bed is formed into nice, straight drills, in a very few minutes. The sowing, after this, is done with *truth*, and the depth of the covering must be alike for all the seeds. If it be parsnips or carrots, which require a wider distance between the rows; or, cabbage plants, which, as they are to stand only for a while, do not require distances so wide: in these cases, other Drillers may be made.

92. In the case of *large pieces of ground*, a hand Driller is not sufficient. Yet, if the land be *ploughed*, furrows

might make the paths, the harrow might smooth the ground, and the hand-driller might be used for onions, or for any thing else.   However, what I did, in America, for *Kidney Beans*, was this.   I had a roller drawn by an ox, or a horse.   The roller was about eight inches in diameter, and ten feet long.   To that part of the frame of the roller, which projects, or hangs over, beyond the roller behind, I attached, by means of two *pieces of wood* and *two pins*, a *bar* ten feet long.   Into this bar I put *ten teeth*; and near the middle of the bar two handles.   The roller being put in motion, *breaks all the clods* that the harrow has left, draws after it the *ten teeth*, and the ten teeth make *ten drills*, as deep, or as shallow, as the man chooses who follows the roller, holding the two handles of the *bar*.   The two pieces of wood, which connect the bar with the hinder projecting part of the frame of the roller, *work on the pins*, so as to let the bar up and down, as occasion may require ; and, of course, while the roller is turning, at the end, the bar, with the teeth in it, is raised from the ground.

93. Thus are ten drills made by an ox, in about *five minutes*, which would perhaps require a man more than a day to make with a hoe.   In short, an ox, or a horse, and a man and a boy, will do twelve acres in a day with ease. And to draw the drills *with a hoe* would require *forty-eight* men at the least ; for, there is the *line* to be at work as well as the hoe.   Wheat, and even peas, are in the fields, drilled by machines ; but *beans* cannot, and especially *kidney beans*.   Drills must be made : and, where they are cultivated on a large scale, how tedious and expensive must be the operation to make the drills,

by line and hoe ! When the drills are made, the beans are laid in at proper distances, then covered with a light harrow ; and after all comes the roller, with the teeth lifted up of course ; and all is smooth and neat. The expense of such an apparatus is, really, nothing worth notice.

94. In order to render the march of the ox straight, my ground was ploughed into *lands*, one of which took the ten rows of kidney-beans ; so that the ox had only to be kept straight along upon the middle of the land. And, in order, to have the lands *flat*, not *arched* at all, the ground was ploughed twice in this shape, which brought the middle of the lands where the furrows were before. If, however, the ground had been flat-ploughed, without any furrow, there would have been no difficulty. I should have started on a straight side, or on the straightest side, leaving out any crook or angle that there might have been. I should have taken two distinct objects, found, or placed, beyond the end of the work, and should have directed the head of the ox in a line with those two objects. Before I started, I should have measured off the width to find where the ox ought to come to again, and then have fixed two objects to direct his coming back. I should have done this at each end, till the piece had been finished.

95. When the seeds, in the garden-sowing, are properly, and at suitable distances, placed in the drills, rake the ground, and, in all cases, *tread it with your feet*, unless it be *very moist*. Then rake it *slightly* again ; for all seeds grow best when the earth is pressed closely

about them. When the plants come up, thin them, keep them clear of weeds, and attend to the directions given under the names of the several plants.

--------------------------------- ➤

TRANSPLANTING.

96. THE *weather* for transplanting, is the same as that for *sowing*. If you do this work in *wet* weather, or when the ground is wet, the work cannot be well done. It is no matter what the plant is, whether it be a cucumber plant, or an oak-tree. It has been observed, as to seeds, that they like the earth to *touch* them in every part, and to lie *close* about them. It is the same with *roots*. One half of the bad growth that we see in *orchards*, arises from negligence in the *planting :* from tumbling the earth carelessly in upon the roots. The earth should be as *fine* as possible ; for, if it be not, part of the roots will remain *untouched* by the earth. If the ground be *wet*, it cannot be *fine*. And, if mixed wet, it will remain in a sort of mortar, and will cling and bind together, and will leave more or less of cracks, when it become dry.

97. If possible, therefore, transplant when the ground is not wet ; but, here again, as in the case of sowing, let it be dug, or deeply moved, and well broken, immediately before you transplant into it. There is a *fermentation* that takes place immediately after moving, and a dew arises, which did not arise before. These greatly exceed, in power of causing the plant *to strike*, any thing to be obtained by rain on the plants at the time of planting

or by planting in wet earth.   Cabbages and Ruta Baga
(or Swedish Turnip) I have proved, in innumerable instances, will, if planted in freshly-moved earth, under a
burning sun, be a great deal finer than those planted in
wet ground, or during rain.   The causes are explained
in the foregoing paragraph ; and there never was a
greater, though a most popular error, than that of *waiting
for a shower*, in order to set about the work of transplanting.   In all the books that I have read, without a single
exception : in the English Gardening books ; in the
English Farmer's Dictionary, and many other works on
English husbandry ; in the Encyclopædia ; in short, in
all the books on husbandry and on gardening that I have
ever read, English or French, this transplanting in
showery weather is recommended.

98. If you transplant in hot weather, the *leaves* of the
plants will be scorched ; but the hearts will live ; and
the heat, assisting the fermentation, will produce new
roots in twenty-four hours, and new leaves in a few days.
Then it is that you see fine vegetation come on.   If you
plant in *wet*, that wet must be followed by *dry ;* the
earth, from being moved in wet, contracts the *mortary*
nature ; hardens first, and then cracks ; and the plants
will stand in a stunted state, till the ground be moved
about them *in dry weather*.   If I could have my wish in
the planting of a piece of cabbages, ruta baga, lettuces,
or almost any thing, I would find the ground perfectly
dry at top ; I would have it dug deeply ; plant immediately ; and have no rain for three or four days.   I
would prefer no rain for a month, to rain at the time of
planting.

99. This is a matter of primary importance. How many crops are lost by the *waiting for a shower !* And, when the shower comes, the ground is either *not dug,* or it has been dug for some time, and the benefit of the fermentation is wholly lost.

100. However, there are some very tender plants; plants so soft and *juicy* as to be absolutely burnt up, and totally destroyed, stems and all, in a hot sun, in a few hours. These, which lie in a small compass, must be *shaded* at least, if not watered, upon their removal; a more particular notice of which will be taken as we proceed in the Lists of the Plants.

101. In the *act* of transplanting, the main things are to take care not to *bury the heart* of the plant; and to take care that the earth be well pressed about the *point of the root* of the plant. To press the earth very closely about the *stem* of the plant is of little use, if you leave the *point* of the root loose. I beg that this may be borne in mind; for the growth, and even the life of the plant, depend on great care as to this particular. See *Cabbage,* paragraph 129, for a minute description of the *act* of planting.

102. As to propagation by cuttings, slips, layers, and offsets, it will be spoken of under the names of the several plants usually propagated in any of those ways. *Cuttings* are pieces cut off from branches of trees and plants. *Slips* are branches pulled off, and slipped down at a joint. *Layers* are branches left on the plant or tree, and bent down to the ground, and fastened, with earth laid upon the part between the plant and the top of the

branch.   *Offsets* are parts of the root and plant separated from the main root.

CULTIVATION.

103. HERE, as in the foregoing parts of this Chapter, I propose to speak only of what is of *general* application, in order to save the room that would be necessary to repeat instructions for cultivation under the names of the several plants.

104. The ground being good, and the sowing, or planting, having been properly performed, the next thing is the *after-management*, which is usually called the *cultivation*.

105. If the subject be from *seed*, the first thing is to see that the plants stand at a proper distance from each other; because, if left too close, they cannot come to good. Let them also be thinned early; for, even while in seed-leaf, they injure each other. Carrots, parsnips, lettuces, every thing, ought to be thinned in the seed-leaf.

106. Hoe, or weed, immediately; and, let me observe here, once for all, that weeds never ought to be suffered to get to any size either in field or garden, and especially in the latter.

107. But, besides the act of killing weeds, *cultivation* means *moving the earth* between the plants while growing.

This assists them in their growth : it feeds them : it raises food for their roots to live upon. A mere *flat-hoeing* does nothing but keep down the weeds. The hoeing when the plants are become stout, should be deep; and, in general, with a hoe that has *spanes*, instead of a mere flat plate. In short, a sort of *prong* in the *posture* of a hoe. And the spane of this prong-hoe may be longer, or shorter, according to the nature of the crop to be hoed. *Deep-hoeing* is enough in some cases ; but, in others, *digging* is necessary to produce a fine and full crop. If any body will have a piece of cabbages, and will dig between the rows of one half of them twice during their growth, and let the other half of the piece have nothing but a flat-hoeing, that person will find that the half which has been digged between, will, when the crop is ripe, weigh nearly, if not quite, twice as much as the other half.

108. It may appear, that, to dig thus amongst growing plants is to cut off, or tear off, their roots, of which the ground is full. This is really the case, and this does great good ; for the roots, thus cut asunder, shoot again from the plant's side, find new food, and send, instantly, fresh vigour to the plant. The effect of this tillage is quite surprising. We are hardly aware of its power in producing vegetation ; and we are still less aware of the distance, to which the roots of plants extend in every direction.

109. Mr. Tull, the father of the drill-husbandry, gives the following account of the manner in which he discovered the distance to which certain roots extend.

I should observe here, that he was led to think of the drilling of crops in the fields of England, from having, when in France, observed the effects of inter-tillage on the vines, in the vineyards. If he had visited America instead of France, he would have seen the effects of that tillage, in a still more striking light, on plants in the Indian corn-fields ; for, he would have seen those plants spindling, yellow, actually perishing, to-day, for want of *ploughing ;* and, in four days after a good, deep, clean, and careful ploughing, especially in *hot* weather, he would have seen them wholly change their colour, become of a bright and beautiful green, bending their leaves over the intervals, and growing at the rate of four inches in the twenty-four hours.

110. The passage, to which I have alluded, is of so interesting a nature, and relates to a matter of so much importance, that I shall insert it entire, and also the *plate* made use of by Mr. Tull to illustrate his meaning. I shall not, as so many others have, take the thoughts, and send them forth as my own ; nor, like Mr. JOHN CHRISTIAN CURWEN, a Member of Parliament, steal them from TULL, and give them, with all the honour belonging to them, to a *Bishop.*

111. " *A Method how to find the distance to which roots* " *extended horizontally.* A piece, or plot, dug and made " fine, in *whole hard ground,* as in *Plate* II. *Fig.* 1.

" The end A. 2 feet, the end B. 12 feet, the length of " the piece 20 yards ; the figures in the middle of it are " 20 turnips, sown early, and well hoed. The manner of

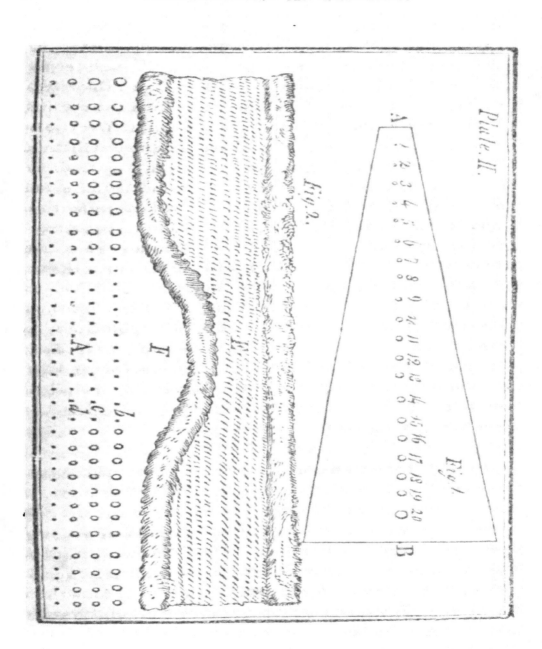

" this hoeing must be, at first, near the plants, with a
" spade, and each time afterwards, a foot distance, till
" the earth be once well dug ; and, if weeds appear
" where it has been so dug, hoe them out shallow with
" the hand-hoe. But, dig all the piece next the out-lines
" deep every time, that it may be the finer for the roots
" to enter, when they are permitted to come thither. If
" the turnips be all bigger, as they stand nearer to the
" end B, it is a proof that they all extend to the outside
" of the piece, and the *Turnip* 20, will appear to draw
" nourishment from six foot distance from its centre. But
" if the *Turnips* 16, 17, 18, 19, 20, acquire no greater
" bulk than the *Turnip* 15, it will be clear, that their
" *roots* extend no farther than those 'of the *Turnip* 15
" does ; which is about four foot. By this method the
" distance of the extent of *roots* of any plant, may be
" discovered.—There is also another way to find the
" length of *roots*, by making a long narrow trench, at the
" distance you expect they will extend to, and fill it
" with salt ; if the plant be killed by the salt, it is
" certain that some of the roots enter it.

112. " What put me upon trying this method, was an
" observation of two lands, or ridges, (see *Plate* II. *Fig.*2.)
" drilled with *Turnips* in rows, a foot asunder, and very
" even in them ; the ground, at both ends and one side,
" was hard and unploughed. The *Turnips* not being
" hoed were very poor, small, and yellow, except the
" three outside rows, *b c d*, which stood next to the land
" (or ridge) E, which land, being ploughed and harrowed,
" at the time the land A ought to have been hoed, gave a
" dark flourishing colour to these three rows ; and the

" *Turnips* in the row *d*, which stood farthest off from the
" new ploughed land **E**, received so much benefit from
" it, as to grow twice as big as any of the more distant
" rows. The row *c* being a foot nearer to the new
" ploughed land, became twice as large as those in *d*,
" but the row *b*, which was next to the land **E**, grew
" much larger yet. *F* is a piece of hard whole ground,
" of about two perch in length, and about two or three
" foot broad, lying betwixt those two lands, which had
" not been ploughed that year ; it was remarkable that,
" during the length of this interjacent hard ground, the
" rows *b c d* were as small and yellow as any in the land.
" The *Turnips* in the row *d*, about three foot distant from
" the land **E**, receiving a double increase, proves they
" had as much nourishment from the land *E* as from the
" land A, wherein they stood, which nourishment was
" brought by less than half the number of *roots* of each
" of these *Turnips*. In their own land they must have
" extended a yard all round, else they could not have
" reached the land **E**, wherein it is probable these few
" roots went more than another yard, to give each tur-
" nip as much increase as all the roots had done in
" their own land. Except that it will hereafter appear,
" that the new nourishment taken at the extremities of
" the roots in the land **E**, might enable the plants to send
" out more new roots in their own land, and receive
" something more from thence. The row *c* being twice as
" big as the row *d*, must be supposed to extend twice as
" far ; and the row *b*, four times as far, in proportion as
" it was of a bulk quadruple to the row *d*."

113. Thus, then, it is clear, that tillage amongst grow-

ing plants is a great thing. Not only is it of great benefit to the plants ; not only does it greatly augment the amount of the crop, and make it of the best quality ; but it prepares the ground for another crop. If a *summer fallow* be good for the land, here is a summer fallow ; if the ploughing between turnips *prepare the land for wheat,* the digging between cabbages and other crops will, of course, prepare the land for succeeding crops.

114. *Watering plants,* though so strongly recommended in English Gardening books, and so much in practice, is a thing of very doubtful utility in any case, and, in most cases, of positive injury. A country often endures present suffering from long drought ; but, if even all the gardens and all the fields could, in such a case, be watered with a watering-pot, I much question whether it would be beneficial even to the crops of the dry season itself. It is not, observe, *rain* water that you can, one time out of a thousand, water with. And, to *nourish plants,* the water must be prepared in clouds and mists and dews. Observe this. Besides, when rain comes, the earth is *prepared* for it by that state of the air which precedes rain, and which makes all things *damp,* and *slackens* and loosens the earth, and disposes the roots and leaves for the reception of the rain. To pour water, therefore, upon plants, or upon the ground where they are growing, or where seeds are sown, is never of much use, and is generally mischievous ; for, the air is dry ; the sun comes immediately and bakes the ground, and vegetation is checked, rather than advanced, by the operation. The best protector against frequent drought is frequent *digging ;* or, in the fields, *ploughing,* and always *deep.* Hence

will arise a *fermentation* and *dews.* The ground will have *moisture* in it, in spite of all drought, which the hard, unmoved ground, will not. But always dig or plough in *dry weather,* and, the drier the weather, the deeper you ought to go, and the finer you ought to break the earth. When plants are *covered* by *lights,* or are in a *house,* or are covered with cloths in the night time, they may need *watering,* and in such cases, must have it given them by hand.

115. I shall conclude this Chapter with observing, on what I deem a vulgar error, and an error, too, which sometimes produces inconvenience. It is believed, and stated, that the ground *grows tired,* in time, of the *same sort of plant ;* and that, if it be, year after year, cropped with the same sort of plant, the produce will be small, and the quality inferior to what it was at first. Mr. Tull has most satisfactorily *proved,* both by fact and argument, that this is not true. And I will add this fact, that Mr. Missing, a barrister, living in the parish of Titchfield, in Hampshire, and who was a most excellent and kind neighbour of mine, has a border under a south wall, on which he, and his father before him, have grown *early peas,* every year, for *more, now, than fifty years ;* and if, at any time, they had been finer than they were every one year of the four or five years that I saw them, they must have been something very extraordinary ; for, in those years, they were as fine, and as full bearing, as any that I ever saw in England.

116. Before I entirely quitted the subject of *Cultivation,* there would be a few remarks to be made upon the

means of preventing the depredations of *vermin*, some of which make their attacks on the *seed*, others on the *roots*, others on the *stem*, others on the *leaves* and *blossoms*, and others on the *fruit;* but, as I shall have to be very particular on this subject in speaking of *fruits*, I defer it till I come to the Chapter on Fruits.

117. Having now treated of the Situation, Soil, Fencing, and Laying out of Gardens; on the making and managing of Hot-beds and Green-houses; and having given some directions as to Propagation and Cultivation in general, I next proceed to give Alphabetical Lists of the several sorts of plants, and to speak of the proper treatment for each, under the three heads, *Vegetables and Herbs; Fruits;* and *Flowers.*

CHAPTER V.

Kitchen-garden Plants, arranged in Alphabetical order, with Directions relative to the Propagation and Cultivation of each sort.

————————

118. THE plants which are cultivated in the kitchen-garden are either such as are for food, or for medicinal purposes. The former are generally called *vegetables,* and the latter, *herbs ;* and then there are pot-herbs and medicinal herbs, which, altogether, forms a strange jumble and inconsistency ; every thing being a vegetable that grows out of the earth, from a blade of grass to an oak-tree. The best and most consistent way, therefore, is to give the name of Kitchen-garden plants to all the things grown in the kitchen-garden, except fruits, which will have a distinct Chapter allotted to themselves. The alphabetical order is also the best, because each article is referred to with so much convenience. The reader will please to bear in mind what has been said in the fore-going Chapter with regard to propagation and cultivation in general ; that Chapter being written for the express purpose of preventing the necessity of repeating, under every particular article, directions for selecting the sorts, for saving and preserving the seed, for sowing, for trans-planting and for after cultivation. The rules there laid down are applicable to all kitchen-garden plants ; some additional rules given in this Chapter, will apply to each

plant respectively. After this preface, I begin the list of kitchen-garden plants in the manner before described.

119. ARTICHOKE.—This plant is propagated either from *seed* or from *offsets*. If from the former, sow the seed in rows a foot apart, in the month of March ; thin the plants to a foot apart as soon as they are an inch high ; keep them cleanly weeded, and the ground moved, now-and-then, during the summer ; and, in the autumn, they will be large enough to plant out where they are to stand and to bear. They are things that require a good deal of room, and a very rich soil. Dung, which would be mischievous in some cases, can do no harm here. The ground ought to be fresh dug in the month of October, the plants taken up, and the points of the roots tipped with a sharp knife. They should be planted in clumps, at three feet apart in the row of clumps, and the rows should be about five feet apart. Each clump should have four good plants in it, and these should be well fastened in the ground, each plant standing at about nine inches from the other. When winter comes on, if hard frosts come, the clumps should be covered pretty thickly with litter, which, however, should be taken off again as soon as the frost is *out of the ground;* but no plant which has been covered to be protected from the frost, should be uncovered, and the sun left to come upon the ground where it stands, before the thaw has completely taken place. In the spring, the ground about the clumps should be moved up a little with a fork, and nicely broken in dry weather, in March or April. These plants will bear fruit the first year ; and, if properly managed, will continue to bear for a great many years. When their

roots reach stagnant water, or any soil which they do not like, the plants begin to give out; but otherwise, they will keep bearing for a great number of years. The next spring, that is to say, the second spring after having been planted out, you will find that they have sent out great numbers of side-shoots or offsets; you should, therefore, move the earth away a little round the clump, and take off these offsets, which would otherwise prevent the great bearing of the plant. When you take off these offsets, you will find some very stout, while others will be very weak; and, if you want a new plantation, these offsets are as good plants as any; and, if stout, they will bear the first year, but, and very conveniently, they will come into bearing after the old plants have done. The artichoke, although so robust a plant, is very sensible of the frost. Therefore, each clump should have the earth drawn up pretty much about it in the fall of the year, but in dry weather if possible, and, in very severe weather, some litter should be laid on the top of each clump, being always taken off as soon as the frost is completely out of the ground. In the spring, the whole of the ground ought to be carefully dug, and the earth levelled down from the sides of the clumps; the offsets should now be taken off, and the plants left to produce their crop. The rows of plants being five feet apart, affords an opportunity for planting other things between them; but, this can hardly be done to any great advantage except you be in very great want of room; for, what you gain in this way, you lose by the imperfect culture of the artichokes. They love *cool* ground, though, not stagnant water at the bottom; and, perhaps, the best situation for them would be under the South side hedge of the outer garden. One row of clumps along under that hedge, and at three feet from it, would contain fifty clumps, which would, if well cultivated, produce enough for any family in the world. The artichoke is a large, rude and tall thing, and, thus situated, it would not intercept the view of prettier crops. If part of that shady hedge were wanted for other things, you might have two rows of Artichokes, extending half the length of the row before mentioned. Those who are very fond of Artichokes might have some few clumps in an earlier spot; and, to have them late in the year, the latest should be cut off with stems as long as possible, and these stems stuck into moist earth or sand in a cool shed or in a cellar; preserved in which manner, many people have them to eat in January. There are *two sorts* of this plant, the difference of which consists, I believe, solely in the fruit, or rather of the flower; for, after all, the seed is the fruit. One of these sorts bear a conical head, and the other a head which is round. The latter is larger than the former, but I never heard that there was any difference in the quality. If you wish to save the *seed* of this plant, you ought to let some of the earliest heads remain uncut, they will flower like a thistle in the summer, and the seed very much like that of the Sun-flower, will be ripe in the Fall. Gather it when perfectly dry, rub it out of the husk, and put it by in a very dry place, where it will keep good for three years at the least.

120. ASPARAGUS.—This plant is raised from seed only. It is contained in small berries which are first green and then red, each of which contains two or three black seeds which are ripe in the month of Octo-

ber. The seed should be then gathered, made perfectly
dry. The pods kept whole and hung up in a dry place
for use ; when wanted to be sown, it should be rubbed
out of the pod.   Out of the pod, the seed will keep four
or five years ; but, if in the pod and kept dry, it would
probably keep twenty.   To have asparagus *beds*, there
are two ways of going to work : first : sowing the seeds
in the beds at once ; and, second, raising the plants elsewhere, and transplanting them into beds.   The beds
ought to be four feet wide, and not more, because you
ought to be able to cut the asparagus without going upon
the beds.   If the ground where the beds are to be, have
a dry bottom to a great depth, the beds may stand pretty
nearly upon a level with the common earth of the garden ;
but, if the bottom be wet, the paths between the beds
ought to be deep ; they ought to serve as trenches ; for
asparagus does not like to have its roots sopping in wet ;
and yet it likes rich and rather moist ground.   It is understood that the whole of the garden has been trenched
to the depth of three feet nine inches, to which depth,
however, the root of the asparagus will not be very long
in going ; for, if the culture be good, and the bottom
free from stagnant water, a plantation will last for a good
long life-time, or more.   The ground being manured
well, well-dug, and made very fine, lay out your beds in
March in dry weather ; or, indeed, in good ground, any
time in April may do very well.   Suppose, four beds to
be wanted, each of them as long as the width of one of
the plats in the garden.   Lay out the four beds at the
west end, for instance, of plat *g* ; and the beds will, of
course, run from north to south : each bed is to be four
feet wide, and each alley between the beds, two feet, or

F

two feet and a half wide. As you mark out your beds, drive down, at each corner, a pin of some durable wood, about the size of your wrist (if it be a stout one), and going down into the ground a foot and a half at least, leaving six inches to be above ground; these pins being always ready to apply the line to, will prevent the beds from ever getting out of their proper shape. Having laid out the beds, make three lines along each, placing the first line at six inches from the outside of the bed. The lines are to be a foot apart, and that will leave six inches from the outside line to the outside of the bed; sow the seed along these lines, press it well down into the ground, and cover it lightly. The plants will be up in June; and, as soon as they are fairly up, thin them to a foot apart, and keep them very clean and nicely hoed all the summer. They will, in the autumn, have stalks or haulm about a foot high, which will turn yellow in the month of November. When it do so, cut it off, and cover the bed an inch or two deep with a mixture of wood ashes or other compost. Thus the beds will lie all the winter. In the spring, March or early in April, move the tops of the beds with a *fork,* and carefully pick out all weeds that make their appearance; and then throw upon the beds earth about two inches deep from the alleys, making that earth very fine, and keeping the edges of the alleys very smooth and straight. The plants will now send out several shoots from each crown, and, if kept clean during the summer, the haulm will attain the height of three feet. This year, the plants will bear some seed; but, no notice is to be taken of that; and, in the month of November, when the haulm becomes yellow, you cut it off again close to the ground, and lay on good, well prepared compost, partly consisting of rotten dung to the depth of two inches or a little more. In the spring, in March, throw upon the beds three inches deep of earth out of the alleys. Break it very fine, and attend to keeping the sides of the bed very smooth and erect. This is the third year after sowing; and, if the ground be good in its nature, and, if all these instructions be duly attended to, there will be some heads of asparagus fit to cut. The four beds will contain 588 stools or crowns; and, if you were to cut only four heads of asparagus from each crown, you would have above twenty hundred bundles of asparagus, a hundred in each bundle. However, unless the crowns be very strong, it would be best to wait another year; and then, without cutting any but what would be very fine, you would have more than any family of reasonable size would want to consume. In the fall of this third year, cut down the haulm as before; put on manure again as before; and in the next spring, take another two and a half inches of earth out of the alleys and put on the beds as before. The alleys will now be deep enough, and you need never throw any more earth upon the beds, except the shovellings up of what has fallen into them from the beds by washing or crumbling; and this ought to be done every spring, in March. Every fall, the haulm ought to be cut off; and some little matter of manure, rather of a littery sort, scattered on; and this ought to be forked up every spring, previous to the shovelling up of the alleys. One very great fault in the management of asparagus beds, is, to suffer the seed to drop and to remain on the beds. This seed will grow and become plants; and, in a short time, you have the bed all in confusion, young ones growing at the top, and old ones growing underneath. Therefore, the haulm ought to be cut off before the seed drop ; and, if it should, by accident, drop, in the cutting of the haulm, the seed ought to be swept carefully up with a broom and carried away. It is the practice of many persons, and of most persons, to sow lettuces, onions and radishes, upon asparagus beds, which are taken off before the haulm of the asparagus arise to any considerable height ; but this is a very bad practice : these plants rob the asparagus, they prevent its due cultivation ; and, in short, the injury to you as a gardener is much greater than its good. In the cutting of asparagus, great care must be taken to use a proper instrument, and to make the cut in a proper manner. The instrument is a knife made with teeth, like a saw, which ought to be put down close by the side of the shoot which you are going to cut off, and then you separate the shoot from the crown by a push almost perpendicular ; for otherwise, you might destroy three or four shoots in the cutting off of one. Those shoots which you do not cut off for the purpose of eating, are left to go on to become haulm, and these are cut down annually at the time and in the manner described. Such is the manner of raising asparagus from seed. The manner of raising from plants is this : you sow the aspara-gus in March or April, in the same manner as described for the beds, in some other spot ; and, when the plants come up, you thin them carefully to the distance of about three inches apart, keeping them very clean all the sum-mer. In October, or in March the next year, you make your beds as before ; and, instead of sowing seed in the three rows upon each bed as before directed, plant these plants at a foot apart in these rows, placing their crowns about half an inch below the top of the ground, and then covering the beds over an inch or two deep with good compost, or fine manure of some sort or other, having amongst it some salt, not too much, or a pretty good portion of wood-ashes. You then proceed with these beds, autumn and spring, precisely in the same way with the beds of sown asparagus; and you may, perhaps, have them fit to cut a year earlier; and, if great care be taken, that will certainly be the case. The asparagus is so excellent a plant; it is so good, and is so great a favourite, that it is one of the few garden plants that is worth the trouble and expense of a hot-bed, and particularly as the trouble which it gives is in an inverse proportion to its value. To have asparagus in hot-beds, which you may have if you will, from November until the time that it comes in the open ground, this is the method; make a bed, according to the rules laid down in Chapter III. The bed ought to be strong or weak; that is to say, high or low, according to the season of the year. In November, for instance, you want but little heat: in January and February a great deal: less in March, and scarcely any in April. To have the plants, make a bed, the rows on which should be seven inches apart, and the plants six inches apart in the row. Fill this bed with plants that have stood one year elsewhere in the manner before-mentioned. Let them stand two years in this bed, and be managed there just in the same manner as if they were going to stand there for ever. At the end of these two years, as soon as the haulm turns yellow, the plants will be fit to take up to put into hot-beds. When you have made your bed, and the heat be sufficiently up, put good earth upon it four inches deep or thereabouts. Then take up the plants, or, rather, the crowns from their bed, and place them upon the earth in the hot-bed as near together as they can conveniently stand. Take care that the crowns are all of the same height in the hot-bed, and bring them from the garden beds with their balls of earth to them, and their roots as little torn as possible. When you have the crowns all neatly and evenly arranged upon the beds, fill all the interstices between them with fine earth, give the whole a gentle watering, and then covet the crowns over with fine earth six inches deep. If the bed be a pretty strong one, and, if you give air judiciously, and keep frosts effectually out, you may cut asparagus in twenty days from the time that you put the crowns into the bed ; but, you must be watchful to give as much air as the season will permit, otherwise the asparagus will be spindling, will be of a pale colour, and will have very little taste. It may so happen, that, when you are ready to put your asparagus into the bed, the crowns will be locked up from you by frost. To be prepared for this, put, in due time, more litter, or straw, upon your stock of crowns than the frosts can penetrate through. If you wish to have but one hot-bed of asparagus every year, your annual provision of crowns will, of course, be accordingly. These crowns will give you, in the hot-bed, asparagus for a month or six weeks ; and that, too, if you please, in January or February. When they have borne their crop, they are of no more use, and will, of course, be flung away ; but, they are worth the trouble, and I know of nothing that is more sure to be attended with success. If the weather should prove very severe while the crowns are in the bed, not only thick coverings, but *linings*, must be resorted to, and these you will find fully described under the head of CUCUMBER. As to the sorts of asparagus of which some people talk, I, for my part, could never discover any difference: some talk of red-topped and some of green-topped; but I am convinced that all the difference that there is, is to be traced to the soil, the climate, and the culture.

121. BALM.—This is a herb purely medicinal. A very little of it is sufficient in any garden. It is propagated from seed, or from offsets. When once planted, the only care required is to see that it do not extend itself too widely.

122. BASIL is a very sweet annual pot-herb, being of two sorts, the dwarf and the tall. It should be sowed in very fine earth early in the spring, and transplanted into earth equally fine, with very great care. But, let me here speak of the place for herbs in general. They should all be collected together in one spot if possible. The best form is a long bed, with an alley on each side of it, the bed too narrow to need trampling in order to reach the middle of it. The herbs should stand in rows made across this bed, the quantity of each being in due proportion to the consumption of the family; for it is a mark of great want of judgment to occupy great spaces of ground with things that can be of no possible use. We often see, in a gentleman's garden, as much parsley growing as would be sufficient for the supply of a large country town; and, as to *mint*, I have often seen it covering several rods of ground, when the sensible original

intention was that it should be confined within the space of a couple of square yards. Mint, however, forms an exception to what has just been said about collecting the herbs together in one place ; for its encroachments are such that it must be banished to some spot where those encroachments can occasionally be restricted by the operations of the spade.

123. BEAN.—Bean is the name given to two plants having very little resemblance to each other in almost any respect. In the French language, they have two different names wholly dissimilar to each other. That sort which we call our bean, and which is an upright plant, rising very high, producing a very large seed, and is called *garden-bean* or *horse-bean :* that species the French call *fève ;* that species which we call *kidney-bean* (because the seed is exactly in the shape of a kidney), or *French bean,* because, I suppose, it came originally from France, the French call *haricot ;* which latter name has given rise to an application of it, very curious, but quite congenial to the turn of mind and taste of those by whom it has been adopted. Thus, we see, a dish of stewed mutton, made richer than its own means would afford, by all manner of ingredients, call a *haricot* of mutton ; whereas the French mean by a haricot of mutton a dish full of haricots or beans, with a little morsel of mutton stewed along with them. The English bean, which is that that we have now to speak of, has several varieties, the favourite amongst which, is the *broad bean,* or *Windsor bean.* The *long-pod* is the next best, though there are several others of nearly the same form, size and quality. But, there is one bean which is called the

Mazagan, which comes earlier than the rest, and which, on that account, is justly esteemed by those who like this sort of vegetable, which, I must confess, I do not. All this tribe of beans thrive best in moist and stiffish ground; but, if we desire to have them early, we must sow them early; and, near a wall, facing to the south, they may be sowed in November and even in October; and, if kept earthed up pretty nearly to their tops, and in very sharp weather, covered from the frost, they will stand the winter pretty well; and will be a little earlier than those which are sowed in the latter end of February or beginning of March. Another way to have these early beans, is, to sow a small patch, and to let them come up within an inch of one another. Standing thus upon a small piece of ground, they are easily protected in sharp weather; and are ready to be removed, by transplanting in the first mild weather in March; but even then they should go into the warmest part of the garden. Another sowing, even of these, should take place in the latter end of February, or very early in March, which is the time also for sowing the Windsor bean, the long-pod, and all the other varieties. Of the Windsor bean and the long-pod another sowing should take place in April, and in every month until July; that is to say, if the family like them. The sowings ought to be of small extent, however, for the crop is large, and the plant, when it has shed its blossom, is no great beauty, though exceeding almost all others in the sweetness of its flower. Mice are great enemies of beans, or, more properly speaking, they *love them too much,* as the cannibal said of his fellow-creatures. This love, however, sometimes proves extremely inconvenient to the bean-planter ; and, therefore, these gentry must be kept down, which they easily are, however, by brick-traps, which gardeners know very well how to set. The depth at which the larger beans are sowed is about three inches, and the smaller ones about two inches and a half ; but, in every case, all the earth drawn out of the drill, should be put in again upon the beans, and trodden down upon them with the whole weight of the body of a stout man ; for the more closely they are pressed into the ground, and the ground is pressed upon them, the more certainly and the more vigourously will they grow ; and the more difficult, too, will it be for the mice to displace them.

124. BEAN (KIDNEY), which the French call HARICOT.—The varieties here are perfectly endless ; but there are two distinct descriptions of the kidney-bean, *dwarfs*, and *climbers*. The mode, however, of propagating and cultivating is the same in both cases, except that the dwarfs require smaller distances than the climber, and that the latter are grown with the assistance of poles which the former are not. This is a plant, very different, indeed, in its nature, from the *fève*, or, English bean : it is a native of a warm climate ; very sensible of frost, and only one degree more hardy than the cucumber, and not at all more hardy than the squash. The very slightest frost checks the growth of the plant and changes the colour of the leaves ; and, the leaves are absolutely scorched up by frosts not sufficient to produce ice no thicker than gauze ; so that, we have here a summer plant to all intents and purposes ; a plant that must be cultivated under cover of some sort, except at times when there is a complete absence of frost. The general

time for sowing kidney-beans, in ground quite open,
when there is no shelter of any sort, and where covering
is wholly impracticable, is the *first of May*. I beg the
reader to bear this in mind : I have tried the thing often
enough : nine times out of ten, earlier sowing does no
good ; and even sowing at this time has frequently been
found too early. I have had my kidney-beans all cut off
in the month of June ; and, therefore, if crop be the
object, the first week in May is quite early enough,
especially for the climbers. But, people wish to have
some small portion, at any rate, of so capital a vegetable,
as early as they possibly can. Those who have the
means, have them all the winter in hot-houses ; but a
hot-bed or hot-beds are insufficient for such a purpose.
In our case, therefore, we must be content with the south
face of a wall, which, if made proper use of for this
purpose, will produce beans from twelve to twenty days
earlier than they can be had in perfectly open ground.
A single row put in, two inches deep, close to the wall,
the beans at about three inches apart in the row, about
the tenth of April, and earthed up to the seed leaf as soon
as they are above ground, and kept carefully screened
from frost every night by the leaning of a board or some
other thing against the wall ; a single row of these beans,
being also of the earliest sort, will, in the south of
England, produce beans fit to gather in the last week of
June ; while the same sort of beans sowed in the open
ground at the same time, will either rot in the ground
and never come up ; or will, after coming up, be so injured by the weather as to be overtaken by beans sowed
early in May, and will, after all, not produce a crop half
so abundant. A good general time for sowing the first

dwarf beans for a crop, is, the first of May : to have a constant supply, you should sow on the first of every month, August inclusive. The climbing beans should be sowed about the 10th of May. The culture of beans is a very easy matter. For the dwarf sorts, you make drills two feet apart and two inches deep, lay the beans along at three inches asunder, lay the earth over them and tread it down hard. As soon as they are up, which is very quickly, draw the earth from both sides (but not when it is wet) close up to the stems, quite as high as the bottom of the stem of the seed leaf, and then give all the ground a good deep hoeing. The dwarf beans want nothing more than this : they push on at a great rate : they begin to show their blossoms in ten days, and if the frosts keep away, you have beans in a very short time. Even while they are producing, you can, if you please, dig along the centre of the intervals, and there have another crop of beans ; or, if you like better, savoys, broccoli, or other things for the autumn or the winter. The beans are soon taken off, and your ground is ready for any succeeding crop. As to the climbers, they are sowed and cultivated in the same manner ; and they will, if you please, creep about upon the ground ; but that is not the best way. They should be planted in a double row, same depth as the dwarf beans, and the two rows about six inches apart. Then there should be an interval between each two double rows, of five or six feet ; they should be earthed up in the same manner as described for the dwarf beans, and, as soon as earthed up, the poles should be put to them. The poles ought to be about eight feet long, and there ought to be two rows of poles to every double row of beans, not placed upright,

but diagonally; and placed on the internal side of the
beans. The poles on one side of the double row ought
to point one way, and those on the other side, the other
way, forming, together, a sort of rough trellis-work.
Beans will go on climbing and bearing till they get to
the top. There are two very distinct varieties of these
climbers. One has a white seed, and has the perfect
kidney shape, the pod is very long and perfectly smooth.
This is called the Dutch runner, and is very highly esteemed. The other variety has a seed not so flat, of a
black and red colour, it has a short pod, compared with
the other; and that pod is rough, instead of being
smooth, and the blossom is red instead of being white
as in the case of the Dutch runner. But there is a white
sort of this bean also : like the red-blossomed bean in all
other respects, but having a white seed and a white
blossom. These are called *rough runners*, because the
pod differs from that of other kidney-beans in being
rough instead of smooth. These are most admirable
plants: they bear prodigiously; their product is, perhaps, the most delicate of all ; and, from the latter end
of July, until the actual coming of the frosts, they continue to blow and to bear without the least relaxation,
let the weather be as hot or as dry as it may. The
Dutch-runner is not a very great bearer, and it gives out
in a comparatively short space of time : it will, too,
have good cultivation and favourable aspect ; whereas
the rough-runners will grow in the shade, will climb up
hedges and trees, will suffer their stems to be smothered
with weeds, and will continue to ornament whatever they
cling to, and to produce in abundance at the same time.
But, there is one precaution, applicable to all sorts of

kidney-beans, which must be by no means neglected; and that is, to take care that no pods be left upon the plant, to contain beans approaching to a state of maturity; for, the moment there be such pods, they draw away all the strength of the plant to themselves, and it would produce no more pods fit for use. It is the same with the cucumber, suffer one cucumber to become large and yellow, and to begin to ripen its seed, and not another young cucumber will come upon the same plant. As to the sorts or varieties of dwarf beans, the yellow dwarf, that I have imported from America, I have found to be the earliest, by several days, and also the greatest bearer. There is the black dwarf, which is deemed early also. The speckled dwarf is a great bearer, but not so early. The best way, probably, is to sow one row of each on the same day; and, though the difference in the time of coming in may not be much, it may be something, and nothing ought to be neglected in the case of a vegetable so universally and so justly esteemed. It is curious, that the Americans should follow the example of the French with regard to the use of the produce of the kidney-bean. They eat them as we do, in the pod; or, rather, they eat the pod, as we do; but they eat them more frequently in the bean itself, and that at two different stages, first, when it has got its full size in the pod, and when, to me, it appears a very nasty thing; and second, they eat them as a winter vegetable: they soak them and boil them. The French do the same, and I can by no means discover that this was ever the practice in England. The seed of the kidney bean may always be saved in England with great facility, if we would but take the proper means; that is to say, forbear from eating the earliest pods. We ought always to set apart a row or a piece of a row for seed, and resolve never to touch it till the seed be ripe. This is hardly ever done : we keep eating on : above all things, we take the first : those that we save for seed are such as have had the good fortune to escape us, so that, our seed of this important plant is generally very bad ; it is but half ripe, and a great deal of it rots as soon as it is put into the ground. If the seed of this plant be well ripened, it will keep good, *if kept in the pod*, for several years ; but, if taken out of the pod, it cannot be relied on after the first year. It is always the best way to keep it in the pod until it be sown, if that be practicable. It continues to be nourished there, and nature has excluded it completely from the air.

125. BEET.—Some people enumerate several varieties of the beet, and these of different colours. There are but two cultivated in our gardens, and the great sign of their perfection, is, their deep blood colour, a deficiency in which respect is regarded as an imperfection. One of these is tap-rooted, like a carrot, and the other pretty nearly as much a bulb as the common garden turnip. The seed of the beet is a little, round, rough pod, thick and hard, and containing within it sometimes two and sometimes three black seeds. The pod is sowed for it is next to impossible to get the seed out of it and to separate one from the other. To have fine beets, the ground should be dug very deeply and made very fine. There ought to be no clods in it, especially for the tap-rooted beet ; for clods turn aside the tap-root and spoil the shape of the beet. No fresh dung, by any means ;

for that causes side shoots to go out in search of it, and thereby makes the root forked instead of straight; and, as in the case of carrots, a forked root is never considered to be a good one. The ground being well and deeply dug and broken, drills should be nicely made about two feet apart, and the seed laid along at the depth of about an inch and a half, and at about a couple of inches from each other. The earth that came out of the drill should be put back upon the seed, and should be pressed down upon it very hard, with the head of the rake, the foot of man being too rude for this purpose. When the plants come up, they should be thinned to about nine inches apart in the row: the ground should be nicely flat-hoed and kept clean during the summer: in October the roots should be taken up, the leaves cut off within a quarter of an inch of the crown, the roots put to dry in the sun for a week or more, and then put away in some dry place, or packed in sand like carrots, for winter use. Beets may be transplanted, and will, in that way, get to a very good size, but they are apt to be forked. They should remain in the seed bed till about the size of a radish such as we eat at the table, and be put in immediately in very fine earth, and they will do very well, though they will not be so smooth as those that are left to stand where they are sowed.

126. BROCCOLI.—There are two distinct species or kinds of the broccoli; the *purple*, and the *white*. There are, besides, a sort that is of a *brimstone colour*, and another that is greenish; but these only come from a mixture of the other two sorts. One of which is white, or, rather, cream colour, not so white as a cauliflower;

and the other is of a bright purple colour. Broccoli is eaten from about the beginning of November, to about the middle of April. The purple sort comes earliest ; and the white is not generally in much perfection until about the middle of February. There is a purple sort which is called *Cape* broccoli, which comes earlier, I believe, than any of the other purple, this being a purple too. Gardeners talk of early broccoli seed, and of late ; and, doubtless, by dint of great care in saving seed from the earliest heads, the habit of early produce in the plants may be produced ; but, while I do not think there is much in this, it ought to be attended to when people go to purchase seed. The time for sowing the purple broccoli is about the beginning of April, if you wish to have it in the autumn and in the beginning of winter, and, if you wish to have it in the spring, the beginning of May is a proper time to sow. Something, however, depends upon the goodness, as well as the earliness, of the ground ; for, in good ground, especially if it be in a warm situation, you may venture to sow either earlier or later than the times here mentioned. The first week in May is quite time enough to sow the white broccoli ; for, if sowed earlier, it gets too much heat before the summer is over ; it begins to form a head or flower before the frost comes ; and, if the head be only closely approaching towards outward appearance, sharp frost will destroy it : it will rot ; and as this sort of broccoli never sends out sprouts from the side, you lose the produce altogether. Now, as to the manner of sowing the seed, as to the manner of treating the plants after they are up, as to the manner of transplanting them where they are to stand to produce, and as to the cultivation while they are going on towards a state of producing.   These are all the same as directed in the case of the CABBAGE, under which head I shall give full and minute instructions relative to all these operations.   But, there is this difference between the cabbage and the broccoli, that the latter, being a much larger plant than any of the garden cabbages, must have a greater space to grow in.   The rows ought to be three feet apart, and the plants at two and a half feet apart in the rows.   The broccoli plants have long stems; and, therefore, the earth should be, at different times, during their growth, drawn up to them, not only for the purpose of keeping them upright, but for the purpose of nourishment also; for roots will start out of the sides of the stem and communicate great vigour to the plants.   The same ought to be done, indeed, in the case of cabbages; but with more care in the case of the broccoli.

127. BRUSSELS SPROUTS. — The plant that has generally had this name given to it in England, is a thing quite different from the real Brussels sprouts. This plant rises up with a very long stem, which has a spreading open head at the top, but which sends out from its sides great numbers of little cabbages, round and solid, each being of the bulk of a large walnut, and each being a perfect cabbage-head in itself. This little cabbage comes out just above the leaf which starts from the main stem, and it is in fact lodged in the socket of that leaf; and, as the leaves are numerous, there are frequently from thirty to fifty cabbages coming out of each stem. The large leaves are broken down in the month of August in order to give the little cabbages room to grow; and in

November these begin to be in perfection, and continue to be an excellent vegetable all the winter. The time of sowing the seed is the fore-part of April. The treatment of the plants, until planted out, the same as that of the cabbage; and the distances at which the plants ought to stand, the same as those mentioned for the broccoli, these being also tall things and requiring much room. Much care is necessary in the saving of the seed of this plant, which, as I have observed before, has an open spreading crown at the top. If you mean to save seed, you must cut off this crown, and let the seed-stems and flowers come out no-where but from the little cabbages themselves. It is, most likely, owing to negligence, in this respect, that we hardly ever see such a thing as real Brussels sprouts in England; and it is said that it is pretty nearly the same in France, the proper care being taken no-where, apparently, but in the neighbourhood of Brussels.

128. BURNET is a very well-known grass, or cattle-plant. Some persons use it in sallads, for what reason I know not, except that, when cut or bruised, it smells like cucumber: its taste is certainly most disagreeable: it appears to me to be of no use in a good garden: it is perennial, and, if curiosity should induce any one to have it in a garden, it can be propagated either from seed, or from a parting of the roots, and one square foot of ground will be certainly enough to let it have.

129. CABBAGE.—Very different, indeed, is this article from the last; for, here we have a plant, universally used, growing easily in almost every sort of soil, and

forming part of the table supply, in one shape or another, from the first day of January to the last day of December. Under this head, therefore, I shall be very minute in my instructions, more especially as the instructions under this head have been, and will be, so frequently referred to. FIRST, of the *manner of sowing*. I will speak of the seed, and of the sorts and of the season for sowing by and by; but let me first speak of the manner of sowing. This manner I have already described in great part in the fourth Chapter, where I speak of the drawing of drills across a seed-bed. Make a seed-bed of the extent that you want, and make the earth very fine : then mark it out in little drills. Drop the seed thinly along these drills, put the earth back upon the seed, and press it down very tightly upon it. When the seed comes up, which will be very quickly, thin the plants to an inch apart, or, perhaps a little more; and do not delay this work by any means; for, small as the roots are, the plants injure one another if they stand crowded for even a short space of time while in the seed-leaf. At the same time that you thin the plants, hoe the ground all over very nicely with a small hoe, and particularly near the plants. When the plants have got four or six rough leaves, they will touch one another, and ought to be removed from the seed-bed. They are too small as yet to be transferred to the spot where they are to come to perfection; but they ought now to be removed for the purposes now presently to be mentioned. Prepare for the purpose a bed three feet wide, and as long as the number of your plants may require. Take up the plants with a trowel or a stick, or something that will heave up the earth, and prevent the breaking of the roots too much as they come out of the ground. Then, with a little sharp-pointed stick, replant them in this new bed at the distance of three or four inches apart every way. This is called *pricking out*. If you have more plants than you want, you throw away the small ones · if you want all the plants that you have got, it is adviseable to divide the lot into large and small, keeping each class by itself, in the work of pricking out; so that when you come to transplant for the crop, your plants will be all nearly of the same size; that is to say, the large will not be mixed with the small; and there is this further convenience, that the large ones may make one plantation and the small ones another. This work should be done, if possible, in dry weather, and in ground which has just been fresh dug. In a very short time, these plants will be big enough to go into their final plantation: they will come up with stout and straight stems, without any tap root, and so well furnished with fibres as to make them scarcely feel the effect of transplanting; whereas, if you were to suffer them to stand in the seed-bed until large enough to be transplanted, they would come up with a long and naked taproot, ungarnished with fibres, and would be much slower in their progress towards perfection, and would, in the end, never attain the size that they will attain by these means. The next operation is, to put the plants out in a situation where they are to produce their crop. They are to stand in rows, of course; and I will speak of distances by and by when I come to speak of the different sorts of cabbages. At present I am to speak only of the *act of planting*. The tool to be used is that which is called a *setting-stick*, which is the upper part of the handle of a spade or shovel. The eye of the spade is the handle of the stick. From the bottom of the eye to the point of the stick should be about nine inches in length. The stick should not be *tapering*; but nearly of equal thickness all the way down, to within an inch and a half of the point, where it must be tapered off to the point. If the wood be cut away all round, to the thickness of a dollar, and *iron* put round in its stead, it makes a very complete tool. The iron becomes bright, and the earth does not adhere to it, as it does to wood. Having the plant in one hand, and the stick in the other, make a hole suitable to the root that it is to receive. Put in the root in such a way as that the earth, when pressed in, will be on a level with the butt-ends of the lower, or outward leaves of the plant. Let the plant be rather higher than lower than this; for, care must be taken not to put the plants so low as for the earth to fall, or be washed, into the *heart* of the plant, nor even into the inside of the bottom leaves. The stem of a cabbage, and stems of all the cabbage kind, send out roots from all the parts of them that are put beneath the surface of the ground. It is good, therefore, to plant as deep as you can without injury to the leaves. The next consideration is, the *fastening of the plant in the ground*. I cannot do better than repeat here what I have said in my Year's Residence, Paragraphs 83 and 84 : " The hole is made deeper than the length of the roots ; " but the root should not be *bent* at the point, if it can " be avoided. Then, while one hand holds the plant, with " its root in the hole, the other hand applies the setting " stick to the earth on one side of the hole, the stick being " held in such a way as to form a sharp triangle with the " plant. Then, pushing the stick down, so that its point go " *a little deeper than the point of the root*, and giving it a

" little *twist*, it presses the earth against the *point*, or
" *bottom* of the root." And thus all is safe, and the
plant is sure to grow. The general, and almost universal, fault, is, that the planter, when he has put the root
into the hole, draws the earth up against the *upper part*
of the root, and, if he press pretty well there, he thinks
that the planting is well done. But it is the point of the
root against which the earth ought to be pressed, for
there the fibres are ; and, if they do not *touch the earth
closely,* the plant will not thrive. To know whether you
have fastened the plant well in the ground, take the tip
of one of the leaves of the plant between your finger
and thumb. Give a pull. If the plant resist the pull, so
far as for the bit of leaf to come away, the plant is properly fastened in the ground ; but, if the pull bring up
the plant ; then you may be sure that the planting is not
well done. The point of the stick ought to twist and
press the earth up close to the *point of the root ;* so that
there be no *hollow* there. Pressing the earth up against
the *stem* of the plant is of little use. As to *distances,* they
must be proportioned to the size which the cabbages
usually come to ; and the size (difference of soil aside)
varies with the *sort.* However, for the very small sorts,
such as the *early dwarf* and *early sea-green,* a foot apart in
all directions is enough ; for there is no occasion to
waste garden ground ; and you do not want such things
to stand long, and the plants are in plenty as to number.
The next size is the *early York,* which may have sixteen
inches every way. The *sugar-loaf* may have twenty
inches. The *Battersea* and *Savoy* two feet and a half.
The large sorts, as the *drum-head* and others, three feet
at least.—Now, with regard to *tillage,* keep the ground

clear of weeds. But, whether there be weeds or not, hoe between the plants in ten days after they are planted. You cannot *dig* between the plants, which stand at the smallest distances; but you may, and ought, to dig once, if not twice, during their growth, between all the rest. To prevent a sudden check by breaking all the roots at once, in hot weather, dig *every other interval*, leave the rest, and dig them a week later. All the larger sorts of cabbages should, about the time that their heads are beginning to form, be *earthed* up; that is, have the earth from the surface drawn up against the stem; and, the taller the plants are, the more necessary this is, and the higher should the earth be drawn.. After the earth has been thus drawn up from the surface, *dig*, or *hoe deep*, the rest of the ground.——Thus the crop will be brought to perfection.——As to *sorts*, the earliest is the *early dwarf*; the next is the *early sea-green*; then comes the *early York*. Perhaps any one of them may do; but the first will head ten days sooner than the last. The greatest thing belonging to cabbages, is, to have heads, loaved and white, to cut early in the spring; and these you cannot have unless you sow the seed in the last week of July or first week of August; and unless that. seed be of the early sort and true. The manner of sowing seed and of pricking out has already been described. The plants should be put out into rows of two feet apart, and about fifteen inches apart in the row; and this work should be done about the latter end of October. If, however, the season have brought the plants very forward, they may go out a little before; but, if the weather prove very mild, it is a very good way to dig them up and plant them again immediately, each in its own place, about the middle of

November ; for, if they get too forward, they will either be greatly injured by a sharp winter, or will, by a mild winter, be made to run up to seed in the spring, instead of having heads. In general, in the south of England, these cabbages, if properly treated, and of a right-early sort, will have good white loaves early in April, or, at latest, by the middle of April. These are succeeded by others sowed early in the spring ; especially by the sugar-loaf, which, if sowed in the spring, will produce fine heads in the months of July, August, and September, and some sowed a little later will carry you through to the month of November. *Early Yorks* sowed in June will follow these. For winter use, there really needs nothing but the savoy, and the *dwarf green* is the best of that kind. When true to its kind, it is very much curled, and of a very deep green. It should be sowed about the middle of April, pricked out in the manner before described, but at larger distances, because it is a larger plant, and because it ought to acquire a good size of stem before it goes out into the ground, the time for final planting being in the hot month of July, and the distances being more extensive than those of the smaller cabbages. Some savoys sowed about a month after the main crop, and planted out six weeks later than the main crop, will give you greens in the winter, far preferable to any Cale. Early cabbages also, sowed and put out about the same time ; and planted in rows very close to each other, afford greens all the winter long. By November, the green savoys, first planted out, will have large and close heads. The drum-heads, and other large cabbages, are wholly unfit for a garden. The red cabbage is raised and cultivated in the same manner as the early cabbages.   It is put out in the fall of the year; but it is large and must have the same distances as broccoli. They form their heads in the early part of the summer and are hard, and fit for pickling, towards the end of it.   There remains now to speak of the manner of saving cabbage seed, which is a matter of great importance, because the trueness of the seed is a circumstance on which depends the earliness and goodness of the plant.   The cabbage is a biennial.   When it makes its loaf in the summer, you cut the loaf off in a sloping cut.   The plant will then throw out side-shoots; but, in a month after cutting the head, the stump should be taken up and laid by the heels, which will check the growing of the sprouts. In the month of November these stumps should be put out into rows where they are to stand for seed.   There should be two rows about eight inches from each other, the stumps in one row being opposite the intervals of the other row; and then there should be an interval of five feet between the rows in order to give you a clear passage for putting stakes and rods to hold up the seed-branches; and, also, for the purpose of going freely into the plantation to keep off the birds, many of which are great purloiners of cabbage-seed.   When the seed-pods begin to turn brown, cut the stems off close to the ground, and place them upon a cloth in the sun.   When perfectly dry, thrash out the seed; put it by, and keep it in a dry place. The ground where the seed is grown should be kept perfectly clean. The stems of the plants should be hilled up in the same manner as directed for a crop of cabbages; and the whole of the ground in the intervals should be dug in the month of March, an operation that will add greatly to the crop of seed. For a garden, two or three plants are sufficient ; but great care should be taken that they stand not near to any thing of the cabbage, or broccoli or cauliflower kind that is in bloom at the same time.

130. CALABASH. — This is a species of crooked squash, good for nothing as food, but is a very curious thing, having a large and long shell, small in one part and big in the other, and, when the big part is scooped out, becomes a ladle with a long handle to it. A thing very well worth growing for the curiosity, and grown in exactly the same manner as the squash.

131. CALE or KALE.—By some called *Borecole*. This is a species of cabbage which is used in winter only. It does not head, or loave, but sends forth a loose open top and numerous side-shoots, particularly after the top is taken off. It is a very hardy plant, resists all frosts ; but it is, at the same time, but a coarse sort of thing. It is to be sowed in the month of April, the plants treated in the same way as that of the cabbage ; the distances at which it is finally planted about two feet each way. There are two sorts, one a bright green, and the leaf very much curled, and the other of a reddish brown colour, and not curled at all. The green is generally thought the best ; but, as the green savoy will stand the weather if sowed rather later in the year than mentioned under the head of CABBAGE, full as well as the Cale will, there really seems to be very little reason for troubling one's self with this very coarse vegetable ; for, it is ridiculous to seek a variety in getting bad things to take their turn with good.

132. CALE (SEA).—This is a plant which is a native of the sea-beach : it is, in fact, sea-cabbage. It has a bloom not much unlike that of the cabbage, a seed also, only larger; the leaf strongly resembles the cabbage-leaf; but this is a perennial, whereas all the cabbage kinds are biennials. This plant soon gets to have a large stem or stool, like the asparagus, out of which the shoots come every spring. These stools are covered over pretty deep with sand or coal-ashes or some such thing, and sometimes with straw or leaves; and the shoots, coming up under the ashes or sand or earth, are bleached, until they come to the air, and these shoots are cut off and are applied for table-use just after the manner of the asparagus; and, though in point of goodness, they are not to be put in comparison with the asparagus, they come a month earlier in the spring, and, for that reason, they are cultivated. They are propagated by seed, and also by offsets. The mode of sowing, and of planting may be precisely the same, in all respects, as those directed for the asparagus, except that you may begin to cut the cale for eating, the second year. You cut down the stalks in the fall of the year just in the same manner as you cut down those of the asparagus; and the treatment all through may be just the same, except that there may be a greater depth of ashes or of sand over the cale than of earth or manure over the asparagus. While you can have asparagus in a hot-bed, it can hardly be worth while to have the cale in that way; but if you chose to do it, you might, and the method is the same, except that the covering in the bed must be deeper for the cale than for the asparagus. Gardeners sometimes, after having covered the crowns well over with sand or

ashes, or some other thing, cover the point of each crown with a large flower-pot, which, keeping the sun and air from the shoots, these are bleached even after they come up above the ashes or the sand. This appears to be a very good way; for it saves the trouble of putting on litter or leaves, which are very ugly things in a garden.

133. CAMOMILE is a perennial medicinal herb of great use. It may be propagated from seed, but it is most easily propagated by parting the roots. One little bit of root will soon make a bed sufficient for a garden. The flowers, which are used in medicine, should be gathered before they begin to fade, and at a time when they are perfectly dry; and then put into a shady and airy place to dry, which they will do perfectly, but not in less than a month. When perfectly dry, they should be put into a paper bag, hung up in a dry place, and kept from all dust.

134. CAPSICUM.—This is a plant of a hot country. It is sowed in the natural ground of the United States of America, though it is a native of countries which are never cold. The seed is, in this country, sowed in a gentle hot-bed, in the month of March. In the middle of April, they may be moved out, and planted under a warm wall, so as to be covered by a frame and lights, or by hand-glasses. And so as to have air given them in the warm part of the day. When no more frost is to be expected, and when the general earth becomes warm; that is to say, about the third week in June, the plants, very carefully taken up and with the earth not much shaken off from their roots, should be transplanted in a

bed of fine rich earth; but still in a warm part of the garden. The bed should have hoops placed over it; the plants should be shaded by mats every day for about a week, if the sun be hot; and if the nights be very cold afterwards, the beds should have a little shelter in the night for a fortnight or three weeks. The plants will be in bloom in July, and, in the month of October, their pods, which have a strong peppery taste, would be fit to gather for pickling. There are several sorts of the capsicum, some with red pods, some with green ones, I do not know which is the best in quality; and a very small quantity of these plants will suffice for any family.

135. CARAWAY is cultivated for its seeds, which are used in cakes, and for some other purposes. Sow the seed in the spring, about the first of April, and leave the plants at about seven or eight inches apart in every direction. A small quantity of this plant will be sufficient, as it is not a thing in very general request.

136. CARROT.—Read the article Beet; for the same soil, the same manure, the same preparation for sowing, the same distances, the same intercultivation, the same time of taking up, and the same mode of preserving the crop, all belong to the carrot; but, the carrot ought to be sowed as soon as possible after the coming of mild weather in the spring; and great care must be taken to watch the coming-up of the plants; for there are several kinds of weeds, the seed-leaves of which are so much like those of the carrot, that it requires long experience and attentive observation to distinguish one from the other. Carrot-seed lies long in the ground; and, there-

fore, the seeds of innumerable weeds are up long enough before it. Great care must therefore be taken to keep down these weeds in time without destroying the carrots ; and it is next to impossible to do this, unless you sow the carrots in rows, no fresh dung should be put into the ground where carrots are sowed, for that would be sure to bring abundance of seed weeds. To save carrot-seed, as well as beet-seed, you must take some of the last year's plants, and put them out early in the spring. When the seed is ripe, the best way is, with regard to the carrot, to cut off the whole stalk, hang it up in a very dry place, and there let it remain until you want the seed to sow. Kept in this way, it will grow very well at the end of three or four years ; but, if separated from the stalk, it will not keep well for more than one year. There is some care necessary in the sowing of carrot-seed, which it is difficult to scatter properly along the drill on account of the numerous hairs which come out of the seed, and make them hang to one another. The best way is, to take some sand, or ashes, or very fine dry dust, and put a pint of it to a pint of seed, rubbing both together by your hands. This brings off the hairs from the seeds and separates them from each other, and then they may be very nicely and evenly sowed along the drills. There ought to be no digging between carrots, beets, or any other tap-rooted vegetables ; because the moving of the earth in the intervals invites the fibres to grow large, and to become forks : deep cultivation is wrong here, for the very same reason that it is generally good. Carrots are sometimes raised in hot-beds, but I shall speak of this under the head of Radishes.

137. CAULIFLOWER.—The cauliflower is, in fact, one sort of cabbage and the French call it *Choufleur,* or flower-cabbage. Its product, as a vegetable to eat, is a lump of rich pulp, instead of being a parcel of leaves folding in towards a centre, and lapping over each other. There is this distinction besides, that it is an annual instead of being a biennial. The head, or flower as it is called, sprouts off into real flower-stalks ; flowers come upon these stalks ; seed-pods and seed follow the flowers, and the plant bears seed within twelve months after it is sown. As much care as possible should be taken in obtaining good and true seed, which, as it is always pretty dear, is apt to be adulterated. Some persons have talked of an early sort and a late sort ; but I believe there is but one. The manner of sowing the seed, and of thinning out the young plants in the rows, is precisely that of the cabbage. The season of sowing for cauliflowers to be eaten in the spring, is about the middle of the month of August. To guard against the effects of the difference in seasons, the best way would be, perhaps, to make three sowings, one on the first of August, one on the fifteenth of August, and one on the 31st. for, the day which would be the proper day in one year, would not be the proper day in another. When the plants are of the same size as the cabbage-plants have been directed to be before pricked out, they should be pricked out also ; but in a more careful and regular manner than was thought neces- sary in the case of the cabbage-plants. The spot should be one of the warmest in the garden ; and it should not be a wet spot by any means. The cauliflower is a tender plant, and, in severe weather, will want covering of some sort, and, to say the truth, it is almost useless to attempt

to rear them unless you have glass to put them under in
very severe weather. They should be pricked out, therefore, in such manner as to allow of frames or hand-
glasses being placed over them. They should not be
covered, however, until the weather demand it, and, in
the meanwhile, you should hoe nicely between them very
frequently, and, by that means, keep the earth as dry
about their stems as the season will permit. In very
severe weather, they must be covered ; but never any
longer than is absolutely necessary ; for, too much covering, and too much deprivation of air, makes them
weak and disqualifies them for bearing. From these beds,
you may plant them out in rows like cabbages, only at a
little greater distances, and, taking care to move a little
earth along with them, about the middle of March ; and,
in those rows, give them good cultivation, and earth them
up in the manner directed for the broccoli. But, greater
pains than this is generally taken ; for, in the month of
November, they are generally put out in clumps of three,
four, five, or six in a clump, and there stand the winter,
covered by hand-glasses, or bell-glasses, which are taken
off when the weather is fine, and raised up at the bottom
by the means of bricks, to prevent a drawing up of the
plants. Towards spring ; that is to say, in the month of
March, the weakest of the plants in each clump are taken
up and planted elsewhere, and the glasses are continued
to be put over the other plants, and to be raised higher and
higher at the bottom according to the season and state of
the weather. At last, the plants become too big for the
glasses, and the weather too warm for any covering to be
required. The glasses are then wholly taken away and
the plants are left to produce their heads. As the dry

weather approaches, the earth is drawn round the clumps so as to form a dish for each; and, when the heads begin to appear, it is the practice to pour water into these dishes. If the ground be very rich, this watering is certainly unnecessary; but, the earth should be very frequently moved round the stems of the plants, and, as the intervals ought to be not less than five feet wide, a good and clean digging of those intervals ought to take place in the month of April. This would probably prevent the necessity of watering, in all cases; and I am disposed to recommend it, being of opinion that it would be more efficacious for the purpose intended. Cauliflowers begin to have good heads in the month of May; sometimes earlier and sometimes later according to the season; and, in their commencement, as well as in their duration, they are the formidable rivals of green peas. To have cauliflowers in the autumn, you must sow early in the month of March, in a hot-bed of no very great heat; and to which a great deal of air should be given; these plants should be pricked out in April, in the manner before directed, and planted out in rows when they attain the proper size; that is to say, when they become strong and bold plants. To have this vegetable very late in the fall, and even in December, sow in the open ground, in the first week in May: prick out and plant out as directed in the last instance. If no hard frosts come early, these will have tolerable heads in the month of November, and then, if there be some of them with very small heads, no bigger than a crown piece, you may, by taking the plants up, and putting their roots in sand in a shed or cellar, have some tolerably good cauliflowers at Christmas. I, having endeavoured one year, to raise cauliflowers in Pennsylvania, where they will not flower in summer on account of the excessive heat, which continually keeps the heart open and prevents the head from coming up, took my plants, in the month of November, when their heads were just beginning to appear, and buried them in the garden, according to the fashion of that country, observed in the burying of cabbages ; that is to say, to place the cabbages along in a row, close to each other, the head upon the level ground, and the roots standing up in the air, and then to go on each side with a spade, and throw up earth in such a manner as completely to cover the heads and the leaves of the cabbages. Indeed, my cauliflowers went into the ground in company with some cabbages ; and, to my great surprize, when we took up the part of the stock in which the cauliflowers were, the greater part of them had heads as big as an ordinary tea-cup. But, this method would not do in England ; for we have wet as well as frost ; and, in Pennsylvania, when once the earth is safely locked up by the frost, there comes no wet to sink into little ridges such as I have described. I think, however, that, if hung up by the heels in a barn or a shed in November, cauliflowers would augment their size as much as if put into sand in a cave. If you attempt to save cauliflower-seed, no pains that you can take would possibly be too great. First look over your stock of heads : you will see some of them *less compact* than the others : more uneven, and more loose : round the edges of the heads, you will see almost perfect smoothness in some, and, in others, you will see a little sort of fringe appearing even before the head comes to its full bigness ; and these heads which are not so compact as the others, will be less white, and drawing towards a cream colour. Now observe, it is the compact, the smooth, the white head, of which you ought to save the seed ; and, though it will bear much less seed than a loose head, it will be good : you can rely upon it ; and that is more than you can upon any seed that you purchase, though it come from Italy, whence this fine vegetable originally came. There remains to notice only, that the sun is apt to scorch the heads of cauliflowers, and to make them of a brownish hue, which prepares them for rotting if much wet afterwards come upon them. To protect them from this, bend and break down a couple of the large outer leaves, which will be protection against both sun and wet while the head is arriving at maturity.

138. CELERY.—There are three sorts of celery, the *white*, the *red*, and the *solid*. The bottoms of the leaves of the two former, become hollow ; that is to say, of the outside leaves ; and it is desirable that the part which is eaten should not be very hollow ; but the solid celery is, by no means, of so fine a flavour as the other. The red is hardier than either of the other two ; and, like most other hardy things, it is not so good as the more tender. It is too strong ; and has a smell and taste somewhat approaching to the hemlock. Celery is a winter plant ; but, as its seed lies very long in the ground, it ought to be sowed early. It is difficult to make come up ; and, though it might do very well to sow it in a warm place in the month of March, the easiest way, is, to sow it upon a little bit of a hot-bed, though not on a greater extent of ground than might be covered with a hand-

glass; and, that space will contain a sufficiency of plants for any garden however large. The plants come up very much like parsley, and, when small, are hardly distinguished from young parsley plants. As soon as they have two rough leaves, the glass may be taken off, and they may be exposed to the air. About six trenches of celery, running across one of the plats, from North to South, would give about 600 roots; and, as it is not in use for much more than about a hundred days of the year, here would be six roots for *every day*, which is much more than any family could want. When the plants get to have about four or five rough leaves, they ought to be pricked out upon a little bed of very fine earth, by the means of a little pointed stick; and they ought to stand in that bed at about four inches apart, having their roots nicely and closely pressed into the ground. This operation would take place by the middle of May, perhaps, and here the plants would attain a considerable size by the month of July, which, a little earlier or a little later, is the time for putting them out into trenches. Knowing the number of plants that you would want, you need prick out no more than that number; but, if you were to put out a thousand instead of six hundred, you might have some to give to a neighbour whose sowing might happen to have failed; and this, observe, is a thing by no means to be overlooked; for, you will be a lucky gardener, indeed, if you never stand in need of like assistance from others; and this is one of the great pleasures of gardening, that one has almost always something to give away from one's superabundance; and here the gift is accompanied with no ostentation on the one side, and without it being deemed any favour on the other side. Your plants being ready, about the middle of July, perhaps, make the trenches a foot deep and a foot wide, and put them at not less than *five feet* asunder. The ground that you make the trenches in should not be fresh dug; but be in a *solid state*, which very conveniently may be; for celery comes on just as the peas and early cabbages and cauliflowers have gone off. Lay the earth that you take out in the *middle* of the space between the trenches, so that it may not be washed into them by the heavy rains; for it will, in such case, cover the *hearts* of the plants, and will go very nearly to destroy them. When you have made your trench, put along it some good rich compost manure, partly consisting of *wood ashes.* Not *dung ;* or, at least, not dung fresh from the yard ; for, if you use that, the celery will be *rank* and *pipy,* and will not keep nearly so long or so well. Dig this manure in, and break all the earth very fine as you go. Then take up your plants, and trim off the long roots. You will find, that every plant has offsets to it, coming up by the side of the main stem. Pull all these off, and leave only the single stem. Cut the leaves off so as to leave the whole plant about six inches long. Plant them, six inches apart, and fix them, in the manner so minutely dwelt on under the article CABBAGE, keeping, as you are at work, your feet close to the outside edges of the trench. Do not *water* the plants ; and, if you plant in *fresh-dug* ground, and fix your plants well, none of the troublesome and cumbrous business of *shading* is at all necessary ; for the plant is naturally hardy, and, if it has heat to wither it above, it has also that heat beneath to cause its roots to strike out almost instantly. When the plants begin to grow, which they quickly will do, *hoe* on each side and between them with a small hoe. As they grow up, *earth their stems*; that is, put the earth up to them, but not too *much at a time*; and let the earth that you put up be finely *broken*, and not at all *cloddy*. While you do this, keep the stalks of the outside leaves close up to prevent the earth from getting between the stems of the outside leaves and the inner ones; for, if it get there, it checks the plant and makes the celery bad.——When you begin the *earthing*, take first the *edges of the trenches*; and do not go into the middle of the intervals for the earth that you took out of the trenches. Keep working backwards, time after time, that is earthing after earthing, till you come to the earth that you dug out of the trenches; and, by this time, the earth against the plants will be above the level of the land. Then you take the earth out of the middle, till, at last, the earth against the plants forms a *ridge*, and the middle of each interval a sort of gutter. Earth up *very often*, and do not put much at a time. Every week a little earth to be put up. You should always earth up when the ground is dry at top; and, in October, when winter is approaching, earth up very nicely to within four or five inches of the very top. When you want celery for use, you begin at the end of one trench, remove the earth with the spade, and dig up the roots. The wet, the snow, aided by the frosts and by the thaws, will, if care be not taken, rot the celery at the heart, particularly the wet, which descends down from the top, lodges in the heart, and rots it. To prevent this, two boards, a foot wide each, form the best protection. Their edges, on one side laid upon the earth of the ridge, formed into a roof over the point of the ridge, the upper edge of one board going an inch over the upper edge of the other, and the boards fastened well with pegs : this will do the business effectually ; for it is the wet that you have to fear, and not the frost. If long and hard frost be apprehended, a quantity of celery should be taken up and laid in a bed of sand or light earth in a shed or cellar; for, when the ground is deeply frozen, it is sometimes impossible to get it out without tearing it to pieces ; and it keeps very well for several weeks in a shed or cellar. To have the *seed* of celery, take one plant or two, in the spring, out of the ridge that stands last. Plant it in an open place, and it will give you seed enough for several years ; for the seed keeps good for ten years, at least, if kept pretty much from the air, and in a dry place.

139. CHERVIL.—This, like celery, spinage, and some few other garden plants, is very much liked by some people, and cannot be endured by others. It is an annual plant : its leaves a good deal like those of double parsley : it is used in salads, to which it gives an odour that some people very much like : it bears a seed resembling that of a wild oat ; it is sowed in rows late in March or early in April ; and a very small patch of it is enough for any garden : it bears its seed, of course, the first summer, bears it, too, in great abundance, and, if properly preserved, the seed will last for six or seven years at the least.

140. CIVES.—A little sort of *Onion*, which is perennial : it may be propagated from seed ; but the easiest way is by parting the roots which are bunches of little bulbs like those of crocuses or snow-drops. The greens only

of this plant are used ; and a very small patch is sufficient for any garden. Five or six clumps in the herbbed would be sufficient.

141. CORIANDER is an annual plant that some persons use in soups and salads. It is sowed early in April. The seed is also used as a medicine. A yard or two square of it will be sufficient.

142. CORN (Indian).—Infinite is the variety of the sorts of Indian corn, and great is the difference in the degrees of heat sufficient to bring the different sorts to perfection. Several of the sorts will seldom ripen well with the heat which they get in the state of New York, requiring that of Carolina or Virginia, at least. Other sorts will ripen perfectly well as far north as Boston ; and there is a dwarf sort which will ripen equally well on land 500 miles to the north of the last-mentioned place. Whether this be the same sort as that which I cultivate, I do not exactly know ; but mine never fails to come to perfection in England, be the summer what it may. This is a very fine garden vegetable. The ear is stripped off the stalk just at the time when the grains are full of milk. The ears are then boiled for about twenty minutes : they are brought to table whole ; each person takes an ear, rubs over it a little butter, and sprinkles it with a little salt, and bites the grains from the stalk to which they are attached, and which, in America, is called the cob. In the Indian corn countries, every creature likes Indian corn better than any other vegetable, not excepting even the fine fruits of those countries. When dead ripe, the grains are hard as

any grain can be; and, upon this grain, without any grinding, horses are fed, oxen are fatted, hogs are fatted, and poultry made perfectly fat by eating the grain whole tossed down to them in the yard. The finest turkeys in the whole world are fatted in this way, without the least possible trouble. Nothing can be easier to raise. The corn is planted along little drills about three or four feet apart, the grains at four inches apart in the drill, any when during the first fortnight in May. When it is out of the ground about two inches, the ground should be nicely moved all over, and particularly near to the plants. When the plants attain to the height of a foot, the ground should be dug between them, and a little earth should be put up about the stems. When the plants attain the height of a foot and a half or two feet, another digging should take place, and the stems of the plants should be earthed up to another four or five inches: after this, you have nothing to do but keep the ground clear from weeds. The corn will be in bloom, and the ears will begin to show themselves in the latter end of July: in the latter end of August, there will be some corn fit to eat; and, as some ears will always be more backward than others, there will always be some in proper order for eating till about the latter end of September. Those ears which are not gathered before October, will become ripe, and the grains in them hard: two or three of the finest ought to be saved for seed, and the rest given to poultry: about three rows across one of the plats in the garden would be sufficient for any family.

148. CORN-SALAD.—This is a little insignificant annual plant that some persons use in salads. It is,

indeed, a *weed*, and can be of no real use where lettuces are to be had. It bears abundance of seed, and a little of it may be had by sowing in April, if any one should have the strange curiosity.

144. CRESS is excellent in salads, with lettuces. It is a peppery little thing, far preferable to mustard or rape. It is an annual, and bears prodigious quantities of seed. A small quantity should, in the salad season, be sowed every six days or thereabouts; for, it should be cut before it come into rough leaf. It is sowed in little drills made with the tops of the fingers, and covered slightly with very fine earth: it is up almost immediately, and quite fit to cut in five or six days. This and other small salads may be very conveniently raised, in the winter time, in any hot-bed that you happen to have.

145. CUCUMBER.—The instructions relative to the raising of cucumbers naturally divide themselves into two sets; one applicable to the raising of cucumbers in hot-beds, and the other to the raising of cucumbers in the natural ground, or with some little portion of artificial heat. I shall first speak of the former; for, the produce of this plant is a very great favourite; it is a general desire to have it early; and it is unquestionably true that the flavour of the cucumber is never so delicate, and the smell never so refreshing as when it is raised in a hot-bed, or, at least, by the means of some artificial heat. To do this, however, at so early a season as to have cucumbers fit to cut in March, requires great attention, some expense, but particularly great attention. I shall, therefore, endeavour to give directions for the doing of this, in

as plain a manner as I possibly can; and, the reader will please to observe, that the directions given for the rearing of cucumbers will also apply to the rearing of *melons*; or, at least, they will thus apply in very great part, and with those exceptions only which would be mentioned under the head of melons. In Chapter III. we have seen how a hot-bed is to be made; make such a bed, four feet high, in the last fortnight of December. Make it, however, for a frame of *one light* only; and let it extend every way to a foot on the outside of the bottom of the frame. Put on the frame as directed in Chapter III., ascertain when the heat is what it ought to be according to the rule laid down in that Chapter, cover the bed over four inches deep with dry mould, a good provision of which you ought to have prepared and kept in a shed. Then, and at the same time, put about a bushel of earth in a flattish heap in the middle of the bed, and lay about another bushel round the insides of the frame, at the same time. Turn this earth over with your hand, once or twice in twenty-four, or forty-eight hours, giving the bed air in the middle of the day; then level the bushel of earth very nicely, and put in some early-frame cucumber seeds in as great number as you may want, at half an inch deep, cover them over, and press the earth gently down upon them. They will appear above-ground in a very few days; but, you must take care to give the bed as much air as it will endure, even before the seed comes up; and, after that, air must be given in as great quantity as the weather will permit, to prevent the plants from being drawn up with slender shanks. If the weather be very severe, litter or straw should be laid all round the bed, and quite up to the top of the frame, to keep out the frost and to keep in the heat ; but, above all things, as much air as possible ought to be given ; for, there is always a steam or reek in a hot-bed ; and, if this be not let out, it destroys the stems of the plants, and they very quickly perish.   Yet, there may be snow, there may be such severe frost, as to render this giving of air very perilous.   In the night-time, it will frequently be neces- sary to cover over the top of the lights, not only with *mats* (which always ought to be done at this time of the year) ; but with straw to a considerable thickness, besides the mats.   In this case, you first lay the mat over the glass : then put the straw upon the mat : then put another mat over the straw, and fasten that mat securely all over the frame, which is best done by billets of wood about a foot and a half long and three inches thick each way, with a tenter-hook at one end, to hang it on to the mat.   This is much better than tacking the mats on to the frame by a hammer and nails ; for this is a carpenter- ing sort of work to be performed twice a-day.   If the weather be tolerably favourable, if it be not extremely untoward, and if you have taken the proper pains, the plants will be fit to be *put into pots* in about four or five days from the time of their coming up.   The time for doing this, however, is best pointed out by the state of the plants, which, as soon as you see the rough leaf peeping up, are ready for potting.   You then get your pots about five inches deep, six inches over at the top, and four inches over at the bottom, measuring from out- side to outside.   You put a small oyster-shell, the hollow part downwards, over the hole at the bottom of the pot. You fill the pots about three parts full of earth, heave the plants out of the ground with your fingers, put two plants into each pot; holding the head of each towards the rim, while you put in more earth with the other hand to fill the pot up to the rim. Then take the pot and gently rap the bottom of it upon the edge of the frame three or four times, which will settle down the earth sufficiently, and will leave the earth about half an inch below the rim. You may then press the root of each plant a little with the point of your finger, and put on a little more earth to make all smooth. Observe, that the shanks of the plants are to go so deeply down into the pot as to leave the seed leaves but a very little above the level of the earth in the pot. The earth will come out of the heap to fill the pots with; and a very small part of it will suffice. You will now draw the earth from the sides of the frame towards the middle of the bed, and, having formed it into a broader heap than before, put the pots down into the mould up to the rim, taking care that they stand perfectly level, and taking care also, that the tops of the plants do not stand too far from the glass; for that would cause them to be drawn up and be made weak. About six inches from the glass is quite enough. I am supposing that your first cucumber-bed, for the producing of fruit, is to have four lights. You will therefore want but four pots of plants, but it will be better to have double the number; the supernumeraries cost nothing, and they may save a neighbour the trouble of making a seed-bed. In this state the plants stand until they go into the bed where they are to bear. They will be fit for removal as soon as they have made two fair rough leaves, and have begun to exhibit the appearance of shoots or runners coming forth. But, while the plants are in this situation, you must be careful to top them or stop them.

From between the seed leaves, there will come out a shoot which will presently have one rough leaf on each side of it; then between these two rough leaves you will see a shoot rising. The moment this is clearly distinguishable, pinch it clean out with your fore-finger and thumb; and this will cause shoots to come out on both sides from the sockets of the two rough leaves which have been left; and, by the time that these side-shoots become an inch and a half long, the plants ought to be removed into the large bed where they are to grow and to bear; for, by this time, they will have filled the pot with roots; and, if they stand in the pots much longer, some of these roots will become matted together on the outsides and at the bottom of the pot, where they will perish, and cause the plants to be stunted. At this age, therefore, they should be removed into the new bed, of the making and managing of which we must now speak. The dung for it should be put into a heap and turned beforehand in the manner described in Chapter III.; and, about a week, or a little more, before the plants be ready to come out of the seed-bed, this new bed must be made, full four feet high, or four feet and a half, in the manner directed in Chapter III. The frame should be put on, the state of the heat ascertained, in the manner there directed, and, in this case, the frame ought to fit the bed as nearly as possible, and the bed ought not to extend beyond the sides of the frame as in the case of the seed-bed; for here there are to be *linings*, the purpose of which we shall see by and by. This bed having arrived at the proper heat, should be covered all over with dry mould to the depth of four inches; then about three quarters of a bushel of

similar mould ought to be laid in the centre of each
light, rather nearer, however, to the back, than to the
front of the frame ; and at the same time, three or four
bushels of mould, or more, ought to be laid round
against the frame on the inside.   The mould in the heaps,
as well as that round the sides of the frame, and, indeed,
the mould all over the bed, ought to be stirred once, at
least, every day, and air ought to be given to the bed,
though there are, as yet, no plants in it.   Every thing
having been thus prepared, take four pots of the plants ;
those which appear to be the finest, of course ; put the
mould into a round heap under the middle of each light
of the new bed, make a hole in the centre of the heap
suitable for your purpose.   Take the pots of plants, one
at a time, put the fingers of one of your hands on the top
of the earth of the pot, then turn the pot upside down,
give the rim of it a little tap upon the edge of the frame,
pushing the oyster-shell with the fore-finger of the other
hand, and the plants and earth will come clean out of
the pot in a connected ball, which, with both hands, you
are to deposit in the hole which you have made in the
heap in the centre of the light.   When you have thus
deposited it, draw the earth of the heap well up about
the ball, and press it a little with your fingers, taking
care of two things, first, that the hole be sufficiently
deep to admit the ball down into it so low that the earth
of the hill, when drawn up about the plants, may come
up quite to the lower side of the stem of the seed-leaves,
and, second, taking care that the points of the leaves of the
plants be not more than six inches distance from the
glass.   While the plants were in the seed-bed, it might
have been necessary to water them once or twice, and

especially about four days before their removal out of the
pots; and now again, at this final transplanting, a little
water should be given, gently poured on in one place,
between the stems of the two plants, and the hole that
that water makes should be covered over again with a
little fresh earth.   The other four pots of plants which
you do not want, may be sunk in the earth in any part of
this new bed, being watered occasionally, and finally flung
away if you do not want them.   But, at this time of the
year, the water must not be cold : it must have stood in
the bed, in a small watering-pot, to get warm, and this
must be observed continually until a much later season
of the year.   By the time that you have these plants in
the bearing-bed, the latter end of January will have
come, and you will have all the difficulties of hard
weather to contend with.   The bed itself will not have
a sufficiently strong heat for more than about a fortnight,
and, therefore, *linings* must be prepared, the dung for
which must be got ready in time, as mentioned in Chapter III., and the lining is to be made thus : the first lining is put at the back, or north side, of the bed. It is,
in fact, another narrow hot-bed, built up along at the
back of the original one, perpendicular, as near as may
be, till you approach the top, twenty inches through,
made of good materials, and put together with the
greatest care.   It is to be carried up even to the height
of the top of the frame, where a board is to be laid on
upon it, close against the frame, in order to prevent the
steam, arising from it, finding its way in upon the
plants.   This lining will send great heat into the bed,
and will continue so to do for a great while ; but still a
fresh supply of heat will be wanted ; and, therefore, in

about another fortnight, you are to put a similar lining to both ends of the bed ; and, in a fortnight from that time, or thereabouts, according to the weather and the state of the bed, another similar lining in the front of the bed, the dung having, in all these cases, been duly prepared as noticed in Chapter III. As these linings sink, they ought to be topped up, keeping them always as nearly as possible to the height of the top of the frame. If very sharp weather come before these linings, or before some of them, have been made, good quantities of litter, or of straw, ought to be brought temporarily to supply their place, so that frost never reach the bed. Even when there are linings, it is good, in very sharp weather, to put litter and straw round the outsides of *them* ; for, dung being moist, the frost soon reaches it, and then it becomes inactive at once. To these precautions relative to the heat, must be added the not less important ones relative to air and light ; for, without these, no plant will thrive, nor will it live but for a short space of time. At this season of the year, the glasses must be covered over in the night time, as was before-mentioned in the case of the seed-bed ; but, these coverings should remain on in the morning never longer than is absolutely necessary. Though there be no sun, there is light, and plants crave the light at the time when nature sends it. As to air, it is given to the plants by the means of pieces of triangular wood, which every one knows how to make. The light is lifted up at one end, and the tilter, as it is called, is put under the middle of the light to keep it up to the height required. You sometimes give air on the back side of the frame and sometimes on the front, according to the direction in which the wind is coming.

To give directions respecting the quantity of air, one can only say, that it must be in proportion to the heat of the bed and the state of the weather ; but it may be observed as an invariable rule, that strong heat, and a good quantity of air are the sure means of having early cucumbers. When the air is kept excluded or supplied in niggardly quantities, because the heat is not powerful enough to counteract its chilling effects, the plants will linger on alive, to be sure, but their colour will be approaching to a yellow, their leaves small, their shoots slender, their blossoms small and feeble, the fruit, if they show any, will not swell ; and, if they bear after all, it will not be before pretty nearly the month of May, instead of a decent bearing in the month of March. A good strong bottom heat, with a great deal of light, and with a liberal quantity of air, are the great means of having cucumbers. The next thing to be noticed is, the after-cultivation of the plants, and, first, with respect to the shoots or runners that come out of them. There will come two shoots out of each plant, and these will soon begin to grow in a horizontal position, and, indeed, go along the ground, which it is their nature to do ; but these two shoots would not be sufficient ; for they would soon get to the outside of the bed, leaving the middle of the bed not half covered with vines ; therefore, when these runners have got three joints, and are beginning to make a fourth, pinch off the top of each runner. New side-shoots or runners will then come out from the three joints. When these have got four joints, which will be very quickly, pinch off the fifth as soon as it appears. Each plant will now have a dozen or two of runners, and that is enough for one light. After this, you may let the runners go on, giving their heads a better direction, now-and-then, in order to cover the ground in the bed ; for they will need no more topping. But, there must be *earthing up,* as well as topping. As the plants advance above ground, so they will below ground, and you must keep putting up earth to the hills in order to supply fresh food for the roots which you will find pushing out in every direction. It is the practice of some gardeners, to be everlastingly drawing the earth away from the side of the hills till they come to the plants, in order to take the points of the roots up and put earth under them, so as to give the roots a horizontal direction. This is sheer nonsense. All that is necessary, is, to keep the hills continually made larger and larger in circumference, as the roots approach the outside, and until you have got all the bed level to the tops of the hills. As you extend the circumference of the hills, the runners will advance upon you ; and, that the bed may be covered evenly with the vines, the runners should be occasionally held down by little pegs of wood with hooks at the top of them. At last the bed is even and level all over. And, finally, it is covered with the vines, and should always be kept quite clear of the innumerable weeds that will start in such a favourable situation ; but, long before this, there will be blossoms and even fruit, if the plants be in good health. The first fruit that appears generally remains small, and never swells to any size ; but these are soon followed by others that swell and that come to perfection ; and, if all these directions be attended to, and, if the weather be not worse than it is one year out of twenty, you can hardly fail to have cucumbers to cut about the middle of March, which is a very fine thing for a gardener to say ;

and, though here is a great deal of detail, though here are a great number of things to do, there is much more of words than of deeds in the thing : it takes two or three sentences to describe how a plant is to be put into or turned out of a pot ; but the act itself is performed in half a minute.   Care ought to be taken that there be not too great a quantity of vines in the bed ; for, if the mass of leaves be too great, they shade part of the vines, shade the blossoms and the fruit ; and, instead of having more fruit from the abundance of vines, you have, perhaps, none at all.   This over-stocking of the bed with vines is a great and prevalent error.   For my part, I think one plant enough for each hill, and I never kept but one in a hill, and, if I put two into a pot, it was by way of precaution lest one should fail.   One will bring more weight of fruit than two, two more than three, and so on, till you come to a number that would give you no fruit at all. The plants thus crowded, rob one another ; their roots interfere with those of each other.   They cease to bear sooner than they would if they stood singly ; and, in short, my experience and observation induce me strongly to urge the reader never to have in a hot-bed, whether of cucumber or melon, more than one plant in a light.   As the season advances, a greater proportion of air is to be given, of course, and there is to be less covering in the night-time, dependant, however, more on the state of the weather than on the precise time of the year ; for we have frequently mild weather in February and severe weather in March.   When the weather becomes such as that water will have the chill taken from it by being placed under a south wall or in a hot-bed, water thus prepared, may do very well ; but, until then, the water should be a little warm. Every one will be a judge when the earth is so dry as to require water ; but care should be taken not to let the water fall in great quantities just upon the stems of the plants at any stage of their growth, for that is apt to rot them. This early cucumber bed will keep on bearing very well until the latter end of May, by which time, another bed, made about the middle or latter end of March will have succeeded it. The plants for this second crop of cucumbers are to be raised in pots put into the cucumber-bed, last mentioned. They are to be managed like those for the first bed, except that they must be sown in a pot, instead of being sown in a hill. The bed for these plants need not be above two feet and a half high, or thereabouts. It will probably want a slight lining ; but the materials need not be equal to those made use of in the making of the early bed. In the case of this latter bed, much air may be given, and the covering of a mat, or two at most, and that only in the night-time, will be sufficient. In April, some more plants may be sown in a pot in this last bed, and repotted as before ; and, in the middle of June, these may go out into hills (under hand-glasses or without) in the open ground, there to produce cucumbers for pickling, or, indeed, for using in any other way, from the middle of July until the time that the frost comes. Thus, will there be a succession of cucumbers, from the middle of March to the month of October. As to sorts, great attention must be paid ; for, some sorts produce their fruit a great deal quicker than others. There is one called the *early frame cucumber* ; another is called the *early cluster cucumber*, another the *long prickly cucumber*. The early frame has doubtless been found to be the quickest in coming to perfection ; but the cluster is a very great bearer, and comes not much later than the other. There are several other sorts, but the long prickly cucumber is most generally esteemed ; and, therefore, ought to be sowed for those who want a general crop. With regard to sorts, however, people generally save the seed themselves of this plant, or get it from some careful and curious neighbour ; and every one sows that which happens to suit his fancy. If you wish to save the seed of a cucumber, let some one fine fruit remain ; but expect the plant, on which this fruit is, to cease bearing as soon as the seed cucumber begins to ripen. This fruit must hang upon the vine till it pretty nearly rots off : you then take the seeds and separate them from the pulp as clean as you can, place them to dry in the sun ; but do not wash them with water : when perfectly dry, but not before, put them away in a dry place, and they will keep good for a great many years. Guard them against mice, for, if they get at them, not one seed will they leave with the kernel of it not eaten. After all, if you have no hot-bed at all, a couple of wheel-barrow fulls of hot dung put into a hole a foot deep, and with good mould a foot deep laid upon the dung, is a very good situation for cucumbers which you may sow there about the middle of May. Two or three plants upon such a hill or bed, and, if you have a hand-glass, keep the plants covered with that in the night-time and when the days are cold, always giving air, however, when the sun is out, and, in time, raising the glass upon bricks and letting the vines run out under it. Even if you have no hand-glass, you may cover, with the help of hoops and a mat or a cloth, until the weather be such as to render it safe for the plants to be at large. Finally, in very rich and warm ground, you may sow cucumber-seed in the natural earth, the ground having previously been well dug, and being kept very clean afterwards ; and, though there be a chance of your having no crop, you may have, and generally will have, a great quantity of cucumbers to pickle by the latter end of August. Before I dismiss this article, let me observe, that I have omitted to say any thing about what is called *setting* the fruit by poking the centre of the male blossoms into the centre of the female blossoms ; because I deem it to be arrant nonsense. The reader ought, before I entirely quit this article, to be informed, that the hot-bed in which the cucumber plants were first raised, may be turned to very good account after the plants come out of it ; asparagus may be put into it immediately ; or, it may be sowed with radishes, onions, lettuces, small-salad, or with carrots. Many purposes will suggest themselves to every man. And, if the bed should fail of its original purpose altogether ; or, if, owing to some accident, the four-light bed should fail of its purpose, still, these hot-beds will be found to be of great use for other purposes, and will be quite sufficient in point of strength for plants of a more hardy nature.

146. DILL is an aromatic herb, very much like, only smaller than, fennel, and it is used by many amongst cucumbers to give an additional relish ; as it is also in soups. It is a hardy biennial plant, and a small patch in the herb garden of two feet by six will be enough for any family. Sow in drills six inches apart, in the spring, making the ground fine first, and raking fine earth lightly over the drills. Thin the plants out when they are a

couple of inches high, and let them then remain where they are ; and you will have abundance of self-sowed plants every spring for renewing your bed.

147. ENDIVE.—This is a plant used for salads, and is sometimes used, perhaps, in cookery. There is a *curled* sort, and one that is *plain*, or smooth-leaved. The curled is generally preferred to the other, but perhaps there is very little difference in the quality. The lettuce, when to be had, is decidedly preferred to the endive ; and therefore this latter is used for salad in autumn, and through the winter as long as it can be had. If any one wish to have endive in summer, it must be sowed early ; but, about the middle of the month of July, or, perhaps, a little before, is the main time for sowing endive. If sowed much before, it generally runs off to seed, and, in fact, it is so much ground and trouble thrown away. Make a bed very fine, and sow the seed in drills at eighteen inches apart, and about half an inch deep in the drill, the earth being pressed down very closely upon the seed. The plants, which will be quickly up, must be thinned as soon as possible to eighteen inches in the row, and thus they will stand, throughout the bed, at eighteen inches from each other. The leaf of the endive goes off horizontally, and lies flat upon the ground ; and, if the ground be good and rich, as it ought to be, and kept perfectly clean, the points of the leaves will meet all over the ground, though at distances so great ; but, if cramped for room, endive can never be fine. When the plants have got something like their full size, they are to be bleached before they be eaten ; for, they have a bitter and disagreeable taste, and are quite a coarse and dis-

agreeable thing unless made white. The manner of bleaching them is this. You take the plant, put your fingers under all the leaves that touch the ground, gather the whole plant up in your hands into a conical form, and then tie it round with matting, which is to go several times round the plant, and which is to cause the plant to end so pointedly at the top as to prevent rain or dew from reaching the inside. When the plant has remained thus for about a fortnight, you cut it off at the stem, take off the matting, and you will find that all the leaves, except those of the outside, are become white and crisp, and free from bitterness of taste. To have a succession of these in good order, you should begin at one end of the bed and tie up a dozen or two once or twice a week; and, when you cut, always cut those that were tied up first; but it is very important to observe that this work of bleaching or tying-up must never be performed except when all the leaves of the plants are *perfectly dry*. The great difficulty in the case of endive, is, to have it to use in winter; for, though it is hardy enough, it will rot, if it stand tied up too long; and it is difficult to preserve it, on account of this tendency to rot. One way is to take up the roots with balls to them in the month of October, when they are perfectly dry, tying the plants up, as before-mentioned, at the same time, planting these balls in sand or earth, in a shed. But, as this can hardly make the plants reach, for use, beyond the middle of December, the only effectual way to have endive in winter, is, to cover them with glazed frames in the fall of the year, or to do the same very well with hoops and mats, taking all covering off in mild weather, just protecting the plants from hard frosts, and going on bleaching and cutting for use as directed for the autumn.   Endive may be transplanted, but it does not transplant so well as lettuce, and the plants are never so fine as those that remain on the spot where they were sowed. If transplanted, they should be put at about twelve inches apart, hoed nicely between and kept clear from weeds.   Endive, if sowed early in the spring, ripens its seed that same summer ; but the best way is to save two or three good plants that have stood the winter, and let them go to seed.   They will produce a great abundance, which, if carefully preserved, will keep good four or five years, at the least.   I have mentioned the middle of July as the time of sowing for the main crop ; but some may be sowed later, as it does not require any great deal of room.

148. FENNEL is a perennial herb, propagated from seed or from offsets, sowed in the spring, or the offsets planted in the fall. The plants should stand about a foot asunder. The leaves are used in salads, or for the making a part of the sauce for fish. In winter, the seeds are bruised, to put into fish-sauce, and they give it the same flavour as the leaves of the plant. It is a very hardy thing ; two yards square in the herb-bed will be enough for any family ; and, once in the ground, it will stand for an age.

149. GARLICK may be propagated from the seed ; but is usually propagated from offsets. It is a bulb which increases after the manner of the hyacinth and the tulip : the offsets are taken off in the spring and planted in rows at a foot apart, being merely pressed into the ground with the finger and thumb and covered over with a little earth· The ground ought to be kept perfectly clean during the

summer, and, though it ought to be good, it ought, by no means to be wet. When the leaves begin to get brown and to die, the root should be taken up and laid upon a board in the hottest sun that is going until they be perfectly dry: then, tied up in bunches by the leaves, and hung up and preserved in a dry place.

150. GOURD is a sort of pumpkin; but I know not any use that it is of. If any one wish to cultivate it, out of mere curiosity, the directions will be found under " PUMPKIN."

151. HOP.—The hop-top; that is to say, the shoot which comes out in the spring and when it is about four or five inches long, being tied up in little bunches, and boiled for about half an hour, and eaten after the manner of asparagus, is as delightful a vegetable as ever was put upon a table, not yielding, perhaps, during the about three weeks that it is in season, to the asparagus itself. What the hop is, in the hop plantations, every one in England knows; but the manner of propagating the plant is by no means a matter of such notoriety. The hop may be propagated from seed ; but it never is. The mode of propagation is by cuttings from the crown or the roots. Pieces of these, about six inches long being planted in the ground with a setting-stick either in spring or in autumn, shoot up and become plants. The hills or clumps in the hop-plantations are generally formed by plants which have stood a year or two in a nursery where the cuttings have been planted. About four or five of these plants are put into a clump, little sticks are put to them the first year to hold up their slender vines, the

next year rods, the next year small and short poles, upon which they begin to bear, and the next year poles of the full length sufficient to carry a crop. The vines which have gone up during the summer and borne the crop are cut off to within two feet of the ground when the hops are gathered ; in the spring of the year, the earth is drawn away all round from the hill, and all the top part of the plants is cut off, leaving the crown to look like a piece of cork ; from this crown, which is lightly covered over with earth, fresh shoots come again in great numbers, a part of the finest of these go up the poles, the weak ones are suffered to hang about the ground for some time ; they are then cut off close to the ground, and the earth is drawn over the crown of the hill, forming a pretty large heap altogether before the summer be over. To have hop-tops in a garden, therefore, about a dozen or twenty hills might be planted along, and pretty near to, one of the hedges. The cultivation should be after the manner above directed ; but, as there must be some vines to go up to the full length, there might be a pole or two to each hill to carry up four or six stout vines. The poles need not be long, and, if they were not permitted to bear, the plant would be the stronger. These hills would, every spring, send forth a prodigious number of shoots to serve as tops. These, as was said before, are to be cropped off close to the ground when they are four or five inches long ; and the hills, when once established, will last for a life-time with the culture before-mentioned and with a good digging of the ground once every winter.

152. HORSE-RADISH. — As a *weed*, I know of

nothing quite so pertinacious and pernicious as this : I know of nothing but fire which will destroy its powers of vegetation ; and I have never yet seen it clearly extirpated from ground which had once been filled with its roots and fibres. But, as a vegetable, it is a very fine thing : its uses are well known, and to those uses it is applied by all who can get it. It is generally dearer, in proportion to its bulk, than any other vegetable, and much dearer, too. The trouble which its cultivation gives ; that is to say, its encroachments, causes it to be banished from small gardens ; and, therefore, it is scarce, though so difficult to be destroyed. Any little bit of it, whether of fibre or of root, a bit not bigger than a pea, not longer than the eighth of an inch, if it have a bit of skin or bark on it, will grow. The butts of the leaves will grow, if put into the ground, and it bears seed in prodigious abundance. The best way to get horse-radish, is to make holes a couple of feet deep with a bar, and to toss little bits down to the bottoms of the holes, and then fill them up again. You will soon have a plantation of horse-radish, the roots long, straight, thick and tender. A square rod of ground, with the roots in it planted a foot apart every way, will, if kept clear of weeds, as it always ought to be and never is, produce enough for a family that eats roast beef every day of their lives. The horse-radish should be planted in the south-east or south-west corner of the outside garden, near to the hedge, and it ought to be resolved to prevent its encroachments beyond the boundaries of the spot originally allotted to it. Every autumn, that part of the ground which has been cleared during the year, which might be about one third part of the piece, ought to be deeply dug and replanted as before ; and thus there will be a succession of young long roots ; for, after the horse-radish has borne seed once or twice, its root becomes hard, brown on the outside, not juicy when it is scraped, and eats more like little chips than like a garden vegetable : so that, at taverns and eating-houses, there frequently seems to be a rivalship on the point of toughness between the horse-radish and the beef-steak ; and it would be well if this inconvenient rivalship never discovered itself any where else.

153. HYSSOP is a sort of half-woody shrub, something between a tree and an herbaceous plant. The flower-spikes are used, fresh or dry, for medicinal purposes. It is propagated from seed or from offsets. A very little of it is enough : a couple of plants in the herb-bed may suffice for any family.

154. JERUSALEM ARTICHOKE.—This plant bears at the root, like a potatoe, which, to the great misfortune of many of the human race, is every where but too well known. But, this artichoke, which is also dug up and cooked like a potatoe, has, at any rate, the merit of giving no trouble either in the cultivation or the propagation. A handful of the bits of its fruit, or even of its roots, flung about a piece of ground of any sort, will keep bearing for ever in spite of grass and weeds ; the difficulty being, not to get it to grow, but to get the ground free from it when once it has taken to growing. It is a very poor, insipid vegetable ; but, if you have a relish for it, pray keep it out of the garden, and dig up the

corner of some field, or of some worthless meadow, and throw some roots into it.

155. LAVENDER. — A beautiful little well-known shrub of uses equally well-known, whether used in the flower or in the water which is distilled from it. Like all other plants and trees, it may be propagated from seed; but it is easiest propagated from slips, taken off early in the spring, and planted in good moist ground in the shade. When planted out, the plants should stand three feet apart. The flower-stalks should be cut off, whether for preserving in flowers, or for distillation, before any of the blossoms begin to fall off. Just, indeed, as those blossoms begin to open wide. The lavender plant grows large, and it should therefore be in the outer garden.

156. LEEK.—This is a plant, which, for certain purposes, is preferred to onions. The time for sowing is as early in the spring as the weather and the ground will permit; the latter end of February, or very early in March. Sow in little drills made across a bed of fine earth, put the rows eight inches asunder, and thin the plants to three inches apart in the row. Keep the ground clean by nice hoeing until the middle of July or thereabouts; then take the plants up, cut the roots off to an inch long, and cut off the tops of the leaves, but not too low down; make deep drills with a hoe at two feet apart. Plant the leeks in these drills with a setting-stick, fastening them well in the ground, and leaving the drill open. As the plants grow, put to their sides the earth that came out of the drill, after that, draw more up to them on each side from the interval; and, if your

ground be really good, as it ought to be, each leek will
be as big as your wrist in the month of October. They
will stand the winter perfectly well without any covering
at all ; but, as a provision against hard frost, some plants
should always be taken up and put into earth or sand in
a shed or in a cellar, for the same reasons as those stated
under the head of Celery. Three or four leeks that have
stood the winter may be left at the end of one of the
rows, or, if you please, moved to another spot to produce
seed which would be ripe in the month of August, and
give you enough for yourself, and for two or three
neighbours.

157. LETTUCE.—This great article of the garden
is milky, refreshing, and pleasanter to a majority of
tastes than almost any other plant. So necessary is it
deemed as the principal ingredient of a good salad, that
it is, in France and America, generally called " Salad,"
and scarcely ever by any other name. It is therefore a
thing worthy of particular attention, not only as to propagation and cultivation, but as to sorts. The way to
sow lettuce in the natural ground is this ; make the
ground rich to begin with, draw the drills across the bed
fifteen inches apart, sow the seed thinly in these drills,
and press the earth nicely down upon them, which work
i to be done as early as you can do it well, in the month
of March. When the plants come up, thin them quickly
to four inches apart. When they get to be about four or
five inches high, leave one and take up two throughout
all the rows, and then hoe the ground nicely between
the remaining plants, having before-hand made another
bed to receive the plants thus taken up ; plant these in

rows across a bed, the rows fifteen inches apart and the plants fifteen inches apart in the row : this is done with a little setting stick with which you must carefully fix the point of the root in the ground, as directed in the case of the cabbage plant. Another sowing in April, managed in just the same way, may be the last for the summer ; for, if sowed later, it is very rarely that the plants will loave or be good for any thing. This is what every man may do that has ground in sufficient quantity and well-situated ; but the lettuce is a thing which people desire to have very early in the spring, and, if possible, in the winter. To have lettuces to eat in the winter, they must be sowed in August or September, in the natural ground, in the manner before-described, and, in November, before they have been mauled by the frost, they must be taken up without much disturbance of their roots, and put into a pretty good hot-bed made for the purpose, the mould for which ought to be eight inches deep, at the least. They should be watered a little, at planting, should stand nine inches apart every way, should be shaded from the sun, if there be sun, for a couple of days, should then have as much air given to them constantly as the weather will permit, should be kept clear from rotten leaves and putrified matter of every description, should have a lining to the bed, if the weather require it, should, above all things, have as much air as the weather will permit, and should, however, be kept safe from being touched by the frost. If all these things be attended to, and if the season be not uncommonly adverse, you may have fine lettuces by the latter end of December, and through the months of January and February, an object the accomplishment of which would be insured by having a second bed made at the same time, to contain plants a fortnight or three weeks younger. To have lettuces *early in the spring*. You sow in August, or early in September, as before, transplant the lettuces in October into the warmest and best-sheltered spots that you have. In beds about three feet wide with hoops and rods placed over the beds soon enough, in order to cover with mats in severe weather; or, instead of hoops and mats, cover with a glass frame, and, in very sharp weather, with mats over that; but, whatever the covering may be, take it off, the moment the weather will permit you to do it with safety. There are, indeed, sorts of lettuce that will generally stand the winter without any covering, in a warm place, and especially on the south side of a wall. But these are the flat sorts that bring round heads, and are poor, soft, slimy things compared with the coss lettuces; though even these are better than none. The coss lettuces grow upright, fold in their leaves like a sugar-loaf cabbage, have a crispness and sweetness which the others have not. If any of these, or, indeed, of any other sort of lettuce, have stood uncovered until any part of January or February, they may be then moved into a hot-bed, and will be very fine in March: if left to stand in the ground, and kept clear of slugs, they will still be a good deal earlier than lettuces sowed in the spring, even if sowed in a hot-bed. But, with all these means, so few can generally be had early in the spring, that, for general use; that is to say, for kitchen-gardeners to get them for tradesmen's families pretty early in May, they must be first raised in a hot-bed, sowed there early in March, or late in February, or sowed under glass upon cold earth, in the fall of the year, and preserved as mere plants to plant out, having been kept from the frost and the wet during the winter. This sowing takes place in September; the lights are placed in such a way as to let no wet get into the frames; the lights are taken off entirely in mild weather; a great deal of air is given; and, in March, these plants are fit to go out into the natural ground, where they are sometimes injured by the frost, but generally they are not. This is the way in which the great crop of early lettuces is generally raised; and, that it is the best way, the long experience of the market gardeners has amply proved. As to the *sorts* of lettuces, the *green coss* and the *white coss* are the best: the former is of a darker green than the latter, is rather hardier and not quite so good. Among the *flat* sorts are the *brown Dutch*, the *green cabbage*, and the *tennis-ball*: there are many other sorts, as well of upright as of flat, but it would be useless to enumerate them, as it would only bewilder the reader in his choice. As to the saving of the seed, half a dozen plants that have stood the winter will be quite enough. The seed will be ripe in August; birds must be kept from it, or they will have all the best before you gather it. The stalks ought to be cut off and laid, till they be perfectly dry, in the sun, the seed then put away in a perfectly dry place, and in a place where no mice can get at it; for, if they get at it, not one good seed will they leave you in a very short time.

150. MANGEL WURZEL. — This may be called *cattle-beet*; but some persons plant it in gardens. It is a coarse beet, and is cultivated and preserved as the beet is.

159. MARJORAM.—One sort is *annual* and one *per-*

ennial. The former is call *Summer* and the latter *Winter*. The first sowed as early as possible in the spring; and, the latter propagated by *offsets*; that is, by parting the roots. The plants may stand pretty close. As the winter sort cannot sometimes be *got at* in winter, some of both ought to be preserved by *drying.* Cut it *just before it comes out into bloom,* hang it up in little bunches to dry, first, for a day, in the sun; then in the shade; and, when quite dry, put it in paper-bags, tied up, and the bags hung up in a dry place.

160. MARIGOLD.—An annual plant. Sow the seed in spring; when the bloom is at full, gather the flowers; pull the leaves of the flower out of their sockets; lay them on paper to dry, in the *shade.* When dry, put them into paper-bags. They are excellent in broths and soups and stews. Two square yards planted with marigolds will be sufficient. It is the *single* marigold that ought to be cultivated for culinary purposes. The *double* one is an *ornamental* flower, and a very mean one indeed.

161. MELON.—The melon is a hot-country plant, and must be raised in England in precisely the same manner as directed for early cucumbers, the rules laid down for which apply here equally well in every respect, except two; namely, that the lights for melons should be larger or more extensive than those for cucumbers; and that the earth for melons should not be light and loose, as in the case of cucumbers, but should consist chiefly of *very stiff loam.* The finest plants of melons that I ever saw were raised in stiff loam, approaching to a clay, which had been dug out before, and turned three or four times

in a heap, mixed with dung from a sheep-yard, about one fifth dung and four-fifths loam. This loam should be turned in a heap several times during one summer and one winter, and then it is fit for use. You should begin to raise melons a month or six weeks later than you begin with early cucumbers. Your seeds may be sowed in a pot in the cucumber-bed, if you have one; if not, you must make one for the purpose, as in the case of the early cucumbers; though the season when you begin will be later, the bed must be equally warm with that for the early cucumbers; there must be linings, and every thing necessary to keep up a steady bottom heat. A second crop of melons may succeed the first, in the same way that the two crops of cucumbers succeed each other; but, as to putting melons out upon ridges to be covered with hand-glasses or paper-frames, it never succeeds, one time out of twenty. Melons want hotter ground than is hardly ever to be had in England. There should be but one plant in a hill. I have had ten fine melons from one single plant, and I never saw the like of that from any hill that contained two or three plants. If once the plants get spindling, they never bear fruit of any size or goodness. You will see many fruit appear before any one begins to swell. If a solitary one should begin to swell before the vines have got to any extent, pinch it off; for, if left on, it will generally prevent the plant from bearing any more. There should be three or four upon a plant beginning to swell together, or about the same time, in order to encourage you to expect a fine crop. Melons are very frequently raised, as pines sometimes are, in *pits*, with foundations for frames built upon the ground, or, going a little way beneath the top of the ground. Upon these walls a wooden coping is fixed, and across this coping, the lights slide up and down. These are very convenient places for melons; but, as they do not enter into the plan of my garden, it would be useless to take up the time of the reader with a more particular description of them. When the fruit of the melon is perceived to be fairly swelling, a piece of glass or of tile should be laid under each fruit to keep it out of the dirt, and, indeed, to add a little to the heat that it would receive from the sun; for, melons require heat from the sun as well as heat from the earth; and, take what pains we will, we have never fine melons in a shady or wet summer. As to the sorts of melons, some are finer than others, and some come into bearing sooner than others. In speaking of sorts, I cannot do better than to take the list from the *Hortus Kewensis,* written by Mr. Aiton, gardener to the King; for, surely, that which contents his Majesty, may very well content any of us. This list is as follows: *Early Cantaleupe, Early Leopard, Early Polignac, Early Romana, Green-fleshed Netted, Green-fleshed Rock, Bossé's early Rock, Black Rock, Silver Rock, Scarlet-fleshed Rock.* In America, they divide the melons into two sorts which are wholly distinct from each other: one they call the *Musk Melon;* that is to say, any melon which belongs to the tribe of those that we cultivate here, and they call these musk melons because they have a musky smell. The other species they call the *Water Melon,* which has no smell, which never turns yellow, which is always of a deep green, in the inside of which, instead of being a fleshy pulp, is a sort of *pink-coloured snow,* which melts in the mouth. This melon very frequently weighs from twenty to forty pounds, and is not deemed much of a fruit unless it weigh fifteen or sixteen. I raised some of these once very well at Botley from seed that was brought from Malta. They are a totally different thing from the other tribe; and, being so much better, I have often wondered that, where people have great space under glass, and great heat at command, they do not raise them in England. There is only one fine *musk* melon that I ever saw in America; which is called the citron melon, having the flesh nearly white and being of the shape of a lemon. The mode of cultivating the water-melon is the same as that of cultivating the other; but it requires more room. If you wish to save the seed of melons, you must take it out when you eat the fruit, and do with it precisely as is directed in the case of the cucumber seed; but, to have the seed true to its kind, it must not be saved on a spot near to that in which grow, and have blowed, cucumbers, squashes, pumpkins, or any thing of that sort; nor on a spot where any other sort of melon has been in bloom at the same time. The greatest possible care must be taken in this respect, or you will have fruit quite different from that which you expect.

162. MINT.—There are two sorts: one is of a darker green than the other: the former is called *pepper-mint*, and is generally used for *distilling* to make mint water: the latter, which is called *spear-mint*, is used for the table, in many ways. The French snip a little into their *salads*; we boil a bunch amongst green peas, to which it gives a pleasant flavour; chopped up small, and put, along with sugar, into vinegar, we use it as a sauce for *roasted lamb*; and a very pleasant sauce it is. Mint *may* be propagated from seed; but, a few bits of its roots will spread into a

bed in a year. To have it in winter, preserve it precisely like *marjoram* (which see), and, instead of *chopping* it for sauce, crumble it between your fingers.

163. MUSHROOM.—This is one of a numerous tribe of funguses; but it is the only one that is cultivated for culinary purposes, and this one is scarcely ever seen in any gardens but those of noblemen, or gentlemen of fortune. In their gardens it is cultivated in order to be had at *all times of the year,* for every body knows, that, in most parts of England, it comes up spontaneously in the meadows and elsewhere. It is cultivated no how but in hotbeds; but there in two distinct ways. The first, is, on hotbeds *out of doors,* and the hot-bed is made and managed in the manner that I will now describe. Take stable dung that is not fresh and fiery, or, if you have no other, mix with it an equal quantity of old hot-bed lining, throw it together in a long ridge, where rains will not fall on it, to ferment, and, in about three weeks it will be ready for use. Then take and mark out the outline of the base of your bed, just as I directed in my instructions about hotbeds in Chapter III.; but, as this one is to go up in a sloping direction on both sides like the roof of a house, you need not have the upright stakes nor the edge-boards that I there recommended. Three or four feet will be quite wide enough. The length you regulate according to the quantity of mushrooms that you wish to grow. Begin, then, with your bed, shaking the dung up well, and, if it be long, beating it well, just as in the case of the cucumber-bed, only keep drawing it in by degrees till you have it in the shape of the roof of a house : beat it on the top as you carry it up, but, particularly, beat it

I

at the sides, for there you will want it to be perfectly even and firm. Having finished it, you will guard it from rains and from the sun by covering it over with long straw, old thatch, or mats; for it must be neither too wet nor too dry. Let it remain in this way a week, or till you find, by forcing your fore-finger down into it, that the heat is *moderate*. Then put on a layer of fresh mould to about an inch thick. In this you will stick little pieces of spawn of mushrooms at about eight inches apart every way. Cover over these with mould to about another inch in thickness, and pat it down nicely with a spade; and still keep the covering of straw or matting over the whole bed as before, for neither wet nor sun must get to it immoderately. Success now greatly depends on the proper moisture of the bed. If in summer time, take off the covering now and then to admit of gentle showers falling on it; or, if in a very dry season, water now and then. But, if in winter, keep out the *cold* at all times. The *in-doors method* of cultivating mushrooms was introduced to this country from Germany. It is usually by means of a small house in any awkward, or out-of-the-way corner of the garden, about ten or twelve feet wide and twenty or thirty feet long. With a fire-place on the outside of one end, and a flue going from it straight down under the middle of the floor of the house and back again to the fire-place; with one door, and two or three small windows, which latter are generally kept shut close with unglazed shutters. All along the two sides of this house are shelves arranged in three tiers, one close to the bottom, another at about three feet up, and another at about six feet up, and these shelves are about three feet in breadth, made of good stout plank, with a front board

of nine or ten inches depth to keep in the dung and the
earth. Whoever has seen the births in a barrack-room,
or in the state-room of a ship, has seen precisely what
the shelves of a German mushroom-house are. These
shelves are to be filled with the dung or compost in
which you are to plant your mushroom spawn, and, as to
preparing compost, you proceed in this manner : take a
quantity of fresh horse dung, with as little long litter as
possible; the less the better ; that has not been exposed
to wet and that has not fermented ; mix it with a fourth
part of fresh mould, and, if you can, get the scrapings
of a horse-track of a mill-house of any sort ; mix all
well together, and, in your shelves, or in as many of
them as you mean to put to work at once, put a layer six
inches thick of this mixture, beating it down as hard as
you can with a wooden bat. This will reduce it down to
the thinness of four inches, or less. Then put in another
layer, rather less thick, and beat that down in the same
way; observing that, towards the wall at the back part
of your shelf, you can afford to increase the thickness of
your layers, as there is the wall to support them; and
the thicker you make these layers, the stronger will be
the bed. Having done this, observe the fermentation
from day to day, as it goes on, and when it is palpably
on the decline, make a parcel of holes in the compost at
from six to nine inches asunder, and put in the spawn ;
and then cover it over with a covering of mould about an
inch thick. Water may be given out of a very fine-rosed
watering pot, when the weather is very warm, and then
it is recommended to scatter a little straw over first, and
water on that, the mushroom being inclined to rot from
any over quantity of moisture, however little. These

beds are not generally of long duration, but particularly those in the shelves. From eight to twelve weeks may be looked upon as a good duration, and, therefore, to have mushrooms *continually*, there must be renewals of the beds, in the house and out of the house; but a very little attention brings it to a regular system in the *in-door* method. The times when the vegetation of this fungus is most successful, are, the spring and fall, as with every vegetable. To procure spawn, you need only apply to the seedsmen, almost all of whom sell it; but you may procure it and propagate it yourself, by bestowing a little care and attention on it. Dig up, in August or September, a parcel of mushrooms, taking a good three or four handfuls of the earth immediately round them; you will find a quantity of small bulbs, as it were, of mushrooms, and of stuff like coarse thread. Put this in ridges on an old cucumber bed, and keep off heavy rains, and, when you find that these have extended themselves, and are formed into a quantity of mouldy looking flakes, take them up and keep them in any dry place till you want them, when you plant little pieces of the size of the top of your thumb, or a little bigger. There is some danger of mistaking other funguses (and less innocent ones) for mushrooms, therefore, observe that the mushroom comes up precisely in the form of a little round white button, which gradually opens itself, till, if permitted to stand long enough, it becomes almost flat on the top. It is white everywhere but on the under side of the crown, which is of a pale red, becoming of a brownish colour as it advances in age. I cannot conclude without observing that some of these funguses are deemed extremely unwholesome; some people even think them poisonous, and that the mushroom is only the *least noxious*. I once ate about three spoonsful at table at Mr. TIMOTHY BROWN's at Peckham, which had been cooked, I suppose, in the usual way ; but I had not long eaten them before my whole body, face, hands and all, was covered with red spots or pimples, and to such a degree, and coming on so fast, that the doctor who attended the family was sent for. He thought nothing of it, gave me a little draught of some sort, and the pimples went away ; but I attributed it then to the mushrooms. The next year, I had mushrooms in my own garden at Botley, and I determined to try the experiment whether they would have the same effect again ; but, not liking to run any risk, I took only a tea-spoonful, or rather, a French coffee-spoonful, which is larger than a common tea-spoon. They had just the same effect, both as to sensation and outward appearance ! From that day to this, I have never touched mushrooms, for I conclude that there must be something poisonous in that which will so quickly produce the effects that I have described, and on a healthy and hale body like mine ; and, therefore, I do not advise any one to cultivate these things.

164. MUSTARD.—There is a *white-seeded* sort and a *brown-seeded*. The *white* mustard is used in *salads* along with the *cress*, or *pepper-grass*, and is sowed and cultivated in the same way (see CRESS). The *black* is that which the *flour* is made of for table-use. It is sowed in rows at two feet apart, early in the spring. The plants ought to be thinned to four or five inches apart. Good tillage between the rows is necessary. The seed will be ripe in

July, and then the stalks should be cut off, and, when quite dry, the seed threshed out, and put by for use.

165. NASTURTIUM.—An annual plant, with a half-red half-yellow flower, which has an offensive smell ; but it bears a seed enveloped in a fleshy pod, and that pod, taken before the seed becomes ripe, is used as a thing to *pickle*. The seed should be sowed very early in the spring. The plants should have pretty long bushy sticks put to them ; and four or five of them will bear a great quantity of pods. They will grow in almost any ground ; but, the better the ground the fewer of them are necessary.

166. ONION.—This is one of the main vegetables. Its uses are many, and they are all well known. The modes of cultivation for crop are various. *Three* I shall mention, and by either a good crop may be raised. Sow early in March. Let the ground be *rich*, but not from *fresh dung*. Make the ground *very fine*; make the rows a foot apart, and scatter the seed *thinly* along a drill two inches deep. Then fill in the drills ; and then press the earth down upon the seed by *treading the ground all over.* Then give the ground a *very slight* smoothing over with a rake. When the plants get to be three inches high, thin them to four inches, or to eight inches, if you wish to have very large onions. Keep the ground clear of weeds by *hoeing*; but, do not *hoe deep,* nor *raise earth* about the plants; for these make them run to *neck* and not to *bulb.* When the tips of the leaves begin to be brown, bend down the necks, so that the leaves lie flat with the ground. When the leaves are nearly dead, pull up the onions, and lay them to dry, in order to be put away for

winter use.   Some persons, instead of sowing the onions
all along the drill, drop four or five seeds at every six or
seven inches distance ; and leave the onions to grow thus,
in clumps ; and this is not a bad way ; for, they will
squeeze each other out.   They will not be *large ;* but, they
will be ripe *earlier,* and will not run to neck.   The third
mode of cultivation is as follows : sow the onions any
time between mid-May and mid-June, in drills *six* inches
apart, and put the seed *very thick* along the drills.   Let
all the plants stand, and they will get to be about as big
round as the top of your little finger.   Then the leaves
will get yellow, and, when that is the case, pull up the
onions and lay them on a board, till the sun have withered
up the leaves.   Then take these diminutive onions, put
them in a bag, and hang them up in a dry place till
spring, taking the biggest for pickles.   As soon as the
frost is gone, and the ground dry, plant out these onions
in good and fine ground, in rows a foot apart.   Make, *not
drills,* but little marks along the ground ; and put the
onions at six or eight inches apart.   Do not *cover* them
with the earth ; but just *press them down upon* the mark
with your thumb and fore finger.   The ground ought to
be trodden and slightly raked again before you make the
marks ; for *no earth should rise up* about the plants.   Proceed after this as with sowed onions ; only observe, that,
if any should be *running up to seed,* you must *twist down
the neck* as soon as you perceive it.   But, observe this :
the *shorter* the time that these onions have been in the
ground the year before, the *less likely will they be to run
to seed.*   This is the *sure* way of having a large and early
crop of onions.   Preserving onions is an easy matter.
Frost never hurts them, *unless you move them during the*

time that they are frozen. Any dry, airy place will, there-fore, do. They should not be kept in a *warm* place; for they will *heat* and grow. The neatest way is to tie them up in ropes; that is to say, to tie them round sticks, or straight straw, with *matting.* For seed, pick out the *finest onions,* and plant them out in rich land, in the spring. To grow this seed upon a large scale, plough the land into four feet ridges, lay plenty of dung along the furrows, plough the ground back over the dung, flatten the top of the ridge a little, and put along, on the top of the ridge *two rows* of onions, the rows seven inches apart, and the onions seven inches apart in the rows. When the weeds come, hoe the *tops* of the ridges with a small *hoe,* and plough first from and then to the ridges, two or three times, at the distance of two or three weeks. When the seed is ripe, cut off the heads and collect them in such a way as not to scatter the seed. Lay them, on cloths, in the sun, till dry as dust; and then thresh out the seed, winnow it, and put it away. The seed will be dead ripe in August, and turnips or early York cabbages, or even Kidney dwarf beans, may follow upon the same ground, the same year. In a *garden* there always ought to be a crop to succeed seed-onions the same summer. There are several *sorts* of onions, of which the *red* is the hardiest and the hottest, and the *white* the tenderest and the mildest, and the best for pickling. The straw-coloured sort is, perhaps, the best for a main crop.

167. PARSLEY.—Known to every human being to bear its seed the second year, and, after that, to die away. It may be sowed at *any season* when the frost is out of the

ground. The best way is to sow it in spring, and in very *clean* ground; because the seed lies long in the ground, and, if the ground be foul, the weeds choke the plants at their coming up. A bed of six feet long and four wide, the seeds sowed in drills at eight inches apart, is enough for any family in the world. This would be enough about parsley; but people want it all the year round. There are some winters that will destroy it completely if it be wholly unprotected, and there are no means of preserving it dry in the manner which has been directed for other herbs. Therefore, if you perceive sharp weather approaching, lay some peas-haulm or straw, not very thickly, over the bed, and do not take it off until after the thaw has completely taken place. The rotting of vegetables is occasioned by thawing in the light, more than by the frost. When the thaw has completely taken place, the peas-haulm or the straw may be taken away, and, by these means, parsley may be safely kept through any winter that we have in England; for it can be thus kept even in America, where the frost goes down into the ground full four feet.

168. PARSNIP.—As to the season of sowing, sort of land, preparation of ground, distances, and cultivation and tillage, precisely the same as the *Carrot*. But, as to preservation during winter, and for *spring use*, the Parsnip stands all frost without injury, and even with benefit. So that, all you want is to put up for winter as many as you are likely to want during a hard frost, and these you may put up in the same manner as directed for carrots and beets. If the parsnips be to stand out in the ground all the winter, the greens should not be cut off in the fall.

To save the seed of the parsnip, let four or five of the plants stand through the next summer, or remove them to a more convenient spot. They will bear a great quantity of seed. When it turns ripe, cut the seed stalk off, lay it upon a cloth in the sun until perfectly dry ; then take off the seed, put it in a paper bag, and put it in a very dry place : it keeps well for only one year.

169. PEA.—This is one of those vegetables which all people like. From the greatest to the smallest of gardens, we always find peas, not to mention the thousands of acres which are grown in fields for the purpose of being eaten by the gardenless people of the towns. Where gardening is carried on upon a royal, or almost royal scale, peas are raised by means of artificial heat, in order to have them here at the same time that they have them in Portugal, which is in the months of December and January. Beneath this royal state, however, the next thing is to have them in the natural ground as early as possible ; and that may be, sometimes by the middle of May, and hardly ever later than about the first week of June. The late king, George the Third, reigned so long, that his birth-day formed a sort of season with gardeners ; and, ever since I became a man, I can recollect that it was always deemed rather a sign of bad gardening if there were not green peas in the garden fit to gather on the fourth of June. It is curious that green peas are to be had as early in Long Island, and in the sea-board part of the state of New Jersey, as in England, though not sowed there, observe, until very late in April, while our's, to be very early, must be sowed in the month of December or January. It is still more curious, that,

such is the effect of habit and tradition, that, even when
I was last in America (1819), people talked just as
familiarly as in England about having green peas on the
King's birth-day, and were just as ambitious for accom-
plishing the object ; and I remember a gentleman who had
been a republican officer during the Revolutionary War,
who told me that he always got in his garden green-peas
fit to eat on old *Uncle George's birth-day.* This, however, is
the general season for the coming in of green-peas in
England ; but, to have them at this season, the very
earliest sort must be sowed ; they must be sowed, too,
in November, or as soon after as the weather will permit, and they must be sowed on the South-side of a wall,
or of a very close and warm hedge, the ground not being
wet in its nature by any means. The frosts will be very
apt to cut them off, and, if the weather be mild, they
will be apt to get so forwatd as to be cut off in January
or February. They should, therefore, be kept earthed
up a little on both sides ; and, if hard frosts approach, they
should be covered with peas-haulm or straw, and these
should be taken off as soon as the thaw has completely taken
place. It will not do to place the row of peas nearer than
about four feet distance from the wall, because, they grow
high, and they would interfere with, and do injury to,
the fruit trees. Three or four rows of the very earliest
peas might be in the border *e,* on the south side of the
wall. Some more rows might be in the outer garder *c,*
on the south side of the wall there. The whole of these
borders need not be devoted to this purpose, but only
such part of them as would be deemed requisite. A
second sowing should take place a month or six weeks
after the first ; but this may take place across the plat

b or *g*. Sow again early in March, and, then, once in a month or three weeks, until the end of May. Too many should not be sowed at a time, and less of the tall sorts than of the low sorts. The manner of sowing peas is the same in all cases. You make a drill with a hoe, three inches deep, in ground as rich as you can make it, sow the peas along not too thick, put back upon them the earth that came out of the drill, and tread it down with your feet pretty nearly as hard as you can, and then, especially in winter time, keep a sharp look out after the mice. When the peas come up, you ought, in all cases, to hoe the ground nicely about them, and draw a little earth to them even immediately, drawing up more and more earth on each side as the plants advance in height, until you have, at last, a little ridge, the top of which would be six or seven inches above the level of the ground; this not only keeps them upright, but supplies them with food for roots that will shoot out of the stems of the plants. Peas must have sticks, and these sticks must be proportioned to the height which the sorts respectively generally attain. For the *early-frame* pea, two feet and a half, or three feet, above the ground, is sufficient; for the next in height, four or five feet. For the tall sorts, from six to eight, and even nine feet. The distances at which the rows are to be sowed must be somewhat in proportion to these heights, the smaller peas may stand at three feet apart, but the taller ones, and especially the tall ones of all, ought to be at six or seven feet apart at the least. You get nothing by crowding them, nor do you get any thing by sowing double instead of single rows of peas. If you try it, you will find that a single plant standing out away from all others, will produce more fruit than any six plants standing in a common single row, though the soil be the same, and though the stick be of the same height. This is enough to convince any one of the mischievous effects of crowding. If you plant the taller peas at distances too close, or, indeed, any peas, the rows shade one another; there will be no fruit except just at the top, that part of the plant which should bear early will not bear at all, those that come at top will be pods only about half full; and, if you plant tall peas so close, and with sticks so short as to cause the wet to bend the heads of the plants down, you will literally have no fruit at all, a thing which I have seen take place a hundred times in my life-time. My Gardener had once sowed, while I was from home, a piece of garden with the tall marrowfat pea, and had put the rows at about three feet apart. I saw them just after they came up. The ground was such as was very good, and which I knew would send the peas up very high; I told him to take his hoe and cut up every other row; but they looked so fine and he was so obstinate, that I let them remain, and made him sow some more at seven feet apart very near to the same place, telling him that there never could be a pea there, and that, if it so turned out, never to attempt to have his own way again. Both the patches of peas were sticked in due time, they both grew very fine and lofty; but his patch began to get together at the top, and just about the time that the pods were an inch long, there came a heavy rain, smashed the whole of them down into one mass, and there never was a single pea gathered from the patch, while the other patch, the single rows of which were seven feet apart, produced an uncommonly fine and lasting crop. The destroyed patch of peas was however of precious advantage; for it made me the *master of my gardener*, a thing that happens to very few owners of gardens. A sufficient distance is one of the greatest things in the raising of peas, whether they be sticked or whether they be not; and they never ought to be sowed too thickly in the row. I never tried it, but I verily believe that a row of peas each plant being at two or three inches distance from the other, would bear a greater crop than if sowed in the usual way. At any rate, never sow too thick, on any account, at any time of the year. As to *sorts* of peas, the earliest is the *early-frame*, then comes the *early-charlton*, then the *blue-prussian* and the *hotspur*, then the *dwarf-marrowfat*, then the *tall-marrowfat*, then *knight's pea*. There are several others, but here are quite enough for any garden in the world. If all these tall sorts be sowed in March, and some more of them again in April, not too many at a time, they will come in, one after another, and will keep up a regular succession until about the latter end of July, or even later. After this, all peas become mildewed and their fruit good for very little. As to *saving the seed* of peas, it is impossible to do it well in a kitchen garden, where you must always have more than one sort of pea in bloom at the same time. If you be very curious about this matter, you must sow somewhere in the corner of a field, and not gather any of the peas to eat; but let them all stand to ripen. When ripe, they are to be threshed out and put by in a dry place. Peas want no watering, but there should be a good digging between the rows just about the time that the bloom begins to appear, for that furnishes new food to the roots at the time when it is most wanted. Great care must be taken to keep slugs and snails away from peas ; for if they get amongst them and are let alone for a very little while, they bite the whole off, and they never sprout again to any good purpose.

170. PENNYROYAL.—A medicinal herb, that is perennial. It is also used for some few culinary purposes. A little patch, a foot square, in the herb bed, is quite sufficient. You must keep this patch well cut off round the edges ; for, one root, if left alone for a summer, will extend over two or three yards square in good ground.

171. POTATOE.—I am going to speak here of this vegetable, as a thing to be used merely in company with meat; and not to be used as a *substitute for bread*, having proved, in various parts of my writings, and proved it beyond all contradiction, that, as a substitute for bread, it is the most wasteful thing that can possibly be used. It has, too, now been acknowledged by various writers, and it has been established by evidence taken before committees of the House of Commons, that, to raise potatoes for the purpose of being used instead of bread, is a thing mischievous to the nation. As a substitute for bread, therefore, I speak not of the fruit of this plant. As food for cattle, or pigs, I know it to be inferior to cabbages, to swedish-turnips, to mangel-wurzel, and to be much more expensive, weight for weight, than either of those articles. I know of no animal that will even *live* for any length of time, upon uncooked potatoes, while I know

that sheep and horned cattle will live, and even fat, to a certain extent, upon either cabbages, mangel-wurzel, or swedish turnips; and, while I know that pigs will live and thrive upon either of these articles, neither of which, weight for weight, demand half the expense that the potatoes demand. As a mere vegetable, or sauce, as the country people call it, it does very well to qualify the effects of fat meat, or to assist in the swallowing of quantities of butter. There appears to be nothing un-wholesome about it, and, when the sort is good, it is pre-ferred by many people to some other vegetables of the coarser kind; and though I never eat of it myself, find-ing so many other things far preferable to it, I think it right to give directions for the cultivation of the plant upon a scale suitable to a gentleman's garden. There are an infinite variety of *sorts*. The skin of some of which is red, that of others of a whitish yellow colour: the first are denominated red potatoes, and the latter white. The red potatoes are of the coarser kinds, as are also several of the white. Those who plant these things in gardens and for their own use, will not plant the coarse ones. I shall speak of only three sorts. First, of a little round white potatoe, which comes very early, or rather, is but a very short time in coming to perfection. The second sort are called *ladies-fingers*, being long and about an inch through when in their usual full size, and these also are white. The other sort are called *kidney-potatoes*, which grow to a pretty large size, are flat, and very much in the shape of a kidney. This is the sort which is planted for the main crop to be preserved during the winter. They have generally a small part at one end of them of a reddish purple colour, which is the sign of their genuine quality. As to the planting and cultivation of potatoes, they are, in the fields, laid along a little trench made by the plough, then covered with manure of some sort, and then covered over with a furrow of earth. Some people lay the potatoe upon the manure, in place of under it. In a garden the ground ought to be rich enough to bear potatoes without any manure at all; for the manure, though it adds to the number of potatoes, makes the size of them very various, and, as in all other cases, gives a strong taste to the vegetable. Drills made with a hoe three feet apart and four inches deep, the sets laid along the drill at eight inches apart, then covered over with the earth that came out of the drill and trod down with the foot, are sufficient for the planting. But, care must be taken to prepare the *sets* properly. The potatoe must be cut in pieces, and there must be but one eye, or two at most, left to each piece. A very small part of the pulp is necessary to be left. It is the eye only which grows, and, if a potatoe were peeled pretty deeply, the peeling itself would do; and it is a common practice amongst the poorer people, to eat the potatoe and plant bits of the peelings. As to the *cultivation*, as soon as the plants are up, and are three inches high, the whole of the ground should be flat-hoed, and should be carefully moved close to the stems of the plants. When the plants get to be seven or eight inches high, they should have earth drawn up to their stems with a hoe, going along the interval and drawing the earth from the middle to form little ridges about four inches high. As the plants advance in height, more earth should be drawn up to them, and when they are about a foot high above the top of the ridge, the intervals should be well dug with a spade, and the earth well broken. After this, a little more earth should be drawn up to the plants, the heads of which would begin to fall down and spread about, and, all that will be wanted in future, will be to pull out any weeds that appear. In the fall of the year, the leaves will drop off and the haulm will die; and, when this death of the haulm takes place, the potatoes should be dug up. I am now speaking of the kidney potatoes which are to be kept for winter use; and they should not be planted too early; because they will be ripe too early in the fall, and will not keep so well through the winter, and until the spring. The last week in April, or the first, or even the second, week in May is quite soon enough to plant. The crop will then be fit to take up in the latter end of October, which is quite soon enough. When taken up, they should, if the weather will permit, be suffered to dry in the sun; all the dirt should be rubbed clean from them; they should then be placed in a cellar, in a barn, or in some place to which no frost can approach: if you can ascertain the degree of warmth just necessary to keep a baby from perishing from cold, you know precisely the precautions required to preserve a potatoe above-ground; for, under ground, they will lie safe and sound during the whole winter, if placed individually, if the *frost* do not actually reach them. I know of no other seed or root; I know of no apple even; I know of no loaved cabbage, that will not bear freezing, if *covered over with the ground.* I have, this year, had a piece of ground, in which potatoes (planted by my predecessor) grew last year, covered over twenty times by the over-flowings of the Thames, and when this piece of ground was dug up in the spring,

the potatoes were as sound and as fresh as ever. We
did not perceive one single rotten potatoe in the whole
piece. There was a great quantity, and the men who
dug the ground, took them home to eat. But, if above
ground, your care must be great, especially if the heap
be considerable. There must be no rotten ones, and no cut
or broken ones. The heap may ferment, and then rottenness will come : you must therefore be careful to turn it
over frequently and pick out every thing approaching towards rottenness. Potatoes are frequently kept in heaps
formed in a conical shape on the ground, and covered over
with straw and earth ; but this is a thing that cannot be required in a case like that which I have in view. The
ladies'-fingers, which are certainly more delicate in taste
than the kidney-potatoes, may be planted at the same
time, and treated in the same manner ; and they will be
better than the larger potatoes all through the winter,
though the crop will not be so large. Some of these,
however, if planted early in March, will be very good for
use from the end of June to the latter end of the summer.
As to the first sort, the little round white early potatoes,
they may be raised so as to be fit to eat in June, and
even earlier. This sort of potatoe has no blossom.
It is a small round white potatoe, the leaf of which is
of a pale green, very thin, very smooth, and nearly of
the shape and size of the inside of a middle-sized *lemon*
cut asunder longways. This potatoe, if planted with
other sorts in March or April, will be ripe six weeks
sooner than any other sort. The ladies' fingers come
much quicker than the kidneys ; but, the early
potatoe comes much quicker still. If you once get
this sort, and wish to keep it true, you must take

care that no other sort grow near it; for potatoes mix
the breed more readily than any thing else, though, in
this case, there be no bloom. It is very difficult, for
this reason, to get this sort true and unmixed. If these
potatoes be planted early in March, or late in February,
it should be in warm and dry ground; and you must
take care to cover the ground where they are planted
with litter or straw, if you perceive that frosts are
approaching, for if the root be once frosted, it immediately becomes water. You may dig up some of these
potatoes in June as big as walnuts or bigger. They are
not ripe in June; but they may be ripe by the latter end
of July; they increase in size as you go on, and the
quantity need not be large, for, by the time these are exhausted, the ladies' fingers come in for use. A small
quantity will be enough for seed for the next year. You
should pick out five or six of the truest plants to stand
for seed; when the haulm dies, take up the roots; put
them by carefully and preserve them till Spring. If you
wish to have potatoes still earlier than this, you must
resort to artificial heat. One way of doing this is as
follows: dig out the earth in the border opposite the
South side of a wall, but at four or five feet from it
in order to give room for the operations to be performed.
Take the earth out to the depth of two feet, and make
a hot-bed there of good, and rather long, dung, causing
the bed to rise about a foot above the level of the
ground. Put part of the earth upon this bed, and lay
the rest as a bank on each side of it. Give the bed a little
time to heat and to sink, and have the earth upon the
bed about eight or nine inches deep. Plant the sets of
potatoes in the earth upon this bed, and about six inches

down into that earth. The sets may be put in at about a foot apart, and then you may sow all over the bed radishes, onions and lettuces. These will come up immediately, and the management of the bed is this. In the first place, you put hoops across it, leaving about eighteen inches between every two hoops; then tie straight and smooth sticks, long-ways of the bed upon the hoops; then have mats good and sound, to lay over the hoops; and the bed ought to be of the width that a mat will completely cover. At all times, when the radishes will bear the open air, that is to say, when there is no frost, the mats ought to be off in the day-time; and, if it be extraordinarily warm for the season, and you are sure that no frost will come in the night, they may be off in the night; for, if the plants be drawn up, the radishes, lettuces and onions will come to nothing, and the potatoes will be spindling and will not produce. By the time that the radishes have been all drawn and used, the potatoes will have come up, and will have attained the height of six or seven inches: the young onions will have been used also, and the lettuce plants taken away and planted out in the open ground; so that the potatoes only will remain, and these will be fit for use in May, and, perhaps, early in May. Under the head of radishes, I shall have to speak of a mode of getting potatoes still earlier than this, though, perhaps, this is as early as any one need wish for. The bed need not be long. From twelve to twenty feet is, perhaps, enough, for any family. After the potatoes are used, the earth should be drawn off the bed, the dung taken out, and applied to the manuring of the garden, the earth put back again to the place whence it was dug out, and the ground applied to the producing of some crop for the latter end of the Summer. Potatoes may be raised from *seed*, that is to say, from the round pods that grow upon the haulm; and from these seeds new varieties come, as in the case of the Strawberry and many other things. The pods should be gathered when dead ripe. The pods should be squeezed to pieces, the seed separated from the pulp, made very dry, kept dry till April or early in May. They should be sowed in little drills, two feet asunder, the plants thinned out to a foot apart, they should be cultivated like other potatoes, and they will produce little roots fit to plant out for a crop next spring. Few people take the pains to do this, the sorts being already as numerous as the stones of the pavement of a large city.

172. PUMPKIN.—A thing little used in England, but of great use in hot countries. They are of various sorts, the fruit of some of which are of immense size, and the fruit of others in very common use in the making of pies, where, however, they require the assistance of cream, sugar, nutmeg, and other spices; but, when so prepared, are very pleasant things. They are by no means bad cattle food, especially for milch cows, during two months in the fall of the year; and I have no doubt that they would produce twenty ton weight upon an acre of land. The time for planting them in the natural ground is the middle of May. They are not so sensible of frost as the Cucumber. They will be up in the first week of June, and you have nothing to do but to keep the ground clear of weeds. The best way is to put three or four seeds in a clump, and put the clumps at ten or twelve feet apart. The runners should have a proper direction given to

them, should be fastened down to the ground with pegs at every two or three feet, and the runners will then send new roots down into the ground. You know when the pumpkins are ripe by their turning yellow, and striped, and when the leaves begin to die. If you wish to save the seed, you must let the pumpkin be quite ripe, and then manage the seed as in the case of the Cucumber. Different sorts must not grow near one another. If they do, they will mix.

173. PURSLANE.—A mischievous weed, eaten by Frenchmen and pigs when they can get nothing else. Both use it in salad, that is to say, raw.

174. RADISH.—There are two distinct species of Radishes, the *tap-rooted*, and the *turnip-rooted*. Of the latter, there are red and white. The former are all red, some, however, of a deeper dye than others. The great thing in the case of radishes, is, to have them early in the Spring, and, for this purpose, the tap-rooted kinds only are used, as they come quicker than others. In the open natural ground, radishes are sowed in the latter end of February, or early in March, and a few once a fort-night, until the beginning of May. If sowed later than that, they are hot and disagreeable, and very few people care for them. The turnip-rooted sorts should be of the latest sowings; but even they become hot, if sowed after the first of May. I shall hardly prevail upon any body to sow radishes in little drills as directed for cab-bages; but that is the best way; and, as soon as they are up, they should be thinned to an inch apart; for, if thicker, you gain nothing in point of quantity, and you

lose in point of quickness in coming. They should be sowed in shallow drills six inches apart, thinned to an inch apart in the drill as soon as they come up, and the ground should be kept clear of weeds by a little hoe. We have seen how radishes may be had early by sowing them upon a potatoe-bed; if you wish to have them still earlier, you must make a bed on purpose, and cover it with a frame and glass. The manner of making a hot-bed has been described in Chapter III. A bed for radishes, made as early as December, if you like, need not be so strong as a bed for early cucumbers. Proceed, in the making of the bed, in just the same manner as directed for cucumbers; but, you need not make the bed to be above three feet high. You must let the heat be gone off more in this case than in the case of cucumbers, before you put on the mould; and before you put on the mould for radishes, take all the lights off the bed for a whole day unless in case of severe frosts, snow or rain. Put the mould on eight inches deep; or, if it be nine inches, it is better still. The mould should be made very fine, and it should be rich without dung. There is no room to spare in a hot-bed, and, therefore, you should make the drills with your finger about two inches apart, and put the seed along in the drills in a very even manner. When the plants come up, thin them to an inch apart. That will give you seventy-two radishes; that is to say, six dozen upon every square foot; and, if your frame be twelve feet long and four feet wide, this hot-bed will give you two hundred and eighty-eight bunches, a dozen in a bunch. Now mind, your success will depend upon two things. Keeping out frost, and giving all the air that you can possibly give, without letting in the frost. If it be fine open weather, whether wet or dry, the lights should be taken entirely off during the day; and even in sharpish weather there should be plenty of air given in the day-time. In open weather, there should be air given by night as well as by day; and the lights should be entirely off in the day-time, except in frosty weather, or during very heavy rains. For, if your radishes be drawn up, they will come to nothing; and they will be drawn up unless they have plenty of air. The heat of the bed, will, in time, diminish so much as to let in the frost, in a severe winter. In such weather therefore, you must *line* the bed in the same manner as is directed for cucumbers. As to covering, in sharpish weather, a single mat over the glass will do. It seldom happens that more than a double mat could be required for a radish-bed; but, if the bed become cool, there must be covering sufficient to keep out the frost; this is to remain on, however, for as short a time as possible; and, even during a hard frost, if the sun come out, the lights should be taken off during the time that the sun is within two hours of its highest pitch; for, in this country, it never, I believe, freezes in the sun, and, to keep away frost is all that you require in the way of covering. Two square feet, or four at most, in one corner of the frame, will give you mustard and cress a plenty for salads, if you take care to make repeated sowings in proper time. In this bed early potatoes may be planted in the manner directed for the potatoe-bed mentioned under the head of the potatoe. A few young onions may be raised here also to be eaten green; and also some lettuce plants, to be removed about the time that the radishes are all drawn. In just the same way, and, with a bed of about the same strength, *early carrots* may be raised. Some people like them, and the trouble is a great deal less than any one would imagine, seeing that it requires so many words to explain the method of doing the thing. Now, as to the sorts of radishes for the hot-bed, there are two, the *early scarlet*, and the *early short-top :* the colour of the former is indicated by its name, that of the latter is between a red and a purple. Some tastes prefer one sort, and some the other. I know no difference in the flavour : the scarlet is the most pleasing to the eye, and is, therefore, the sort that market-gardeners cultivate ; but the short-top is the earliest ; that is to say, the quickest in coming to perfection ; or, at least, I think so ; for I never actually tried one against the other ; and they certainly eat more crisp than the scarlet. The finest radish of all for the flavour, as well as for crispness, is called the *salmon-radish*, from its colour being precisely that of salmon when in season ; but it does not come so quickly as the other two sorts. If you have the early radishes in beds, the salmon-radish ought to be the first to sow in the open ground. With regard to the turnip-rooted sorts, they are all greatly inferior, in point of flavour, to the tap-rooted ; and, as to the *black Spanish radish*, it is a coarse thing that will stand the winter about as well as a turnip ; and is very little superior to a turnip in point of flavour. It is called a radish, and may be had with hardly any trouble even in the winter time ; but it is, in fact, not fit to eat. In all sowings of radishes, the greatest care must be taken to keep away the birds, until the radishes be fairly up, and even begin to show rough leaf ; for, they are extremely fond of these seeds, and they are sowed at a season of the year when bird-food is scarce. The sparrows will see you when you are sowing, will know very well what you are at ; and though you bury the seeds very safely, they will watch the first peeping up of the head, and you will not have a single radish, if you sow in winter or early in the spring, unless you take the proper precautions to keep off the birds. When you take the lights off the hot-bed of radishes, you must cover the bed over with a net. When you tilt up the lights to give air, the birds will go in unless you hang nets over the opening. The market-gardeners, who want great quantities of radishes pretty early in the spring, sow them in the month of January in the natural ground in warm situations. As soon as they have sowed, they cover the beds with straw, half a foot thick. Under this straw, the radishes, sheltered from the frost, come up ; and then the straw is taken off in the day-time, and put on again at night ; and this opening by day, and covering by night, is kept up until mild weather come in March, when the radishes are fit to take up for sale. The same may be done in a private garden ; but the straw makes a great litter about the ground : it makes a pretty place ugly, and the advantage is not sufficient to counterbalance the eye-sore. Radish-seed, like all others, becomes untrue, if plants of different sorts bloom and ripen their seed near each other. This, therefore, must be guarded against ; if you want to save seed, refrain from drawing a few of the very earliest of your radishes ; let them stand in the bed until the middle of March or first of April ; then take them up, transplant them into the natural ground, and they will well ripen their seed during the summer. Though, observe, they will not ripen *all* their seed, for, like the beet, the buckwheat, and many other plants, they continue to blow long after part of their seed is nearly ripe. Therefore, if you were to stop till all the seed ripened, before you gathered any, you would stand a chance to lose the whole; for the birds would have eaten the first seed long before all the flowers were off the plant. The best way, therefore, is to pull up the plants when the first seed is ripe; and that gives you plenty of time to put the whole plant to lie and wither in the sun, without which, too, it is very difficult to get the seed out of the pods. A very good way is, first to make the whole plant, pods and all, dry in the sun, and then to hang the plant up by the heels in some dry and airy place, and rub the seed out of the pods as you want it. In the pod, it will keep a great many years, perhaps twenty, and, perhaps, fifty; but, out of the pod, it will keep well, not above two.

175. RAMPION.—This is the smallest seed of which we have any knowledge. A thimble-full, properly distributed, would sow an acre of land. It is sowed in the spring, in very fine earth. Its roots are used in soup and salads. Its leaves are also used in salads. A yard square is enough for any garden.

176. RAPE.—This is a *field-plant* for sheep; but it is very good to sow like *white mustard*, to use as salad, and it is sowed and raised in the same way.

177. RHUBARB.—The *dock*, which is a mischievous weed, is the native English rhubarb. Its name is found in the list of seeds in Chapter IV., because that list is the same as the list in my American Gardener; and, in

America, dock-leaves are eaten in the spring, and are
carried to market in great quantities to be sold.   But, in
this country, where the winter does not sweep every
thing green from the face of the earth, nobody thinks of
cultivating the dock, which is one of the most mischievous weeds that we have.   In that list also is the
dandelion; because that plant also is used as greens |in
the spring; and, if the plants be fine, and you lay a tile or
bit of board upon them to bleach them, or tie them up
as directed for endive, they make very good salad in the
month of April; but, not being worth cultivation in a
garden, and being a mere weed, they have not been
mentioned by me as articles to be cultivated.   I am now
to speak, not of the dock, but of the foreign rhubarb,
of which there are two sorts, the stalks of the leaves of
the one being pretty nearly red, and those of the leaves of
the other being of a greyish green colour.   The latter is
the finer of the two, grows larger than the other, and
the flavour is better.   The uses of the rhubarb are very
well known, and it is known also that the only part used
is the inside of the stalk of the leaf, which is fit for
use towards the latter end of April, when it supplies, by
anticipation, the place of green gooseberries in all the
various modes in which these latter are applied.   The
propagation of the rhubarb may be either from seed or
from offsets.   It bears seed in prodigious abundance, and
that seed precisely resembles the seed of the dock.   It is
sowed any time in the spring, in the same manner as directed for cabbages, and, when the plants come up, they
ought to be thinned to six inches apart in the row.   In
the fall, the plants are taken up and planted in rows at
three feet apart, and two feet apart in the row.   During

the first summer after this, none of the leaves ought to be stripped off for use. If the plants throw up seed-stalks, these should be kept cut down. During this summer, the plants will become very strong, and the next spring, they will produce leaves, the stalks of which will be fit for use. They will stand and flourish for any length of time on the same spot, and their produce will be prodigious. When taken off for use, their leaves should be stripped off, and not cut. It is perfectly hardy, and all that it requires, is, digging the ground in the intervals and between the plants in the month of November, and again early in April, and giving a moderate supply of manure, once in two years. If propagated from offsets; that is to say, shoots taken off from the sides of the old stools, the offsets ought to be planted at the distance before-directed ; and, if they be stout, and planted out in the fall, you may begin using the leaves the next spring.

178. ROSEMARY is a beautiful little shrub. One of them may be enough in a garden. It is propagated from *slips*, taken off in the spring and planted in a cool place.

179. RUE.—Still more beautiful. Propagated in the same manner. One plant of the kind is enough.

180. RUTABAGA.—(See *Turnip*.)

181. SAGE is raised from seed, or from slips. To have it at hand for winter, it is necessary to *dry it ;* and it ought to be cut, for this purpose, *before it comes out into bloom,* as, indeed, is the case with *all other herbs.*

182. SALSAFY.—The seed of the salsafy very nearly resembles that of the wild oat. It is a tap-rooted plant, resembling the parsnip in colour, and not very much unlike it in flavour. It is usually sowed late in February or early in March, in drills a foot apart, and, when the plants come up, they are thinned to six inches apart in the row. Hoeing between to keep down the weeds is all that is required. Though it is usually sowed so early in the spring, it ought not to be sowed till May, and even the middle of May; for, if sowed earlier, many of the plants will run up to seed, and then they become good for nothing for use. It is as hardy as the parsnip. It stands in the ground all the winter, without the smallest injury, and need not be taken up to be put in house except as a precaution against frost. Some people let part of their plants stand until the spring, when they send up their seed-shoots very early, which are cropped off and used in the same manner as asparagus. Two or three plants left to run up to seed will be sufficient. The seed-pods, when ripe, should be cropped off, made perfectly dry in the sun, and then put by and preserved in a dry place.

183. SAMPHIRE is propagated from seed or from offsets. It is perennial, and is sometimes used as a pickle, or in salads. The time for sowing is April, and the same time may do for putting out the offsets. It is, however, an insignificant thing, and hardly worth serious attention.

184. SAVORY.—Two sorts, *summer*, and *winter*; the former is annual, the latter perennial. Both may be propagated from seed, sowed in a little patch early in spring; but the latter may also be propagated from offsets. To have these herbs in winter with the least possible trouble and in the greatest possible perfection, they should be cut and dried in the manner directed for sage.

185. SAVOY.—(See *Cabbage*.)

186. SCORZENERA.—This is only another kind of salsafy, growing a little larger than the salsafy, the root being of a dark colour on the outside instead of being of a whitish colour, and it is propagated and cultivated and used in precisely the same manner as the salsafy.

187. SHALOT.—A little perennial onion, propagated from seed, if you please, but much more easily propagated from offsets, like the garlick, which it perfectly resembles in the manner of its growing. The offsets ought to be planted out in rows six or eight inches apart in the month of March, and the plants ought to stand four inches apart in the row. The ground should not be wet at bottom, and should be kept very clean during the summer. As soon as the leaves die, the bulbs should be taken up and made perfectly dry in the sun; then tied in bunches, and hung up to be preserved in a dry place.

188. SKIRRIT is a plant very little known now-a-days; but, if any one has a mind to cultivate it, the manner of doing it is the same as that directed for the salsafy. It is, however, a perennial, and may be propagated from offsets.

189. SORREL.—This is no other than the wild sorrel cultivated. The French, who call it *oseille*, make large messes of it. But a short row is quite enough for an English garden. It is perennial. May be propagated from seeds, but, much more readily, from offsets.

190. SPINAGE.—Every one knows the uses of this excellent plant. Pigs, who are excellent judges of the relative qualities of vegetables, will leave cabbages for lettuces, and lettuces for spinage. Gardeners make two sorts of spinage, though I really believe there is but one. One sort they call *round spinage*, and the other *prickley spinage*, the former they call summer spinage, and the latter winter ; but I have sowed them indiscriminately, and have never perceived any difference in their fitness to the two seasons of the year. The spinage is an annual plant, produces its seed and ripens it well even if sowed so late as the month of May. It may be as well to sow the round spinage for summer, and the prickley spinage for winter, but the time of sowing and the manner of cultivating are the only things of importance ; and great attention should be paid to these, this being a most valuable plant all the year round, but particularly in the winter and the spring. It has something delightfully refreshing in its taste, and is to be had at a time when nothing but mere greens or broccoli is to be had. It far surpasses them both, in my opinion, the use of it never being attended with any of those inconveniences as to bodily health which is the case with both the others. In the summer, there are plenty of other things ; but for the winter crop, due provision should always be made. The time for sowing for the winter crop, if the ground

be good, is the last week in August, and, if the ground
be poor, a fortnight earlier. Sow in shallow drills, eight
inches apart, and thin the plants to six inches apart in
the row : keep them clear of weeds, hoe about them
before winter sets in, and draw the earth close up to the
stems of the plants, taking care that the dirt do not fall
into the hearts. The ground should be rather of the drier
description ; for, if wet, and the winter be severe, the
plants will be killed. They will have fine leaves in the
month of November, or before : for use, the outside
leaves should be taken off first, or, rather, these only
should be taken off, leaving all the rest, and they should
be pinched off with the finger and the thumb close to the
stem of the plant. The plant will keep growing, more
or less, all the winter, except in very hard weather, and
will keep on yielding a supply from the beginning of
November to the latter end of May, when the seed
stalks will begin to rise, and when the summer spinage,
sowed in the latter end of February and cultivated in the
same way as the former, will be ready to supply their
place. About the first of May, another sowing of summer spinage should take place ; but this will be generally supplanted by peas, beans, and other summer crops.
If, however, the reader wish, like me, to have it all the
summer, he must sow again in the month of June, and
again in the month of July. These two latter sowings
being made in the coolest and least sunny part of the
garden. As to saving the seed of the spinage, a few
plants of each sort will be sufficient. The plants must
be pulled up before the seed be dead ripe, or the birds
will have every grain. It is a coarse-looking seed, with
a thick husk upon it ; but the small birds are very fond

of it, and will begin to hammer it out of the husks while these are still green. The seed-plants, when pulled up, should be laid in the sun to become perfectly dry, and the seed should be then rubbed off and put by in a dry place.

191. SQUASH, sometimes called VEGETABLE MARROW; and, though the thing is certainly very good, as a vegetable, and the former name not very flattering, the latter is certainly beyond its merits. This plant, or, rather, this tribe of plants, are of the pumpkin kind. There are several sorts, some for summer use, and some for winter use. The summer kinds that I have, are the *flat bush*, the *long bush*, the *crooked-necked bush ;* that is to say, they grow upright, and branch out like a little bush ; whereas the winter sorts run upon the ground like cucumbers and melons. The time for sowing all the sorts in England is, about the middle of May, in the south, and perhaps, the first week in June, in the north. The squash is not so tender as the cucumber, and will stand any little frosts that we have in June, though such frosts check them in their growth. To have them early, they should be sowed in a gentle hot-bed in April. Put out into pots in the manner directed for cucumbers. They should be *topped*, while in the pots, in the manner directed for cucumbers : about the middle of May, the pots should be taken out and sunk in the natural ground, and a frame set over them, or they should have a covering of hoops and mats for the night-time, just to keep off the frosts. About the middle of June, they should be planted out in the open level ground, which need not be exceedingly rich. The distance for the bush sorts ought

to be five feet at the least, and for the running sorts, of which I have the *white winter squash*, and the *bell shaped winter squash*, should be six feet, at the least. The ground should be kept very clean. When the plants are put out of the pots the balls should be sunk in the ground to a level with the ground, a little water should be given to each ball after it is fixed in the earth, and a little dry earth should be drawn up round the stems of the plants to the height of the seed-leaf. In about a fortnight, a very nice hoeing should be given to the whole of the ground. In another fortnight, a very nice digging to the whole of the ground, and the summer-sorts will begin to produce for use, by the latter end of July. If the first crop fail, or appear to be likely to fail, you may sow again in July, and even in August; that is to say, the summer-sorts, and, I dare say, the winter sorts, too, but I have no experience upon that head. I sowed some in the month of August last year; about five and twenty plants in number, and had bushels of squashes fit for use before the frost came. All the bush squashes are of a yellow colour before they are fit for use, though I have seen them in the markets in England for sale when still green. Of all the sorts, the flat-bush is the best for the summer, and the long white for the winter. The manner of cooking them is very simple. They are merely washed clean, and boiled for about twenty minutes; but by running a fork into them, you know when they are done, in the same way that you judge in the case of a turnip. The summer sorts must not hang on the plant long, except you wish to save the seed. You soon discover what is their usual size, and, as soon as they arrive at that, they are fit to be gathered.

They require no peeling, as a turnip does ; and, if they be (as the winter squashes will be) much larger than they are wanted, for one time, you may cut a part off, and leave the rest for use another day. They are certainly far preferable to the best of turnips ; and, though they are not actually marrow, they are a very delightful vegetable, and their produce is prodigious. If well cultivated, I dare say that a single plant of the flat bush squash would produce a bushel of fruit ; but, like the cucumber and all other plants of the same description, if you wish the plant to continue producing for a long while, you must take care to gather every fruit as soon as it becomes fit for use, and before it begins to ripen its seed. The small ones ; that is to say, the fruit gathered at a very early stage, when not much bigger than a large walnut, for instance, make excellent pickles, much better than cucumbers. If you wish to save the seed, you must proceed in exactly the same manner as directed in the case of the cucumber.

192. TANSEY.—A perennial culinary and medicinal herb, propagated from seed, if you like ; but from offsets is the easiest way : a plant or two would be sufficient for a garden, and, when once it had taken root, it would remain there for a life-time.

193. TARRAGON is a very hot, peppery herb, used in soups and salads. It is perennial, and may be propagated from seed sowed at any time in the spring, or from offsets put out in either spring or fall. Its young and tender tops only are used. It is eaten with beefsteaks in company with minced shalots. A man may,

doubtless, live very well without it; but an orthodox clergyman once told me, that he and six others once ate some beef-steaks with shalots and tarragon, and that they " voted unanimously, that beef-steaks never were so eaten !" If you will have it in winter, you must dry it, in the manner directed for sage and other herbs.

194. THYME.—There are two distinct sorts of this popular, and most fragrant herb. One is called *common thyme*, and the other *lemon thyme*, both are perenniel, both may be propagated from seed, but both may also be propagated from offsets or partings of the roots, and this is the easiest way. The winter sometimes destroys thyme. Some of both sorts should be preserved for winter use, cut at the same stage as is directed for the sage; and, as in the case of all other herbs, cut when perfectly dry, and dried in the shade, in some place where it receives no wet either from rains or dews, during the drying.

195. TOMATUM.—This plant comes from countries bordering on the Mediterranean. Of sorts there are the *red*, the *yellow* and the *white*. The fruit is used for various purposes, and is sold at a pretty high price. The plants must be raised in a gentle hot-bed pretty early in April, or late in March, put into small pots when they are two inches high, and turned out into the natural ground about the first week in June; but even then they must be put on the south side of a wall, or in some other warm and sheltered situation. If close to a wall, their runners may be trained up it by the means of shreds when the leaves and fruit make a very beautiful appearance. If not close to a wall, there must be sticks put to train the vines up,

and to tie them to. The ground in which they are planted, should be kept very clean, and frequently stirred about them. If you intend to save the seed, you should have a plant or two very early placed against a south wall.

196. TURNIP.—I am here to speak of turnips to be cultivated in a garden for table-use, and not to be cultivated in a field for the use of cattle; but, as the *Swedish turnip*, or *ruta baga*, yields most delicate greens, for use in March, a few of these might find a place in a garden. It is true, that they are to be found upon almost every farm; but you must go to the farm to get them, and get leave to take them into the bargain; so that, a couple of rows across one of the plats ought to find a place in the garden. The *garden-turnip* is called the *stone-turnip* by some; by others, the *early white Dutch-turnip*; some say that they are both the same; there is another turnip which has a long and taper root, and not a large bulb in proportion; and this is called, in Hampshire at least, the *mouse-tailed turnip*. But, the finest turnip for eating that I ever saw, I never yet saw in England. It is a little flat turnip. The bulb lies almost wholly upon the top of the ground, sending down, from the centre of it, a slender tap. This bulb is about four or five inches diameter in general, and not above two inches through, in depth. The flesh is of a deep yellow colour. This sort of turnip is in universal use throughout the northern States of America. Some farmers in England cultivate the yellow Scotch turnip as it is called; and, if this turnip really did come from Scotland, there is something good that is Scotch, at any rate. This yellow turnip is cultivated in Herefordshire under the name of the ox turnip; and I

remember that Mr. PALMER of Bollitree told me that it far exceeded, in point of richness, and in point of standing the weather, all other turnips, except the Swedish: I think his account was, that, weight for weight, it was half way between the common turnip and the Swedish, as food for cattle. However, the chances are that, as people like white better than yellow in a turnip, they will prefer the early white Dutch or early stone to any other. The manner of propagating and cultivating all the sorts is the same. Spring turnips, or, rather, early summer turnips, are very poor things : the plant must have cold weather, to make it really good : do what you will, it will be hot if you have it to eat in the early part of the summer ; but, if you wish to have them at that time, you must sow them in March. The manner of sowing is, in shallow drills a foot or fifteen inches apart, and the plants thinned to eight or nine inches in the row. The fly, or, rather, the *flea,* is apt to take them off, and, in that case, there is no remedy but sowing again. The ground between them should be kept clean, and it should not be fresh dunged, for that will be sure to make them rank and hot. Depend rather upon the TULLIAN principle of causing growth by tillage. For autumnal and winter use, turnips are very good and very convenient, seeing that they may be so easily preserved from the frost, even in the severest winters. To insure a crop, you should sow in the last week of July, or the first of August, in the south of England, and a week or two earlier, towards the north. It is a very good way to sow again in the last week of August, especially in good and warm soil, for these will be sound in the month of March, and, if the winter be mild, quite large enough, while those sowed earlier, will become woolly by that time. But, there is a way to prevent this woolliness; that is to say, by taking up the turnips, and taking off their greens and roots early in November, keeping them in a cellar or some other convenient place, taking care to exclude all bruised, broken, or rotten turnips or parts of turnips. A small conical heap made in the garden, upon the top of the ground, covered first with straw and then with earth, will keep the turnips perfectly sound until March, so that, be the winter what it may, you may always have turnips ready for use ; and, as they are not in a state to grow, they will not become woolly.

197. WORMWOOD is a herb purely medicinal. It may be propagated from seed, from slips, or from offsets : it is perenniel, and a foot square in the herb-bed is enough to be allowed to it. It loses its leaves in the winter ; and, therefore, for winter use, it must be cut and dried, in the manner directed in the case of other herbs, and put by and preserved in paper bags.

198. *Nota Bene.* BORAGE.—I omitted the insertion of this plant in due alphabetical order, and, as the printer treads closely upon my heels, I am obliged to mention it here.—This is a very pretty flowering plant. One sort of it has *blue* flowers, one *red*, and another *white*. The only use that I ever saw Borage put to, was putting it into wine and water, along with nutmeg, and some other things perhaps, the mixture altogether being called, *cool-tankard*, or by the shorter name, *cup*. If once you have it growing upon any spot, you need not take the trouble to sow. It bears an abundance of seed, some of which

is ripe, while the plant is still in bloom. If you wish to have it young at all times, you may sow in the spring, in the summer, in autumn, or, at any time. The plants should not stand too thick upon the ground, and the ground should be kept clean. Any awkward corner under one of the hedges will do very well for borage, which, however, is by no means unornamental in a flower-garden, both flower and leaf being very pretty.

CHAPTER VI.

Fruits. Propagation, Planting, and Training and Pruning, whether wall-trees, espaliers, or standards, with an Alphabetical List of the several Fruits, and with observations on the Diseases of Fruit-trees.

---

199. ALL the fruits to be treated of here, with the exception of the Cranberry, the Melon and the Strawberry, are the produce of *trees*, or of *woody plants*. In treating of them I shall pursue the following course : first, give instructions as to the Propagation, next, as to the Planting, next, as to the Training and Pruning ; next I shall give the List of Fruits ; and, lastly, I shall make some remarks on the nature and tendency of the Diseases of fruit-trees, and on the remedies proper to be applied.

PROPAGATION.

200. ALL fruit-trees, from the loftiest cherry, down to the gooseberry, may be propagated by *seed* ; and this would be the proper way ; but nature has so contrived it, that the seed of fruit-trees will not bring trees to produce the same sort of fruit except by mere accident ; so

that, gardeners are compelled, in order to insure the sort
of fruit which they wish to have, to raise the trees from
some part or other of the wood of the tree the like of which
they wish to have. The several parts of the wood, taken
and used for this purpose, are SLIPS, LAYERS, CUTTINGS,
and BUDS. The different methods of propagation suited
to each kind will be mentioned under the name of the
kinds respectively in the Alphabetical List which will
form a part of this present chapter. In this place,
therefore, I am to describe the several methods generally, and the general management suited to each.

201. SLIPS are little branches of one or two year's
growth, pulled off from a limb or larger branch of the
tree by a downward jerk of the hand. You then take a
sharp knife, trim off the ragged bark from the bottom of
the slip, and cut the tip of the slip off at the same time,
leaving the slip altogether to be about a foot long. The
time of the year for taking off slips is about the beginning of March ; and, if it were a little earlier, it might be
as well. You then plant them as you would a little tree,
but three or four inches deep in the ground, and in a
shady place, a most convenient place for purposes of this
sort would be near the hedge on the south side of the
garden. They should be put in a row or rows about
eighteen inches apart, and about a foot apart in the row.
In this situation they will make shoots in the summer,
and make roots. They should be watered a little at the
time of planting, and occasionally a little in the spring
and summer, until they have shoots two or three inches
long. There are many sorts of apples that will admit of
propagation in this way, as quinces also will ; and the

common codling apple may be raised in this manner with the greatest facility. In a very dry and hot season, it may not be amiss to lay a little litter upon the ground in which the slips are planted in order to keep it cool.

202. LAYERS.—You take a limb, or branch, of a tree in the fall, or *early* in spring, or at Midsummer, and pull it down in such a way as to cause its top, or small shoots and twigs to lie upon the ground. Then *fasten* the limb down by a peg or two, so that its own force will not raise it up. Then prune off all the small branches and shoots that stick upright; and, having a parcel of shoots lying horizontally, *lay* earth upon the whole, all along upon the limb from the point where it begins to touch the ground, and also upon all the *bottoms of all the shoots.* Then cut the shoots off at the points, leaving only two or three joints or buds beyond the earth. The earth laid on should be *good*, and the ground should be fresh-digged and made very fine and smooth before the branches be laid upon it. The earth laid on should be from six inches to a foot thick. If the limb, or mother branch, be very *stubborn*, a little cut on the upper side of it will make it more easy to be held down. The ground should be kept clean from weeds, and as cool as possible in hot weather. Perhaps rocks or stones (not large) are the best and coolest covering. These layers will be ready to take up and plant out as trees after they have been laid a year. In cases where the branches intended to be laid cannot be bent down sufficiently near to the ground without danger of breaking them off, a box of earth or a pan with notches in the sides to lay the branch in, may be used. Vines may, by means of pots with opening sides, be laid as they are growing in the grapery or against the wall ; and this is frequently done by the gardeners as matter of curiosity mixed with utility. They lay a shoot, in this manner, in the spring, and, when it has rooted and is in full bearing in the fall, they cut it off immediately below the pot, and produce at table a growing tree covered with ripe fruit. The earth, however, in boxes, or pans, or pots, being in small bodies, necessarily dry up sooner than when not so ; and, therefore, when this method of laying is adopted, great care must be taken to water constantly, so as to keep up the required moisture. And not only does the limb require this moisture to make it root, but when rooted, the young roots require it, to keep them alive. To cause the limb to put forth roots, it is a common practice to prick it nearly through, in two or three directions, at one of the joints that are to be buried under ground ; or to cut a notch nearly half way through the limb. At these wounds, matter oozes out which quickly causes the putting forth of young roots.

203. CUTTINGS are short pieces cut from trees in the month of February. You take a shoot of the last year and cut it off with a small piece of the preceding year's wood at the bottom of it, if that be convenient. The shoot should be a sound and strong one, and it is not *absolutely necessary* that it should have a piece of the preceding year's wood. The cutting should have, altogether, about six joints or buds, and three of these should be under ground when planted. The cutting should be fixed firmly in the ground, and the cuts should be performed with a sharp knife, so that there may be

nothing ragged or bruised about the bark. As to situation, watering, and the rest, follow precisely the directions given in the case of the slips. Currants and gooseberries, some apples, and a great number of flowering shrubs are universally propagated from cuttings.

204. BUDS are little pieces taken out from the side of a shoot in the summer, containing a newly-formed bud, which is fixed into the side of a branch growing upon another tree; but, as buds will be more fully described when I come to the act of budding, nothing more is necessary upon the subject in this place.

205. STOCKS.—The general way of obtaining fruit-trees of the larger kinds is by *grafting* or *budding;* and this grafting or budding is performed by putting cuttings or buds upon other trees. They may be put upon large trees, which are already bearing; so that, by these arts, you may have numerous sorts of fruit upon the same tree; but, what I am to treat of here is, the manner of raising young trees; and, to have these, there must be stocks previously prepared to receive the grafts or the buds; therefore, I now proceed to give directions for the making of this previous preparation or provision. Under the name of the different fruits, I shall speak of the sort of stocks suitable to each; but I may observe here, that the stocks for apples are crabs, or apples; that the stocks for pears, are pears, quinces or hawthorn; and that the stocks for peaches and nectarines, are plums, peaches, nectarines, or almonds; that the stocks for apricots are plums or apricots: that the stocks for plums are plums; that the stocks for cherries, are cherries; and that the

stocks for medlars are pears or hawthorn. In many of the cases, stocks may be raised from suckers, and they are so raised ; but never ought to be so raised. Suckers are shoots that come up out of the ground, starting from the roots of trees, and are very abundant from pears and plums, and sometimes from cherries. They run to wood, and produce suckers themselves in abundance, which trees do not that are raised from seeds, cuttings, or layers. Suckers, therefore, never ought to be used to graft or bud upon ; for, if you graft a pear, for instance, upon a pear sucker, the tree begins to send out suckers almost immediately ; and, in America, where this hasty and lazy practice prevails, I have seen a pear orchard with all the ground covered with underwood forming a sort of coppice. I will, therefore, say no more about suckers, but proceed now to the proper mode of obtaining stocks, first speaking of those which are to be obtained from the *pips*, and then of those which are to be obtained from the stones. The pips of crabs, apples, pears and quinces, are obtained from the fruit : the three former in great abundance when cider, perry, or verjuice are made ; the last with some difficulty, on account of the comparative rareness of the fruit, but quince stocks are so easily obtained from cuttings or layers that this is not a matter of much consequence. The pips are, of course, collected in the fall of the year ; and when collected, make them dry, put them immediately into fine dry earth or sand, and keep them safe from mice until the month of March. When that month comes, dig a piece of ground well and truly, make it rich ; make it very fine, form it into beds three feet wide, draw drills across it at eight inches distance, make them from two to three inches deep, put in the seeds pretty thickly, cover them completely, tread the earth down upon them; and then smooth the surface. When the plants come up, thin them to about three inches apart; and keep the ground between them perfectly clean during the summer. Hoe frequently; but *not deep near the plants*; for, we are speaking of *trees* here; and trees do not renew their roots quickly as a cabbage or a turnip does. These young trees should be kept, during the first summer, as *moist* as possible, without watering; and the way to keep them as moist as possible, is, to keep the ground perfectly clean, and to hoe it frequently. I cannot help observing here upon an observation of Mr. MARSHALL: "As to *weeding*," says he, "though seedling trees must "not be *smothered*, yet some *small* weeds may be suffered "to grow in summer, as they help to *shade* the plants "and to keep the ground *cool*." Mercy on this gentleman's readers! Mr. MARSHALL had not read TULL; if he had, he never would have written this very erroneous sentence. It is the root of the weed that does the mischief. Let there be a rod of ground well set with even "*small weeds*," and another rod *kept weeded*. Let them adjoin each other. Go, after fifteen or twenty days of dry weather; examine the two; and you will find the weedless ground moist and fresh, while the other is dry as dust to a foot deep. The root of the weed sucks up every particle of moisture. What pretty things they are, then, to keep seedling trees *cool!*—To proceed: these seedlings, if well managed, will be eight inches high, and some higher, at the end of the first summer. The next spring they should be taken up; or, this may be done in the fall. They should be planted in rows, four feet apart, to give room to turn about amongst them; and at two feet apart in the rows, if intended to be grafted or budded without being again removed. If intended to be again removed, before grafting or budding, they may be put at a foot apart. They should be kept clean by hoeing between them, and the ground between them should be *digged in the fall*, but not at any other season of the year. The plants will grow fast or slowly according to the management; and, the proper age for budding or grafting is from three to five years; but it is better to have a strong stock than a too weak or too young one. The younger they are the sooner they will bear, but the sooner they, also, decline and perish. To speak of the *kind* of stocks most suitable to the different kinds of fruit-trees is reserved till we come to speak of the trees themselves; but there are some remarks to be made here, which have a *general application*, relative to the kinds of stocks. It is supposed by some persons, that the nature of the stock affects the nature of the *fruit*; that is to say, that the fruit growing on branches, proceeding from a *bud*, or a *graft*, partakes, more or less, of the flavour of *the fruit which would have grown on the stock* if the stock had been suffered to grow to a tree and to bear fruit. This is Mr. MARSHALL's notion. But, how erroneous it is must be manifest to every one, when he reflects, that the stock for the *pear* tree is frequently the *white-thorn*. Can a pear partake of the nature of the *haw*, which grows upon the thorn, and which is a *stone-fruit* too? If this notion were correct, there could be hardly a single apple-orchard in all England; for they are all grafted upon *crab-stocks*; and, of course, all the apples, in the course of years, would become crabs.

Apricots and peaches are generally put on plum-stocks, yet, after centuries of this practice, they do not become plums. If the *fruit* of the graft partake of the nature of the stock, why not the *wood* and *leaves*? Yet, is it not visible to all eyes, that neither ever does so partake?— The bud, or graft, retains its own nature, wholly unchanged by the stock; and, all that is of consequence, as to the kind of stock, is, whether it be such as will *last long enough,* and supply the tree with *a suitable quantity of wood.* As to the stocks raised from stone-fruit, the stones must be taken from the fruit when the fruit is ripe, made perfectly dry in the sun; then packed in perfectly dry sand, and kept there until the month of November, when the stones must be sowed in just the same manner as described for the pips, except that they ought not to be closer than an inch from each other in the drill, and should be covered to the depth of three inches, or, perhaps a little more. The plants will come up in the Spring, and will attain a good height the first Summer. They should be transplanted in the Fall, first taking off the tap root, and shortening the side roots. In the next month of April, they should be cut down to the ground and suffered to send up only a single stalk for grafting or budding upon. They should now be planted in rows at four feet apart and at a foot apart in the row, in order to give room for the operations of grafting and budding. There are cases when stocks raised from *layers* are preferred; these cases will be mentioned under the head of the fruit to which they apply, and the reader already knows how to raise stocks from layers, because it is done in just the same manner as when the layer is intended to be a tree to bear fruit without budding or grafting. I cannot dismiss this part of the subject without exhorting the reader never to make use of suckers as stocks : by a very little additional care, you obtain seedling stocks ; and, really, if a man have not the trifling portion of industry that is here required, he is unworthy of the good fruit and the abundant crops which, with proper management, he may generally make himself sure of.

206. GRAFTING.—When I come to the alphabetical list of fruits, I shall speak of those circumstances connected with grafting in which one sort of fruit differs from another; but the mode of performing the operation of grafting, and the mode of doing other things relative to the stock and the scion, are the same in all cases, therefore I shall in this place give the instructions necessary for a knowledge of the arts of grafting and budding. There is another thing, too, which is equally applicable in all cases, and which ought to be mentioned before I enter upon the subject of *grafting* and *budding ;* and that is this, that the stock ought to stand one whole *summer* upon the spot where it is grafted or budded before that operation is performed upon it. If stocks be planted out in the Fall the sap does not rise vigorously enough in the Spring to afford a fair chance for the growing of the graft ; but, another remark of equal importance is that fruit-trees should stand only *one summer* on the spot whence they are to be removed to their final destination, because, if they stand longer than this, they will have large and long roots, great amputations must take place, and the tree suffer exceedingly.

207. Grafting is the joining of a *cutting* of one to another tree in such a way as that the tree, on which the

cutting is placed, sends up its sap into the *cutting*, and makes it grow and become a tree. When a cutting is thus applied it is called a *scion*. Certain stocks have been found to be suited to certain scions, but these will be particularly mentioned hereafter in the articles treating of the respective kinds of fruit. It is best that I confine myself here, as much as possible, to instructions as to the time of grafting, the mode of preparing the scion, the mode of performing the operation of grafting, and, lastly, to the treatment of the plant grafted. The time of grafting is, generally, from the beginning of February to the end of March, beginning with the earliest sorts of trees, as plums, cherries and pears, and ending with the latest, as apples. But seasons are different, and in a backward season, the season for grafting will be backward, and in such case, the fulness and bursting appearance of the buds of the stocks, and the mildness of the weather, must be our guides. Not but much more than the necessary importance is attached to this matter by us; for I have seen an American negro-man, sitting by a six-plate stove, grafting apple trees in the month of *January*, and then putting away the grafted plants in a cave there to wait 'till *April*, before he planted them! However, it is certain that mild weather with occasional showers, is the best time for grafting. The mode of preparing the scion comes next : take from the tree from which you mean to propagate, as many branches of last-year's wood as you think will cut into the quantity of scions that you want : but in choosing what branches to take, let the vigour of the tree guide you in some measure. If it be a healthy, flourishing, and young tree, take your branches from the outside side shoots, for the upright ones at the top, or those near the middle, are more likely to be given to produce wood than fruit. Yet do not take branches from the very lowest part of the tree if you can avoid it, as these are sure to be more puling in their nature. In case the tree be old, or weakly, then chuse the most vigorous of its last-year's shoots, no matter where they grow. Keep these branches uncut 'till you arrive at the season of grafting, keeping them in the meanwhile buried in dry mould : and when that season arrives, take them up and cut them into the proper lengths for grafting. The middle part of each branch will generally be found to be the best ; but your branches may be scarce, and few in number, and then make use of every part. Each scion should have from three to six eyes on it ; but six will, in all cases, be quite enough, as there is no use in an extraordinary length of scion ; but, on the contrary, it may be productive of much mischief by overloading the head with young shoots and leaves as summer advances, and thereby making it more subject to accident from high winds or heavy rains.

208. *The operation of Grafting* is performed many ways, though no one of them differs from any of the others in the *main principle*, which is that of bringing the under, or inner, bark of the scion to bear upon the same bark of the stock ; so that, the scion is (as I said before) a branch of another tree, brought and made to occupy precisely the place where a branch, or stem of the stock, was cut off. The sap of the stock flows upward towards the scion, and it will flow on into the scion, *provided it find no interruption.* Here, therefore is the nicety : to fit those two barks so closely the one upon the other that the sap shall proceed onward into the scion just as it would have done into the amputated branch, causing the scion to supplant the branch. I shall only mention and illustrate

two modes of grafting, namely, *tongue-grafting*, and *cleft-grafting*. These two it is necessary for me to speak of separately, and thoroughly to describe, for they are not both of them applicable in all cases, the former being used in grafting on small sized stocks, and small branches of trees, and the latter on large stocks and large branches.

209. *Tongue grafting.*—Suppose you to have your stock of the proper age for grafting (and for all about which, see above, the article on Stocks), you cut it off at three or four inches from the ground, and with a very *sharp, straight and narrow-bladed grafting-knife,* cut a thin strip of wood and bark upward from about two inches below the top of your already-shortened stock. Make this cut at one pull of the knife, inserting the edge rather horizontally, and, when it has gone through the bark and into the wood a little short of the middle, pull straight upwards (plate 3. *fig.* 1. *a b*).

PLATE 3.

FIG. 1.   FIG. 2.   FIG. 3.   FIG. 4.   FIG. 5.

Then, at less, rather, than half way down this cut, and with the blade of your knife across the cut, and downward, cut a very *thin tongue* of not more than three-eighths of an inch long (plate 3. *fig.* 1. *c*). Proceed nearly in the same way with the bottom part of the scion : cut first a narrow strip of wood and bark out, but not putting the knife in horizontally as you have done with regard to the stock at *fig.* 1. *a*., nor bringing it out straight to the end to make a shoulder or angle, as you have done with the stock at *fig.* 1. *b*.; but make a sloping cut (plate 3. *fig.* 2. *a. b.*) of about the same length as the cut in the stock, or a little less if any thing; then make a tongue (plate 3. *fig.* 2. *c.*) to correspond with that in the stock, but recollect that this must be cut *upward* instead of *downward*; then place the scion upon the stock, inserting the tongue of the scion into the tongue of the stock. Bring the four edges of bark, that is, the two edges of the cut in the top of the stock, and the two corresponding edges of the cut in the bottom of the scion, to meet precisely ; or, if the scion be in diameter a smaller piece of wood than the stock, so that its two edges of bark cannot both meet those of the stock, then let only one meet, but be sure that that one meets precisely. But observe well, that this can never be, unless the first cut in the stock and that in the scion (plate 3. *figures* 1 and 2, *a* and *b*.) be as even as a die, and performed by a knife scarcely less sharp than a razor. Take a common pruning-knife, and attempt to make a cut of this kind, and you will find, when you come to fit the scion on, that, squeeze them together as you may, you will, in most cases, see light between the parts of the stock and the scion that you are trying to join so effectually as that the *sap shall flow out of the one and into the other unconscious of any division at all !* But I will not suppose any body so ungain (as it is called in Hampshire) as to go about so nice an operation as this without being prepared with the proper instrument for performing it ; and, therefore, I now suppose the scion put on properly and presenting the appearance as in plate 3. *fig.* 3. But this is not all : the operation is not yet complete. The two parts thus joined must be bound closely to one another by matting, or bass, as the gardeners call it (pl. 3. *fig.* 4). A single piece tied on to the stock an inch or so below the part grafted, and then wound closely up till it reach the very top of the stock, will, if well done, almost insure the junction ; but, lest parching winds should come and knit up all vegetation, it is usual to put on, besides the bandage of matting, a ball of well-beaten clay, sprinkled over with a little wood-ashes, or the fine siftings of cinders, to cover completely the parts grafted, that is, from an inch below them to an inch or so above them (pl. 3. *fig.* 5.) ; and even to prevent this ball of clay from being washed off by heavy rains, it is well to tie round it a covering of coarse canvass, or else to earth up the whole plant as you do peas or beans, drawing a little mound round it so as nearly to reach the top of the clay. Something now remains to be said on the *future treatment* of the grafted plant. In a month's time, at least, you will see whether the scion have taken ; it will then be either bursting forth into leaf, or it will be irrecoverably dead. In this latter case, take off immediately canvass, clay, bandage and dead scion, and let the stock push forth what shoots it please, and recover itself. In the former case, how-

ever, you must, as soon as the scion is putting forth
shoots, cut off, or rub off, all shoots proceeding from the
stock between the ground and the clay, as these, if suffered to push on, would divert the sap away from the
scion and probably starve it ; then carefully stake the
plant, that is, put a small stick into the ground at within
three inches, or thereabouts, of the root, and long
enough to reach a few inches above the scion, which you
will tie to it slightly with a piece of wetted matting.
This is really necessary, for, when the shoots proceeding from the scion, become half a foot long, they,
with the aid of their leaves, become so heavy, that
when blown to and fro by the wind, will break off
immediately above the clay, or become loosened down
at the part joined to the stock. The staking being
done, you need do nothing more till about the end of
June, when you should take off the whole mass of canvass, clay, and bandage ; but be very careful, in taking
off the clay, not to break off the plant at the junction.
It should be done by a careful hand, and after a day or
two of rainy weather, as then the clay is moist and comes
off without so much danger to the plant as when it is
not. On taking off the clay, there is found a little sharp
angle left at the top of the stock ; this should now be
cut smooth off, as is marked by the dots at *a* in *fig.* 3.
The bark of the stock and that of the scion will heal
over this, and the union is then complete. Lastly, it is
frequently found that mould, and sometimes small vermin,
have collected round the heretofore covered parts of the
plant, according as the clay has been cracked by the sun.
Rub off all mould with your fingers. No instrument
does it so well ; and kill all vermin in the same way ;

and it is not amiss to finish this work by washing the joined parts with a little soap and water, using a small painting-brush for the operation. All these things done, you have now only to guard against high winds, which, if the plants be not staked as is above described, will very likely be broken off by them, and, in this work of destruction, you will have the mortification to see the finest of your plants go first.

210. *Cleft grafting.*—This, as I said above, is a species of grafting adopted in cases where the stock is large, or where it consists of a branch or branches of a tree headed down. In either of these cases, saw off horizontally the part you wish to graft, and smooth the wound over with a carpenter's plane or a sharp long-bladed knife (plate 4. *fig.* 1).

PLATE 4.

FIG. 1.   FIG. 2.   FIG. 3.

Prepare your scion in this manner: at about an inch and a half from the bottom, cut it in the form of the blade of a razor, that is, make it sharp on one side and let it be blunt at the back, where you will also take care to leave the bark whole (plate 4. *fig.* 2. *a*). Having thus prepared the scion, make a split (plate 4. *fig.* 1. *a.*) in the crown of the saw-cut, downwards, for about two inches, taking care that the two sides of this split be perfectly even. Hold it then open by means of a chisel or a wedge (or when the stock is but a small one, your knife), and insert the scion, the sharp edge going inwards, and the bark-side, or razor-back, remaining outward, so that, on taking out the wedge or chisel, the cleft closes firmly upon the scion (plate 4. *fig.* 3.), the two edges of bark formed by the cleft squeezing exactly upon the two edges of bark formed by the blunt razor-back. To make the two barks meet precisely, is, the reader will see, the only nicety in this operation; but this is so essential that the slightest deviation will defeat the purpose. In this sort of grafting, the stock on which you graft is generally strong enough to hold the scion close enough within its cleft without the aid of binding, and then it is better not to bind; but, as it is also necessary to prevent air circulating within the wounded parts both of the stock and the scion, use grafting-clay to cover them over so as effectually to exclude that air, and cover the clay with a piece of coarse canvass, wetting it first and then binding it on securely. In this way, the stock being strong, you may insert several scions on the same head, by making several different clefts and putting one scion in each; but this can only be to insure your having two to succeed, for, if all the scions that you put upon one head, take, you must chuse the two most eligible, and sacrifice the rest, as more than two leading limbs from such head ought not to be encouraged. The season for performing this sort of grafting, and the mode of preparing the scion, and the future treatment of the tree, are precisely the same as in *Tongue grafting.*

211. I have mentioned an application of clay to be used in grafting ; but it may be as well here to give some particular instructions as to preparing this, before I end this article on grafting. The object being to put something round the wounded parts of the stock and the scion that shall exclude water and air, it is necessary, of course, that the application be adhesive and close. Pure yellow or blue clay is both, if you beat it well with a good stout stick, now-and-then pouring on a little water to make it work. Get it, in this way, to be perfectly pliable in the hand. Beat it upon a hard stone, or a boarded floor, or a brick floor swept clean first ; but beat it again and again, returning to it for two or three days, and taking a spell each day. If you suffer it to remain hard, besides the danger of unsettling the scion in squeezing round it this untractable mass, it cracks, the very first hot day, and is utterly useless. Let it, therefore, be so loose that the man who follows the grafter to put it on, can take off a piece and readily flatten it out into a kind of pan-cake, an inch or so thick, and wrap it, without any exertion on his part, or any resistance on the part of the plant, round the grafted tree. Then he should sprinkle a little wood-ashes over the whole to dry it and take off the immediate effect of the sun.

212. BUDDING is performed for precisely the same purpose as grafting, and, like grafting, it is performed in many different ways ; but I shall only notice the most usual, and, as long experience has ascertained, the best, method : namely, that of *T budding*, so called from the form of the two cuts that are made in the bark of the stock to receive the bud (*pl.* 5. *fig.* 1.) ; or *shield budding*, as it is sometimes called, from the form of the piece of

bark on which the bud is seated (pl. 5. *fig.* 2.) assuming the shape of a shield when it is prepared to be inserted within the T cut in the stock. The only solid difference

PLATE. 5.

FIG. 1.   FIG. 2.   FIG. 3.

between budding and grafting is this, that, whereas, in grafting, you insert on the stock *a branch* already produced, in budding, you insert only the *bud.* I shall proceed, in treating of this matter, in the same way that I did in the preceding article ; namely, as to the *season proper for budding, the choosing and preparing of the bud, the operation of budding, and the future treatment of the plant budded.*

213. The *season for budding* is, generally, from the latter end of July to the latter end of August, the criterions being a plump appearance of the bud formed on the spring shoot of the same year, seated in the angle of a leaf ; and, a readiness in the bark of the stock to separate from the wood.

214. In *chusing and preparing the bud,* fix on one seated at about the middle of a healthy shoot of the Midsummer growth. These are, generally speaking, most

inclined to fruitfulness. Choose a cloudy day, if you have a choice of days at this season, and, if not, perform your work early in the morning, or in the evening. The time being proper, you sever the branch on which you find buds to your liking. Take this with you to the stock that you are going to bud. Holding the branch in your left hand, the largest end downward, make a sloping cut from about an inch and a half below the bud, to about an inch above it, suffering your knife to go through the bark and about half way into the wood, cutting out wood and all. This keeping of the wood prevents the bud and its bark from drying while you are preparing the incision in the stock ; and, if you wish to carry buds of scarce sorts to any distance, you may do so safely by putting their ends in water or in damp moss, but it is always safer, as well in grafting as in budding, to perform the operation with as much expedition as possible, but particularly it is so in budding.

215. *Operation of budding.* Cut off the leaf under which the bud is seated, but leave its foot-stalk (*pl. 5. fig. 2. a.*) and, by this, hold it between your lips, while, with your budding-knife, you cut two straight lines in the stock at the place where you wish to insert the bud, and this should be at a place where the bark is smooth, free from any bruises or knots, and on the side rather from the mid-day sun. Of these lines, let the first be horizontal, (pl. 5. *fig.* 1. *a.*) and let the next be longitudinal, beginning at the middle of the first cut, and coming downward (pl. 5. *fig.* 1. *b*). Let them, in short, describe the two principal bars of the Roman letter T. You have now to take out from the bark on which your bud is, the piece

of wood on which the bark is, and which has served you
up to this time, to preserve the bark and bud from drying and shrinking.   But this is a nice matter.   In doing
it, you must be careful not to endanger the root, as it is
called, of the bud, because in that is its existence.   The
bark (if the season be proper for budding) will easily
detach itself from this piece of wood, but still it requires
very careful handling to get it out without endangering
the *root of the bud*.   Hold the bud upon your fore-finger
and keep your thumb on the wood opposite ; then, with
the fore-finger and thumb of the other hand, bend backward and forward the lower end of the shield, and thus
coax the wood to disengage itself from the bark ; and
when you find it decidedly doing so, remove your thumb
from it and the whole piece of wood will come out,
leaving you nothing but a piece of bark of about two and
a half inches long, with a bud and foot-stalk of a leaf on
it.   If the root of the bud be carried away with the piece
of wood, you will perceive a small *cavity* where it ought
to be.   In this case, throw away the bud and try another.

216. Having succeeded in a second attempt, now open
the two sides of the longitudinal bar of the T, with the
ivory haft of your budding-knife (pl. 5. *fig.* 1. *b.*) ; but, in
doing this, raise the bark clearly down to the wood, for
the inside of the piece of bark belonging to the bud
must be placed directly against this.   Having opened
these sides wide enough to receive the longest end of
bark, insert it nicely : taking especial care that its *inner
side lie flatly against the wood of the stock*.   Then cut the
upper end of the bark off so that its edge shall meet precisely the edge of the horizontal bar of the T (pl. 5. *fig.*1.*a.*).

With your finger and thumb, bring the two sides of the longitudinal bar over the bark of the bud, or, rather, the shield, and, with a piece of well-soaked matting, begin an inch below this bar and bind firmly all the way up to an inch above the horizontal bar, taking good care to leave the bud peeping out. Bind in such a way as to exclude the air, for that is the intent of binding in this case. Tie your piece of matting on first, and then wind it round and round the stock as you would a ribbon, taking care not to twist the matting. Wind it *slowly,* and every time you have gone completely round, give a gentle pull to make it firm.

217. *Future treatment.*—In a fortnight's time from the operation, you will discover whether the bud have taken, by its roundness and healthy look ; and, in a fortnight after that, loosen the bandage to allow the whole plant to swell ; and, in about five weeks from the time of budding, take away the bandage altogether. In this state the plant passes the winter, and, just as the sap begins to be in motion, in the following spring, you head down the stock at about half an inch above the bud, beginning behind it, and making a sloping cut upward to end above its point. Some gardeners leave a piece of the stock about six inches long for the first year, in order to tie the first summer's shoot to it, to prevent its being broken off by the wind. This may be well, when the plant is exposed to high winds, but, even then, if you see danger, you may tie a short stick on to the top part of the stock and to this tie the young shoot, and then the sap all goes into the shoot from the bud, instead of

being divided between it and the six inches of stock left in the other way.

218. There are some advantages that *budding* has over *grafting*, and these I think it right to mention. In the first place, universal experience has proved that certain trees succeed very much better when budded than the same trees do when grafted : such are, the peach, nectarine, apricot, plum and cherry ; indeed, the rule is, that all stone fruits do better budded than grafted. That they are, when budded, less given to *gum*, a disease peculiar to stone fruits and often very pernicious to them. You may, also, by budding, put two or more branches upon a stock that would be too weak to take so many grafts ; and you may bud in *July* when grafting *has failed* in *March* and *April*. The disadvantage of budding, is, that the trees are rendered one year later in coming into bearing than when you graft.

219. PLANTING.—Under the heads of the several trees in the list which will follow hereafter, directions will be given with regard to the age, the size, and other circumstances which will be found to vary according to the several purposes, and situations for which the trees are intended. I shall here, therefore, confine myself merely to the act of planting ; that is to say, the manner of removing a young tree from one spot and placing it in another; the rules here being applicable to all trees. The first thing to be observed is, that, though trees will grow if kept out of the ground for a considerable time, they ought to be kept in that state as short a time as possible, and, during even that short time, the roots

ought to be exposed as little as possible to the sun and wind. The taking up of a young tree ought to be performed with the greatest possible care, especially if it have stood in the place whence it is taken for more than one year. And here let me stop for a minute in order to re-impress upon the mind of the reader the importance of the observation which I made in paragraph 206. After having read that paragraph again, the reader will please to observe, that all long roots must be pruned off to within at most four or five inches of the stem of the tree; and that, if the tree have stood too long in its place before its final removal, this loss of root will render it absolutely necessary to cut off the upper part of the tree very near to the ground; and even after that, will make it very slow to re-enter upon vigorous growth. If, therefore, you be not ready for the transplanting of your trees, at the time when they might be transplanted, rather than let them stand to get these long roots, take them up in the fall of the year, give the roots and heads a pruning, and plant them again, so that you may not experience the great check at the final transplanting.

220. I return now to the taking up of the tree, which ought to be done without tearing any of the roots, and which is not done without such tearing one time out of twenty. You ought to dig some earth away a little distance all round the tree to a considerable depth, and nearly let it tumble down of itself; for, if you pull, you break a root; and, if that root be large, and break off near the stem of the tree, the tree will have a bad root and will never grow finely. Having taken the tree fairly out of the ground, you begin by pruning the root. All

the larger shoots of the roots you cut off to within six inches of the stem, and you take entirely out all the hairy fibres ; for they never grow again and they are apt to mould and to keep the earth from closely touching the roots out of which the new shoots are to come. Having pruned the root, you proceed to plant the tree. The hole must be much deeper and wider than is required for the mere reception of the root. The earth ought to be broken very finely at the bottom of the hole. When that is done, the root of the tree ought to be placed upon it in such a manner as for the tree to stand about an inch higher above the ground than it stood before it was removed. If the tree be to be placed against a wall, the head should lean gently against the wall, and the bottom of the trunk about eight or ten inches from it : if the tree be to be planted in the open ground, the trunk should be held perfectly upright : while thus held, very fine earth should be put upon the roots : if it were sifted, so much the better : the tree should be joggled or shaken a little to cause the earth to go down and in amongst the roots and fill up all the cavities, so that the fine earth may touch the roots, and lie closely round them in every part. If you tumble in the rough earth, which would leave part of the roots untouched, the parts so untouched will mould, will perish, or become cankered. When the roots are all covered with very fine earth, you may fill up the hole with the earth that has come out of it, only taking care to break it very fine. Before you have put in quite all the earth, give a gentle tread all round the tree with your foot, treading first at a foot distance from the tree, and approaching all round to within three or four inches ; then put the rest of the earth over the treading, and leave the surface round the treading in the form of a dish.

221. If you plant late in the spring, lay a little short litter into the dish, and give the tree a watering occasionally until the month of July, unless the weather obviously render such operation unnecessary. I am particularly anxious that the reader should attend to this part of my instructions; for, nine times out of ten, when failure takes place, careless planting is the cause. If you purchase trees, you should look well at the roots; and, if they be very large, or at all torn, it is much better to fling the trees away than to plant them; for what are a few shillings, or even a few pounds, when compared with the *loss of years*, in providing yourself with fruit?

TRAINING AND PRUNING.

222. TRAINING and pruning go together : they are two parts of the same act, because you lay the branch in its proper place at the same time that you cut it. They are, therefore, inseparable as matters to be treated of. There are, however, different sorts of training : one against walls or pales, or against a house; and the trees thus situated are called *wall-trees*. After these, come *espaliers* and dwarf trees in various shapes for a garden. These will be spoken of by and by; and, at last, I shall speak of the planting of standard trees for an orchard. The main principles of pruning are the same in all cases :

the objects are, to render trees productive, to preserve their health, and to keep them in regular and convenient form ; for, in this case, as well as in almost every other, though nature does a great deal, she will not do all : she will not do every thing : she must be and will be assisted ; and certainly the management of fruit-trees may be considered as one of the principal parts of the art of gardening.

223. I shall now give instructions for the pruning of peach trees placed against walls. If I were to stop at every particular part of the instructions, in order to point out the difference between the pruning of a peach tree and that of the apricot and other trees, the mind of the reader would be bewildered : therefore, I shall keep the peach tree solely in my eye while giving these instructions ; and, as this head of training and pruning will immediately be followed by an Alphabetical List of Fruits, the reader will find, under the name of each fruit, such remarks as are required to point out to him in what respect he is to differ in his training and pruning from the rules laid down in the case of the peach. He will, therefore, please to observe, that, in the instructions which I am now about to give, I have the peach tree solely in my eye.

224. Training and pruning involve so many circumstances, such a great variety of objects and of operations, that to give minute instructions upon the subject absolutely demand a great space ; and, after all, it is fortunate, when mechanical operations are to be described by words; it is extremely fortunate, if the writer

make himself clearly understood; and, indeed, it is impossible for him to do it unless he have the best *attention* of the reader : it is not a clear statement of a fact ; it is not a mere affirmation or negation, that is required here ; nor is it in the construction of an argument and the drawing of a conclusion : here we have to describe innumerable minute acts to be performed with the hands and the fingers ; and, I have always found, that to be intelligible, in such a case, is the most difficult thing that one experiences in the use of words. Hence it is that this is hardly ever attempted without the assistance of drawings, or of something that teaches through the channel of the eye. I shall do my best to make myself clearly understood ; and, if I have the strict *attention* of the reader, I have little doubt of success. I shall first offer some preliminary observations, and to these I request the reader's extraordinary attention.

225. The time, or rather times, of pruning, are common to all fruit trees. The winter pruning is performed in February, March and April, beginning with the earliest sorts of trees (with reference to their blooming) and ending with the latest, forming this series : apricot, peach, plum, pear, cherry, apple. Quinces and medlars will be spoken of sufficiently under the names of those trees, as will gooseberries, currants, and raspberries. It may be matter of indifference, perhaps, whether the winter pruning of the above mentioned trees take place in one of the afore-mentioned months or the other ; but three things are to be observed in the case of all trees ; that pruning ought not to be done during the time of flowering ; and that the summer pruning ought not to be done

'till after the fruit has attained a considerable size; that
it is essential always to prune with a very sharp knife;
that the cut ought to be from below, upwards, beginning
behind a bud, and finishing near its opening, taking good
care not to hurt it.   A rubbishing pruning-knife, a thing
made of bad stuff, or in bad shape, will spoil any set of
trees in the world.   The best pruning-knives that I have
ever seen are made by MR. RICHARDSON of Kensington.

226. *Preliminary observations.*—First: The sap of trees
tends always to mount perpendicularly from the root to
the top, flowing through the straight branches, and there
producing wood instead of fruit.   Therefore, when you
wish to restore equality between two branches of which
one is more weak than the other, bend the more vigorous
one down a little and raise the other, and it will soon
overtake it.   Also, when you wish a tree to furnish well
at bottom, you must prevent the sap mounting to the
head by inclining the upper branches downwards and
pruning them long, and, if necessary, by means of the
annulary incision.

227. Second : the less the sap has of direct channels;
the less it can freely circulate between the bark, the
more it will produce of branches and fruit-buds. Thus, it
is, perhaps, that the graft and the annulary incision, by
stopping the progress of the sap, augment the quantity,
and improve the quality of the fruit.   So, when a tree
runs to wood, bend the branches downwards ; stop the
sap, and force it to produce fruit.

228. Third : the sap flies more strongly into a short-

ened branch than into another, and the more the branch be shortened, with the more force will the sap be drawn to it. Therefore, when one part of a tree becomes less strong than the other, prune it shorter, so that the sap may go there in greater abundance and reinforce the weakened part.   This shows, too, that, to have fruit, you should prune long; and short, to have wood.   For instance, if you cut down to within two or three buds, you will have nothing but strong wood; but cut off in the middle, the extremity will then furnish wood, the middle spurs, and the lower end, fruit shoots; so also, prune not at all, and incline horizontally, and you will have nothing but blossom-buds.   From these premises, it may be concluded, that, when you have a branch given to bear, instead of pruning it long, as is the practice with most gardeners, it should be pruned short to produce an influx of sap sufficient to nourish and perfect the fruit; and that the vigorous wood shoots, which the French call *gourmands*, or gluttons, should be pruned long.

229. Fourth : If you cut a branch completely off, the sap goes to the neighbouring branches and shoots. When a branch, therefore, becomes diseased and is difficult to cure, sacrifice it without hesitation.   The neighbouring branches will soon replace it, and, perhaps, in less time than it would have taken in the cure, if that had been possible.

230. Fifth : Every shoot that has been topped or dis-budded, throws out, from superabundance of sap, a quantity of shoots and fruit buds.   So, if by means of

bending, you cannot prevent a branch throwing out wood, top it and pinch off the side buds when they are bursting, and it will then tend to fruit.

231. Sixth : The duration and the strength of a tree depend upon an equality existing constantly between its head and its roots, as well as between the different parts of its head.   You should never, therefore, cut back a tree to its main limbs or to its trunk unless there be a corresponding deficiency in the roots, either from old age or from accident. This proves the necessity of pruning very short on transplanting. If one part of the branches, by strong growth, take the sap destined for the other part, these decline rapidly, and finish by complete decay, in which they do not fail to involve the whole tree.

232. Seventh : The more a tree is forced into bearing, the more it is exhausted ; but the more it is suffered to put forth wood, the more it is vigorous.   This principle proves that we should never suffer a tree to become overloaded with fruit-branches, or that we expose ourselves to lose it altogether in a few years, or, at least, to see it barren for one, two, or even three, years. But an intelligent gardener will always take care to provide an even quantity of branches both for wood and fruit ; and the result will be that he will have a greater quantity of fruit, and of finer quality, and that he may rest assured of this annually without injuring the tree or shortening its duration.

233. These principles are applicable to all fruit-trees, but there is another which applies more particularly to

the stone-fruits, and, of these, mostly to the peach-tree.

234. Eighth : The fruit-buds, particularly of stone-fruits, to form and bring to maturity their fruit, should be accompanied by shoot-buds, which draw the sap towards them. Every fruit-branch which has not these dries up and dies without bearing. It often happens that the severity of the winter destroys the shoot-buds which are coming alongside the fruit-buds ; and those who prune before this can be discovered, stand the chance of leaving fruit-branches without wood-buds, and consequently, of seeing these dry up and die as soon as they have flowered. Every fruit-branch which has, at its extremity, nothing but a wood-bud, should be shortened unless you wish to preserve it for a wood-branch ; but do this only in the last extremity, because it will always remain sterile below.

235. Between the stone-fruits and the pip-fruits, there is a great deal of difference in the manner of bearing. The latter bear on little branches of from two to three inches long, called spurs. These are two or three years in forming, and they generally come upon other small branches. The first year, a spur has three leaves, the second, five, and the third, seven. The stone-fruits, as the peach for instance, bear their fruit on branches of one year's growth, which should, therefore, be shortened at every winter pruning. The fruit-buds of these last are easily recognised. They are round and ruddy, and garnished with a cotton envelope ; whereas the wood-buds are, on the contrary, long and of a green colour.

236. Any form may be given to a tree, so that it be suited to its nature, to the aspect, and to the soil. For instance, the *wall-tree* is placed flat against a wall well exposed to the sun ; the *espalier, pyramid, bush,* and *dwarf* trees, generally grafted on stocks which yield but little sap, are placed in the borders of the garden, and produce little shade, and require a less deep soil than the standard or half-standard. The stocks on which it is proper to graft these trees will be mentioned in the articles treating of the particular management of each.

237. The French method of pruning, as practised at Montreuil, is that to which the peach-tree is subjected. And, as the peach-tree is the most delicate, and the most difficult to manage, I will take it as the model of a good form, and I shall refer to this article in speaking of other trained trees, which ought all to be pruned in the same manner, with the slight exceptions of keeping the fruit-branches of the pip-fruits a longer time, because they do not bear till about the second or third year, though they last much longer ; and of leaving on these branches fewer wood-buds, because they are not wanted for such constant succession. These differences will be treated of in the articles on each particular sort of fruit.

238. The wood-branches of the peach-tree are known by their vigour, by their thickness, equal to, if not surpassing, that of the little finger ; by their length of about from three to six feet, and by their bark, which is grey from the first year. The fruit-branches, at most not larger than a large quill, are from six inches to two feet

long ; their bark is very smooth, green on the side
towards the wall, and red on the side towards the sun.
Sometimes the flower-blossoms are assembled in clusters
round a short shoot, or spur of one or two inches long,
with a wood-bud at the end sufficient to draw the sap
which is necessary to nourish the fruit.

239. *First Year*—Suppose the young tree placed against
a wall, the first shoot of the graft (or bud) never having
been pruned (plate 6. *fig*. 1.).   Cut it off at six or eight

PLATE 6.

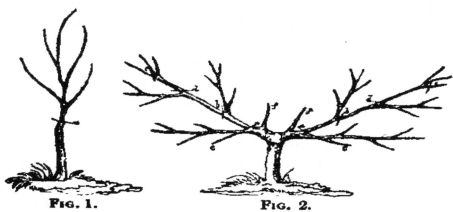

Fig. 1.   Fig. 2.

inches above the stock (pl. 6. *fig*. 1. *a*) ; and then, when
it has sent out its shoots, nail them, after having taken
off all that come before or behind.   It is a general rule
never to leave any shoots but such as come at the sides of
the branches.   Choose, amongst your young shoots, two
of equal vigour, one on each side, by which means to
form your two principal branches that are always to remain ; and, having done this, cut off all the rest.   If one
of them become longer or more vigorous than the
other, incline it downwards to suffer the other to gain the
advantage.   If one of the two perish, train the other
straight again, prune it precisely as you did the graft, and

procure other two branches from it. The only mischief
is, that your tree is thus thrown back a year. When you
nail up the two main, or mother, branches, extend them
so as to form a very wide letter V (say an angle of ninety
degrees), but being cautious never, on any account or
at any age, to bend or arch them, or assuredly the secondary branches run off with all the sap, and your tree
is deformed.

240. *Second Year.*—Do not attempt more than to procure a lower secondary branch and to lengthen the
mother-branch. (plate 6. *fig.* 2. *a.*) Therefore prune
close to the old shoot, that is at two buds from it, and
of these two buds, the end one must be an upper one,
to prolong the mother-branch, and the under one will
throw out the lower secondary branch. Nail, and that is all.

241. *Third Year.*—This year you must procure an
upper secondary branch, fruit-branches (plate 6. *fig.* 2.
c.) on the lower secondary branch, and again a lengthen-
ing of the mother-branch. For these purposes prune the
mother-branch at two buds again, but let both buds be
on the upper side of the branch, the end one to carry
on the mother-branch, and the other to form the upper
secondary branch. (plate 6. *fig.* 2. *b.*) If two successive
buds should not be found thus placed, prune them at
three buds from the last year's wood, but, in this case,
rub off the intermediate bud which will be on the under
side. To obtain lateral branches from the lower secondary branch, prune it in the same manner.

242. *Fourth Year.*—Lengthen the mother-branch, and
get a second lower secondary branch. (plate 6. *fig.* 2. *d.*)

243. *Fifth Year.*—Same operation ; but get a second upper secondary branch. (plate 6. *fig.* 2. *e.*)

244. *Sixth Year.*—Same operation.   Third lower secondary branch ; and, if the tree have been taken care of, and its form have not been sacrificed to a too great eagerness to get fruit quickly, the peach-tree is formed. And if it have all the requisites, that is to say, health in its nature, a good aspect, and suitable land, it ought to extend to between twelve and twenty feet in length, and eight in height over the surface of the wall.

245. All trees will not so readily assume this form ; therefore I will anticipate a few cases, and point out the means of remedying the evil.   Though a gardener, thoroughly embued with these principles, and applying them under all circumtsances, can never be in error.

246. If the upper secondary branches, favoured by their more perpendicular position, flourish at the expense of the mother-branch, incline them downward, even, if necessary, to touch the mother-branch, to re-establish the equality.   And you may also leave some fruit-buds to slacken the sap ; and, at the time of nailing, shorten the mother-branch at a strong wood-bud, whilst you take care to prune at a weak one on the branch or branches that you have lowered.   In order that both the sides of the tree may be alike, the corresponding secondary branches, both upper and under, should be pruned at buds of the same vigour and at the same height.   The same with regard to the mother-branches.

247. The secondary branches ought to be separate enough to allow of nailing the fruit-branches that they throw out, say about two feet; but it ought not to be more, because a well-trained tree ought never to leave any space vacant. In a tree completely formed, the wood-branches are pruned at the point where they begin to diminish in size. But this is not a universal rule, for a feeble tree should be pruned shorter to give it strength, and a young and vigorous tree should be pruned much longer. In fruit-branches, too, prune according to the greater or less degree of vigour apparent in them. Those branches, the eyes of which are accompanied by a wood-bud, may be shortened to *two* or *four* eyes; but the short branches, or spurs, having clusters of eyes, should *not be* pruned at all if they have a wood-bud at the extremity. Both, however, should be cut clean off if the wood-buds perish, as they would be sterile. When two branches form a fork, cut out the most feeble. As the fruit-branches bear but once, it is indispensable that they be renewed every year; and do not, as some very unskilful gardeners would do, prune very long and suffer the bud at the extremity to furnish the new fruit-branch; for it inevitably results from this, that the branch, besides being weak from one end to the other, will be perfectly barren below the last year's shoot, and will end by dying at the end of two or three years, during which time it will have furnished nothing but thin, long, disproportionate and unproductive twigs; but, by shortening every year the branch that has borne, and replacing it by one of its own lower buds, you have every year good and vigorous wood, and placed as near as possible to the respective wood branches. This shortening should be

performed as soon as the fruit is all gathered. At Montreuil they call it the *remplacement,* or replacing.

248. Some persons train their trees in what is called the *fan* form : that is, instead of having but two mother-branches, they will have three or four or even five or six ; but, for simplicity's sake, I have given a specimen of a tree trained purely in the French fashion, leaving at *f. f.* in *fig.* 2. two branches that might have been carried on to form this tree in the *fan*-fashion. According as their mother-branches are numerous, they are obliged to incline them downward more or less. The principle is, not to deviate from the angle of ninety degrees, or right-angle, more than is necessary for the nailing in of the fruit-branches between the secondary branches ; so that the two lower principal, or mother-branches, may be horizontal, and never more inclined. When they have three or five mother-branches, they train the middle one upright. In other respects they prune these mother-branches as the French do those à la Montreuil ; excepting, that, as they furnish more, they should be pruned much longer during the two or three first years.

249. *Summer pruning* belongs most particularly to the most tender of fruit trees, and, of course, to the peach-tree; I shall, therefore, treat of it here to finish the subject of pruning. The operation is generally performed in the month of May, when the young shoots are not more than from eight to ten inches long, and it consists in taking off the superfluous ones. It may be done by the hand, but it is less dangerous for those that you determine to leave, to do it with a pruning-knife. All the

shoots that come immediately before or immediately behind should be severed, and those that you leave at the sides will profit by it. Recollect always that the shoot you save for a wood-branch should be healthy and vigorous; and if the one best suited to your purpose as to locality, be not so, reject it and fix on a lower and healthier. When the fruit is set, all the shoots proceeding from the bearing branches, should be removed, with the exception of those neighbouring ones which tend to nourish the fruit by drawing the sap to it, and of those that have been fixed on for the purpose of succeeding the whole branch. Should all the blossoms of a branch be sterile, prune immediatly down to one or two buds.

250. NAILING is also an essential part of training. It is performed after the prunings both of winter and summer, only that in the latter, it is not done 'till the shoots are strong enough to bear the constraint without danger of breaking. It may be well deferred, especially in old trees, 'till the month of July, or even August ; or better still never to do it 'till the trees are found to require it. The *object* is to keep the branches in their proper and assigned position, and it is done (when there is no trellis against the wall) by means of shreds, and nails driven into the wall, by which the branches are supported. When there is a trellis, you tie with matting. To nail well, you must bend the shoots and branches without effort, without making sharp angles, and yet make them stretch to their utmost in the form of a wide V. So manage it that each branch and its shoots shall assume the form of the tree ; so that every part of the tree be furnished, the middle, the sides, and the upper and lower

parts ; and so that all the ramifications of the tree be spaced according to their size, without confusion or entanglement, and that the eye may follow them with distinctness.

251. Before I conclude my instructions relative to the pruning of the peach against the wall, let me speak of an operation which is not probably of modern invention, and which is applicable to all fruit trees : it is called the *annulary incision*, or operation of ringing, which is the cutting out of a narrowish strip of bark all round the collar of a tree, or round one of its branches only. It may be done with any sharp instrument. The annulary incision is performed a few days before the blossoming of a fruit tree, and, by retarding the flow of sap, causes it to tend to fruit ; but fine fruit obtained in this manner weakens the tree or the branch on which it is borne ; and according as the plant is more or less strong and the operation is renewed more or less often, it is sure to perish. This operation may be performed on plants or parts of plants of which the too vigorous sap thwarts the plans of the gardener in the training of his trees ; but let him consider it only as a remedy against superabounding sap, and let him be cautious in the use of it even then.

252. Having now done with the wall-tree training and pruning, with the exception of what is to be said as peculiarly applicable to each sort of tree, the rules for pruning and training which differ from those for the peach, and which additional observations are, as I before observed, to come under the names of the different trees respectively, I shall proceed to speak of the mode of

managing those fruit-trees which are not placed against a wall.' There are divers modes of training, the *pyramid*, the *goblet*, the *bush*, the *half-standard*, the *arching* ; and, which is the great method of all, *espalier*, after which will come the instructions for rearing of standards for the orchard. I shall give my reasons for preferring the old-fashioned espalier to every other species of training of trees not against a wall, and also my reasons for wholly excluding all standards from the garden. I think all the other methods, except the espalier, of training fruit-trees (for a garden) very bad : I have never seen them attended with success, to say nothing of the irregularity of their appearance, and the various inconveniences which attend them. Nevertheless, I will mention them here one by one, that the reader may, if he chuse, make use of them.

253. PYRAMID FORM. Some think that the *distaff* and *pyramid* forms are different ones, and that the former requires less pains than the latter. No doubt this error arises from their having taken for the former some neglected and ill trained trees, whilst they have seen trees of the pyramid form well trained by a skilful hand. Be that, however as it may, the first year prune the graft at 5 or 6 inches from the bottom, saving 3 or 4 eyes to form lateral branches and to carry up the stem ; but these first lateral branches are most essential, for they will furnish the requisite abundance of wood below, which, when the tree has obtained a certain height, cannot be obtained, and yet which is absolutely necessary to the beauty as well as utility of the pyramid. Suffer no other shoots this year than from the 3 or 4 buds mentioned above. Stop the upright stem every year when

it has shot to the length of 12 or 18 inches, and this will force it to send out every year a set of lateral shoots, and of these you make your election of 3 or 4 to save. At the pruning time, shorten the lateral branches more or less according to the vigour of the tree and the just distribution of sap amongst all the branches. If you wish to *raise* a branch, prune at an upper bud ; and at a lower bud to *lower* a branch. If you wish to cause a branch to tend to the right or the left, chuse a bud situated on the right or left side to prune at. In either case to prevent the branch going straight, you have nothing to do but prune a little way above a bud. Thus the training continues ; and, as the lowermost branches are always a year older than the upper, this gradation should be preserved in the length of the branches, which of course, must diminish by stages all the way up, from the base to the summit. This sort of training conduces at once to the fruitfulness and to the duration of the tree.

854. THE GOBLET OR CUP FORM is very little other than an espalier, but of which you bring the extremities of the two sides round in a circle to meet each other, and to form a large vase or goblet open at the top and tapering down to an inverted cone at bottom. To procure this, prune the young tree so as to have 4 or 5 branches as near to one another as possible at the top of the stem. Manage these principal branches as you do those of the wall-tree ; but rub or cut off all shoots or buds that are putting forth towards the inside of the goblet; as these would soon fill it and destroy the form. The principal branches are brought into form by means of one or two hoops, as occasion requires.

255. BUSH TRAINING is rarely exercised excepting in the case of dwarf apple trees, of which the gardeners will sometimes have a square. It is, suffering the tree to take its own natural form, and pruning only for the purpose of keeping up an equal quantity of wood and bearing branches.

256. HALF-STANDARDS. — If the plant have been grafted where it is to stand, nothing can be done the first year; but if it be a young transplanted tree, shorten the graft down to 2 or 3 buds. The next year chuse the strongest bud to lengthen the stem, and pinch the others off at about 6 inches length to favour the one you have saved, and which is to form the trunk of the tree. If, out of this, there come lateral shoots, prune them short, in little stumps, that is, at one or two buds, and let them remain 'till the autumnal pruning, when you must cut these off close to the stem as well as those that you pinched off to favour the first saved shoot. And thus you continue heightening the tree more and more every year, 'till it shall have reached the height you wish, whether of standard or half-standard. If, before it get to the height you desire, it should fork, pinch off the weakest of the two shoots as soon as it is 3 or 4 inches long, and cut it clean out at the winter pruning succeeding; or if it should become distorted, or should break off by some accident, either pinch off, or cut, immediately below the damaged part, and in the winter pruning, shorten it down to the strongest bud below that you have, one that you have been favouring for the purpose since you perceived the mischief above, and that will supply you with a fresh undamaged stem. If the tree arrive at the height

you desire in the summer, pinch it off a little above
that point, and cut down to the exact height you wish
it is your first succeeding winter pruning; and then cut
off again all the other shoots of the summer that you
have before only pinched off. Then in the following
spring, having now got the trunk of your tree, watch
narrowly the shoots that the last year's wood will send
out, and chuse from among them the three or four most
vigorous and most equally placed of them for principal
branches, and pinch off all the rest as before directed.
When these branches send out their shoots, pinch off
those that come too close to one another, and prune
them close in winter. In the autumn, prune the principal branches and their shoots that are designed to be secondary branches, precisely as we have directed with
regard to wall-trees above; and when you have done so
two or three years, you may let the tree alone to nature,
only cutting out the dead branches as they occur. A tree
well formed, and in good ground well cultivated, will last
more than a century. Sometimes a vigorous branch will
do harm to more fruitful ones, and yet you may, for
sound reasons, wish to preserve it. In such a case,
slacken its vigour by pruning it very long, or even by
ringing it.

257. ARCHING is done by bending in the form of a
half-hoop, more or less open, the branches, and in this
way you bring them pointing towards the earth. This
situation retards the circulation of the sap, and forces it
to betake itself to leaf buds and to transform them into
wood-buds.

258. *Espalier.* This is the form which, in my opinion is the only one suited for the open ground of a *garden.* The fanciful affair of arching for vines or any other tree is more a matter of pleasure-garden than of kitchen garden: the other forms are intended to promote bearing and they are all vastly inferior to the espalier in this respect. Apricots obtained in any way except against a wall or a house are seldom good for much; there are a few of the sorts which will bear in other situations; but the fruit is good for very little. Apples, pears, plums, cherries, and quinces and medlars, all do exceedingly well as espaliers; and it is notorious, that the fruit is always larger, and of finer flavour when the tree is trained in this form than when the limbs are suffered to go in an upright direction. There are several sorts of pears which will be very fine on espaliers on the very same spot of ground where they will scarcely come to anything like perfection on a standard tree or upon any tree the limbs of which are suffered to go upright.'

259. Espaliers are managed in the following manner: Suppose it to be an apple-tree which has been grafted in the manner before directed, and which has a good strong shoot coming up from the graft. Take the tree up, and plant it in the manner directed under the head of Planting in this Chapter. Whether planted in the fall or in the spring, let the tree stand in the spring till the buds begin to break, then cut the shoot down to within three buds of the bottom. Cut sloping and let the cut end pretty near to the point where the top bud of the three is coming out. These three buds will send forth three shoots, and all the three will take an upright direction.

About the middle of July, take the two bottom shoots, one of which will be on one side of the stem or trunk, as it must now be called, and the other on the other side, place a couple of little stakes to each of these shoots, and tie the shoots down to the stakes so that they may lie in a horizontal direction, suffering the top shoot to go on; but, about the latter end of July, take the top off from that shoot. Thus, when winter comes, you will have one upright shoot and two horizontal ones. In the spring, cut off the top shoot again, leaving five buds. Two of which you will cut out in order to prevent them from sending out shoots. You will again have two side-shoots, and the top shoot will again be going on upright. You must now have longer stakes in order to give these side shoots a horizontal direction; but, the stakes that serve for the new shoots will serve also for those of the last year; but then, as the shoots of the last year will be going on, there must be additional stakes to tie them to. The next year you proceed in the same manner; and, if you do the work carefully you will finally have these lateral shoots in perfectly regular order, and they should be at about from seven to nine inches asunder, the lowest within a few inches of the ground, and the highest just according to your fancy; but it is not desirable to carry the tree to a height beyond that of about five or six feet. As these side-shoots or limbs increase in size and length, they will need loftier and stouter stakes; and this, like the growing of peas in a neat manner, and to produce fruit most abundant in quantity and most excellent in quality; this staking, as in the case of peas, has been the great obstacle to the cultivation of espaliers. A stake of any ordinary wood will last not above two years, and espe-

cially in garden ground: it rots off at the point where
it begins to touch the earth, and there is an everlasting
trouble and expense. To have espaliers, therefore, and
to have them in neat order, the old fashion was to have
stakes of *spine-oak,* an inch one way, and two inches the
other; such stakes would last ten or fifteen years, according to the wetness or dryness of the land. The best
stakes would be the trunks of young locust trees, planted
within two feet of each other, and suffered to grow to
the height of about twelve or fourteen feet. They
would do this, in good ground, in the course of four or five
years. Cut down in winter, and the branches trimmed off
close, they would make espalier stakes to last for a
good long life-time. While the limbs of espaliers are
small, they should be fastened to the stakes by good fresh
matting, or bass, as it is called, to be occasionally renewed: when the limbs get stout, I have seen brass wire
used; though, perhaps, the matting might still be sufficient; for, when the limb has once got to be an inch or
two through, it wants little supporting except merely
towards its point, or when heavily laden with fruit.
Espaliers are to be planted in *rows* if there be a considerable number of them in a garden; and they should
not stand nearer, if intended to be permanent trees, than
at *twenty feet* from each other. That they should be
planted in straight line is obvious enough. The best
situation for them is along by the sides of walks and not
more than about three feet distant from the edge of the
walk. Their symmetry is very beautiful; and, what can
be more beautiful than an avenue of fruit-trees in bloom,
and trained in form so regular and neat? The crops they
bear are prodigious compared with those standard trees

upon the same spot. I remember a gentleman who had an espalier apple-tree of about twenty feet in length, and two very large standard trees of the same sort of fruit, in the same garden and very near to the same spot. All the three trees were well laden with fruit : I stood looking at them for some time, making an estimate of the crop; and I came to the conclusion that the espalier had more fruit than both the great standards put together, while its fruit was of double the size, or nearly so. I asked him why he did not chop down those two great trees that shaded and spoiled so much of his garden, and plant a couple of espaliers. He had the new-fashioned taste of despising the espaliers, and talked of grubbing this particular one up. In remonstrating with him, I said that the espalier had a greater quantity of fruit upon it then than both the other trees. This appeared to him to be so monstrous, that he offered to bet me a hundred to one, or more, against my opinion. I declined the bet ; but he promised, that, when he gathered the fruit, which was to be done in a few days, he would have it measured and give me an account of the result, which, to his utter astonishment, he found to be that the espalier contained half a bushel more than both the other trees put together. The eye always deceives itself in comparing things irregularly placed with things placed with regularity. So much, then, for the training of espaliers. The *pruning ;* that is to say, the pruning of the limbs, is as follows. Apples, and, indeed, all the other trees which I have spoken of to be planted for espaliers, bear upon *spurs,* some shorter, and some longer ; not like peach-trees which have their fruit upon shoots of the last year. Sometimes, indeed, apples, and these other trees will bear upon the last year's wood, but generally they bear upon spurs, which come out of the sides of the limb itself until it gets to be very large, and afterwards come out of the lower buds of little side-shoots that have been cut off; and these spurs last for a great many years. When you gather an apple in the fall, you will, if the tree be in vigour, see a blossom-bud, ready, coming out of the same spur, to bear the next year; and I ought to observe here, that the greatest possible care should be taken (as it never is) not to pull off the spur when you pull off the apple. Gentlemen who are curious in these things actually cut off cherries with a scissors, except the morellos, and one or two other sorts, which bear pretty generally on the last year's wood, to avoid the danger of pulling off the spurs. It being the fact, that the trees bear upon spurs, there needs no new supply of limbs or of shoots; and, therefore, the little side-shoots that come out of the limbs ought to be cut clean out about the latter end of July, unless there be a deficiency of spurs upon the limb; and, in that case, the little side-shoots should be cut off, leaving one bud, or, perhaps, two, if the joints be short, and these will frequently send out spurs. Let us now go back to the second year after planting the tree, when we had got two lateral shoots running horizontally, and one upright shoot. Each of these lateral shoots will send out two side-shoots near their point, and one at their point, to go straight forward: that one is to be suffered to go on, but the others must be shortened to *one bud:* the same thing will happen next year, when the same operation is to be performed, and at the same season: thus, at last, you have a limb ten feet long, furnished with spurs from one end to the other. When your room will suffer you to carry the limb no further, you cut off the point. Let any one judge, then, what a saving of room here is ; how much sun and air, and how regularly admitted, compared with what is to be expected from the half-standard or any other form. How are you to prune in this careful and yet easy manner a tree of irregular shape? My real opinion is, that, an acre of ground well stocked with espaliers, the rows at ten feet apart, and the plants at twenty-feet apart in the row, would produce, on an average of years, three times the weight of fruit to be obtained from trees in any other form ; besides which, the ground between the rows might, a third part of it, at least, produce cabbages, cauliflowers, broccoli, crops of any sort that did not mount too high. The great fault in orchards is, a want of pruning ; and, indeed, such an operation on standard trees is next to impossible. People pretend to object to the *formality* of the espalier. Just as if formality were an objection in a kitchen-garden where all is straight lines, and must be straight lines ! The little border between the espalier trees and the walk should not be crowded with plants of any kind, and should have no plants at all that grow to more than six or seven inches high. On the other side of the espaliers nothing should grow within about four feet ; but, how small, still, is the space of ground which even a large espalier would occupy ! Very little more than *half a rod*, while you can have no tree in any other shape that will not occupy and render useless five times the quantity of ground to produce the same quantity of fruit ; and, if I were to say ten times, I should be much nearer the mark. Then, there is the inconvenience of fruit-trees in all the other forms. They must stand at a considerable distance from the walk, or they extend their branches over it. It is a circle of ground that they occupy or shade; and the plat in which they stand can only be partially cultivated for other things. If they mount above the reach of the hand, to get at the fruit *is* a business of great trouble; and, after all, there can be no regular and true pruning; no minute inspection: no picking off of caterpillars with exactness: no detection and destruction of other insects; and, in the case of cherries, what a difficult business it must always be effectually to protect the fruit against birds on any other tree except wall or espalier! I have seen the thing attempted some hundreds of times, and never saw it effected in my life. Monstrous must be the expense and trouble to keep the net extended all round and held clear off the tree at top, where the finest cherries always are. In short, the net lays upon the top of the tree; birds come and eat the fine cherries there, and leave you the sour ones beneath. An espalier, on the contrary, is, with the aid of a few long stakes, and a good net, protected as completely as if it were within a hand-glass. Espaliers were always the great reliance of our gardens until within the last sixty or seventy years. An objection is made to their formality, their stiffness of appearance! Alas! the objection is to what is deemed the *trouble*, or *labour*; and, SWIFT observes, that labour is *pain*, and that, in all his family, from his great grandmother to himself, nobody liked pain. This, however, is a great error; for, as in an infinite number of cases, some of which occur to every man almost every day of his life, pains-taking, *at the first,* produces ease and leisure in the sequel.

260. STANDARD TREES.—After what I have said, I do most anxiously hope, that, if any gentleman ever should make a garden after the plan that I am recommending, he never will suffer it to be disfigured by the folly of a standard-tree, which, the more vigorous its growth, the more mischievous that growth to the garden. But, an orchard is another thing; and especially if that orchard be to be a pasture as well as an orchard. In this case, it is necessary to keep the branches of the trees out of the reach of cattle; and they must have a clear trunk to a considerable height. The usual way of going to work is this: to purchase trees with a clear trunk of the length which is desired: to plant the trees at suitable distances, and to shorten the shoots of their heads at the time of planting. A dreadful amputation of roots must take place. It is impossible that there should be a due supply of sap for the first summer at least; the bark becomes clung to the wood. The shoots that come out the first summer are poor feeble twigs; the trees, if unpropped, are blown nearly out of the ground before the summer is over; therefore, a propping takes place; sometimes with one stake, hay-bands and cord; sometimes with two: there must be three, to keep the tree upright, so that here is a tripod with a stump coming up in the middle. The tree gets something in the head, and, at least, a parcel of leaves, the wind works the trunk about in spite of the bandages, and, nine times out of ten, a breaking of the bark and the foundation of a canker takes place. In short, the tree must be sup-

ported by something like carpentering work; or it is
sure to lean on one side; and every reader must know
that a rarer sight is hardly to be seen in England than an
apple-tree with an upright stem. Indeed, more than one
half of such trees totally fail, and those that do not, are
so crippled in their roots that they become poor weakly
things, and, if not unproductive altogether, bear very
mean fruit. The true way to have a fine orchard would
be, to plant the trees when young, having been previously
moved, as directed under the head of PLANTING in this
Chapter. After planting, the trees should be cut down
just before the buds begin to burst, to one bud, or two,
at most, for fear of accidents. If to two buds, only one
should be suffered to send up its shoot. All things having been done rightly, this shoot would be strong, and
fed by a root which would have fairly started in the progress with itself. To insure stoutness of trunk, take
care that no side-shoots be suffered to remain for any
length of time, even the first summer. The second
spring after planting, cut the new shoot down to within
three buds of its bottom : it will send out three shoots,
rub off the two lower ones, and suffer the top one to go
on; and this shoot will now, in good ground, attain the
height of a man's head. The next spring, shorten down to
four or five or six shoots, according to the strength of the
trunk, and during the summer, take off the side shoots;
and you will have in the fall, a trunk seven or eight feet
high. That is the tree. Nature will teach it, after that,
how to form its head; and your business will be to keep
the inside of the head clear by cutting off the shoots
that there cross or interfere with each other. Apple-trees,
and the same may be said of all other fruit-trees, would

have as straight trunks as the oaks in the weald of Surrey, if this method of planting orchards were pursued. But it will be objected, how are these trees to be protected from cattle during their growth ? Why, if you must have the pasture, and still wish to have straight-trunked, wide-spreading, healthy and durable trees, you must surround each of them with an effectual fence to prevent the possibility of cattle reaching either trunk or branches. It is a great object to have a good orchard, or it is not : if it be, then this expense is not a thing to be thought of; and, if it be not, why plant any trees at all ? The truth is, however, that, if you reckon the expense of great trees, the stakes and the bandages, the loss of many of the trees, and the bushes or other miserable protections, which, after all, you resort to, and are compelled to resort to to keep the sheep from barking the trunks, or the cows from rubbing them to pieces ; and particularly if you reckon the loss that you sustain in the tardy arrival of the crop ; if you reckon these expenses and these losses, they very far exceed in amount the expenses of the way that I recommend. The usual practice in America very much resembles the practice here, and is attended with much about the same consequences. Those who do the thing well there, break up the pasture, and cultivate grain of different sorts, or Indian corn, until the trees have attained a size to set all cattle at defiance. The finest orchard that I ever saw belonged to Mr. PLATT in the township of North Hempstead in Long Island. The rows of trees were at about thirty feet apart, and the trees at about twenty-five feet apart in the row, the trees of one row placed opposite the intervals of the other row. This

N

gave him about six hundred trees upon ten acres of land. When I saw the trees, they had attained pretty nearly their full size, and had come to within a few feet of causing the extreme branches of one tree to touch those of another. It is the fashion in that country to shake down the apples that are intended for cider, and to gather those only that are intended for eating. As soon as the apples are shaken down, they are put up into heaps in the form of haycocks, in which state they lie till they are removed to be made into cider; and, I remember seeing them in this state in Mr. PLATT's orchard, the cocks being as thick upon the ground as those of a middling crop of hay. This gentleman, from whose orchard came the first cuttings that I received from America, had a very pretty nursery of his own, and solely for his own use. In that he propagated all his fruit-trees, and he planted them out very small in his orchards, taking care, when he sowed the orchards with grain, not to suffer the wheat or the rye or the oats to stand too close to the young trees. After the trees get to be stout, and able to resist cattle, the land is laid down for grass, and in so hot a country, the shade of the trees is no injury to the grass; but appears to be the contrary; for the cattle there will feed under the shade of trees, when they will not feed elsewhere. The after-pruning of orchard-trees consists in constantly taking off all shoots that come out any where in the middle of the tree, and in carefully cutting away every bit of dead wood, whether occasioned by blight, by wind, or by any other cause. As to the *cultivation* of orchards, when the trees begin to give out bearing, or to bear poor or small fruit, they, in America, first put manure to a good distance round the tree;

but, they are soon after that compelled to plough up the whole of the land, to manure it, and to take a crop or two of grain, most frequently buck wheat, ploughing always as deep as they can : after this, they lay the land down with grass again ; and thus they keep up the bearing of their orchards. Mr. PLATT had a curious mode of making strong cider : in the month of January or February, he placed a number of hogsheads of cider upon stands out of doors. The frost turned to ice the upper part of the contents of the hogshead, and a tap drew off from the bottom the part which was not frozen. This was the spirituous part ; and was as strong as the very strongest of beer that can be made. The frost had no power over this part ; but the lighter part which was at the top, it froze into ice. This, when thawed, was weak cider. This method of getting strong cider would not do in a country like this, where the frosts are never sufficiently severe. As to the sorts of apples and of other fruit-trees, they will be spoken of under the respective heads in the Alphabetical List.

ALPHABETICAL LIST OF FRUITS.

261. APPLE.—Apples are usually grafted on crab-stocks ; but when you do not want the trees to grow so very tall and large, it is better to raise the stocks from apple-pips ; because they certainly come into bearing sooner, Some graft apples upon stocks raised from

layers; and these certainly bring trees to bear quicker.
The layers being raised in the manner before-mentioned,
from the limbs and shoots of apple-trees. See the word
layer in the Index. Every thing having before been said
relative to the propagating, the planting, the training,
and the pruning of apple-trees, there remains to be
spoken of here nothing but the different sorts. To give
an opinion as to the best sorts would perhaps be useless,
where the sorts are so numerous, and when tastes are so
different. I shall, therefore, with regard to eating
apples, simply give from Mr. AITON's *Hortus Kewensis*, a
list of the apples grown in the King's gardens: I shall then
give the names of some of the American apples of the
eating kind; after which I shall make an observation or
two upon cider apples. Those of the king's gardens are
as follows: *Borstoff Apple, Golden Harvey, Golden Rennet,
Golden Russet, Juneting, Margill, Common Nonpareil,
Scarlet Nonpareil, Nonsuch, Brookes' Pippin, Cockle Pippin,
Court of Wick Pippin, Downton Pippin, Fearn's Pippin,
Frankland's Pippin, Golden Pippin, Padley's Pippin, Red
Ingestrie Pippin, Ribston Pippin, Robinson's Pippin, Ronald's
Pippin, Summer Pippin, Spice Pippin, Pomme d'Api, Pomme
Noire, Pomme Grise, Quarenden, Sack-and-Sugar, Syke
house, Bigg's Nonsuch, Summer Codlin, Autumn Codlin,
Spring Codlin, Costard, French Crab, French Minchin,
Mawthorn dean, Kirke's Scarlet Admirable, Lemon Pippin,
Minier's Dumpling, Norfolk Beaufin, Autumn Pearmain,
Scarlet Pearmain, Winter Pearmain.* On the American
apples I can offer some opinion. The earliest is *Woolley's
Summer Pearmain*; and I call it Woolley's, because Mr.
WOOLLEY of North Hempstead introduced me to the
knowledge of it and gave me some of the fruit in the

year 1817. It is a long apple, shaped somewhat like the old English pearmain, beautifully striped red and white, and ripe in the month of August. I have very few of these. The apple which succeeds this is the *Fall Pippin*, and it continues to be good to eat until the middle of November. Then comes the *Greening*, which continues to be very good to eat until February; and then comes the *Newtown Pippin*, which, if properly preserved, is very good to eat until the month of June. For my own part, I should wish for no sorts but these, except I added *Conklin's Pie Apple*, the reputation of which is very great. There is the *Doctor Apple* of exceeding beauty, and very good until late in November; but, indeed, after January comes, there is no apple wanted either for eating raw or cooking, but the *Newtown Pippin*, which, to the qualities of fine relish and long keeping, adds the other great quality of being a surprisingly great bearer. It hardly ever totally fails, even when other trees do; and it generally has a large crop. I have a tree in my garden at Kensington, which was covered with fruit in 1826. It stood against a wall, and I was afraid that it would be killed by a foul drain oozing through the wall from the out-premises of one of my neighbours: I moved it, therefore, in the month of April, 1827, to another part of the garden, and, large as it was, it is now (May, 1828) well-loaded with fruit. I never saw any thing more beautiful than the tree now is, whether in shoot, leaf, or fruit. The cuttings, which came from Mr. PLATT at North Hempstead, were put upon the several little limbs of an old dwarf standard-tree; but the whole now appears as if it had been all from a young original stock. There are numerous sorts of excellent American apples; but I do not think it necessary to speak of any others. Something, however, may be said about apples for cooking. There are our own *codlings*, which come earliest : *Conklin's pie-apple* I have mentioned, the *Russettings* are very fine for this purpose, and they keep a long while : the *Spitzen-berg Pippin* is a fine large apple for this purpose, keeps through the greater part of the winter, and bears surprizingly. In Herefordshire the apples most highly esteemed for this purpose are the *Quining*, or *Queening*, and the *Boovey red-streak*, they are both very fine apples, but particularly the former. There are some excellent sorts in Devonshire; but, as to sorts, people will generally be directed by their taste, or by the fashion of the neighbourhood. With regard to cider apples, it would be useless to speak of sorts, and rather beside my subject, seeing that I am treating of things not to make liquor of, but to be used for the table. To preserve apples throughout the winter is a thing of great consequence. First, the sort is to be attended to ; for an apple that is not of a keeping nature will not keep. If the quantity be small, I have found that wrapping each apple in a piece of paper and packing in a chest is the best way. In all cases, they should be carefully hand-gathered, *laid* in the basket which you use in the gathering, and not *tossed* into it ; for, the smallest bruise leads with certainty to rottenness. They should be quite ripe before they be gathered ; and yet, when quite ripe, they fall with the least shake of the limb. Here is one of the great advantages of *espaliers*, the limbs of which cannot be shaken with the wind ; while, as every one knows, much about half the crop is shaken down by the wind from the greater part of standard-trees long before the apples are ripe.   When apples are gathered, they should be laid upon cloths or mats in the sun, or in some dry airy place, until they become perfectly dry in every part of them.   If the quantity be large, they ought to be laid upon a floor or upon broad fruit-shelves ; but not one upon the other.   Clean straw laid under them is very good ; but I have found a single new mat to be better : they should be looked over frequently to see if they begin to rot, and such as do begin ought to be immediately taken away.   When there is frost, all that you have to do is, to keep the apples in a state of total darkness until some days after a complete thaw has come.   In America they are frequently frozen as hard as stones : if they thaw in the *light*, they rot ; but if they thaw in darkness, they not only do not rot, but lose very little of their original flavour.   This may be new to the English reader ; but he may depend upon it that the statement is correct.

262. APRICOT.— With regard to the propagation, the planting, and the training of the tree, the instructions have already been given under the head of Training and Pruning.   The pruning differs from the peach in that the apricot generally bears upon spurs, some of which are formed by nature, and others may be formed in the manner directed in the case of the espalier apple.   The apricot does not require so much attention as the peach and the nectarine in the providing of new wood ; because those trees bear only upon the last year's wood ; but, occasionally new shoots ought to be laid in to supply the place of branches taken off by the *blast*, which very frequently takes off a whole branch, and even a whole limb, without any apparent cause.   The apricot tree is not

subject to mildew, and to the various blights to which
the peach and other fruit-trees are subject; but it is subject to this blast, of which I have never heard a reasonable cause assigned. The proper situation for the apricot-
tree is a wall facing the east or the west. Facing the
south is as good, perhaps, but that situation is wanted
for the peaches, the nectarines and the vines. The
apricot is a prodigious bearer, and of life equal to that of
an oak. It will bear, and bear prodigiously, too, after
the trunk is perfectly hollow, and there is nothing left of
it but the mere shell. It is well-known that the young
fruit, when of the size of a half-grown walnut, is used
for the making of tarts, and for other purposes; and,
though, in my opinion, inferior to green gooseberries, is
more highly esteemed, because it is more rare. Whether
part of the fruit be gathered for this purpose or not,
courage should not be wanting to thin the fruit so as not
to leave it at nearer than six inches at the most from
each other upon the tree. A tree eight feet high, and
spreading seven feet from each side of the trunk, will
cover a space of a hundred and twelve square feet: the
fruit, at six inches apart, would be four apricots to a
foot, that is to say, four hundred and forty-eight apricots
upon the tree, or pretty nearly thirty-eight dozen. It is
not to be supposed, however, that the fruit would be distributed equally over every part of the tree; but, suppose you have half the number, what prodigious quantities must come from either of the end walls of the
garden! There is no greater error than that of permit-
ting trees to bear too great a quantity of fruit. Generally speaking, you have the same weight in half
the number that you have in the whole number if too

numerously left : then, you prevent the tree from bearing the next year ; for it has not strength to provide for blossoms, while it is strained to its utmost in the bearing of fruit. This being a matter of so much importance, and applicable to all sorts of fruit-trees, I beg the reader to observe how fully this opinion is supported by the two instances which I am about to cite. Under the head CUCUMBER, I have observed (and the fact is notorious to all gardeners), that if you leave one fruit to stand for seed, the plant instantly ceases to bear : it is the same with kidney-beans. " Gather cucumbers and *have* cucumbers, gather kidney-beans and *have* kidney-beans," are maxims as old as the hills. These are annual plants ; and, therefore, the consequences of causing them to make the grand exertion of ripening their fruit are apparent the same year. As to fruit-trees, it is notorious that, in this country, orchard trees seldom bear great crops two years running ; but here the matter is irregular owing to the *blights,* and, therefore, the effect of over-bearing is a fact not so well established as it is in America where there are no blights. In that country, the thing is so well known, that nothing is more common than for a man, going into one part of the country from another, to ask whether that is the bearing year in that neighbourhood ; and it never yet was known that two bearing years succeeded each other with regard to the same tree. Some sorts of apples (and the Fall Pippin is one of them) bear upon some limbs of the tree one year, and upon other limbs of the tree another year ; and you will frequently see a limb or two loaded with fruit while not an apple is to be seen on any other part of the tree. This doctrine, therefore, I take to be firmly established.

With regard to apples and fruit of about the same value, the consequence is not very great; but, in the case of wall-fruit, you want a crop every year; and, therefore, you must take away one year that which would prevent bearing the next. Cherries may, perhaps, be an exception here; because they take care to make the superabundant fruit drop off at a very early age; but, then, there is another consideration with regard to which even cherries form no exception; and that is, that, if the fruit be too numerous, it is smaller than it ought to be. Perhaps in hardly any case, the greater number produces any thing like a proportionate weight to the smaller number: and, as to the quality, the superiority of the small number is great indeed. The apricot should not be gathered until it be almost ready to fall from the tree; and, if the sort be good, it is preferred by many persons to the peach. As to sorts, the following are those mentioned by Mr. AITON in the *Hortus Kewensis:* the *Black*, the *Brussels*, the *Masculine*, the *Moor Park*, and the *Royal Orange*. For my part, I recommend the *Moor Park*, and the *Turkey*. The former is fine, and a good bearer: the latter not a good bearer, but superlatively fine. Mr. MARSHALL recommends the *Breda*, to ripen in September. The *Masculine*, the *Brussels*, and the *Black*, are cultivated only because they come early: they are in my opinion very poor fruit: they might be planted as espaliers in very warm situations; but are certainly unworthy of a good wall. Besides the use of apricots as fruit from the tree, they make the most delicious of all preserves; and, while, in the season of their ripeness, mixing them with apples in pies and tarts, make a great improvement in the article. The apricot is, on all accounts, a tree deserving of the greatest attention : it usually blows in February, or March at the latest, and ought to be pruned before the blossom buds begin to burst. .As to the protecting of the blossoms from frost, I shall give general directions for that under the head of Peach.

263. BARBERRY.—This fruit is well .known. The tree or shrub on which it grows is raised from the seed or from suckers or layers. It needs little care ; and should stand in the outer part of the garden, and in the shade of the hedge ; for, the hot sun tends to prevent the fruit from growing large.

264. CHERRY.—Cherries are budded or grafted upon stocks raised from cherry-stones, of the manner of raising which stocks I have spoken under the head of PROPAGATION. If you wish to have the cherry tree for a wall or an espalier, the stocks should be raised from the stones of the *Morello,* or the *May-Duke.* As to the management of the tree in its early stages, and the planting of it out, directions have been given under the head of PLANTING. Cherry trees, except the *Morello* and one or two more, bear upon spurs ; and great care should be taken in the forming and the preserving of these spurs, all the rules for doing which have been mentioned under the head of espalier apple. Cherry trees do exceedingly well as espaliers ; and, as standards, though they bear prodigiously, the crop is for the birds and not for the gardener. As espaliers, they may, as I have before observed, be most conveniently covered with a net. In the gathering, too, the espalier form is of

great advantage : the fruit may be clipped off with a sharp-pointed scissors, without exposing the spurs to injury. As to the sorts of cherries, those mentioned in the *Hortus Kewensis*, are as follows : *All Saints, Bigarreau, Elton, Carnation, Crown, Kentish, May-Duke, Late Duke, Morello, Ronald's Superbe, Harrison's Heart, Black Heart, White Heart.* The Kentish cherry, good for very little, is the earliest ; the May-Duke the next ; and then come the others. The May-Duke is one of the finest of all the cherries, and is the only one made use of in forcing. If suffered to hang until it be quite ripe, it becomes nearly black, and then it is better, perhaps, than any other cherry. Besides these garden cherries, there is the little black cherry, which are vulgarly called merries, by a corruption of the French word *merise*. This is the cherry of the common people, and is too well-known to need any particular description. The Bigarreaus are very large and very fine ; but they require a good wall, or a very warm situation as espaliers.

265. CHESNUT.——This is an inhabitant of the woods. It is generally called the Spanish chesnut : those from America grow to a greater height, but have smaller, though sweeter, fruit. Chesnuts are raised from the seed ; though to have the very fine ones that grow in Brittany, the cuttings are generally got from that country, and put upon chesnut stocks in England. To preserve chesnuts, so as to have them to sow in the spring, or to eat through the winter, you must make them perfectly dry after they come out of their green husk ; then put them into a box or a barrel mixed with, and covered over by, fine and dry sand, three gallons of

sand to one gallon of chesnuts. If there be maggots in any of the chesnuts, they will come out of the chesnuts and work up through the sand to get to the air; and thus you have your chesnuts sweet and sound and fresh. To know whether chesnuts will *grow*, toss them into water: those that swim will not grow. To raise a chesnut tree with a straight stem or trunk, follow precisely the directions given for the planting and raising of orchard trees.

266. CRANBERRY.—This fruit is not much cultivated in England, notwithstanding its excellent qualities in the making of tarts, and in the making of sauce to be eaten with mutton or venison. The finest cranberries come from America, where the plants creep about upon the ground in the swamps. If cultivated in England, they must grow in some wet place, and be kept clear of weeds: the plant creeps over the ground, like other creeping plants; and I saw them bearing very well by the side of a running stream at Aldbury in Surrey. Cranberries make an excellent preserve, and they may be kept throughout the winter in their natural state, either laid in a heap in a dry room, or put into a barrel amongst water. I have imported them from America, sometimes barrelled up in water, and sometimes not; and always sound and good.

267. CURRANT.—This, though a low shrub, bears a fruit at once popular, plentiful, and excellent in its qualities; and, it is one of the great fruits of England, though not the same in many other countries. It is raised with the greatest facility by cuttings of the last year's wood, taken off in February, and planted in a cool

place after the manner directed under the head of *cuttings,* which word see in the Index. The cutting gets roots the first summer, and the next fall or spring, it may be removed to the spot where it is finally to stand. Some currant trees may be placed in a warm situation so as for the fruit to come early; but the finest currants are those which grow rather in the shade; the fruit becomes larger there and has not the disagreeable tartness which it acquires if ripened in a hot sun. This shrub flourishes and bears well under the shade of other trees, as is seen so frequently and to such great extent in the market gardens near London. When the young currant tree is planted out, it ought not to be suffered to have any limbs within five or six inches of the ground; but should be made to have a clear and straight trunk to that height. When the limbs come out, or rather the shoots that are to become limbs, there should not be more than four or six suffered to go on as principal limbs. By shortening the shoots at the end of the first year, you double the number of limbs. These, as in the case of the espalier apple-tree, are to be kept constantly clear of side-shoots by cutting off, every winter, the last summer's wood within one bud or so of the limb; and when the limbs have attained their proper length, the shoot at the end of each limb should also be annually cut off, so that, the tree when it has received its pruning, consists of a certain number of limbs, looking like so many rugged sticks, with bunches of spurs sticking out of them, as in plate 7. On these spurs come the fruit in quantities prodigious. If you neglect to prune in the manner here directed, the centre of the tree becomes crowded with wood, and the small quantity of fruit that comes near the point of the limbs, is very poor and small. This method of pruning currants (and, as will be seen by and by, that of gooseberries is the same) is amongst the very greatest of improvements in gardening, and is a discovery to be as-

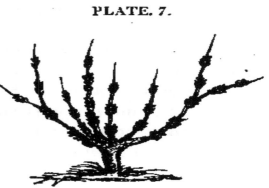

PLATE. 7.

cribed solely to the market-gardeners in the neighbourhood of London, like a great many other things in the art of gardening, in which they far excel all the rest of the world. Mr. MARSHALL in his book on gardening, and the French authors in all their books, describe a method very different indeed, from this, which is, at once, so simple and so efficacious, causing to be produced such immense quantities of fruit and always of the best quality : hanging to one single joint of a currant tree, in the market gardens, you frequently see as much fruit as will fill a plate. One tree pruned in this manner is equal to more than six trees pruned in the manner practised in general throughout the country. But, these gardeners excel all the world in every thing that they undertake to cultivate : they beat all the gentlemen's gardeners in the kingdom : nothing ever fails that depends upon their skill, and I should be ungrateful, indeed, if I did not acknowledge that I have learned more from them than from all the books that I have read in my life, and from all that I ever saw practised in gentlemen's gardens. There are three sorts of currants, distinguished by their different colours of *red*, *white*, and *black*, and the several uses of all these are too well known to need any description.

268. FIG.—There are several sorts of figs, but some of them will not ripen in England. Figs are raised either from cuttings or layers, which are to be treated in the manner directed under those heads, which see in the index. The fig must stand against a wall, and a warm wall, too. The great difficulty with regard to figs, is, that they must be suffered to grow in their own way, without much training or pruning ; and are therefore very unsightly things. The ground in which they stand should be made as rich as possible. They have the singularity that some of their fruit is hardly formed at a time when part of it is ripe, and that thus a succession of bearing is kept up until the frost comes. As far as my observation has gone, comparatively few people like figs, on account of their mawkish taste ; but, in a very fine summer, the fruit is good and rich, and the number of the fruit is generally very great.

269. FILBERD.—This is a fruit well known to us all. The tree, or rather, lofty shrub, is raised from suckers or layers : the latter is best because those raised from suckers, infest the ground with suckers. You cannot propagate a filberd from seed, it being one of those plants the seed of which does not, except by mere accident, produce fruit equal to that of the tree from which it comes. The plants raised from layers, or the suckers, ought to be put into a nursery in rows two feet apart, and at two feet distance in the row. They will then become little trees by the end of two years, and they

should not stand there longer before they be finally re-moved. A very good situation for filberds would be not far from the hedge in the outer garden ; where they should never be suffered to grow to too great a height ; never higher than to make it a matter of no difficulty to gather the fruit with the hand. In Kent, which county produces more filberds than all the rest of the country put together, the trees are planted in rows at about ten or twelve feet apart, and at about the same distance apart in the row. Care is taken to have a clear stem or trunk about a foot high, after which limbs are suffered to come out in every direction. Care is taken to prevent any limbs from going upright above a certain height, and an annual pruning takes place in the winter to take out all dead wood, all shoots that cross one another, and to keep the middle of the tree clear, so that the sun and air find their way to every part of it. Filberds, like every description of hazel, will grow and bear under the shade of lofty trees ; but the fruit is not so abundant and not nearly so fine. To preserve filberds for use through the winter, and until the spring, follow precisely the direction given in the case of the chesnut. There are two sorts of filberds, the *scarlet* and the *grey,* those being the colours of the skins of the kernals. Filberds are really never good till they are quite ready to drop out of the husk, or green shell, and until the bud ends of them are white : if taken out of the husk at an earlier stage than this, the kernels will shrivel.

270. GOOSEBERRY.—This is a fruit, which, in all its qualities, is upon a par with the currant, whether for eating in its natural state, for cooking, or for preserving ; for, though we in England do not commonly make use

of green currants, in America, they always make use of them in preference to green gooseberries : in which respect, as in a great many others, the people of that country have taken their habits from the northern parts of England. When the *green* currants are used in a cooked state, the *ripe* gooseberries are used in that state. Gooseberries are propagated, planted out, trained, and pruned, in precisely the same manner as directed for currants. See paragraph 266. Neither of these little shrubs should be planted by the side of walks, where they interfere in a very troublesome manner with the cultivation of the plats and borders. They should have a piece of ground devoted to their exclusive occupation, and should be planted at distances sufficient to allow of going round them conveniently to gather the fruit. For gooseberries and currants there might be plenty of room in a part of the wall between the hedge and the garden. Sometimes currants are placed against a wall facing to the north ; and their fruit if properly protected will hang on to the latter end of October or later. These two very useful fruits have most destructive enemies in the small birds, especially the sparrows and the finches, which feed upon their fruit-buds, and upon the fruit when very young ; and the black-birds, thrushes, and some others, which feed upon them when ripe. To keep the birds off in the spring is a very difficult matter. Frequent shooting at them, or the attendance of some person constantly upon the spot to frighten them away, is necessary ; and these means can be but partly efficient ; for, who is to rise so early as birds, which are always upon the wing for their food, not only before sun-rise, but sometime before day-light. As to the preserving of currants and gooseberries until late in the fall, if you have preserved them until they be ripe, it is a much easier matter. If the currant-tree be against a wall, nothing is more easy than to cover it over with a mat nailed to the wall; and a standard tree is covered completely by a couple of good new mats, well joined together and closely drawn round at the bottom, and fastened round the stem of the tree. Trees, however, subjected to this discipline do not bear so well the next year. The sorts of gooseberries are very numerous. The following is the list cultivated in the King's gardens : *Claret, Early Lincoln, Golden drop, Goliah, Green-gage, Imperial, Keen's seedling, Lomax's victory, Old Briton, Pope, Rumbullion, Warrington.* The *Keen's seedling*, raised by MR. KEEN at Islington, is valued very much on account of its *thorns*, which are so numerous and so sharp and so well placed as to keep the small birds from the buds and the young fruit. For many years it has been the fashion to give the preference to gooseberries of a large size, and the people of Lancashire (chiefly the weavers) have been famous for their success in this way; but, as quality is far preferable to size, I regret the almost total disappearance of the little smooth black gooseberry, and of the little hairy red gooseberry, both of which have very thin skins, and are of flavour delicious. The big gooseberries are nearly all skin, and the pulp is of a very mean flavour. For several years I have not seen a black gooseberry tree in any garden except that of some old farm house; but I would earnestly recommend to the reader to obtain these two sorts if he can.

271. GRAPE.—See VINE.

272. HUCKLEBERRY.—I do not recommend the cultivation of this in a garden ; though two or three rod of ground may very well be bestowed upon it. It grows wild in the heaths of Surrey, Sussex and Kent, and in many other parts of the kingdom, and is a very good fruit for tarts, when mixed with currants, and by no means bad to eat in its raw state. The benefit of cultivation would doubtless make the fruit larger and of finer flavour.

273. MEDLAR.—A very poor thing, indeed, propagated by grafting on pear stocks or crab stocks. It is hardly worth notice, being, at best, only one degree better than a rotten apple.

274. MULBERRY.—This tree is raised from cuttings or from layers after the manner directed under those heads. It is planted out like an apple or a pear tree. It should not stand in the kitchen garden for it grows to a great size, and should have grass beneath to receive the falling fruit, which is never so good when gathered from the tree. It is well known that silk-worms feed on the mulberry leaf, especially on that of the white mulberry, which is cultivated for that purpose in France and Italy, and which grows wild in America, bearing prodigiously. The other sort is the red mulberry, or purple, as it ought to be called, and this is the only sort that is common in England.

275. MELON.—As to the rearing of melons, that has been fully treated of in the foregoing Chapter. The sorts is all that we have to do with here. The following s the list of those cultivated in the King's gardens.

Early Cantaleupe, Early Leopard, Early Polignac, Early Romana, Green-fleshed netted, Green-fleshed rock, Bossé's Early rock, Black rock, Silver rock, Scarlet-fleshed rock. In America, there is a melon of oblong shape, of small size, and of most delicate flavour. They call it the nutmeg melon; the vines are very slender. It is quick in bearing, its colour, when ripe, is of a greenish yellow, and its flesh very nearly approaching to white. This is the finest melon that I ever tasted. The great things that come from France sometimes, are very little better than a squash or a pumpkin. I had some white-coated melons the seed of which came from Spain : they weighed from eight to twelve pounds a-piece; but were, in point of flavour, not a bit better than a white turnip. The rock melons of various sorts are, in my opinion, but very poor things ; there is no part of them, except just the middle, that is not *hard*, unless you let the fruit remain till it be nearly rotten. Indeed all the red-fleshed melons are hard; and I never have seen any melon of that description that I really liked to eat. The little American melon which is grown there in great quantities in the natural ground, may be eaten all out with a spoon, leaving a rind at least not thicker than a shilling : it has twice the quantity of eatable pulp as a great rock melon. But there is the water-melon, resembling other melons only in its manner of growing, and somewhat in the shape and size of the leaf. The size of these may be put down at from ten to thirty pounds weight. The flesh is not at all like that of other melons. From the skin inwards, an inch wide, it is white, like the flesh of a green cucumber, but harder ; after that, towards the centre of the fruit, come ribs resembling long honey-combs, and, except that the colour is pink, or between pink and scarlet, looking precisely like so much frozen snow. This is the part that is eaten ; and the fruit is called the *water-melon*, because these ribs actually instantly turn to water in your mouth.   This is the favourite fruit of all ranks and degrees, and of all ages, in hot countries ; and, when the weather is very hot, the refreshing effects of tasting the fruit are really surprising.   In England, this sort of melon may be cultivated in the same manner, though with somewhat more difficulty than the common sorts, or musk melons ; but they want greater heat and more room.   I have grown them very fine in England ; and I have now a pot of plants to repeat the attempt this year (1828).   The seed is large and black, and the coat, after the melon gets to be of considerable size, is always of the deepest green.   One great difficulty is, to know when the fruit is ripe ; for it emits no odour, like the musk melon, and never changes its colour, not even after the whole of the inside is rotten.   In America, there is only here and there a man skilful enough to ascertain, by rapping his knuckles upon the fruit, whether the fruit be ripe.   Unskilful people *plug* them ; that is to say, take out a piece, as you do out of a cheese, to taste it, and then replace the plug.   Other melons generally become ripe in about 5 or 6 weeks after they begin to swell ; in the case of water melons, the best way would probably be to write down the time of setting and beginning to swell of each fruit ; and to allow seven weeks, perhaps, instead of 6 weeks, before you cut the fruit.

276. NECTARINE. — To be propagated, planted, trained and pruned, precisely in the same manner as di-

rected for the peach. Nectarines rarely succeed in England so well as peaches. They do not ripen so well: they get into a shrivelled state before they are ripe, the cause of which I never have been able to ascertain. The sorts are numerous. Those cultivated in the King's gardens are the following : *Early Newington, Late Newington, Brugnon, Violette hâtive, Du Tellier's, Elruge, Fairchild's, Late Genoa, Murray, White.* There are two other nectarines, the *Sweet Violet,* and the *Temple.* I recommend the *White French,* a very beautiful fruit, and a great and constant bearer, the *Violette hâtive,* and the *Du Tellier's.* I have never known the rest to ripen well. The White French, though not of so very fine a flavour as the other three, is so beautiful a fruit and so great a bearer that no garden should ever be without it. To preserve the blossoms will come under the head of peach ; and the thinning of the fruit has already been spoken of under the head of apricot. The rules there given relative to this matter being applicable to all fruit trees that grow against a wall or in espalier.

277. NUT.—The mere hazel-nut such as is produced in the coppices, and in quantities so prodigious that, in the year 1826, it was calculated that there were a greater number of four-bushel sacks of nuts, at Weyhill Fair, than of bags of hops ; though all the hops grown at Farnham and a considerable part of those grown in Kent, are taken to that fair. Of course this is not a thing for a garden nor even for an orchard ; but, there are certain nuts called *Cob-nuts,* of three times the bulk of the common nut, and with kernals of nearly as fine flavour as that of the filberd. These are propagated, planted,

trained and pruned, in precisely the same manner as the filberd ; for the seed will not produce a tree to resemble the fruit of the original tree, except by mere accident.

278. PEACH.—The propagation, planting, training and pruning, have already been spoken of fully; but I have here to speak of the preserving or protecting the blossoms of wall-trees. The peach, like the nectarine, will bear, and sometimes ripen the fruit well, against a wall facing the west ; facing the east, neither does well ; and the proper situation of both, is, a wall facing the south. Here the situation is as warm as our climate will suffer it to be ; but the bloom comes out at so early a season that that season is always a time of anxiety with the gardener, on account of the frosts by which the blossoms are frequently so severely attacked as to prevent the coming of any crop at all. To protect the blossoms, therefore, against the frost is a matter of great import-ance. The boughs of the yew-tree and other evergreens ; or, the spreading parts of fern, are used for this purpose, Some people nail up mats in the evening and take them off in the morning ; but to mat is very tiresome ; and, as to the boughs and the fern, they must remain on day and night ; and, what with the putting them on and the taking them off and their keeping off the sun and air from the buds and the fruit, they generally do as much harm as good. Frosts descend ; that is to say, their destructive effect comes down upon a tree perpendicularly. It is not the *cold* that destroys the germ of the fruit. It is the wet joined to the cold. That which is dry will not freeze ; frost has power on those things only which have moisture in them ; and though there is moisture in the

blossom, that is not sufficient of itself to give the frosts the power of destruction. When frosts come without rain or dews, they do very little harm to blossoms. Therefore, the thing to be desired, is, something to keep off the wet during the time that the blossom is becoming a fruit. The best way of doing this is to have something going out from the top of the wall to about a foot and a half wide, which might remain day and night, until the dangerous season were over. The thing recommended by a very able and experienced French writer, M. DE COMBLE, is, a board of that width, supported by posts at convenient distances. These posts, however, besides their unsightliness, I object to on account of the holes that must be made for placing them in the ground. To obviate this, and to cause the operation to be little troublesome, I would, in the building of my wall, have, in the row of bricks next to the top row, what the bricklayers call a wooden brick, at suitable distances. In these wooden bricks (to be made of the most durable wood), might be holes for the purpose of admitting the end of a stout piece of iron, about, perhaps, two feet long, besides the part necessary to enter into the brick. When the blooming season arrived, and just before the blossoms began to burst, these pieces of iron would be put into the holes in the bricks and there fastened by means easily to be invented; upon these pieces of iron the boards might be laid all along the wall; the boards might be fastened down to the pieces of iron by holes made in the former to admit a small cord to fasten the former to the latter, and thus the whole would remain safe against the power of the winds until the season arrived when the fruit would be out of danger. The board might be

o

placed rather in a sloping direction, in order to prevent rains from pouring upon it and running down the wall. When done with, these protecting materials might be safely laid aside until the next year : here is a method, at once little expensive, little troublesome, not at all annoying to the trees, and perfectly effectual. As to the *thinning of the fruit*, greater care is, if possible, necessary here than in the case of the apricot. No single shoot should, on any account, be suffered to bear more than two peaches ; and, if it be not a strong shoot, not more than one ; and this for the reasons amply given under the head of apricot ; where I ought to have observed, that it is not the producing of the *pulp* which requires the great effort from the tree ; but the bringing of the *seed* to perfection ; so that, though you are to have the same weight of peaches on a tree that should bear a hundred as on a tree that should bear two hundred ; still the effort required from the tree would be only half as great in the former case as in the latter ; because, in the former, there would be only half the number of *seeds*. The *sorts* of peaches are very numerous. I shall first give the list cultivated in the king's gardens, and then give my opinion, founded on experience. *Catherine, Incomparable, Old Newington, Royal Povey, Bear's Early, Bourdine, Chancellor, Early purple, Early Vineyard, French Mignonne, Gallande, Montagne, Noblesse, Persique, Red Magdalen, Royal George, Teton de Venus, Yellow Alberge.* The list of peaches which I recommend are the *Early Anne,* not very fine but early, and a constant bearer, the *Double Montagne,* the *Early Montaubon,* the *French Mignonne,* the *Grosse Mignonne,* the *Royal George,* the *Noblesse,* the *Early Gallande,* the *Late Gallande,* the *Vanguard,* the *Bellegarde,* the *Chancellor.*

and the *Violette hâtive.* These are the best peaches, according to my observation; and, after the *Early Anne,* I have placed them as they appear to me to be best in quality; that is to say, the best first, and the least good last. In point of bearing, the *Royal George* is a famous peach, and it is not much excelled in any other respect. Peaches should never be gathered (and the same with regard to nectarines) until just about to drop from the tree. They are not to be pulled; and if they do not come off with just putting your hand under them and giving them a little touch, they are not ripe; and an unripe peach is a very poor thing. Some people place a net along in front of the tree, tacked on one side to the wall, and supported on the other by little forked sticks, in order to catch the fruit when they fall, and to prevent bruising. And this is a very good way when you have not time to make an individual examination of the fruit; but, if one fall upon another, a bruising takes place in spite of the swagging situation of the net. Peaches and nectarines also may be preserved like apricots; and they make, if possible, still better pies and tarts; though, for these purposes, they should not be quite dead ripe. The greatest possible attention must be paid to have your trees of the right sort. When gentlemen go to a nursery to choose trees, and especially trained trees, they are too apt to be captivated by the appearance of the *plant*; but, as ill weeds grow apace, so it is with fruit trees. A *Catherine* or a *Magdalen* peach would be of twice the size in the same space of time as a *French Mignonne* or a *Montabon*; and, indeed, it may be laid down as a general rule, that, in proportion as the fruit excels, the stature of the tree is puny and its growth slow: it is the same through almost every thing in nature, and it would be strange, indeed, if peach trees formed an exception. With regard to the diseases to which the peach-tree is subject, and the enemies that it is exposed to, mention will be made of these hereafter.

279. PEAR.—The propagating and planting have already been noticed; because every thing in those respects said of the apple is applicable to the pear. In the rearing of orchards of pears also, the rules for the rearing of apple orchards apply in all respects whatever; and the reader should, therefore, now turn to those rules. Pears, in a still greater degree than apples, demand espalier training if they are of fine sorts. Indeed, these fine sorts, the greater part of which have come from France, are worthy of a good wall, facing the west, the east, or the north. As to the training and pruning of them, the rules are precisely those described under the head of *Espalier*, which see. Pears very seldom bear upon the last year's wood; but upon spurs in like manner as the apple does. No standard pear tree, any more than a standard apple-tree, should have place in a garden. All the reasons given for training apples in the espalier form, apply to pears, and with still greater force; for, it is perfectly useless to attempt to get fine pears upon standard-trees. Most trees will bear; but the fruit will not ripen, and will not be of good flavour even if they do. I have mentioned before, that the stocks for pears, are pears raised from the pip, quinces raised from cuttings or layers, or white-thorn raised from the stones. For wall-trees or espalier trees, quince stocks are the best; and that these may be had from the pips, is proved by this fact, that I have now more than a thousand

young pear trees grafted upon quince stocks raised from the pips. I got the pips from America, where quinces are grown in great abundance. It would be difficult to get the pips here, and, therefore, quince stocks must generally be raised from layers or cuttings. The quince-stocks are the best; because they do not force up wood so big and so lofty as the pear stocks. The white-thorn is very durable, and has a dwarf tendency; but it is apt to send out suckers; and certainly does not produce a tree so fruitful in its early stages as the quince-stock: the sorts of pears are almost endless. The French authors mention a hundred and fifty-two sorts. I shall insert the list from the *Hortus Kewensis*, and then mention those sorts which I think may content any man: It is: *Aston-town Pear, Autumn Bergamot, Gansel's Bergamot, Summer Bergamot, Brown beurrée, Golden beurrée, White beurrée, Bishop's Thumb, Winter Bonchrétien, Williams's Bonchrétien, Citron des Carmes, Chaumontelle, Crasanne, Colmar, D'Auch, Jargonelle, Lammas, Martin sec, Red Doyenné, Summer Rousselet, St. Germain, Swan's Egg, Verte-longue, Virgouleuse, Windsor, Catillac, Dr. Uvedale's St. Germain.* The only pears that I think necessary, are, for the summer, the *Green chisel*, which is the earliest of all, and if the fruit come from a tree well trained and pruned, it is by no means a mean pear; the *Catherine* pear, which is a little long pear with a beautiful red cheek; it does not rot at the heart as some pears do, and is nearly as great a bearer as the Green chisel itself, and that is a great bearer, indeed. The *Summer Bergamot*; and the *Summer Bonchrétien.* The autumn pears are, the *brown Beurré*, the *Autumn Bergamot*, and particularly the *Gansel's Bergamot*, which, in my opinion, very far surpasses the *Brown beurrée*. The winter pears that would satisfy me, are, the

Winter Bonchrétien, the *Colmar,* the *Crasanne,* and the *Poir d' Auch,* that is to say, the pear of the city of *Auch* in France. Pears for cooking are, *Parkinson's pear,* the *Cadillac,* and *Uvedale's St. Germain.* Besides these, there are two pears which I have propagated from cuttings brought from Long Island, and which appeared to have no name there : I call the one the *Long Island Autumnal Pear,* the very finest fruit of the pear kind, without any exception, that I ever tasted in my life. When ripe, which it is early in October, it is of a greenish yellow colour, weighs about three quarters of a pound, actually melts in your mouth, and, with a little care, keeps well to the middle of November. The other is what I call the *Long Island Perry pear,* which is of a middling size, very hard, and very rough to the taste when raw ; but this pear, when baked, or stewed and then preserved, is the finest thing of the kind that I ever saw. To these recommendations may be added, that this tree is as great a bearer as the Green chisel itself; and, which is rather singular of the pear and apple kind, the three years that I was in Long Island, these trees were loaded with fruit every year. Cattle and hogs are turned into the orchards of America to live and fatten upon the fruit : they take up from the ground those which they like best ; or they feed from the lower branches of the trees. I never perceived my cattle extremely anxious about other fruit ; but to get at the perry pears, the steers and oxen used to raise themselves upon their hind legs, which I very rarely saw them do in the case of any other tree. Their strong jaws could mash them; and they, therefore, were able to ascertain their sugary quality. Raw, they will keep all the winter long, and until the month of May ; and still be as solid and as hard as ever. I am sure that this is the best pear in the world for cooking, and, I think, for the making of perry. With regard to the gathering of pears for the table, the rules are precisely the same as those laid down in the case of the apple; though it may be observed that summer pears (which keep but for a short time) ought to be gathered a little while before they be ripe, and especially the *Green Chisel* and the *Catherine.*

280. PLUM.—As to the sort of stock, it must be the seed of the plum, as mentioned under the head of Propagation. The plum is budded in general, and not grafted; so is the cherry; but both may be grafted, and this is the common practice in America. As to the management of the budded plant, and as to planting out, directions have before been given, in the case of the peach, if against a wall; and, in the case of the espalier apple, if in the form of the espalier. Plums do not require so much room as other wall trees; nor do they require so much as apples, or pears, or cherries, in espalier. They bear generally upon spurs, seldom on the last year's wood; for training and pruning against a wall, the rules laid down under the head of APRICOT exactly apply; and, all the objection to standards, mentioned under the head of APPLE, equally apply here. Against a wall, plums are placed on walls facing the east, the west, or the north; and the *Green-gage* (queen of all plums), is finer when it has a northern aspect than when much exposed to the sun: it is not so sugary; but it is larger, comes in more by degrees, and is, in fact, of finer flavour than when exposed to a hot sun. As to the sorts of plums. Those cultivated in the king's gardens are as follows: *Red Bonum Magnum, White Bonum Magnum, Catherine, Coe's Golden Drop, Damascene, Drap d'Or,*

Fotheringham, Blue Gage, Green Gage, German Prune, Imperatrice, Mirabelle, Morocco, Early Orleans, Late Orleans, Blue Perdrigon, White Perdrigon, Précoce de Tours, Queen Mother Plum, Royale de Tours, Simiennes, Wine-sour, or Windsor. The *Green-gage* and the *Orleans* are the most fashionable plums ; though the *Blue Gage,* which comes late in the fall, is, in my opinion, one of the finest of plums ; and it is a very great bearer. All plums may be preserved with sugar : the green gage or the blue gage would be the best ; but *damsons* and *bullaces* are generally used, because they come more abundantly, and, of course, are not so difficult to obtain. The *Magnum Bonums* are fit for nothing but tarts and sweetmeats. *Magnum* is right enough ; but, as to *bonum,* the word has seldom been so completely misapplied.

281. QUINCE.—There is an apple-shaped and a pear-shaped. It is not a fruit to be eaten raw ; but to be put into apple-pies and some other things. They are to be preserved like apples ; and the trees are raised from cuttings or layers.

282. RASPBERRY. — There are two sorts, distinguished by their colours of red and white. There are some of each that bear a second crop in the autumn. The largest of raspberries is called the Antwerp, and a very fine fruit it is. Raspberries are propagated from offsets taken from the old stool: these are taken off in the fall, and they bear the next year. The stools ought to stand in rows at six feet apart, and at three feet apart in the row. It is very curious that in the northern countries of America, Nova Scotia and New Brunswick for instance, the raspberry plant dies completely down in

the fall of the year, and new shoots come up again out of the ground in the spring, much about after the manner of *fern*. These shoots bear the first year, though they do not make their appearance above ground until June; and where the land is clear of high trees, and where the August sun has shrivelled up the leaves of the raspberries, these shrubs form a sheet of red for scores of miles at a stretch. They are the summer fruit of the wild pigeon, and of a great variety of other birds. I once thought that raspberries would never bear upon the shoot of the year in England; but I have frequently, of late years, seen them bear upon such shoots. The stems of raspberries should be prevented from bending down, when loaded with leaves and with fruit, by stakes put along the sides of the rows; and by little rods tied to these stakes. Every stool will send out, during summer, a great number of shoots. When the leaf is down, these should be all taken away, except about four to produce fruit the next year. The shoots that have borne during the summer, die in the autumn : these should also be removed ; and, in November, and again in March, all the ground should be well and truly digged ; and the weeds should be kept down completely during the whole of the summer. One manuring in three years will be sufficient. The common little raspberry is but a poorish thing ; and every one should take care to have the Antwerp if possible. Raspberries, when gathered, will not bear much keeping or pressing : they are a very delicious fruit when taken at the proper time ; but, if put together in too great quantities, whether they be gathered carefully or not, they will taste badly directly, and, in twelve hours, they will be sour. Raspberries, like currants, are sometimes made use of, with the assistance of sugar, to make wine, and, in America, where strength is a great requisite, to make brandy; that. is to say, a parcel of brandy and sugar is put amongst the juice of the raspberries : these things I, for my part, totally disapprove of : that which we call currant wine, is neither more nor less than red-looking weak rum. The strength coming from the sugar; and gooseberry wine is a thing of the same character, and, if the fruit were of no other use than this, one might wish them to be extirpated. People deceive themselves. The thing is called *wine*; but it is *rum*: that is to say, an extract from sugar.

283. SERVICE.—A tree of the woods, where it bears a thing between a sloe and a haw. It is totally unfit to be eaten; and, therefore, I shall say no more about it.

284. STRAWBERRY.—Very different from the last article ! This is a fruit, exceeded in no one respect (except that of keeping) but by very few; and surpassing a very great majority of the fruits of this country. It is so well known, that to describe either plant or fruit would be almost an insult to the reader. I shall, therefore, have to speak only of the different sorts, and to describe the manner of propagating and cultivating the plants, so as to insure, or, at least, give the best chance of, fine fruit and large crops, no man ever having found that he had too much of this excellent fruit. Strawberry plants are raised in the following manner : the plant, while it is bearing, sends forth runners along upon the ground : these runners have several joints, and, at every joint, there comes out a root which penetrates down into the ground. Each of these roots sends up a plant; so that

the runner, if it extend to a yard or two, as it frequently will, would, perhaps, produce ten or a dozen plants. All these plants, if cut from the runner and planted out, would grow; but all of them would not bear the first year if so planted out. The runners begin to start usually in May, not making much progress at first, on account of the coldish weather; but, by the middle of June, the runners have produced an abundance of plants. You take the earliest and stoutest of these, plant them out before the end of the first week in August, and these plants will bear abundantly the next year. Great care must be taken in this planting. The ground should be made rich and fine : the root is but small, and the weather is hot : therefore, the root should be fixed well in the ground with the fingers ; and a little rain or pond water should be given to the plants. They should be attended to very carefully to see that worms do not tear them out of the ground or move them at all : the ground should be moved frequently between them, approaching as near to the plant as possible. By November, the plants will be stout : the winter, however severe, will do them no injury; and, in the month of June, when only a year old, they will produce a crop worth fifty times the labour bestowed upon them. When planted out, they ought to be placed from three to five in a clump, each plant at a few inches from the other. The clumps should be in rows of three feet apart, and, if it were four, it would be so much the better, and at three feet apart in the row. To cultivate strawberries in *beds*, suffering them to cover the whole of the ground with their runners and young plants, is a miserable method, proceeding from the suggestions either of idleness, or of greediness, and sure to lead to the defeating the object of this latter. Strawberries will bear a little in this way, though not much ; but the fruit will be of small and insipid flavour. Neither should even the clumps be suffered to stand to bear for more than two years. I have sometimes tried them the third year, but have never found it answer. But then to have new clumps is so easy that this can form an objection with no one. Having need of a certain number of clumps, you have only to take up those that have borne for two years, and plant just the same number of new ones. To remove strawberries from one place to another is the easiest thing in the world : you have nothing to do but to give a chop with a spade round the clump ; take it up and put it in the place where you wish to have it. This may be done at any time between October and May without the smallest chance of injuring the crop : to all its other excellent qualities, the strawberry adds hardiness of the plant, in a swamp, on a bank, amidst rocks, and upon the tops of walls, I have seen strawberries growing and bearing ; but stifling they will not endure ; and, therefore, if you want the industry and care to plant them at suitable distances and to keep them clear of grass and weeds, never expect a crop of strawberries. Before I come to speak of the different sorts, let me notice three things : preserving strawberries from the birds and slugs ; keeping them from being covered with dirt by the heavy rains ; and giving them water if the ground be at all dry. As to the first of these, the wood-pigeons, the common pigeons, the doves, the blackbirds, the jack daws, the thrushes, and even some of the small birds, invade the strawberry clumps, and, if unresisted, destroy a great part of the fruit. In this case, which happens when there are woods and shrubberies at hand, nothing is a protection but a net, held up by hoops or little forked sticks. The slug is a still more bitter enemy; and, in some seasons, where strawberries are suffered to run together in beds, more than half the fruit is consumed or spoiled by these nasty and mischievous reptiles. The remedy is, to examine the clumps well just as the strawberries are beginning to be ripe. See that there are no slugs about the stems of the leaves, and then make a little circle of hot lime, at half a foot or so at the extremity of the leaves of the clumps. No slug will enter that magic circle; but, if rain come, or even heavy dews, the lime becomes slack and powerless, and a little more must be put upon the circle, the least dust in the world being enough. The other precaution; namely, to keep the fruit from being beaten by the rain down amongst the dirt, short grass-mowings, or moss, the latter being the best of the two, should be laid round the stems of the plants, just as the fruit begins to ripen. This will completely guard against the evil: come what rain will, the fruit will always be clean. The last thing that I have to mention, is the *watering;* and a real good watering with rain-water, or pond-water, should be given just when the blossoms are falling and the fruit begins to set. Blacking the ground over with the rose of the watering-pot is of no use at all: the water should be poured out of the nose of the pot, held close down to the plant; and, one gallon of water, at least, should be given at one time to every clump of plants. If the weather be very hot in June, even while the fruit is ripening, and while you are gathering strawberries, they might have another such a watering, and that would be enough. Nothing have I ever found more difficult than, behind my back, to secure an honest watering. Watering-pots, when full, are heavy; the distance may be great, and few men like to carry heavy things for any long continuation. Just turn your back, and they merely wet the ground; and, if you return, you see that the strawberries have all been watered; but (and mind this), *go the next day*, if the weather have continued fair, and you will then see how you have been cheated. Strawberries like good, deep, and rich land: *holding land*, as the people in the country call it: they will grow almost any where, and will produce more or less of fruit; but, if you mean to have fine strawberries, you must have good land; therefore, make the land as good as you can make it. As to the sorts of strawberries, the *scarlet* is the earliest; and some people like it; the *hautbois* (or high-stalked), the *Kew pine*, the *Chili*, the *White Alpine* and the *Red Alpine*; which two latter are vulgarly called *wood strawberries*. The hautboy has a musky and singular flavour as well as smell, and some people prefer it to all others. But, the great strawberry of all, now-a-days, is that which was some years ago raised from seed by Mr. KEEN of Islington, which is therefore called the KEEN's *seedling*; and this strawberry, which is the only one used for forcing in the King's gardens, has nearly supplanted every other sort. It is early; it is a prodigious bearer; the fruit is large, and very large; and it surpasses, in my opinion, all others in flavour. I gathered some of the *Kew pine* (for many years thought the best of all); at the same time, I gathered some of the *Keen's seedling*: I put the two parcels down upon the table before several persons, who tasted both in order to form a judgment; and every one of them said that the *Keen's seedling* was the best, I having taken care not to let any of them know which was which. But the London market speaks to the character of this strawberry. Notwithstanding habit and prejudice, the London gardeners have found that no other strawberry will sell ; and, in fact, there is hardly any other now brought to the markets. The Alpines are poor hard little things ; and, as to the Chili (nearly as large as a pigeon's egg), it is very little superior in flavour to the potatoe. In my "*American Gardener*," I have recommended the forming of strawberry plantations into *beds*, knowing that it was impossible to prevail upon people in that country to take the pains required to cultivate them in clumps.

285. VINE.—It is the practice in England to cultivate vines only against walls, against houses, upon roofs of houses, and under glass ; but, that it might be cultivated otherwise on many spots in the south of England, the history of the country most amply proves to us. For a series of ages there were extensive vineyards in England ; and wine made here very nearly as good as that of France. I remember seeing, when I was a boy, a beautiful vineyard, in extent, I should think, of two or three acres, in the grounds of the estate called PAINSHILL at COBHAM, in Surrey. The vines were there planted in rows, and tied to stakes, in just the same manner as in the vineyards in France ; and, at the time when I saw that vineyard, the vines were well-loaded with a black-coloured grape. The reasons why this culture has been dropped, are of no importance at present ; but the facts that I have stated are of great importance; because they prove that vines may be raised in espalier in a warm situation in any garden on

the south side of Warwickshire at the least. The grape-
vine is *propagated* from *cuttings* or from *layers*. A layer
is a shoot of the vine, laid into the ground in one part of
it with a little sloping cut on the under side. The
fore part of the shoot is then tacked to the wall, or a
stake is driven into the ground to tie it to. In the fall
of the year this is a young vine with a good root to it;
but, as vines do not remove very well, the usual way is
to untack a shoot from the vine which grows against the
wall, bring it out into the border opposite. Sink a pretty
large flower-pot into the border, place the cut part of
the shoot into the flower-pot three parts filled with
earth, put a nice straight stick down into the flower-pot
at the same time, put a peg on the wall side of the pot to
prevent the shoot from rising up, tie the top of the shoot
to the stick, then fill the pot and the hole full of earth,
and press it down well so as to form a little dish to hold
the water. Soon after this is done, which ought to be
in the month of February, cut the fore part of the shoot
off to within a joint or two of the ground, tie it firmly to
the stick; and, when it sends out its shoots, tie one of
them to the stick, and cut the other away. In the fall
of the year, cut off the back part of the shoot which
attaches the tree against the wall, dig up the pot, and you
have a vine to remove to what spot you please, to be
transplanted by merely turning the ball out of the pot,
just as you would in the case of a pot of cucumbers or
melons. When transplanted thus in the fall, or any time
before the middle of February, cut the vine down to
within one or two buds of the ground, and then you
begin to train as hereafter to be directed. The other
way of propagating vines is by *cuttings*. You cut off,

before the middle of February, a piece of a shoot which came out the last summer : this cutting should, if convenient, have an inch or two of the last year's wood at the bottom of it; but this is by no means absolutely necessary. The cutting should have four or five buds or joints : make the ground rich, move it deep and make it fine. Then put in the cutting with the setting stick, leaving only two buds, or joints, above ground; fastening the cutting well in the ground. Or, another, and, I think, a better, way of propagating vines by cuttings, is, to take in February, a bud of the last year's wood, cutting all wood away except about half an inch above and half an inch below the bud, and shaving off the bark, and a little way into the wood straight down this inch-long piece, only let this shaving be on the side opposite to the bud. Bury the whole, two inches deep in a largish pot filled with good mould, keeping the bud in an upright position. Do not mind covering the bud over; it will shoot up through the mould, and the place behind it, from which you cut out the slice of bark and wood, will send out vigorous roots; and then, as to keeping it cool, see CUTTINGS, under the head of *Propagation*, in this Chapter. As to the training and pruning of vines, I have in my book on *American Gardening*, given instructions for the performing of this work in the espalier form. The very same instructions apply to walls and to houses, and also to roofs, seeing that, on roofs, it is merely a trellis-work lying in a sloping attitude. I have supposed a new plantation of vines to be made expressly for espalier training; and, with several sorts of grapes, this method would succeed perfectly well in the south of England, in warm spots and at no great distance from walls facing the south. I shall, therefore, now repeat, with some little variations as to season and other circumstances, my directions for training and pruning the vines in espalier. First, look at plate 8, which represents, as well as I am able to make it represent, three trellis-works for vines. These trellis-works are to be five feet high, and to consist of little upright bars, two and a half inches by two inches, put two feet into the ground, and made of locust wood. The proper situation for vines would be in a line on the south side of the north wall, or on the south side of the south wall, and at about seven feet from the wall, leaving plenty of room for the work to be performed on the wall-trees as well as on the trellis. The length of such line would be 200 feet; and, allowing for the thickness of the walls, and for the door-way coming into the hot-bed ground (in case you choose the south side of the north wall), and for the door-way going from the inner to the outer garden, if you choose the other wall, there would be *space for twelve vines* at sixteen feet apart. You would, therefore, plant your cuttings or your young vines at that distance. Look now at the plate, which, in fig. 1. represents the cutting become a plant, or the young vine, having made its first year's shoot. There is no difference in the treatment; but, in order to avoid unnecessary words, let us suppose it to have been a cutting, and suppose it to have been tied to a little stake during the summer. The first year of its being a vine, after the leaves are off and *before pruning*, it is exhibited in figure 2. The same year's vine, *pruned in February*, is exhibited in figure 3. The vine, in its next summer is exhibited, *with shoots, leaves, and grapes*, in figure 4. Having measured your dis-

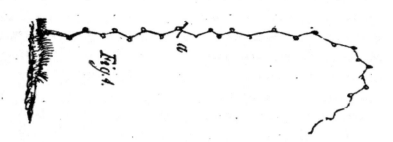

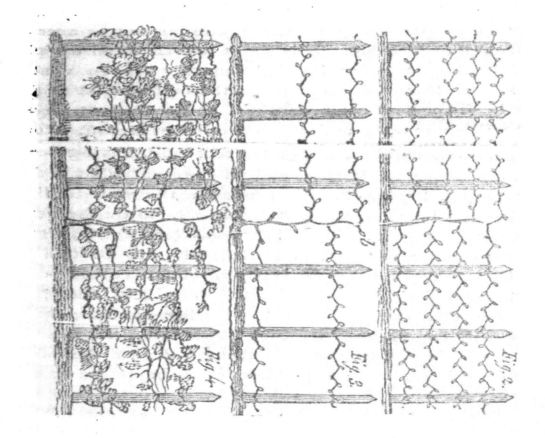

tances, put in a cutting at each place where there is to be a vine, leaving above ground only two joints or buds. From these will come *two shoots*, perhaps ; and, if two come, rub off the top one and leave the bottom one, and, in winter, cut off the bit of dead wood which will, in this case, stand above the bottom shoot. Choose, however, the upper one to remain, if the lower one be very weak. Or, a better way is, to put in two or three cuttings within an inch or two of each other, leaving only *one bud* to each out of ground, and taking away, in the fall, the cuttings that send up the weakest shoots. The object is to get one good shoot, coming out as near to the ground as possible. This shoot you tie to an upright stick, letting it grow its full length. When winter comes, cut this shoot down to the bud nearest to the ground. The next year another, and a much stronger shoot will come out ; and, when the leaves are off, in the fall, this shoot will be eight or ten feet long, having been tied to a stake as it rose, and will present what is described in *fig.* 1. plate 3. You must make your trellis ; that is, put in your upright *locust-bars* to tie the next summer's shoots to. You will want (see *fig.* 2.) eight shoots to come out to run horizontally, to be tied to these bars. You must now, then, in winter, cut off your vine, leaving *eight* buds or joints. You see there is a mark for this cut at *a, fig.* 1. During summer, eight shoots will come, and, as they proceed on, they must be tied with matting, or something soft, to the bars. The whole vine, both ways included, is supposed to go sixteen feet ; but, if your tillage be good, it will go much further, and then the ends must be cut off in winter. Now, then, winter presents you your vine as in *fig.* 2 ; and now you must *prune,* which is the all-important part of the business. Observe, and bear in mind, that little or no fruit ever comes on a grape-vine, except on young shoots that come out of wood of the *last year.* All the four last year's shoots that you find in *fig.* 2. would send out bearers ; but if you suffer that, you will have a great parcel of *small wood,* and little or no fruit next year. Therefore, cut off four of the last year's shoots, as at *b.* (*fig.* 3.) leaving only *one bud.* The four other shoots will send out a shoot from every one of their buds, and if the vine be *strong,* there will be *two bunches of grapes* on each of these young shoots ; and, as the last year's shoots are supposed to be each eight feet long, and as there generally is a bud at, or about, every half foot, every last year's shoot will produce thirty-two bunches of grapes ; every vine 128 bunches ; and the twelve vines 1536 ; and, possibly, nay, probably, so many *pounds* of grapes ! Is this incredible ? Take, then, this well-known fact, that there is a grape-vine, a single vine, with only *one stem,* in the King's gardens, at his palace of Hampton Court, which has, for, perhaps, *half a century,* produced on an average, annually, *a ton of grapes* ; that is to say, 2,240 pounds, avordupois weight. That vine covers a space of about forty feet in length, and twenty in breadth. However, suppose you have only a *fifth part* of what you might have, three hundred bunches of grapes are worth a great deal more than the annual trouble, which is, indeed, very little. *Fig.* 4 shows a vine in summer. You see the four shoots *bearing,* and four other shoots coming on for the next year, from the butts left at the winter pruning, as at *b.* These four latter you are to tie to the bars as they advance on during the summer. When winter comes again, you are to *cut off the four shoots* that sent out the bearers during the summer, and leave the four that grew out of the butts. Cut the four shoots that have borne, so as to leave but *one bud* at the butt. And they will then be sending out wood, while the other four will be sending out fruit. And thus you go on year after year for your life; for, as to the vine, it will, if well treated, outlive you and your children to the third, and even thirtieth generation. I think they say, that the vine at Hampton Court, was planted in the reign of King William. During the summer there are two things to be observed, as to pruning. Each of the *last year's shoots* has thirty-two buds, and, of course, it sends out thirty-two shoots with the grapes on them, for the grapes come out of the two first fair buds of these shoots. So that here would be an enormous quantity of wood, if it were all left till the end of summer. But, this must not be. When the grapes get as big as *peas*, cut off the green shoots that bear them, at *two buds distance* from the fruit. This is necessary in order to clear the vine from confusion of branches, and also to keep the sap back for the supply of the fruit. These new shoots, that have the bunches on, must be kept tied to the trellis, or else the wind would tear them off. The other thing is, to take care to keep nicely tied to the bars the shoots that are to send forth bearers the next year; and, if you observe any little *side-shoots* coming out of them, to crop these off as soon as they appear, leaving nothing but the clear, clean shoot. It may be remarked, that the butt, as at *b*, when it is cut off the next time, will be *longer by a bud*. That will be so; but, by the third year the vine will be so strong, that you may safely cut the shoots back to within six inches of the main trunk, leaving the new shoots to come out of it where they will ; taking care to let but *one* grow for the summer. If shoots start out of the main trunk irregularly, rub them off as soon as they appear, and never suffer your vine to have any more than its regular number of shoots. Thus far with regard to the training and pruning of vines in espalier. I have now to speak of training against a *wall ;* training under *glass in a green-house ;* and training *against a house.* If against a *wall,* you proceed to raise the young vine in precisely the same manner as before directed ; but, in place of carrying the trunk upright, in order to have bearing shoots come out of the side of it, as in plate 8, you cut it down to within two eyes of the bottom. Suppose you have got the vine, *fig.* 2. plate 8. Instead of bringing out from it four shoots of a side, bring out only the two bottom ones, cutting the top of the trunk off pretty close down to the highest of the two first shoots from the bottom. These two shoots may be suffered to bear the first year after they come out ; but these two shoots are then to be suffered to remain to form limbs for the bearing shoots to go out of ; and these bearing shoots are to go up the wall perpendicularly, instead of running horizontally, as they do on the trellis-work. All the rules for cutting out the shoots alternately are the same in this case as in the other. The vine might be trained against the wall horizontally as against the trellis-work ; but it would not be so convenient ; for, the two horizontal limbs left at the bottom may be carried to any length against a wall ; so that, one vine would, in time, be sufficient for a wall of considerable extent. I have seen such limbs, forty feet long, supplying an abundance of bearing wood to cover the wall. If you choose, you may, at every three or four yards distance, cause these bottom limbs to touch the ground, and, if pegged down and covered with a little part of the earth, they would strike root there. The upright bearing shoots should be tacked to the wall in a serpentine manner, which checks the flow of the sap and makes them bear better all over the vine. *Under glass* the training and pruning is precisely the same as that against a wall : two limbs running along at the bottom of the glass, and the shoots coming out, pruned, and tied up in the manner directed in the case of the wall. Against a house, you want a lofty trunk. You carry it to the height that the situation requires, and train by side-shoots, just in the manner directed for the trellis in the case of the espalier. *A roof* is only a wall lying in a sloping direction, and the training and pruning are precisely those directed for the wall. Such is the manner of pruning vines in what is called the *long-pruning* ; but there is a method very different, called the short pruning, which very much resembles the method which I have described for pruning the currant-tree. Instead of alternate bearing shoots, brought out of the trunk, as in the espalier form, for instance, you suffer these shoots, as in plate 8. *fig. 3.* to remain perpetually. They send out annually side-shoots. These you cut off to within one or two eyes of the limb, and, out of these little artificial spurs, come, the next year, shoots to bear the fruit. The vine bears only on shoots that come out of the last year's wood, and therefore, these spurs would become too long in a very short time; so that, you must cut them out close to the limb, at the end of a

year or two, and others will be always coming out to
supply their place. Whether against a wall, under glass,
against a house, or on a roof, you observe the same
rule : your vine is furnished with perpetual limbs instead
of being annually furnished with new and long shoots.
Hoping that I have made this matter of training and
pruning vines intelligible to the reader, I have now to
speak of the management of the fruit, of the soil suitable
for vines, and of the sorts of grapes. When the grapes
get to be of the size of a pea, or thereabouts, they
should be thinned in the bunch with a sharp-pointed
scissors. More than half of them, and those the
smallest, of course, should be cut out, otherwise they
will not be so fine ; and, in some cases, the fruit will be
so closely pressed together on the bunch as to cause
moulding and rotting. It is supposed, and I believe the
fact, that thinning the grapes adds greatly to the weight
of the bunch, and certainly it heightens greatly the
quality of the fruit. As to the soil for grapes, it cannot
be too rich. The ground should be dug about the roots
not only in the fall and in the spring, but even in the
summer. The earliest grape, is what we call the *black
July,* and what the French call the *noir hâtif* ; the *Chas-
selas,* which is a white grape, approaching to a yellow, is
also very early ; the *Black Hamburgh* is a fine grape and a
great bearer, and this is the sort of the famous Hampton Court vine ; the *White sweet-water* is a very fine
grape ; and these four would satisfy me ; but, I shall
here add the Kew list of grapes, and with that list I
conclude this long article. *Burgundy, Black Cluster, Black
July, Common White Muscadine, Parsley-leaved Muscadine ;*
these are called, in the HORTUS KEWENSIS, *wall-grapes ;*

then, as *house-grapes*, come the *Black Damascus*, *Muscat of Alexandria*, *Royal Muscadine*, *Black Frankendale*, *Black Hamburgh*, *Black Prince*, *Black Frontignac*, *Grizzly Frontignac*, *Red Frontignac*, *White Frontignac*, *White Sweet-water*, *Marseilles*, *White Nice*, *Syrian*.

286. WALNUT.—The way to raise walnut-trees, is, this. When the walnuts are quite ripe, make them perfectly dry and preserve them in precisely the manner directed for the filberd. Sow them late in February, and the tree will be a foot high by the next fall. If it be to stand where it is sowed, nothing more is necessary than to keep the ground about it clean, and to prune off the side-shoots at the bottom, always leaving a tolerable head until you have a clear trunk of the height that you desire. If the tree be to be transplanted, you ought to take it up in the fall after the spring of sowing it; for it has a long tap-root, and will remove with great difficulty if you suffer it to remain for two or three years. When you take the young plant up, cut off the tap-root to within six inches of the part which met the top of the ground; transplant it into a nursery; let it stand there for three years, and then it will remove with a good bushey root. Keep the side-shoots pruned off in the manner before-directed, and the head of the tree will form itself. It is said that walnut-trees should be threshed or beaten, a saying which has certainly arisen from the want of a good reason for knocking down the fruit, which, like nuts and filberds, should always hang till it drops from the tree.

DISEASES AND VERMIN.

287. I HAVE reserved until now the remarks necessary to be made upon the diseases to which fruit-trees are subject; and also on the insects and other mischievous living things by which they are injured. I have reserved, too, until now, the observations to be made relative to divers mischievous insects which do injury to the herbaceous plants of the kitchen-garden. I shall now speak of the whole under one head, which would be more convenient to the reader than if the remarks with regard to them had been scattered throughout the book.

288. CANKER.—Apple-trees are greatly afflicted by the canker, which is a rotting of the bark in particular spots; producing, in time, the destruction of the branch or limb. If perceived when at first coming, it may sometimes be cut quite out; and, if that cannot be done, its ravages may be staid by paring off all the perished bark till you come to the quick, and cutting the edges of that quick very smooth with a very sharp knife, this bark will grow a little again and have round edges; the place should be washed once or twice a year with soap and water to keep out the insects, which are always endeavouring to harbour round these wounded spots. As to the putting on of plaister of any kind, I have tried it often, and have never found it of any use. But, observe, neither a tree nor a limb is to be abandoned merely because it is cankered: in many cases, the cankered part of the tree bears best; and it so happens that I have an apple-tree, at this time one limb of which is half cut

off by the canker; that limb bears more than all the rest of the tree; and it was from that very limb that I cut the branch of beautiful fall-pippins that were exhibited last autumn at my shop in Fleet-street. So that, a tree is not to be despised merely because it is cankered. The canker comes very frequently from bruises given to the tree by the carelessness of gardeners, or by the friction of limbs one against another. It very frequently comes from the rubbing of limbs and branches against the stakes; and this makes it so dangerous to plant great trees for an orchard. However, I have seen apple-trees that were old and cankered when I was a boy, and that continue to bear well unto this day. It is a thing to be guarded against, and to be got rid of if possible: it is sometimes fatal, but by no means generally so.

289. COTTON-BLIGHT.—This disease makes its appearance like little bunches of cotton-wool stuck upon the joints or along the shoots of apple-trees, which leave, after they be rubbed off, little round pimples or lumps; and it does the same with regard to the roots that it does to the limbs and the shoots. Under this white stuff, there are innumerable insects, which, when squeezed by the finger, are of the colour of blood. It is a very nasty thing, very pernicious to apple-trees; and it also comes on the joints of vines. There is no cure but rubbing the stuff off mechanically, as fast as it appears, and washing the place well with something strong, such as tobacco-juice. The potatoe, which some people look upon as so nutritious, very nearly poisons the water in which it is boiled; and an Irish gentleman once told me that that water would cure the cotton blight. Rub-

bing the part with mercurial ointment will certainly do it; but then you must get at the root as well as at the limbs and the branches: if you take up a young tree that has the cotton-blight, cut the nobs off from the roots, cleanse the tree perfectly well and replant it, and, it is very likely the disease will not return. If it once get complete possession of a large tree, the tree will soon become useless.

290. MILDEW, which the French call WHITE BLIGHT, seizes the spring shoots of peach and nectarine trees, makes them white as if dusted over with meal or lime, and fixes itself on spots on the fruit. I have heard of, and have seen tried, tobacco smoke, lime water, and several other things as remedies, all of which I have seen invariably to fail. All you can do, is, to cut off the shoots and leaves that have it, and to suffer others to come out. This blight sometimes comes upon apple-trees.

291. LICE.—Prodigious quantities of these come upon the points of the shoots of peaches, nectarines, and cherries, which cause them to curl up, and to become black; and, after this, generally, the branches suffer greatly: the only remedy is, to cut these points off as soon as you perceive them beginning to curl. You may also wash the trees, or fumigate with tobacco.

292. GUM.—All stone fruit; cherries, plums, peaches, nectarines, and apricots, are liable to the gum, which sometimes proceeds from injudicious pruning, and sometimes from the tree having but a poor root. It very

frequently comes after the cutting out of a luxuriant branch, especially if that branch be cut off near to the trunk and in the spring or summer, which it never ought to be if it can be avoided. A tree will sometimes gum, and cease to gum afterwards; and, though it gum, it will bear. If it continue to gum, and the gum appear in several parts of it at the same time, and attack the tree severely, it will soon cease to produce wood fit for bearing, and the sooner it is cut down and thrown away, the better.

293. PEACH-BUG.—This is a thing between louse and bug: it is of a green colour, and clings along upon the wood of the peach trees, and of nectarines of course. These are destroyed very quickly by fumigating the trees with strong tobacco-smoke, or washing them with water in which tobacco has been steeped. It is rather difficult to fumigate against a wall; but, at any rate, the wood can be well washed with tobacco-water. These insects, however, must be destroyed by one means or another; or they will spoil the crop for the year, and spoil the tree too.

294. MAGGOT.—There is a maggot which comes in apple-trees and pear-trees, but particularly the former, just before the tree opens its blossoms. You will see the young leaves that have come out curl up longwise. If you open those curls, you will find enveloped in a very small web, a little maggot that you can hardly clearly discern with the naked eye. From this, its birth-place, it creeps away into the cups of the blossoms and there feeds upon the germ of the fruit; and becomes a visible

maggot a full third of an inch long, having a black head
and a greenish body.   When the blossoms are not
abundant, and sometimes even when they are, this
wretched thing feeds upon the roots or germs of the
buds, as well as upon the blossoms.   It enters down into
the heart of the bud which has just bursted out into
little leaves, and you will see those leaves die in the
month of April, just as you will see cabbage-plants or
lettuce-plants die when attacked by the grub or the wire-
worm.   Of a row of lettuce-plants, you are surprised to
see one lopping its leaves down flat upon the ground,
and the rest standing bolt upright; but, if you take it
up, you will find, that a grub-worm or a wire-worm has
eaten out the heart of its root.   Just in like manner does
this maggot destroy the buds of apple-trees; and, as in
the case of a row of lettuce-plants, it, like the grub or
wire-worm, will, if let alone, go from bud to bud, from
one end of a branch to the other.   The killing of the
buds by these maggots is one great cause of the *canker*
in apple-trees : they make a wound which descends down
to the very wood ;   I have, in numerous instances,
watched the progress of the wound, and have seen it
turn to complete and destructive canker.   As to prevention, in this case, I am not certain of the source of the
maggot ; but I think it proceeds from eggs deposited
upon the bark during the previous summer, and clinging
there until the spring.   What I have done, is, to wash all
the limbs and stout branches of the trees well in the
month of March with a hard-brush, soap, and tobacco-
juice ; and certain it is that my trees have not been in-
fested by these maggots since.   If you find them at
work upon a tree, watch the flagging of the buds ; cut

the flagging buds out with a sharp pen-knife : you will find a maggot in the heart, and will, of course, put an end to its spoliations. This is another reason why espaliers are better than standards : this work is easily performed upon an espalier ; but, on a standard, impossible. Sometimes you see the petals of the blossoms curl up ; and there you find the maggot. It is better to take one blossom out of the bunch at once ; for, if the maggot remain, it will destroy the whole. We very often see whole bunches of blossoms, leaves and all, shrivel up suddenly : the maggot has done this, and is gone before you perceived the mischief. The whole of standard-trees are frequently nearly stripped in this way : people call it blight ; but, in general, appear to know nothing of the cause.

295. BIRDS.—The way to keep birds from fruit, and, indeed, from every thing else, is, to shoot them, or frighten them away, or cover over effectually with nets the object which they covet. I have spoken occasionally of the care to be taken in this respect ; but, in all cases, where birds are very fond of the thing that you have, you must keep them away, or give up the cultivation of the thing ; for it is time and labour thrown away, to raise things and then let them be destroyed in this manner. There is one season when to defend yourself is very difficult ; I mean the spring, when the birds attack the *buds*. There are certain buds which the sparrows will destroy, just when they are sending out their fruit ; but the great enemies of buds are the bulfinches, the chaffinches, and, above all, the greenfinches, which assail the buds of plums of all sorts in a most furious

manner. They are hard driven for food at this time of the year; and they will actually strip whole branches. It is, however, contended by some persons, that, after all, they do no harm; for that, there are insects in the bud which they eat; and that it is not the herbage that they want, but the animal, seeing that birds live upon grain, and pulse, and insects, and not upon green things. This is by no means true : they do live upon green things, or, at least, they eat them as we see fowls eating grass, during a great part of every day. I believe that these little birds eat the buds, and are not at all looking after insects. The wild pigeons in America live, for about a month, entirely upon the buds of the sugar maple, and are killed by hundreds of thousands, by persons who erect bough-houses, and remain in a maple wood with guns and powder and shot, for that purpose. If we open the craw of one of these little birds, we find in it green stuff of various descriptions, and, generally, more or less of grass, and, therefore, it is a little too much to believe, that, in taking away our buds, they merely relieve us from the insects that would, in time, eat us up. To keep birds from buds is a difficult matter. You cannot net all your trees; nor can you fire with shot amongst your trees without doing a greater harm than that which you wish to prevent. Birds are exceedingly cunning in their generation; but, luckily for us gardeners, they do not know how to distinguish between the report of a gun loaded with powder and shot, and one that is only loaded with powder. Very frequent firing with powder will alarm them so that they will quit the spot, or, at least, be so timid as to become comparatively little mischievous.

296. MICE. — Very troublesome creatures. They commit their depredations by night, and must be well looked after. Brick traps are the best things; for, as to poisoning them, you may poison, at the same time, your cat or your dog. Great vigilance, however, is required to keep down mice; but it ought to be resolutely done.

297. RATS.—If the garden be near to a house or out-buildings, and especially near to a farm-yard, where dogs and ferrets are not pretty constantly in motion, the rats will be large sharers in the finest of the fruit that the garden produces. On the walls, in the melon-bed, even in the strawberry-beds, they will take away the prime of the dessert. They do but taste, indeed, of each, but then they are guests that one does not like to eat with. Here there is absolutely no remedy other than those of dogs and ferrets. I have seen a wall of grapes pretty nearly cleared by rats, some farm buildings being at the back side of the wall: these nasty things must, there-fore, be destroyed by one means or another.

298. MOLES.—These cannot get into a garden with a wall round it. If they come through or under the hedge, and make their workings visible, they ought to be caught without delay; for, if suffered to get to a head, they do a great deal of mischief, besides the ugliness which they produce.

299. ANTS.—A very pretty subject for poets, but a most dismal one for gardeners; for it is one of the most mischievous of all things, and the most difficult of all to guard against or to destroy. It is mischievous in many

ways, and all the sorts of ants are equally mischievous. Those which have their nests in little hillocks on the ground; that is to say, the small ant, is the sort which most frequently display their mischievous industry in the gardens. I once had a melon-bed that underwent a regular attack from a community of *horse-ants*, as the country people call them; that is to say, the largest ant that we know any thing of. I know nothing but fire or boiling water, or squeezing to death, that will destroy ants; and, if you pour boiling water on their nest in the grass, you destroy the grass; set fire to a nest of the great ants, and you burn up the hedge or the trees, or whatever else is in the neighbourhood. As to squeezing them to death, they are amongst the twigs and roots of your trees and plants: they are in the blossoms, and creeping all about the fruit; so that, to destroy them in this way, you must destroy that also which you wish to protect against their depredations. Ants injure every thing that they touch; but they are particularly mischievous with regard to wall-trees; where they attack successively bud, blossom, leaf, and fruit. There is no method of keeping them from the wall. They may be kept from mounting espaliers by putting tar round the stem of the tree, and round the stakes that the limbs are tied to; but there is no keeping them from the wall, unless by killing them. Mr. FORSYTH recommended to make the ground very smooth near the bottom of the tree that they attacked; then to make smooth holes with a sharp-pointed stake or iron bar, down into which, as he says, they will go; and then he recommends to pour water into these holes, and drown them. MONSIEUR DE COMBLE recommends the laying of sheep's trotters or cow-heels with the skin on,

near the attacked tree, and that, when these be well
covered with ants, to plunge them into a bucket of
water, drown the ants, then put the sheep's trotters near
the tree again to wait for another cargo. By these
means something may be done, to be sure; but, the true
way is, to find out the nest from which they come; for
they are extremely scrupulous in this respect; it is only
one tribe that makes its attack upon one and the same
object. If you look attentively you will find that, in the
morning, very early, they all come in the same direction,
and that they go in exactly the same way back at night.
Trace them to their fortress; and, when it is, quite
night, treat them to a bucket of water that is as nearly
upon the boil as possible. You kill the whole tribe.
When my melon-beds were attacked by the horse-ants, I
set to work to discover whence they came. I traced
them along a brick wall. Then out of the garden between
the door-frame and the wall. Then along at the bottom
of the edge of the wall on the side of a lawn; then,
after having made an angle along the wall, going, as I
thought, over it into a meadow on the other side. Every
corner of hedge and ditch of that meadow was examined
to discover the nest, but in vain. Looking back to the
spot where I thought they went over the wall, we discovered that they turned along the top of the wall,
and went under the roof of a summer-house that was
ceiled below: having lifted up a tile, there we saw
bushels of ants, with little sticks and straws, the result
of years of their detestable industry. A copper of water
was made to boil against the evening. It was taken to
the spot in a boiling state as nearly as possible; every
thing was prepared for the purpose, and by midnight,

scarcely a handful of them were left alive; and my melon-bed, which I was actually upon the point of giving up as lost, was suffered to proceed unmolested. The greatest care, therefore, ought to be taken, especially if grass ground be near the garden, to hunt out ants' nests, and to destroy them.

300. SPIDER.—I do not know that the common spider does any harm to the gardener, and I know that it frequently does good by killing the flies; but there is a red spider which is very mischievous to vines, especially when under glass. If attended to, however, they are easily destroyed, and the destruction of them should not be neglected. Plentifully washing of the trees with water is the great remedy, and, in hot-houses, syringes are made use of for this purpose.

301. CATERPILLAR.—Very few more mischievous creatures than this infest the gardens. In the first place, it is a most destructive enemy of fruit-trees, apples, pears, plums, quinces and medlars, but particularly apples and plums are literally flayed alive by this nasty insect. Hundreds of trees together are, early in the month of June, very frequently completely stripped of every leaf by the caterpillars. Of their progenitors I know nothing; but I know that they make their first appearance in a web formed into the shape of a bag or sort of wallet attached to the branches of trees. And this bag is a small thing at first; but it grows larger and larger as the caterpillars within it increase in size. If you open one of these bags, a goodly tribe glads your sight; and, if you leave the bag till the caterpillars grow

too big for it and open it themselves, they sally forth in
every direction, and strip the tree of its leaves. Prevention is not, however, in this case, very difficult. If they
come on espaliers, you pick the bag off as soon as you
perceive it, and crush it under your foot. If they come
on standard-trees, you must take a ladder; but a better
way is, to load a gun with powder, and to blow the bags
from the trees. If once they escape from the bag and go
on their travels, you have no remedy. If you shake the
tree and bring part of them to the ground, they crawl up
again. Lime has no effect upon them; and your only
hope is, that your other enemies, the sparrows, will lend
their assistance in delivering you from these; and I do
verily believe, that, were it not for the sparrows, and
other birds, these insects would make it next to impossible to cultivate gardens in England. They have no
slugs and snails in America; but caterpillars they have,
and they sometimes strip an orchard of every one of its
leaves. There are caterpillars which infest the cabbages and the Swedish turnip, and some other herbaceous
plants. These manifestly proceed from the butterfly;
but, unfortunately, they do not make their appearance in
little pockets or bags; but you make the first discovery
of the honour of the visit that they are paying you by
perceiving their gnawings upon the edgings of the leaves
of the plants. Let them alone for a little while, and they
will go from cabbage to cabbage until there is not a bit
of leaf left in the whole patch. They leave you the
skeleton of a cabbage, taking away all the flesh, and
leaving all the bones; that is to say, the stalk of the
cabbage and the ribs of the leaves. These are most
mischievous things; they are wholly insensible to the

powers of lime : in heat they delight ; wet will not injure them ; frost is their only destroyer ; and many a time have I prayed for winter in order to see an end of the caterpillars. In order to mitigate the mischief, and, indeed, in a great measure to put a stop to it, look narrowly among your plants of the cabbage kind about the middle of the summer. If you see the butterflies busy, expect their followers in due time. Watch the plants : as soon as you see one attacked, take it entirely up, shake the caterpillars from it upon the ground, put them to death with your foot, and carry the plant away to the pigs. 'Tis very rarely that the whole or any considerable part of a piece of cabbages is attacked at once ; and, therefore, you may, in some measure, guard against the mischiefs of this pernicious insect of which there are several sorts, some green, some brown, some smooth, some hairy, and all equally mischievous.

302. SNAIL.—From the curious construction of the snail, it is known to every body in town as well as country. It is very mischievous, and especially amongst fruit-trees, where it annoys the fruit, as well as the leaf, but particularly the fruit. It is a great enemy of the apricot and the plum, both of which it will eat whether in the green or in the ripe state. It is very mischievous amongst the plants in the garden in general ; but its size and its habits and manners makes it not difficult to destroy. Its places of harbour are, behind the trunks or big limbs of wall-trees, in a garden, or, round the butts of the trees that form the hedge of the outside of the garden. Snails lie in such places all the winter long, and never stir till they are warmed into life in the spring. Many persons have kept snails for a year or more nailed

up in a box, and have found them just as lively afterwards as if they had never fasted at all. In winter time, in dry and frosty weather, snails should be routed out from all their fastnesses, and destroyed. This is the most effectual way of guarding against their depredations ; for, when the leaves come out, they have shelter, they are exceedingly cunning in availing themselves of that shelter, but though you finally discover and kill them, they spoil your fruit first.

303. SLUG.—This is a snail without a shell, and like the snail, likes neither sun nor frost. Some slugs are black, others whitish, others yellow. The great black slug and the yellow slug live chiefly upon worms, and do not touch plants of any kind. The mischievous thing is the little slug that hides itself in the ground or under grass or leaves, and that comes out in the night, or in the rain, and eats the garden plants of almost every description more or less, and sometimes, pretty nearly clears a field of wheat. Slugs cannot live under the shining sun, nor can they move about much except when the ground is wet or moist from dew or rain ; then it is that they come forth and make up for lost time. They are propagated amongst weeds and grass, and any thing that affords constant shade and tranquillity. A garden constantly clean is, therefore, the most effectual prevention ; but if they come, they must absolutely be killed, or you must give up your crop. The way to kill them is this. Take *hot lime,* in a powdered state, put it into a coarsish bag ; and, after night-fall, or before sun-rise, in the dew, or on the moist ground, go over their haunts, shake the bag and let the fine powder fall upon the ground : some little particle will fall upon every slug

that is abroad; and every slug that is touched with the lime will die. If rain come it will destroy the power of the lime, and then it will be necessary, perhaps, for you to repeat the remedy several different times.

304. ROOK-WORM. — This is an underground enemy; a miner and sapper. It is a short worm or long maggot, as big round as a thick goose-quill, body white, and head partly red and partly black. It is a fact, I suppose, that the May-bug, or chafer, comes from this worm. The French call it the *ver hanneton*, which corroborates that opinion. It attacks the roots of plants, and will even attack the roots of trees, and will now-and-then destroy some young trees. It will clear a patch of cabbages in a very short time. It is underground, and, therefore, not to be guarded against; but a garden may very soon be ridded of it. First, kill every one that you meet with in digging; next, the moment you see a plant begin to flag, dig it up and take up the worm. If the worm be on its travels, you are sure that it is gone towards the next adjoining plant, to the right or to the left. Pursue it both ways with the spade, and ten to one but you overtake it. A little perseverance in this way will soon clear a garden of the rook-worm; but as to our fields, their crops would be absolutely devoured, in many cases; or, rather, the plants would be destroyed, were it not for the rooks, which are amongst the most useful of the animals in this country; and really it is too hard to grudge them a little of the corn when they have so largely contributed towards bringing the whole of it to perfection.

305. BLACK GRUB.—It should be called the brown

grub, for it is not black. In its workings, it is half way between a rook-worm and a caterpillar. It lies snugly under the ground near the roots of the plant in the day-time, and comes up at night, eats the plant off at the stem, or eats out its heart. This is a most perverse as well as a most pernicious thing : it is not content, like the caterpillar, the snail, or the slug, to feed upon the leaves ; but it must needs bite out the heart, or just cut off the plant at the bottom. Lime has no power over it : nothing will keep it off : no means but taking it by the hand : in a garden this may be done, by examining a little about the ground just round the stem of every plant ; for as soon as it has destroyed one plant, it gets ready for another for the next night's work. In a gar-den, this thing may be destroyed, or kept down ; but, in a field it is impossible, and many a field has had its crop almost totally destroyed by this grub.

366. WIRE-WORM.—This is a little yellow worm which, at full growth, is about an inch long ; and it is called wire-worm because it is very tough and difficult to pinch asunder. It is bred in grass-land, and in old tufts of grass in arable land. A piece of land digged or ploughed up from a meadow, or grass-field, will, for a year or two, be full of these worms, which carry off whole fields of wheat sometimes. In gardens they are very destructive. They attack tender-rooted plants, make a hole on one side of the tap-root, and work their way upwards till they come to the heart. When they have done that, they go to another plant, and so on. You perceive when they are at work, by the plant dropping its leaves ; and the only remedy is, to watch the plants narrowly, and, as soon as you perceive the tips of the leaves beginning to

flag, to take it up, and destroy the worms. They are particularly fond of lettuces that have been transplanted; and I have had whole rows of lettuces destroyed by these worms, in spite of every precaution.

307. WOOD-LOUSE.—Is a little grey-coloured insect of a flat shape, and about twice as long as it is broad. When you touch it, or when it sees itself in danger, it forms itself into a ball, and very much resembles a Dutch cheese, and is, by the children in the country, called the *cheese-bob*. Its name of *wood-louse* comes from its habit of living and breeding in rotten wood, and under boards or slabs that are lying upon the ground; but it also haunts very much the cracks in bricks, and the holes in the joints of walls. It feeds upon buds and blossoms, and also upon the fruit itself. When it gets into hot-beds, it hides round the edge of the frame, and does a great deal of mischief to the plants, especially when they are young. Cabbage-leaves or lettuce-leaves laid in a hot-bed or against the edge of the wall, will invite them to take shelter as a place of retreat for the day, all the dilapidations being committed in the night. You lift the leaves in the day-time and kill them; and, further, as to walls, the great remedy is to keep all the joints well pointed, and to fill up any cracks that there may be in the bricks.

308. EAR-WIG.—This is a most pernicious insect, which feeds on flowers and on fruit, and which, if it congregated like the ant, would actually destroy every thing of this sort. Its favourite flowers are those of the carnation kind. To protect very curious plants against

them, the florists put their stages on legs, and surround each leg with a circle of water contained in a dish which is so constructed as to admit the leg through the middle of it, seeing that the ear-wig is no swimmer. Others make little things of paper like extinguishers, and put them on the tops of the sticks to which the carnation-stalks are tied. The ear-wigs commit their depredations in the night, and they find these extinguishers most delightful retreats from the angry eye of man and from the burning rays of the sun. Take off the extinguishers, however, in the morning, give them a rap over a basin of water, and the enjoyments of the ear-wigs are put an end to at once. They are very nasty things in fruit of the stone kind, and particularly the apricot. They make a way in at the foot-stalk of the fruit, get to the stone and live there day and night; so that, when you open a fine apricot, you frequently find its fine juice half-poisoned by three or four of these nasty insects. As soon, therefore, as the wall-fruit begins to change its colour, the tree should be well furnished with extinguishers made of cartridge-paper, and able to resist a shower. By great attention in this way you destroy them all before the fruit be ripe enough for them to enter. But, one great protection against all these creeping things, is, to stir the ground very frequently along the foot of the wall. That is their great place of resort; and frequent stirring and making the ground very fine, disturbs the peace of their numerous families, gives them trouble, makes them uneasy, and finally harrasses them to death.

309. WASPS.—These are enemies of another sort,

and, in some years, most troublesome they are. They
fix upon the finest fruit, and, in some seasons, long
before it be ripe. They will eat a green gage plum to a
shell; and, while they spoil your fruit, they will not
scruple to sting you if you come to interrupt their en-
joyment. The first thing to do, is, to destroy all the
wasps' nests that you can find any where in the neighbourhood. These nests are generally in banks. Discover the nest in the day-time, open it with a spade at
night, and pour in boiling-water. There is a little
bird, called the red-start, that destroys the wasps; but
boys are their great enemies; and about sixpence a nest
will keep any neighbourhood pretty clear of wasps. But,
the great remedy, is, to kill them when they come to
the tree, and that is done in this way: you fill a pretty
large phial half full of beer mixed with brown sugar:
the wasps attracted by this, go down into the phial and
never come out again. The phials must be emptied every
day, if any thing like full, and put up again with fresh
sugar and beer. A string is tied round the neck of the
phial, which is thus fastened round some part of the tree.
There must, however, be a considerable number of these
phials attached to every tree.

310. FLIES.——Great flies, like the flesh-flies, feed
upon all the softer fruits; and even upon apples and
pears. They are destroyed or kept down precisely in the
manner directed for the wasps. Some persons, in order
to preserve fine pears, cover them over with bunting, a
piece of which they tie completely over each pear: this
is a very troublesome, but a very effectual, method.

CHAPTER VII.

The formation of Shrubberies and Flower Gardens; and the
Propagation and Cultivation of the several sorts of Shrubs
and Flowers.

311. ON this part of my subject it is not agreeable to
my plan to be very minute, except as to the several
kinds of shrubs and flowers, the lists of which I shall
make as complete as I can: it is not for the use of
florists that I pretend to write; but for the use of persons who have the means of forming pretty gardens, and
who have a taste for making use of these means; a taste
which, I am sorry to say, has been declining in England
for a great many years.

SHRUBBERIES.

312. As to the form of shrubberies, or pleasure
grounds, that must greatly depend upon adventitious circumstances so various that particular directions must be
inapplicable in nine cases out of ten. There are some
things, however, which are general to all situations, and,
with respect to these, I shall offer my opinion. Shrubberies should be so planted, if they be of any considerable depth, as for the tallest trees to be at the back,

and the lowest in front : if one could have one's will, one would go, by slow degrees, from a dwarf Kalmia to a Catalpa or a Horse-chesnut. Such a slope, however, would require the depth of a mile; and, therefore, that is out of the question. If the shrubbery be of narrow space, the best way is to have no very tall shrubs at all; and to be content with an outside border of lilacs or laurels. The walks, to be beautiful and convenient, should be of gravel of a deep yellow, well-sifted and laid down in the substantial manner directed for the walks of the kitchen-garden. Such walks cannot be kept in neat order without box edgings; and every thing relating to box and to edgings has been said in Chapter II. relative to the walks of the kitchen-garden.

313. *Gravel* walks are not to be kept in neat order without being broken up once a year; and that once ought to be about the middle of the month of May. They are broken up with a pick-axe, newly raked over; and rolled with a stone roller immediately after the raking; and not the whole walk at once; but a bit at a time, so that the top be not dry when the roller comes upon it: for, if it be, it will not bind. So nice a matter is this, that, if a part be prepared for rolling, and if the hands be called off to dinner before it be rolled, mats are laid on to shade it from the sun until their return to work. This is a matter of the greatest nicety : a very good eye is required in those who rake previous to the rolling, and the rollers must have a very steady hand, or there will be unevenness in the walk, which, when properly laid, is certainly one of the most beautiful objects in the world. If proper care have been taken in laying the foundation

of the walk, few or no weeds will come even on its edges; but, if they should they must be eradicated as soon as they appear. Some leaves will fall even in summer, and the walk must be swept with a soft broom once in the week, at least.

314. But *grass* is another great ornament, and, perhaps, if kept in neat order, the greatest of all. If grass be about to be laid down, the ground should be well prepared: if too poor to keep the grass fresh through a hot Summer, it should be made richer, and always deeply moved. The next thing is, to keep the ground, whether on the sides of terraces, on a slope, or on a level, perfectly smooth and even on the surface. To *sow grass* is not the way to have fine grass plats; but to cut the turf from a common or from some very ancient and closely-pressed pasture where the herbage is fine. From our finest Downs, or from spots in our Commons, the turf is generally taken; and, short grass, as the gardeners call it, is seen in perfection, I believe, no where but in England. The old DUKE of ORLEANS, shewing sir FREDERICK EDEN his gardens at Chantilly, coming to a grass-plat, said, here is something that you will like, at any rate; and then he told him that the turf of which the plat was formed was actually imported from England, and cut upon Epsom Down. The grass cut with a turfing-iron made for the purpose, is rolled up, just like a piece of cloth, green-sward inwards, the strips are cut by a line: and cut into pieces of from two to four feet long. These are laid down in the fall of the year on the place where they are to grow: they are placed and pressed up very closely together, being well beaten down with the back

of the spade as the workman proceeds; and when the whole is laid, a roller of iron or of stone, of sufficient weight, is passed over the plat. During the next winter, care must be taken to roll again when the ground is in a dry state, after every frost. In the month of April, it will be necessary to begin to mow; for the grass will grow very well. Grass-plats are the greatest beauties of pleasure grounds if well managed; but, unless you be resolved not to spare the necessary expense for this purpose; if you think that you cannot have the perseverance to prevent your plat from becoming a sort of half meadow at certain times, the best way is not to attempt the thing at all. During the month of May, grass must be mowed once a week. From the first of June, to the middle of July, and especially if the weather be wet, twice a week may be necessary; or, one mowing and one swarding or poling, and sweeping. The mower can operate only in the *dew*: he must be at his work by daylight, and the grass must be swept up before it be dry. It is the general practice to mow every Saturday morning, and to pole or sward the grass in the middle of the week, to knock or cut off the heads of the daisies, and to take away the castings of the worms, which are very troublesome in the greater part of grass-plats. Where the thing is well done, the worm-casts are rubbed off by a pole or rod the evening before the mowing is performed, otherwise they interrupt the progress of the scythe and take off its edge. A good short-grass mower is a really able workman; and, if the plat have a good bottom, he will leave it very nearly as smooth and as even as the piece of green cloth which covers the table on which I am writing: it is quite surprising how close a scythe will go if in a hand that knows how to whet it and use it. If, however, you do not resolve to have the thing done in this manner, it is much better not to attempt it at all. The decay of gardening in England in this respect is quite surprising.

315. It is very much the fashion to have clumps of shrubs, or independent shrubs, upon grass-plats : people must follow their own taste; but, in my opinion, nothing is so beautiful as a clear carpet of green, surrounded with suitable shrubs and flowers, separated from it by walks of beautiful gravel. The edges of grass, whether against walks or against shrubberies, are sure to grow out, and ought, therefore, to be kept in by trimming or paring off very frequently ; for the whole ought to be as smooth as a piece of cloth. If thistles or dandelions, or even daisies, come amongst the grass, the mowing of them off is not enough, for each will make a circle round the crown of its root and will overpower the grass. This, however, is easily cured by cutting these roots off deeply with a knife, and pulling them up. This done during two summers successively, will destroy the dandelions and the thistles ; and, as to the daisies, which have a shallow root, they may easily be kept down, if not extirpated.

316. In the fall of the year, all shrubberies (in the month of November) should be digged completely with a fork : all suckers should be taken away, all dead wood taken out : all leaves carried off or digged in, and better carried off than digged in ; for if digged in, they make the ground hollow, and harbour slugs and other vermin.

The ground should be made smooth, therefore, when it is digged: all hares and rabbits kept out, for they are very mischievous in shrubberies, barking during the winter many of the trees of the most valuable kind. During the summer, there should be two or three hoeings to prevent weeds from growing, and a nice raking once a week to take up any leaves that may have fallen; for no trees or flowers will be seen to advantage unless they stand upon a spot that is in neat order. Shrubs should not be too much crowded by any means; it cramps them in their growth, makes their shoots feeble, makes their bloom imperfect, and they hide one another: a shrubbery should not be a mass of indistinguishable parts; but an assemblage of objects each clearly distinguished from the other. The distribution should be such as to insure bloom in every season that bloom can be had; and, though shade is in some cases desirable, flowering shrubs, to be beautiful, must not be shaded, except in instances so few as not to warrant the supposition that there is ever to be a departure from the general rule.

317. If there be water, every eye tells you that it ought to be bordered by grass; or, if of larger dimensions, by trees the boughs of which touch its very edge: bare ground and water do not suit at all. It was formerly the fashion to have a sort of canal, with broad grass walks on the sides, and with the water coming up to within a few inches of the closely shaven grass; and certainly few things were more beautiful than these Sir WILLIAM TEMPLE had one of his own constructing in his gardens at MOOR PARK. On the outsides of the

grass-walks were borders of beautiful flowers. I have stood for hours to look at this canal, which the good-natured manners of those days had led the proprietor to make an opening in the outer wall in order that his neighbours might enjoy the sight as well as himself; I have stood for hours, when a little boy, looking at this object; I have travelled far since, and have seen a great deal; but I have never seen any thing of the gardening kind so beautiful in the whole course of my life.

318. The present taste is on the side of irregularity: straight walks, straight pieces of water, straight rows of trees, seem all to be out of fashion; but, it is also true that neatness; that really fine shrubberies and flower-gardens, have gone out of fashion at the same time. People, however, must follow their own tastes in these respects; and it is useless to recommend this or that manner of laying out a piece of ground. I proceed, therefore, to speak of the propagation and management of shrubs, in the first place; and shall then give a list of the several shrubs, mentioning under each name any thing worthy of particular attention.

SHRUBS.

319. SHRUBS are propagated in just the same way that fruit-trees are, by cuttings, by slips, by layers, by graft-ing and budding in some instances, and, in every instance, they may be propagated by seed, and that, too, without the same inconvenience that occurs in the case of fruit-

trees; because I know no instance of a shrub the seed of which will not bear a flower like that of the parent tree, though I am not sure that this is the case in every instance. As often as they can be raised from seed, that is the best, though in some instances the slowest way. Cuttings and layers, and the other methods of grafting and budding, do not produce a plant so vigorous and so healthy as if raised from seed; and, though a great number of shrubs are propagated from suckers, these suckers have all the disadvantages which was mentioned when speaking of the propagation of fruit-trees. They send out suckers again, and, in a few years, if left alone, fill the whole ground with them. This is very conspicuous in the case of the lilac, which is always raised from suckers, but which may easily be raised from seed. I now proceed to give a list of the shrubs in alphabetical order, with a short description attached to each.

LIST OF SHRUBS.

320. ACACIA, the ROSE.—Latin, *Robinia Hispida*.—French, *Robinia-Rose*.—A shrub from North America, where it grows to fifteen or twenty feet high; and, in June, and sometimes again in July and August, blows a rose-coloured flower hanging like bunches of grapes. The leaves are larger and more rounded than those of the common acacia, or locust, but otherwise are just like them. The branches are covered with little prickles, when of the first and second year: afterwards these fall off, but this quality has given the species its name of *hispida*, which means hairy. It is not altogether elegant

in its form, but the beauty of its young branches, its luxuriant leaves, and, above all, its delicate and abundant flowers, make it one of the most desirable and esteemed shrubs either for the shrubbery, border, or parterre ; and the facility of procuring and cultivating it is an additional recommendation.   Graft on the common acacia, in just the same manner that you graft apples or pears (see par. 209, for tongue-grafting), and, if you make any difference at all, graft nearer to the ground than is there recommended ; and draw the earth up with a hoe about the clay that you wrap round the grafted plant, and this will keep up a moistness that renders the operation more surely successful.   The plants will flower the first year, but, unless they are in a very sheltered situation, they should have stakes driven in alongside of them, and should be tied to these, for they are exceedingly brittle, and would be blown to pieces by one high wind, without this precaution.   The flowers come on the same year's wood, therefore keep your plants shortened every year, if you wish them to flower low down ; but, if you have them on lawns, or buried at all in the shrubbery, let them have their way, only now-and-then cutting out dead wood or broken limbs.   It is perfectly hardy, and any soil almost suits it, though, like most other things, it flourishes most in the finest soil.   The SMOOTH-TREE ACACIA.—Lat. *Mimosa Julibrissin*—Fr. *Acacie arbre desois*, is a green-house shrub.   It is not ranked by the botanists with the preceding plant, but I put them together as *acacias*, meaning to have done with that genus of plants when I have finished this paragraph.   This plant is a native of the Levant, where it becomes a tree of thirty feet high, blows a rose-coloured flower in August.   It is

propagated either by sowing the seeds, or by laying;
and, in cultivation, it requires a fresh and rather light
mould; and, if put in the open ground, should be very
carefully protected from frosts and cold winds.———
SPONGE TREE ACACIA.—Lat. *Mimosa farnesiana*—Fr. *L'Acacie de Farnèse*, is also a green-house plant, but is rather
less hardy than the preceding. It comes from Saint
Domingo, where it grows to about fifteen feet high. Its
wood is white and hard, and its branches thorny; its
leaves are small, and shut up at the decline of the sun,
as do those of several of the acacias, and in August it
blows a small head of yellow and sweet-scented flowers.
Propagated in the same manner as the last.———PSEUDO-
ACACIA, see LOCUST.

321. ALMOND, *common dwarf.*—Lat. *Amygdalus nana.*
—Fr. *Amandier nain.*—A hardy tree, originally from
Russia, growing about three feet high, and blowing a
pink flower in March and April. Propagated by sowing
in a nursery, or where they are to stay; but the best
sorts are obtained by grafting either on the common
almond, or on the plum tree.———SILVER-LEAVED ALMOND,
Lat. *A. argentea*—Fr. *A. satiné,* is a taller sort, from the
Levant, growing eight or ten feet high, blowing rose-
coloured flowers in April, and having leaves covered on
both sides with a kind of down, of a silver colour.———
DOUBLE DWARF ALMOND, Lat. *A. pumila*—Fr. *A. à fleurs
doubles,* is a third sort, a smaller tree than the last, but
with remarkably double flowers of a pale rose colour,
appearing in May and often again in September. All
these trees are cultivated in the same simple manner.
They are hardy, and very handsome when in flower,

though their not bearing leaves and flowers at the same time, is a remarkable illustration of how much flowers borrow effect from foliage. Propagate by grafting on the bitter almond, or on plum-stocks, and give any situation and almost any soil. Cut out dead wood when it occurs, and that will be all the pruning necessary to these plants.

322. ALL-SPICE, *Carolina.*—Lat. *Calycanthus Floridus.* —Fr. *Calycanthe de la Floride.*—A hardy and exceedingly odoriferous shrub of Carolina, eight feet high, and blows a ruddy brown flower from May to August.—— FRUITFUL CALYCANTHUS.—Lat. *C. fertilis.*—Fr. *C. fertile.* —A hardy shrub of North America, three or four feet high, and blows a reddish brown flower from May to August. Both sorts propagated by layers ; but, as they take root with difficulty, it is best not to remove them until the third year It likes a deep and fresh soil, or still better, heath-mould ; and should not be quite exposed to the sun. If propagated from seed, it should have artificial heat to bring it up, otherwise it lies two years in the ground.

323. ALTHEA FRUTEX.—Lat. *Hibiscus Syriacus.*—Fr. *Ketmie des Jardins.*—A beautiful shrub. A native of Syria, the Levant, and North America, and of which there are four varieties, *the red, the purple, the white, and the striped.* It is a hardy late plant, coming into leaf late in June, and blowing throughout August and September. The flower comes at the side of the last year's wood as well as on the present year's wood ; and its form is very much that of the Lavetera. It grows to eight or ten feet high, generally, in America, and will grow quite

as high here.   Indeed, there is one now before the door
of the farm-house at the Duke of Devonshire's estate at
Chiswick that is full twelve feet high, and that blows regularly every year.   It ripens its seed here in an ordinarily good summer, and, though generally propagated
from cuttings or layers, is far finer when propagated
from the seed, which comes up the first year, and will
do well even when sown in the open ground.   The
young plants make a late shoot in the fall of the year,
which, if frosts come early, will be pinched by them, but
you can cut down below this in the next spring, and your
plant is but the finer for it.   It is not difficult to please
as to soil.

324. ANDROMEDA *the Marsh.*—Lat. *Andromeda poly-
folia.*—Fr. *Andromède d' Europe.*—A heath about one foot
high, which blows a rose-coloured flower in May.   It
grows well in any soil, but prefers shade, and earth which
is light, nourishing, and easy to penetrate.   Propagated
either by suckers or by dividing the roots, and does very
well after transplanting, for which February or March is
a better time than the autumn.   When raised from seeds,
sow in pots under glass ; use a peat soil and cover the
seeds very lightly over ; and put them in fresh pots when
they are an inch or two high, placing them at such distances from each other as shall suffer them to grow
strong.

325. ANTHYLLIS *the silvery, or Jupiter's beard.*—Lat. *Anthyllis barba Jovis.*—Fr. *Anthillide argente.*—A shrub of Provence and the island of Corsica, which grows four or five feet
high, and blows a pale yellow flower in April and May. Pro-

pagated by layers, cuttings, suckers, or seed sowed under a frame. Likes rich earth, and is a green-house plant.

326. ARBUTUS, *or Strawberry-tree.* — Lat. *Arbutus unedo.*—Fr. *Arbousier unedo.*—A large evergreen shrub, and a native of Ireland, which blows in September and October. The flower is of a yellowish white, or red. It bears a fruit very much resembling the strawberry. Propagated by layers, made in February, or the beginning of March; also by seed, sown immediately after it is ripe, in pots of lightish earth, which should be exposed to the south-east till the seed comes up. When the plants are four or five feet high, they are planted in small pots, and put into a house during the winter till they are strong enough to put in the open earth. It is peculiarly suited to lawns and shrubberies, where it makes a good show, and grows to the height of ten or fifteen feet.——ANDRACHNE ARBUTUS is another species, from the Levant. It has larger flowers of a deep red, but it is not so hardy, and, if planted in the open ground, must be secured against frosts.

327. AZALEA, *the white flowered.*—Lat. *Azalea viscosa.* —Fr. *Azaléa visqueux.*—A pretty and hardy shrub from North America, about three feet high, and blowing a white flower in June and July.——*Red-flowered.*—Lat. *Azalea nudiflora,* Fr. *Azaléa nudiflore,* is a hardy shrub, also from North America, about three feet high, and blows in May and June.——*Yellow-flowered.*—Lat. *Azalea pontica.*—Fr. *Azaléa de pont.*—A hardy shrub, found near the Black Sea. It is about three feet high, and blows in May. Propagated by layers or by suckers, which should

not be moved until they have taken root well. They
like black heath mould; but do well in any garden soil.
These are all very ornamental shrubs; they have none
of them much leaf, but the white has the most. The
flower comes at the ends of the branches, and resembles,
in form, that of the common honey-suckle. Cut out
dead wood, and that is all the pruning you need do.

328. BARBERRY.—Lat. *Berberis vulgaris.*—Fr. *Vine-
tier.*—A thorny little indigenous shrub, which bears a
great abundance of small oblong red berries, and it is
for these, either for pickling, or as an ornament, that
the tree is planted in our gardens and shrubberies. It
nevertheless serves to make good hedges, and requires
no pruning, and is contented with any soil. Propagate
by sowing the seeds, or by layers (which ought to remain
two seasons before they are cut off from the mother
plant) or by suckers. There is another sort, the CHINESE,
Lat. *Sinensis.*

329. BLADDER-SENNA.—Lat. *Colutea Arborescens.*—
Fr. *Baguenaudier faux Séné.*—A shrub of the south of
France, Italy and the Levant, which grows ten or twelve
feet high. It blows a yellow flower during the whole
summer, and bears the flower and the fruit at the same
time. Propagated by layers, or by sowing the seed in
rich and rather shady borders, or in an old hot-bed,
where they must stay till the following spring, when
they may be put in a nursery till the autumn, or planted,
at once, where they are meant to stay. Likes chalky
soil.——BLADDER-SENNA *Oriental.*—Lat. *Colutea orientalis.* Fr. *Baguenaudier du Levant.*—A hardy shrub from

the Levant, about six feet high, blows a yellowish red flower in June and July.——BLADDER-SENNA, *scarlet-flowered.* — Lat. *Colutea frutescens.* — Fr. *Baguenaudier d' Etheopie.*—A hardy shrub, originally from Africa, about four feet high, and blows in July. These two latter are propagated in the same way as the first, and are equally hardy, and like the same soil.

330. BLADDER-NUT, *five leaved.* — Lat. *Staphylea pinnata.*—Fr. *Staphylea à feuilles ailées.*—A hardy shrub, common in England, about fifteen or twenty feet high, and blows a white flower in April, May, and June.—— BLADDER-NUT, *three leaved.*—Lat. *Straphylea trifolia.*—Fr. *Straphylea à trois feuilles.*—A hardy shrub from Virginia, not so high as the preceding one, and blows a white flower in May and June. Propagated by suckers planted in the autumn. Any soil or situation suits these.

331. BRAMBLE FLOWERING.—Lat. *Rubus odoratus.*—Fr. *Ronce odorante.*—A hardy shrub, originally from Canada, five or six feet high, and blows, in June and August, a pinkish violet-coloured flower. Propagated by suckers. It likes a moist shaded situation. This plant is also called the *flowering Raspberry.* -

332. BREAD-TREE. — Lat. *Melia Azedarach.*—Fr. *L' Azedarach des jardins.*—A green-house shrub of Asia, which grows ten or twelve feet high, and blows a white flower tinted with purple, in July. Propagated by sowing the seed, as soon as ripe, in the open earth ; but, in a place sheltered from the frost. Orange-tree earth suits its best.

333. BROOM.— See GENISTA.

334. BUCK-THORN, *the common.* — Lat. *Rhamnus Alaternus.*—Fr. *Nerprun Alaterne.*—A hardy shrub from the south of Europe, eight or ten feet high. Blows a greenish yellow flower in April and May, and bears a red berry. Propagated by seed, grafts, and layers. Not particular as to soil, but should be in a sheltered situation. There are two varieties of this plant, the *common,* and the *jagged-leaved,* and they are very fit for shrubberies.

335. BOX-TREE.—Lat. *Buxus sempervirens.*—Fr. *Buis commun.*—An evergreen shrub of France, England, and many other parts of Europe, which grows twenty feet high, and blows a yellowish flower in April. Is most generally propagated by slips or layers, which will strike readily in the open ground, and almost any where. It is most commonly used as an edging to gravel walks, but it is also very handsome as a shrub, and is much used in situations where shade and drip of other trees will allow of scarcely any thing else.

336. CANDLE-BERRY MYRTLE.—Lat. *Myrica gale.*—Fr. *Myrica Galé.*—A hardy shrub, common in the forest of Rambouillet, in France, four feet in height, and has a small red blossom, which appears in May and June. Propagated by sowing, or by dividing the roots. Heath mould suits it best.——CANDLE-BERRY MYRTLE, *common American.*—Lat. *Myrica cerifera.*—Fr. *Myrica de la Caroline.*— A hardy shrub of North America, four or five feet high, and blows in May. The fruit is small, and covered with a white dust.   Propagated by suckers, or by seed sowed in pots.

337. CAPER BUSH.—Lat. *Capparis spinosa.*—Fr. *Câprier de Provence.*—A climber, originally of Provence and the environs of de Grasse and Toulon.   It grows three or four feet high, and blows white flowers in abundance in May and June.   Propagated by seed or by layers, but, as it is *tender,* the sure way to make layers is to cover the stump with earth, and then the shoots which come immediately from it take root easily.   It is a proper green-house plant.

338. ————————. Lat. *Camellia Japonica.* — Fr. *Camellier du Japon.*—A very beautiful evergreen green-house shrub, which blows in February and March, flowers double, semi-double, and single ;   and there are the red, red-and-white, pure white, and the blush, with various others that have been procured by art.   This plant, though strictly speaking, a green-house plant, may be brought to grow and blow in the open ground, if it be planted under a southern wall, and sheltered in the winter by mats or other covering.   It likes a good rich soil, though it is the practice of the great florists to grow it in a mixture of peat and good garden mould, to which some add a small proportion of sand.   It is not difficult of propagation either by cuttings, layers, or by grafting : if by cuttings, take off, in August, ripened shoots of the preceding year's growth, to which you will let there be three buds.   Plant a dozen or so in a pot of six or eight inches diameter filled with sand or sandy loam.   Keep

the pot under a frame or a hand-glass without bottom heat, and shade it from powerful sun. In the spring, you will find them pushing forth ; at least, all such as have struck. Give them water plentifully when they are in a growing state, and sprinkle their leaves also ; and, in the fall, they will be fit to pot off, when you should plant them singly in good-sized pots well drained by placing pot-sherds at the bottom. By layers, proceed as is recommended in Chap. VI. and graft in the manner recommended in that Chapter also, only it is usual to omit cutting a tongue in the stock and the scion as there recommended, because it is supposed to weaken both more than they can bear ; but the greater attention is requisite in the tying, so that the barks of the stock and the scion may not, in the operation of tying, be removed from the point where you have placed them. I will only repeat, that, when growing, and when in flower, this plant requires to be plentifully watered ; and that the broiling mid-day sun of summer it never likes.

330. CATALPA.—Lat. *Bignonia Catalpa.*—Fr. *Bignone Catalpa.*—This is a shrub or tree rising to the height of thirty or forty feet ; and it is sufficiently hardy for almost any part of the south of England. Its flowers, which come like those of the horse chesnut, but not until August, are far more beautiful, and they are pendulous instead of being erect. In every thing else, this tree is the reverse of the hore-chesnut. Its leaf is very large, of a singularly bright green, which it preserves wholly unfaded through the hottest summers, and until the coming of the frost. Catalpas should not be planted in the shade. In very cold and wet summers they do not

blow in England ; they blow, however, five times, perhaps, out of six ; and, if they never blowed at all, they ought to be cultivated for the beauty of the leaf. It is a tree of great durability, as well in tree as in timber. They may be raised from layers ; but with much less trouble from seed, which can, at all times, easily be had from America, which comes up the first year, and which attains a considerable height even during the first summer.

340. CEDAR.—See JUNIPER.

341. CHERRY, the BIRD.—Lat. *Prunus Padus.*— Fr. *Cerisier à grappes.*—A very handsome shrub, growing to the height of six or eight feet, and blowing in May, abundance of white flowers ; these become fruit, some red and some black. It is a native of England, and is propagated either by seeds, suckers, or grafting on the common cherry ; and it is not nice as to soil.——DOUBLE FLOWERING CHERRY—Lat. *Cerasus flore pleno*—Fr. *Cerisier à grande fleurs,* is another species of cherry. It produces a beautiful double flower in April, not so abundant as that of the former kind, but much handsomer ; and the plant is not so tall. Propagation and cultivation the same.——DWARF AMERICAN CHERRY—Lat. *Prunus Pumila.*—Fr. *Cerisier nain de Canada.*—From North America. A dwarf shrub, not more than three or four feet high, blowing small white flowers in April and May upon remarkably slender branches. Propagate in the same manner as for the two last ; and give any soil or situation. These, according to their respective sizes, are very desirable in the shrubbery and on the lawn, and they are so handsome and so easy of cultivation that no excuse can well be found for not having them.

342. CISTUS, or **ROCK-ROSE,** *the laurel-leaved.*—Lat. *Cistus laurifolius.*—Fr. *Ciste à feuilles de Laurier.*—A hardy shrub from the south of France and from Spain, about six feet high, and blows a large white flower in June and July.——Gum Cistus.—Lat. *Cistus Ladaniferus.*—Fr. *Ciste Ladanifère.*——A hardy and very beautiful shrub, about six or eight feet high, and blows, in June and July, a beautiful large white flower, with violet spots in the inside. Propagated by cuttings taken in the summer, which take root in about six weeks, if well ripened young wood be chosen for the purpose, and put under a hand-glass, and not crowded together too much.——Cistus, *the white-leaved.*——Lat. *Cistus Albidus.*—Fr. *Ciste Cotonneux.* — A shrub of the south of Europe; is three or four feet high, and blows a purplish flower in June and July. It will sometimes live in the open ground, but it is best to keep some plants in a house. Propagated by sowing the seed in April, in pots in a hot-bed; and when the young plants have five or six leaves, they must be planted, separately, in very small pots, and put in the shade, or in a shaded bed, to strike. Also propagated by cuttings made in summer.

343. CLEMATIS, or **VIRGIN'S BOWER.** — Lat. *Clematis viticella.*—Fr. *Clématite bleue.*—A hardy plant, common enough in gardens : it is a climber, and is suited to bowers and trellis-work, or for other conspicuous places. Blows a bluish purple flower in July and August, and is easily propagated by layers, or from the seed, which ripens in abundance, or by parting roots. Any soil will suit it.

344. COBEA, CLIMBING.—Lat. *Cobæa Scandens.*—Fr. *Cobéa Sarmenteux.*—A green-house climber, originally from Mexico. Its branches will grow thirty or forty yards in length, and it blows, in August and September, a large and exceedingly handsome flower, which is at first of a pale yellow, but afterwards violet. It is, although a green-house plant, as hardy as the passion flower, and, like that plant, will run over a great extent of wall in one summer, blowing abundance of its magnificent flowers, and ripening seeds in a pod of the size of a walnut ; then, if not very well protected from frost, it will die down. But it is so easily procured either from seeds, or cuttings, that no one need be long at a loss, if his plant even perish during the winter. In green-houses of small extent, it almost prevents your having any thing else, so much room will it occupy in a short time ; therefore it is generally seen in the larger conservatories, where it makes a great show for two months.

345. CORIARIA, or MYRTLE-LEAVED SUMACH.—Lat. *Coriaria Myrtifolia.*—Fr. *Redoul à feuilles de myrte.*—A hardy shrub from the south of Europe, that blows in April. Propagated by suckers, and also by seed.

346. CYPRESS-TREE.—Lat. *Cupressus Sempervirens.*—Fr. *Cyprés commun.*—A hardy shrub from the Levant; grows fifteen or twenty feet high, and blows a yellow blossom in May. The wood is hard, and of a red colour, with a very sweet scent.

347. CYTISUS, or LABURNAM. — Lat. *Cytisus*

Laburnum—Fr. *Cytise des Alpes.*—A hardy and handsome tree, originally from the Alps, twenty or thirty feet high, and blows a yellow flower in May and June.——CYTISUS, COMMON.—Lat. *Cytisus Sessilifolius.*—Fr. *Cytise à feuilles sessiles.*—A hardy shrub of Provence, twelve feet high, blows a yellow flower in May and June.——HAIRY CYTISUS.—Lat. *Cytisus hirsutus.*—Fr. *Cytise velu.*—A hardy shrub of the southern parts of Europe, smaller than the common cytisus, and blows a yellow flower in June. All the three sorts propagated by sowing the seeds in pots or in flower-beds, where they must remain until the following spring, when they must be put in a nursery. They grow well almost every where, producing amazing quantities of blossom and of seed. They require no particular management, and are proper for the inner parts of shrubberies. As they produce their flowers from spurs, which come all along the old wood, prune no more than is necessary to neighbouring trees or other things, and cut out dead wood.

348. DOGWOOD, or CORNELIAN CHERRY.— Lat. *Cornus Mascula*—Fr. *Cornouiller mâle.*—A hardy shrub from Austria, fifteen or twenty feet high, and blows a yellow flower in February. Propagated by suckers, which are taken and planted early in the autumn.—— DOGWOOD, AMERICAN.—Lat. *Cornus Florida.*—Fr. *Cornouiller à grandes fleurs.*—An equally hardy plant from North America, but it there sometimes rises to the height of forty or fifty feet. Grows at the edges of woods, and blows large white and pink flowers at the ends of its branches in May and June. Propagated from seeds ; and but little known in England.

349. DIERVILLA.—See HONEYSUCKLE.

350. DIOTIS SHRUBBY.—Lat. *Diotis candidissima.*
—Fr. *Diotis cotonneuse.*—A hardy shrub from Siberia,
eight or nine inches high, and blows a yellow flower in
August. Propagated by layers, and cuttings will do
under a hand-glass. Likes a stony soil.

351. FONTANESIA, *phillyrea-leaved.*—Lat. *Fontanesia
phillyreoïdes.*—Fr. *Fontanesia à feuilles de filaria.*—A hardy
shrub from Syria, ten or twelve feet high, and blows a
white flower in May. Good to put against walls, for the
purpose of hiding them. Propagated by suckers, cuttings,
and also by seed. Does well in almost any soil, if it be
not too moist.

352. FUCHSIA.—Lat. *Fuchsia coccinea.*—Fr. *Fuchsie
écarlate.*—A pretty *tender* shrub, a native of Chili, where
it grows to the height of three or four feet. Its young
branches are delicate, and of a deep scarlet colour, as are
the tips of its leaves ; and, throughout the summer
months, it blows numerous little pendant flowers, the
upper part scarlet, and, towards the lower, becoming of
a bluish violet. The young shoots strike freely under a
hand-glass, which should frequently be tilted up a little
to give air. A mixture of good loam and peat suits them
well. The green-house is the proper place for this
plant, though in the summer it will do well turned out
into the open ground, and will even live through a moderate winter in England, if cut down and carefully covered
with litter ; but it is generally potted in the beginning of
October, and then, having taken root, is placed in its
winter quarters.

353. GENISTA, or BROOM.—Lat. *Genista tinctoria.*— Fr. *Genêt à balais.*—The common yellow broom every one knows ; and the effect of it in a shrubbery need scarcely be described. There is a white sort, *Genista alba,* which is very handsome. These blow in May ; and are propagated without any difficulty from the seed. Sow them in rows not far apart, in the spring, and keep them cleanly weeded when they are small. The white sort is remarkably handsome for a full month in the spring of the year, and should, by all means, form a part of the shrubbery, though it is rather too tall to be immediately in the front row.

354. GERANIUM.—Lat. *Geranium.*—Fr. *Geranier.*— The botanists have found geraniums in almost all countries, some herbaceous, some woody, some fibrous-rooted and some tuberous-rooted ; but I shall leave all the rest unmentioned, that I may have the more room to speak of the two or three sorts that I deem the most ornamental, and, in every way, the best deserving mention in this work. The English florists have become celebrated for their collections of a vast variety of green-house geraniums, which equal, or surpass, in number that of the auricula, and which certainly does include a set of flowers of unrivalled beauty. This plant is, among English florists, what the tulip and hyacinth are with the Dutch florists : they spare no expense in erecting propagation-houses and conservatories for it, they have shows of it, they give a high-sounding name to every new variety, and whole works have been published laudatory of its beauties.—The common *scarlet* and the *ivy-leaved* are the only two sorts that I shall particularize. The

first is well known in most gardens. It is a woody plant, though its wood is of a succulent nature and is not a match for our winters in the open air ; it grows to the height of four feet or more in good ground in England, and much higher at the Cape of Good Hope or in the south of Africa, where it is indigenous. It has large downy soft leaves of a beautiful luxuriant green, placed at the end of foot-stalks, and it bears its flowers in scarlet bouquets, or bunches, at the end of foot-stalks longer than those of the leaves. It will spread to a great width when planted out, and in a good warm summer. I have had it at Kensington full five feet over, and covered with blossoms from the middle of June to the middle of October. It is said to like a *light* rich mould best. Rich mould it does like, but I never found it do otherwise than well in the deepest and stiffest garden mould that I have occupied, and I have occupied some of the stiffest that I ever saw in my life. In its native country it likes sand, because it has nothing else ; but I look upon it, that a geranium in African sand under an *English* sun, would become a very poor thing indeed. Gravel suits it ill, as do also the extremes of chalk or clay, but a good depth of mould over a bed of either of these latter, with well-rotted manure and good tillage, will make a very fine geranium, and will keep it in blossom four months of the year. As it is infalliby killed by hard frost, unless most cautiously covered over with litter and mats, the way to perpetuate it that I generally follow is this : in July take some cuttings of young wood that is ripening and put them in separate pots of nice mould, observing to have two joints below the earth and one above it. Then plunge the pots up to their rims in a hot-bed of

moderate heat.   Shade them with mats, but do not give
air for a day or two, and then give a little water and air,
but let the water have stood in the watering-pot exposed
to the sun for three or four hours before you give it.
When you find they have struck and are growing well,
re-pot them and place them in the open air, but in a
shady situation, with hoops over them that you may lay
mats on.   Put some siftings of cinders on the ground
before you place the pots on it, and this will keep out
worms.   In this place, let them recover the re-potting;
which they will soon do, and then they are nice fresh
and convenient-sized plants for the green-house, where
they will blow in the winter, and in the following May,
will be your supply for the open ground.   Another way
of propagating is by seed, of which you may generally
gather abundance in July, and, if sowed directly in good
earth and in large pots plunged in a hot-bed, will come
up directly, and, being potted out singly in three weeks
from the time of coming out, and again carefully managed (though not forced), will be fine strong plants by
the end of autumn, and handsomer in form than those
raised from cuttings.   Put them into the green-house in
September, or earlier if the weather be cold, and observe
that you cannot give too much *air*, nor keep the place
too free from *damp*.   Want of air and dampness being
the two main destroyers of these plants.   If their leaves
turn yellow, be sure that there is not air enough; and,
if their joints become mouldy, look to dampness as the
cause.   Prune off dead branches, and always keep the
plant bushey, for otherwise it becomes a long horny
thing, with a small head and few flowers.——The *ivy-
leaved geranium* is a pretty little trailing plant, with

thin branches of a brownish green hue, and little smooth rather fleshy leaves of a dark green with a broad rim of black near the outside edge, and of the shape of an ivy-leaf. It blows clusters of pinkish flowers throughout the summer months; is tender, but does well in the green-house, or in any parlour window of good aspect. Propagate it by cuttings as you do the last-mentioned; and train it up a little ladder, getting wider and wider as it gets high; prune only dead branches. A mixture of vegetable manure and good mould suits it well.

355. ————————. — Lat. *Gordonia Pubescens.*—Fr. *Gordania Pubescent.*—To which BERTRAM, the discoverer of it, gave the name of *Franklinia.* This shrub is a native of the southern States of America. Its flowers are magnificent, and it grows to a height of from ten to twenty feet. It is deciduous; and the seeds of it must be had from America; for though it would blow here very well, it would not ripen its seed. It has long stood the climate of Pennsylvania, where the winters are much more severe than they are in England.

356. GEORGIA BARK.—Lat. *Pinkneyea Pubens.*—Fr. *Pinkneyea Pubescent.*—This is a singularly beautiful shrub, both as to leaf and flower; grows to the height of twenty feet; but must be tender, because it appears to be confined to the southern States of America. It was discovered by M. MICHAUX in 1791, who gave it the name of PINKNEYA, in honour of Mr. PINKNEY, who had been ambassador in France.

357. GUELDER-ROSE. — Lat. *Viburnum opulus.*—

Fr. *Viorne obier.*—A shrub common in most parts of Europe, is five or six feet high, and blows a large round white flower like a ball of snow, in May and June. Propagated by seed, but most frequently by layers or suckers. Not at all particular as to soil.

358. HARE'S-EAR, *shrubby.* — Lat. *Bupleurum fruticosum.*—Fr. *Buplèvre frutescent.*—A rather tender evergreen shrub of Provence, and other parts of the south of France. It grows to the height of five or six feet and blows a yellow flower in July or August. It is very pretty, and suited to winter shrubberies ; but requires to be placed so that it may not push out too much in the summer. Propagated by sowing the seeds in light earth as soon as they are ripe, or by cuttings under a hand-glass.

359. HONEY-SUCKLE.—Lat. *Lonicera caprifolia.*—Fr. *Chèvrefeuille des jardins.*—A trailing shrub of England, France, and other parts of Europe, which grows against walls or trees, and blows a reddish flower from the end of the spring to the middle of summer. Any soil suits it, but it does best exposed to the sun. Propagated by layers made at any time of the year, or by cuttings put in in the spring and autumn.——HONEY-SUCKLE, RED-BERRIED.—Lat. *Lonicera alpigena.*—Fr. *Chèvre-feuille des Alpes.*—A climbing shrub, three or four feet high, from Switzerland Blows a red flower in May.——HONEY-SUCKLE, the PYRENEAN.—Lat. *Lonicera Pyrenaica.*—Fr. *Chèvre-feuille des Pyrénées.*—A climbing shrub of the Pyrenees, three or four feet high, and blows, in May, a flower that is red on one side.——HONEY-SUCKLE, *the*

Trumpet.—Lat. *Lonicera sempervirens.*—Fr. *Chèvre-feuille toujours vert.*—A climbing evergreen shrub from North America. Blows, from May till August, a flower which is red on the outside, and yellow in the inside. Propagated by layers and cuttings. Any soil suits them.—— HONEY-SUCKLE, *the Tartarian.*—Lat. *Lonicera Tartarica.* Fr. *Chameserisier de Tartarie.*—A shrub, originally from Russia and Tartary, which grows to the height of five or six feet, and blows in March and April. As the seeds are one or two years in coming up, it is best to propagate them by layers, which may be planted where they are to stay at the end of eighteen months. They do not like the spring frosts, but hard winters do not hurt them. Any soil suits them, but it is advisable to put them in a good situation and in a warm soil.——HONEY-SUCKLE, *Yellow-flowered.* — Lat. *Diervilla lutea.*— Fr. *Diervilla a fleurs Jaunes.*—A hardy shrub from North America, two or three feet high, and blows a yellow flower in June. Propagated by suckers. Any soil or situation agrees with it.

360. HAWTHORN, *White.*—Lat. *Mespilus Oxiacantha.*— Fr. *Néflier Aubépine.*—A shrub common in many parts of Europe, which blows a white flower in May; but enough of it has been said in paragraph 32. But, besides being a most useful plant for the purpose of making hedges, it is also an exceedingly ornamental shrub, having foliage, flower and fragrance to delight our senses early in the month of May. Propagated from the seeds which ripen plentifully. Gather them in the fall; keep them all the winter in sand, and sow in the spring; and, in two years your plants will be fit to go out.

361. INDIGO, *shrubby bastard.*—Lat. *Amorpha fruti-cosa.*—Fr. *Amorpha élevé.*—A rather hardy shrub of Caro-lina, ten feet high, and blows a violet-coloured flower in June and July. Propagated from seed and from cuttings. Any soil will do for it, but it prefers a light and gravelly soil, and a warm situation. In severe winters it requires sheltering.

362. IVY.—Lat. *Hedera helix.*—Fr. *Lierre commun.*—A hardy climber, common in Europe ; blows a whitish flower in September and October, and is useful to cover old walls.—*H. Canatiensis,* or IRISH IVY, is the best sort : both are easily propagated by layers or cuttings.

363. JASMIN, *common white.*—Lat. *Jasminum officinale.*—Fr. *Jasmin commun.*—A shrub of the coast of Malabar, which grows ten or twelve feet high, and blows a sweet-scented white flower from July to October. Propagated by suckers. Any soil suits it, but it likes a light and warm one best. It is generally trained against walls or trellis-work, and will there grow to a great height.——JASMIN, *yellow Italian.*—Lat. *Jasminum humile.*—Fr. *Jasmin d' Italie.*—A shrub which grows four or five feet high, and blows a yellow flower from July to September. Cul-tivated like the white jasmin.

364. JUNIPER-TREE, or *red cedar.*—Lat. *Juniperus Virginiana.*—Fr. *Genévrier de Virginie.*—An evergreen tree from North America that blows in May, and pro-duces a little blue berry. It grows to forty or fifty feet high, and delights in peat soil ; but is not very nice as to that.——PHŒNICIAN CEDAR.—Lat. *Juniperus Phœnicea.*—Fr. *Genévrier de Phénicie.*—An evergreen shrub from the

south of Europe, which blows in April, and produces a
yellow berry. It grows to about six or eight feet high.
JUNIPER, *the common.*—Lat. *Juniperus communis.*—Fr. *Genévrier commun.*—A shrub common in England ; and bears
a fruit of a blackish blue colour. Propagated by cuttings
and suckers, and, also, by seed, which comes up the
second year, and should be sown in garden mould mixed
with sand. The two foregoing should be propagated in
the same manner.

365. KŒLREUTERIA, *panicled.* — Lat. *Kælreuteria
paniculata.*—Fr.*Kælreuteria paniculé.*—A hardy shrub, ten or
twelve feet high, originally from China, which blows a yellow flower in August. Propagated by seed, and requires great
care for the first two or three years. It is also obtained by
cuttings planted in February in pots, and put into a hot-bed
of moderate heat. They take root in about a month, and
should be separated in the autumn.

366. LAUREL, *or sweet-bay.*—Lat. *Laurus nobilis.*—Fr.
Laurier commun.—That common evergreen which we see
now in all parts of England forming the underwood to
high shrubberies, and the fore-ground of low ones. It is
a native of Italy, but is hardy enough to stand the
winters of the southern parts of England well, though in
the North, and particularly if on high and exposed
situations, it will not outlive a very severe winter. It
blows a yellow small flower in May ; and is easily propagated by layers. It grows to ten or twelve feet high,
when in a sheltered situation, and is more particular as
to this matter than as to soil. Under the tall Scotch
firs in Windsor great Park, immediately adjoining that

barrenest of all spots, Bagshot Heath, there are laurels of eight-and-twenty feet high ! I never saw them any where so large as there.——PORTUGAL LAUREL.—Lat. *Prunus Lusitanica.*—Fr. *Cerisier Azarero.*—Another evergreen, and common enough in England. It is from Portugal, and blows a white flower in June and July, and then produces blackish berries, thinly disposed on its flower-stalk. It will grow to twelve or fifteen feet high (and much higher when raised from seed,) forming a round full head like an apple-tree, and having a no inconsiderable, though very short, trunk. Propagated, from layers or seed, the seed should be sown as soon as ripe in beds. Any soil almost will suit it, but it likes a good deep one best.—— LAUREL ALEXANDRIAN. — Lat. *Ruscus racemosus.* — Fr. *Fragon à grappes.*—An evergreen shrub from the south of Europe, which is about two feet high, blows, in June and July, a flower of a yellowish colour, and the fruit is a beautiful red berry. It is propagated by seed but most commonly by separating the roots (which should be strong) in February or March. It likes a sandy earth, and will thrive in a shady situation.

367. LIME TREE.—Lat. *Tilia europæa.*—Fr. *Tilleuls de Hollande.*—A hardy tree of England, France, Sweden, and other parts of Europe. It would grow to a good height, except that it is generally kept short in gardens, that the branches may grow thicker and form a shade. Blows a yellow flower in May and June. Propagated by cuttings, and sometimes by seed, and likes a soil of good depth.

368. LILAC, *common.*—Lat. *Syringa vulgaris.* — Fr. *Lilas commun.* —A shrub from Constantinople, about

twelve feet in height, blows, in May, a violet-coloured, or white, flower.——LILAC, *Chinese.*—Lat. *Syringa Chinensis.* — Fr. *Lilas hybride.* — A shrub originally from China. Has a violet-coloured flower. Not so tall as the foregoing.——LILAC, *Persian.*—Lat. *Syringa Persica.*— Fr. *Lilas de Perse.*—A shrub from Persia, about eight feet high, and, in May, blows a light purple flower. They are all to be propagated by shoots, suckers, or layers, and they like good deep soil. They are very proper for shrubberies, but the first sort in particular is too tall for the fronts of them.

369. LOCUST.—Lat. *Pseudo-acacia.*—Fr. *Robinier.*— A timber-tree of North America, which I mention here on account of its being one of the most ornamental of our tall shrubbery trees, both owing to its handsome foliage, and its handsome and abundant clusters of white flowers. It is propagated from seed, which is sometimes ripened in this country. The plants come up the first year, and, in the fall of the same year, may be planted out where they are to stand ; though it is certainly better to give them one year in the nursery, cutting them down to within a couple or three inches of the ground every time you transplant. Their only enemies are hares and rabbits, and, if planted out young in a place where these vermin abound, expect not to preserve your locust trees.

370. LOBLOLLY BAY.—Lat. *Gordonia Lasyanthus.* —Fr. *Gordonia à feuilles Glabres.*——This is an evergreen which rises to the height of fifty or sixty feet in America, bearing a white flower, in size and shape very much like that of the dwarf or round tulip. I have never seen one of

them in England, and I suppose that it is about as tender as the Magnolia Grandiflora, as it comes from the
southern States of America.

371. ——————————. Lat. *Symphoricarpos parvixlora.*—
Fr. *Lonicera Symphoricarpos.*—A very pretty dwarf shrub,
that comes out into leaf more early in the spring than
any other that I know of, and has a leaf of singular
beauty.   I raised, the year before last, great quantities
from seed got from America.   The seed lay two years in
the ground ; but the plants grew surprizingly after they
came up.   It blows in August a minute but pretty and
pendant rose coloured flower, which is succeeded by a
small red berry.   This is a very pretty shrub, and easily
propagated from layers, of which every plant affords prodigious quantities.

372. MAGNOLIA.—There are seven sorts of Magnolias, all of which come from North America: They
are called, first, The *Magnolia Grandiflora,* some of which
have white and some purplish flowers.   It grows in the
southern States of North America to the common height
of our elms.   It is rather too tender for exposed situations in England, and is generally placed against a house
or a high wall facing the south.   I have, however, seen
them standard trees, and of considerable height.   Its
flowers are magnificent, indeed.   They are shaped somewhat like the flower of the tulip, and burst open like the
tulip.   The petals are from three to four inches long, and
the flower sometimes, when quite open, forms a circumference of more than a foot, or approaching to a foot and
a half.   From the centre of the petals there arises a

flower-pod somewhat in the shape of a pine-apple, which opens when the seed is nearly ripe, and the seeds come out from the sides of this seed-pod and hang suspended from it from a little sort of string. This magnolia is an evergreen, and has long, large, and beautiful leaves. All magnolias may be raised from the seed ; but that seed must be brought from the country of which the tree is a native. The seed comes up the first year in the natural ground, but the seedlings must be carefully protected during the winter for a year or two.—Second, *Magnolia tripetella*, which the Americans call *umbrella-tree*. This tree is hardy, and will grow as a standard in any tolerable situation in England. The leaves of this tree are some of the largest and finest in the world. I have some now each of which is about twenty-one inches long, and nine inches wide in the middle. The flower is white and has three petals, each of very great length and breadth. This tree loses its leaves in the fall.—Third, *Magnolia acuminata*. This is another variety. It is hardy, and will very well endure the climate of England.—Fourth, *Magnolia cordata*. This has rather a round leaf, and has a yellow blossom. It is about as tender as the Magnolia Grandiflora.—Fifth, *Magnolia auriculata.*—Sixth, *Magnolia macrophylla*. Both varieties of the great magnolia or magnolia grandiflora, and both about as tender as that.—Seventh *Magnolia Glauca*, or *small Magnolia*. This is perfectly hardy, grows in Canada, and in all parts of the United States of America, and is a shrub, take it altogether, excelling every other. It is called the *glauca* on account of the bluish colour on the under-side of its leaves, which are of a bright green on the upper side, and have the solidity and characteristics of the laurel, though the tree is deciduous. It rises to the height of ten or twelve feet ; bears a flower of the shape of the dwarf or round tulip. It is about the size also of the flower of the dwarf tulip, opens by slow degrees, and emits an odour the most delightful that can be conceived ; far exceeding that of the rose ; in strength equal to that of the jonquil or the tuberose, and far more delightful. In the country where this tree grows, a clump of them scents a whole wood. The tree continues to bear flowers for a long while, two months, at the least ; for the flowers succeed each other, some being mere buds, while the petals of others are dropping. This tree will grow in almost any ground : as it is generally found near swamps in America, I thought that it required a low situation in England, until I saw upon a sand-hill partly covered with heath, in a garden which belonged to Sir HERBERT TAYLOR near St. Ann's Hill, one of these magnolias in as vigorous a state and as full bloom as I ever saw one in America. This shrub, like the great magnolia, is raised from layers in England ; but if it were raised from seed, as it very easily might be, the plants would be beyond all measure finer than they generally are. None of the other magnolias are nearly so odoriferous as this ; all but this are somewhat tender : this might be in every shrubbery in England with the greatest ease ; and I cannot help expressing my hope that it may one day become as common as the lilac.

373. MEZEREON. — Lat. *Daphne Mezereum.* — Fr. *Daphné bois gentil.* —A shrub of the most mountainous parts of France, three feet high, and blows a rose-coloured, or white flower, at the end of the winter.

Propagated by cuttings or by seed sown in open earth, in drills or otherwie, but covered two inches thick. It likes a light soil, and a rather shady situation. A very nice plant for the front part of shrubberies.

374. MYRTLE, common.—Lat. *Myrtus communis.*—Fr. *Myrte commun.*—A shrub originally from Asia, Africa, Italy, and the south of France. Blows a white flower during the summer, and the fruit ripens in the autumn. It will grow five or six feet high in pots or against walls, but if not well protected, will not outlive the winter; and it requires a good aspect to make it blossom. It likes a good loamy soil, and I have had it blossom abundantly in such, and in a south-western aspect, in Hampshire. Propagate it by cuttings of young wood placed under a hand-glass, or by layers.

375. OLEASTER, *narrow leaved.*—Lat. *Eleægnus angustifolia.*—Fr. *Chalef à feuilles étroites.*—A hardy tree of Provence, about thirty feet high, and bears a yellow blossom in June and July. Its foliage produces an agreeable effect in parks and large gardens, for which only it is proper. Propagated by layers or by cuttings, but the cuttings require sheltering in the winter. Any soil suits it, but it likes best a light, sandy, and rather warm soil.

376. OLIVE-TREE.—Lat. *Olea Europæa.*—Fr. *Olivier commun.*—A green-house shrub from the south of Europe. Blows a white fragrant flower in May. Propagated by parting the roots, by suckers, and by cuttings. They are often grafted on the common privet.

377. OLEANDER, *or Rose-bay.* —Lat. *Nerium Grandi-florum.*——Fr. *Laurier rose à grandes fleurs.*—A beautiful evergreen green-house shrub, from the south of Europe. Grows six or eight feet high, and from July to September, blows large double pink flowers of the most agreeable and most delicate appearance. It requires a good but rather light soil, water and heat when putting forth its flowers, but little water and no *damp* at other times, as these cause a mould to come round its joints. It is a handsome plant in form, and should be shifted into fresh pots every two or three years. Propagate it by cuttings of the young and just-ripened wood, planted under a hand-glass, and with a little heat under, or by layers which root freely. It is one of the very handsomest of green-house shrubs. —— COMMON RED — Lat. *Nerium Oleander*—Fr. *Laurier rose des jardins*—is another species, not so tender, and not by any means so handsome. It will grow and blow in the open ground, but must be covered carefully in the winter. Propagation the same as for the former.

378. ORANGE-TREE.—Lat. *Citrus.*—Fr. *L'oranger.*— A green-house evergreen shrub of the East Indies and south of Europe, which grows fifteen feet high, and blows a white fragrant flower in June and July. Propagated by sowing in March or April in pots put in a bed of moderate heat, or more easily, by procuring from Italy or France, roots already grafted and pretty strong. These plants require a rich mould, and should be manured with rotten dung. In the north of France, they are generally kept in large square boxes of three or four feet diameter, and these boxes being on wheels, they are easily moved in and out of the conservatory. The sides of the boxes are so constructed as to open like doors, and thus, every year, one side is opened and looked at, and roots are pruned or fresh mould introduced, as the cultivator thinks fit.

379. PAPAW.—Lat. *Anona triloba.*—Fr. *Assiminier.*— a native of Canada, and, therefore, hardy. It bears a beautiful purple flower in the month of July, and rises to the height of twenty or thirty feet. It being hardy, it would be certainly worth the trouble of obtaining the seeds from America.

380. PERIWINKLE, *large* — Lat. *Vinca major.*—Fr. *La grande Pervenche.*—A hardy trailing plant from the south of Europe, grows two feet high, blowing a pretty blue flower during the whole of the summer. Propagated by suckers which come in abundance ; likes any soil, and a shady situation.

381. POME-GRANATE. — Lat. *Punica granatum.*— Fr. *Grenadier commun.*—A shrub belonging to Italy, Spain, and the south of France. About twelve or fifteen feet high, and blows in July and September a beautiful red flower. Propagated by suckers and layers, and cuttings which root easily. There are two sorts which have white flowers, one double, the other single. Require the green-house in England, and a little heat, too, to make them blow strongly. Good loamy soil.

382. PASSION FLOWER.—Lat. *Passiflora cærulea.*— Fr. *Grenadille bleue.*—A climbing plant, originally from South America ; is about forty feet high, and, from July

till October, blows a flower, the exterior of which is a
pale green, and the interior a fine purple. Its branches
will extend over a large surface of wall in one summer,
and, if not well looked to and nailed up, will get into
great confusion and become rather ugly than otherwise.
It may be trained up pillars, over bowers, or it may be
let in at parlour windows. It is, as far as its branches
go, tender, but will live throughout the winter if matted
over with care, and, if not matted, will often only die
down to the root, and spring up again at the approach of
summer. Propagate by striking cuttings in the autumn
under a hand-glass or a gentle heat. Mixture of garden
mould and peat suits the passion-flower well; but it is
not very nice as to soil.

383. PISTACHIO-TREE.—Lat. *Pistachia vera.* — Fr.
Pistachier cultivé.—A tree from Syria, twenty or thirty
feet high, and blows in April and May.——TURPENTINE-
TREE. — Lat. *Pistachia terebinthus.*—Fr. *Pistachier téré-
binthe.*—A hardy shrub from Barbary, where it attains
the height of an elm. Blows in April and May.——
MASTICK-TREE.—Lat. *Pistachia lenticus.* — Fr. *Pistachier
lentisque.*—A green-house shrub from the south of Europe,
where it is generally about ten or twelve feet high, and
blows in April. These all bear berries. Propagated by
seed, sown in pots and put into a hot-bed, in the spring.
Layers can also be made of them, but they are never so
strong. They require a warm situation, and, in the
winter, the roots should be covered with litter.

384 PRIVET, *common.* — Lat. *Ligustrum vulgare.*—
Fr. *Troène commun.*—A hardy shrub, common in Eng-

land ; six or eight feet high, and blows a pretty odoriferous white flower in June and July. Propagated by cuttings, layers, and seed. Does well in any soil or situation. It is generally used for low hedges in gardens and pleasure grounds, where it is suitable; and, when white and red roses are planted with it, makes as pretty a fence as can be conceived.

385. PSORALEA, *bituminous.*—Lat. *Psoralea bituminosa.*—Fr. *Psoralea bitumineux.*—A green-house shrub of the south of France, about three feet in height, and blows a blue flower during the whole of the summer. It will sow itself when in a strong earth, and likes a warm but airy situation.

387. RHODODENDRON.—Lat. *Rhododendrum maximum.*—Fr. *Rhododendron d'Amerique.*—A beautiful American shrub, growing to six, ten, or even, sometimes, twenty feet high ; blowing, in June and July, large flowers of a pale rose colour. Propagated by layers ; or by sowing the seed, which must be procured from America. This is one of the most ornamental of all shrubs, and is proper for either the lawn, front of shrubbery, or the flower-border, and any good soil suits it well.

387. ROSE.—Lat. *Rosa.*—Fr. *Rose.*—Any eulogy of the rose would be childish, and it would not be much less childish to insert a catalogue of roses of more than a thousand in number, from the lists of the florists of France and England. The roses that might content any man not a professed florist, are the following. 1st. *Provence,* white and red. 2d. *Moss Provence,* white and red. 3d. *Damask.* 4th. *Velvet.* 5th. *Striped.* 6th. *Maiden's*

blush. 7th. *Monthly roses,* white and red. 8th. *Yellow double and single.* 9th. *Rose de Maux.* 10th. *Sweet Briar.* 11th. *Austrian briar* (the flower, the colour of that of a nasturtium). 12th. *Chinese,* or ever-blowing. 13th. *Multiflora,* many-flowering. 14th. *Lady Banks.* The three last may be easily raised from cuttings: all the rest from layers or suckers. The Lady Banks is a rosé brought from China by Sir JOSEPH BANKS, and given to the King's gardens at Kew. It is a little white rose, and bears its flowers in bunches, and yields to nothing, in point of odour, except the Magnolia Glauca. The leaf is very delicate, and the tree has *no thorns,* in which respect it differs, I believe, from every other rose in the world. After all, perhaps, leaf, colour, size, every thing taken into account, the Provence rose is still the finest, and they ought to be in abundance in every shrubbery. To cause the rose to continue to produce flowers for a long while, gather the flowers close to the stem, cropping off the seed hip as soon as the petals begin to drop, which, besides the other circumstance, will prevent the ground from being littered by the flowers which become putrid in a short time. Roses may be budded on stocks of any vigorous sort, and stocks may be raised from the seeds of the dog, or hedge, rose. This is the way in which tall standard rose-trees are obtained. The stocks should be managed in the same way as stocks for fruit-trees. Roses never thrive in poor, and particularly, in shallow ground. They like cool, and somewhat stiff ground; and you always perceive the hedge roses finest on the sides of land which is too stiff to be arable land. If, therefore, the ground of your shrubbery be of a very light nature, you ought to move it deep for the roses, and to get something of the clayey or marly kind to mix with it, it being quite useless to plant the shrub unless it be made capable of bearing flowers, which it will not in a poor hungry soil. Roses may be trained against houses, and especially the Chinese rose. In this case, care should be taken to prune out old wood occasionally, and to shorten the shoots so as to keep the tree in bearing condition. If roses, as standards, are required to be of considerable height, occasional pruning must take place to keep the head in order, and to prevent one part from rambling beyond another. All the roses but the Chinese bear upon wood of the last year or some former year; that is to say, there must be wood of a year old or more for a little shoot to come out of to bear the flowers. The height of your dwarf rose must depend upon that of its surrounding neighbours: if they be low, as in a flower-border or flower-garden, the roses must be so pruned down in the winter as to leave no part of the shrub more than a foot high, taking care to leave the strongest and best wood: out of this wood come little shoots that bear the roses. A chinese rose will send out a long shoot from the ground in the spring, which will bear flowers during the same year. If this rose stand in a low border, it must be cut down to within a foot of the ground, or it overtops every thing in a short time.

388. SAGE, *Jerusalem.*—Lat. *Phlomis fruticosa.*—Fr. *Phlomis frutescent.*—A hardy shrub of Spain and Sicily, three or four feet high, and blows a yellow flower in July, August, and September. Propagated by dividing the roots, and by sowing in beds prepared for that purpose. Not particular as to soil.

389. SEA-BUCKTHORN.—Lat. *Hippophae rhamoïdes.* Fr. *L' Argoussier rhamoide.*—A large hardy shrub from the borders of the Mediterranean, and blows in April. Propagated by layers made in black heath-mould. Any soil suits it, but light soil is best.

390. SERVICE-TREE, *true.*—Lat. *Sorbus domestica.*—Fr. *Sorbier cultivé.*—A tree common in England, about fifty feet high, blows a white flower early in the spring, and bears fruit which *may* be eaten. Propagates itself in forests, and is obtained in gardens by seed, and by grafting on the white-thorn.——Mountain Ash.—Lat. *Sorbus aucuparia.*—Fr. *Sorbier des oiseleurs.*—A tree common in the north of Europe, not so high as the preceding one, blows clusters of white flowers in May, and bears clusters of beautiful red berries in the autumn. A most ornamental tree for large pleasure-grounds.——Bastard Service-tree.——Lat. *Sorbus hybrida.*—Fr. *Sorbier hybride.*—A tree common in the north of Europe, and differing from the others in its leaves and flowers only; the former being downy, and the latter smaller. Propagated from seed, and are obtained sooner by grafting on the quince or thorn.

391. SCORPION SENNA.—Lat. *Coronilla emerus.*—Fr. *Coronille des Jardins.*—A shrub originally from the south of France, three or four feet high, bearing, in April and June, a yellow flower; and, if clipt with the scissors, will blow again in the middle of summer. Propagated by seeds or by suckers, or cuttings planted in the open ground early in the autumn. A very pretty plant for the fronts of shrubberies.

392. SNOW-DROP TREE, *four winged.*—Lat. *Halesia tetraptera.*—Fr. *L'Halésia à quatre ailes.*—A hardy tree of Carolina, twenty or thirty feet high, and blowing a white flower in May. Propagated by seed and by layers which do not firmly take root until the third year. It likes a good soil and will grow freely.

393. SPINDLE-TREE, *common.* — Lat. *Evonymus Europæus.*—Fr. *Fusain d' Europe.*—A hardy shrub twelve feet in height, and blows a whitish flower in May. Common in England.——SPINDLE TREE *the warted.*—Lat. *Evonymus verrucosus.*—Fr. *Fusain galeux.*—A hardy shrub from Austria. In May blows a flower of a brownish purple. These shrubs are propagated by their seed sown in light earth in the shade, or by ripened cuttings struck in the open ground in autumn. Any soil suits them; and hey suit large pleasure grounds.

394. SPIRÆA, *Hawthorn leaved.*—Lat. *Spiræa crenata.*—Fr. *Spirie à feuilles crenelées.*—A hardy shrub originally from Siberia, about three feet high, and blows a white flower in June and July.—— SPIRÆA, *Willow Leaved.*—Lat. *Spiræa salici Folia.*—Fr. *Spirée à feuilles de saule.*—A hardy shrub from North America, about six feet high, and blows a purplish red flower in July and August.——SPIRÆA *Germander-leaved.*—Lat. *Spiræa chamædrifolia.*—Fr. *Spirée à feuilles de germandrée.* — A hardy shrub from Siberia that blows a white flower early in the spring. SPIRÆA *Hypericum Frutex.*— Lat. *Spiræa Hypericifolia.*—Fr. *Spirée à feuilles de millepertius.*—A hardy shrub and blows a white flower. From America.——SPIRÆA *Scarlet.* — Lat. *Spiræa tommentosa.* — Fr. *Spirée cotoneuse.* — A hardy shrub from America, and blows a red flower. All these are propagated by layers, slips, suckers, cuttings, and, also by seed. Not particular as to soil. Very desirable shrubs.

395. ST. JOHN'S WORT, *large flowered.*—Lat. *Hypericum calycinum.* — Fr. *Millepertius à grandes fleurs.*— A hardy perennial from the environs of Constantinople, which blows a yellow flower from June to September. Propagated from seed and by dividing the roots in March. Likes a warm situation.——ST. JOHN'S WORT, *hairy.*— Lat. *Hypericum hirsutum.*— Fr. *Millepertius velu.*—A hardy plant common in Europe, growing three feet high and blowing a yellow flower in July and August. Propagates itself. Pretty for the fronts of shrubberies.

396. STRAWBERY-TREE, *red berried trailing.*—Lat. *Arbutus uva ursi.*—Fr. *Arbousier busserole.*—A hardy shrub, common in England. Blows in March and April, a white flower, and bears very pretty red fruit in June. Propagated by seed, sown as soon as ripe, in pots, and exposed to the south east till it is up. When the plants are an inch high, they should be planted in little pots till they are strong enough to put into the open earth. They like heath mould and rather a shady situation. Makes a good show on naked banks.

397. SUMACH, *Venice.*—Lat. *Rhus continus.*—Fr. *Sumac fustet.*—A hardy shrub belonging to Italy and Austria. It is about eight feet high, and blows in July and August.——SUMACH—*virginian.*—Lat. *Rhus typhinum.*

—*Sumac de virginie.*—A hardy and large shrub from North America. Blows a purplish flower in July, Propagated by seed, cuttings and suckers. Likes a light soil with a good bottom. Must be sheltered from the high winds. Its chief property is the handsome red colour of its leaves in the fall, and for this it is admitted to the shrubberies and pleasure gardens of Europe.

398. SYRINGA, *common.*—Lat. *Philadelphus coronarius.*—Fr. *Syringa odorant.*—A hardy shrub of the southern parts of Europe, which grows to from four to ten feet high, and blows a white flower in June and July. Propagated by suckers or by dividing the roots in the Autumn, and any soil suits it. Its powerful odour is disliked by many, but there are few shrubberies in which it has not a place.

399. TAMARISK, *French.*—Lat. *Tamarix gallica.*—Fr. *Tamaris de France.*—A hardy shrub of the south of France, which grows to the height of twelve feet, and blows a purplish white flower from May to October. Propagated by cuttings made in February and put into rich and moist earth, but they must not be transplanted until the end of the following year or the Spring after that. Likes a moist and warm situation.

400. TREFOIL, *Shrubby.*—Lat. *Ptelea trifoliata.*—Fr. *Ptéléa à trois feuilles.*—A shrub from north America, from four to six feet high, and blows in May and June, a greenish yellow flower. Propagated by seed, cuttings and suckers. As hard frosts injure it when very young, it should be put in a sheltered situation.

401. THORN, *evergreen.*—Lat. *Mespilus pyracantha.*—Fr. *Néflier buisson ardent.*—A shrub from the south of Europe. The flower is white, slightly tinged with rose, and it blows in May and June. Propagated by seed, grafts, and layers. There are two more sorts, the double and the rose-coloured, which are more rare.

402. THUJA, *the Chinese.*—Lat. *Thuia orientalis.*—Fr. *Thuia d' orient.*—An evergreen tree, originally from China, about thirty feet high. Blows in March and April. Fit for pleasure-grounds of considerable size, and shrubberies. Propagate from seed, and by layers.——THUJA, *the American.*—Lat. *Thuja occidentalis.*—Fr. *Thuia d' occident.*——A tree belonging to Canada, very much like the preceding one, and blows in February and March. Propagated by seed sown in a warm place, in good light earth. In about two years they should be transplanted at about two feet apart, and toward the fourth year may be put where they are to remain. They are also propagated by layers. Not at all particular as to soil.

403. TRUMPET FLOWER, *ash-leaved, or climbing.* Lat. *Bignonia radicans.*—Fr. *Tecoma grimpant.*—A hardy climber of North America, which grows to thirty or forty feet high, and blows a most beautiful scarlet flower in July and August. Propagated by layers or by suckers, or from the seed, and, whilst the plant is young, the root should be covered with straw during the frost. Common garden soil.

404. TULIP-TREE.— Lat. *Liriodendrum tulipifera.*—Fr. *Tulipier.*—This, in fact, in its native country, is an immense timber-tree ; and, in England, where it is raised generally from layers, it is frequently seen at the height of forty or fifty feet, and is suited only to such shrubberies as are of great dimensions. It bears a flower in the shape of a tulip : like that of the tulip, the flower has no smell ; but not like that of the tulip, the colours of the flower are not at all interesting : the leaf is very beautiful, and preserves its freshness during the hottest summer.

405. VERVAIN, *three-leaved.*—Lat. *Verbena triphylla*—Fr. *Verveine odorante.*—A green-house shrub from Chili. Blows a violet-coloured flower from June till August. Propagated by layers and cuttings, in March and April. Requires rich earth, to be watered frequently during summer, and to be put into a green-house in winter.

406. VIBURNUM, *Laurestine.*—Lat. *Viburnum tinus.*-Fr. *Viorne Laurier-tin.*—A hardy evergreen shrub from the south of Europe, and blows in April a cluster of flowers, red in the outside and white within. Propagated by layers, graffs, and seed. Does well in any soil, grows to six or eight feet high, and is very ornamental in shrubberies and on lawns.

407. WIDOW-WAIL.—Lat. *Cneorum tricoccum.*—Fr. *Camelée à trois coques.*—A little ornamental green-house shrub, originally from the south of France. It blows in the months of June and July a small yellow flower. Suited to a border of winter shrubs, and propagated by sowing the seed under a frame, and transplanting in light soil and in the shade. In the coldest season it requires shelter.

408. ZIZYPHUS, *or Christ's-thorn.* — Lat. *Paliurus aculeatus.* — Fr. *Paliure epineuse.* — A hardy shrub from the south of Europe : blows a yellow flower in June and July. Propagated by suckers and cuttings, under a hand-glass, as well as by seed. Does well in any soil.

---

409. It is not right for me to put this list of Shrubs out of my hand without observing that I, by no means, give it as a complete botanical catalogue. I do not write for the curious in botany, but for the use of those, for the practical application of those, who have the means and the desire to make pretty spots for their pleasure. I might have inserted the names of a great multitude of trees and of shrubs which are very curious, but an account of which would have been wholly out of place in a work like this.

FLOWERS.

410. THESE are annual, biennial, and perennial ; or fibrous, tuberous, and bulbous. The list that I give below will consist of some of each of these, but they will be arranged alphabetically, and not according to the above distinguishing characters. These are called *herbaceous,* to distinguish them from shrubs which are *ligneous,* or woody. And, in their uses, it may be said that the one is the flower of the shrubbery, and the other the flower of the border.

411. Flowers are cultivated in *beds*, where the whole bed consists of a mass of one sort of flower; or in *borders*, where an infinite variety of them are mingled together, but arranged so that they may blend with one another in colour as well as in stature. Beds are very little the fashion now, excepting amongst the florists, who cultivate their tulips, hyacinths, and other choice flowers in this manner; but the fashion has for years been in favour of borders, wherein flowers of the greatest brilliancy are planted, so disposed as to form a regular series of higher and higher as they approach the back part, or the middle, of the border; and so selected as to insure a succession of blossom from the earliest months of the spring until the coming of the frosts. This is easily attained by paying strict attention to the height and time of flowering of plants, both of which I have taken care to notice under each, in the alphabetical list below. In the mixed beds of flowers, there are two things, which, more than all others, tend to give them the desired agreeable appearance: one is, room between the several plants. A mat of the most beautiful flowers in the world, crowded up against each other, and out of all order, never can look like any other than a mass of brilliant weeds. There should be room, and considerable room, too, allowed to every plant; and those plants which spread much, should be carefully kept within their proper bounds. The other, is, the careful tying up of such plants as require it, to sticks of proper height and strength. Many do not want it at all, but many do, and, if this be neglected or put off, a good high wind will tear up the high plants, such as hollyhocks, African marigolds, marvel of Peru, and make them

the means of beating down and destroying the lesser and, perhaps, choicer ones below them.

412. In Chapter IV. I have treated at large of propagation and cultivation *in general*, and, as to the *propagation* and *cultivation* of flowers, I may refer my readers to that Chapter for the general knowledge, and, therefore, I shall now only notice a few particulars that I did not go into there. The plants that I enumerate in the following list are propagated either by *seed*, by *cuttings* or *pipings*, by parting the *roots* or the *tubers*, or by *separating the offsets.*——*By seed.* The general instructions given in Chap. IV. par. 85 to 95, are sufficiently in the reader's mind, and I need say no more upon that.——*By cuttings or pipings*, and by *layers.* The instructions for striking the *carnation* fully explain this.——*By parting the roots.* This is taking up the plant, we will suppose, of the peach-leaved campanula, and dividing it into as many parts as there are complete crowns; each of which, if divided so as for it to have a piece of root left with it, and carefully replanted, will become a flowering plant in the spring following the operation. It is performed generally in the autumn. For parting the tubers of of tuberous-rooted plants, see the article "*Auricula*" or "*Ranunculus.*"——*By separating the offsets.* This is, taking off the two or three young bulbs that, on taking up a bulbous root, you find growing at its side, its root being fixed on at the root, and its body curling up round the body, of the mother bulb. Break these off carefully, and treat them according to the instructions given for each sort under the respective name of each. As to their cultivation, I have spoken so much of it in general, that I will not say any more upon that subject. But there is,

in this division of horticulture, cultivation in pots and also in *glasses*. Potting is a very nice operation; it should always be done (as it very frequently is not) in the most careful manner possible. In the first place, the pots that you are about to use should be thoroughly clean, both inside and outside; for, nothing looks worse than a set of dirty flower-pots, and nothing can thrive in a mass of crusted earth which is often found filling flower pots to a third part of their height, having probably been left in them ever since they were last used. Having a clean pot, put in a handful of broken pot-sherds, put upon this, earth enough to fill the pot a little less than half full, take the plant you are going to put into it, in your left hand, and with as good a ball of earth about its roots as circumstances will admit; hold it in the pot to see if there be enough, or too much earth in. The earth should rise up about the stem of the plant to where it did before you took it up, and neither higher nor lower: nature shows the exact line at which the root ends and the stem begins; and you must follow this. Place the plant on the earth; hold it steady, while, with your right hand, you put in fine earth round the roots so as to touch them in all parts; that done, take hold of the edges of the pot with your two hands, and rap it gently down on the ground two or three times; put on a little more earth, and finish by giving a little water, which will cause the earth to settle immediately about the roots. —If your pots be to remain out of doors, place them on a flat surface that has been previously strewed over with coal ashes, and this will prevent worms getting to them. Always observe to keep pots upright, so that the water which you give them may run out, which, unless this be

observed, it will not, and rotting at the root takes place
assuredly. Water must be given every day in hot
weather, and towards the close of the day. In winter it
need not be given so frequently, and it should be in the
fore-part of the day, as then the plant has time to imbibe
the moisture before the cold of night comes on, which,
coming with the water, might hurt if not destroy it. In
the winter, the greatest care is necessary to keep out
damp ; therefore, watering should be very sparingly performed, and none splashed about the house or room in
which the plants are kept. When there is any appearance of moss on the surface of the earth in the pots, stir
it up with a little stick cut in the form of a knife ; break
the earth fine, and, if you have any in reserve, strew a
little fresh earth over, after taking off that which had
become mossy. If there appear mouldiness at the joints
of the plants, be sure that there is not air enough given, or
that the place is damp. In either case, open the lights
when the sun is out, if it be not exceedingly cold ; and
keep up a steady and moderate fire by night till the place
be thoroughly dry.—In glasses filled with water, bulbous
roots, such as the hyacinth, narcissus, and jonquil, are
blown. The time to put them in is from September to
November, and the earliest ones will begin blowing about
Christmas. The glasses should be blue, as that colour
best suits the roots ; put water enough in to cover the
bulb one third of the way up, less rather than more ; let
the water be soft, change it once a week, and put in a
pinch of salt every time you change it. Keep the glasses
in a place moderately warm, and *near to the light.* A
parlour window is a very common place for them, but is
often too warm, and brings on the plants too early, and

causes them to be weakly. This should be avoided by all means, as it often causes a fine root to blow badly. Of the narcissus kind, the polyanthus narcissuses are, in my opinion, far the most to be preferred for glasses.

LIST OF FLOWERS.

413. ACONITE, or *monk's-hood.*—Lat. *Aconitum napellus.* —Fr. *Aconit napel.*—A perennial plant from Germany; which has been long known in English gardens, and is still cultivated, notwithstanding the warnings of MILLER and many others, who produce evidence of the poisonous effects of the plant in all its parts; and not only poisonous when eaten, but even when injudiciously smelled to. There are several sorts of ACONIT, but I shall only mention this one. Its varieties are, *deep blue, white,* and red. It flowers in the months of May and June, the flowers coming in a spike at the top of a stalk of three feet high. The leaves are of a shining green, and very much divided. It makes a considerable show in the larger flower-borders; likes almost any good soil; and is propagated either by parting the roots in the autumn, or by sowing the seeds in the spring in the flower-nursery.

414. ADONIS, *pheasant's eye.*—Lat. *Adonis annua.*—Fr. *Adonide aunuelle.*—An annual plant, which inhabits the environs of Paris, and a great part of France and Europe; and is generally found in fields, and places which are at all wet. The flower is of a deep red, and

the plant is straight and one or two feet high, and blossoms from July to November. It sows itself, but is difficult to transplant, unless done with great care and with a clod of earth at the roots. There is a perennial kind which grows to about the same height as the former, and blows very handsome and larger and yellow flowers. It may be raised by seeds, or by dividing the roots.

415. AMARYLLIS, *yellow.*—Lat. *Amaryllis Lutea.*—Fr. *Amaryllis jaune.*—A hardy bulbous root of the south of Europe, which blows a yellow flower in September; requires no more care than that ordinarily bestowed on hardy bulbous rooted plants, and is propagated by offsets, which should be nursed two years in a bed appropriated to them. This is the only really hardy kind of this handsome tribe, so much and so justly celebrated by the ancient poets; but there are one or two others, which, though none but those who are curious and careful procure for themselves, are nevertheless easily obtained from the florists who supply us with the choice roots of hyacinth, narcissus, &c. and which I will, therefore, mention.——The GUERNSEY LILY—Lat *Amaryllis sarniensis*—Fr. *Lis de Guernsey*—Is a most beautiful autumnal flower, coming in a considerable cluster upon a slender and elegant stem of about twelve inches high. This stem is unaccompanied by leaf; but, grouped with young seedling geraniums, or any other green plants, they make an uncommonly handsome appearance either in a conservatory or in a room. The roots are procured from Guernsey by our florists, who import them just as they are about to burst into bloom. Put them immediately in pots having pot-sherds

at the bottom, and being filled with turfy loam mixed with some sand and a little peat earth. Give water regularly; not much at a time; see that it drains off well; and keep the plant out of the heat of the sun or it will quickly fade.——BELLADONNA LILY.—Lat. *Amaryllis Bella-Donna.*—Fr. *Belladonne d' Automne.*—A larger plant than the last, bearing much larger flowers hanging downward, five or six in number, and of a pale blush. These are procured in the same manner; but sometimes they arrive in England earlier than at other times, according to the season; but about the first week in September you should enquire for them. As they come when just ready to blow, they come in and are gone, almost in a day. This last plant, if put into the ground deep enough, will live through our winters; but it is properly a frame plant.

416. ANEMONE, *single, or poppy.*—Lat. *Anemone coronaria.* — Fr. *Anémone des fleuristes.* — A hardy tuberous-rooted plant from the Levant. There are double and single sorts, both equally esteemed by the florists, and both cultivated in the same manner: if from seed, sow in January under a frame, having procured fine earth that has received the frost. Make your bed very fine, and sow the seed pretty thickly over it, and cover very lightly indeed with the same earth. Do not let there be more than the thickness of a shilling of earth over the seeds; and give very gentle waterings of soft water, from a fine-rosed watering pot, taking care that frost do not penetrate by night, nor the mid-day sun; for either would destroy the young plants. When the plants are all up and are out in their rough leaves, take

off the glasses unless the weather be very severe, and shade from sun by day; give gentle waterings, or admit showers of rain. When the leaves of these plants have died away completely (which will be about the end of March), take up every tuber carefully and put them by in drawers, till the next October or November, and then plant them in beds or patches where you mean them to blow in the next spring. If you have sowed them in drills in your bed, you will find it a much easier work to take up the young tubers than if you had sowed them broad cast; for you easily follow the rows and pick out the little pieces, which it would puzzle you to distinguish from stones when sowed in the other manner. *By dividing the roots* of anemones you multiply your number very easily. Do this with a sharp knife when you take up your roots that are overblown, cutting them into as many pieces as there are strong and plump buds, each of which will blow strongly the next spring. The *soil* for the anemone is a good, strong, rich garden mould, and the manure rotten cow or horse dung; but the former is mostly preferred, though neither should be put too close to the roots of the plants, but should be digged in at a foot or a foot and a half below the surface of the ground. Avoid planting in a much exposed situation, for the high winds knock the plants about, and severe frost will cause them sometimes to blow less finely than they would do without such. Raise the beds to about three or four inches above the walks, so that rains may not lie upon them; and plant about the latter end of October, though, if your soil be very wet, it may be better to plant later (the middle of February) as the plant has less time to remain dormant and run the risk of rotting. Put in your roots at five inches apart every way, making straight drills of about two inches depth for their reception, and taking care to place them in these at even distances, a great deal of the beauty of these beds depending upon regular order ; and, when all the roots are placed in the drills, cover them over up to the edge of the drills with fine earth.   The bud, I need hardly say, of the root, or tuber, should be uppermost, and the roots, which will have the appearance of brown coarse threads, downwards.   The anemone, though a very hardy thing, certainly blows the finer if not pinched during its growth by frosts, and it is, therefore, the practice with all the florists to be prepared with a suitable covering of wheaten or barley straw as the winter approaches, so that the first intimation of frost is a warning to them to cover over their beds of these and other similar roots.   They are, however, careful not to endanger vegetation by keeping these coverings on unnecessarily, when they would assuredly cause the roots to become mouldy and eventually rot ; but they watch for frosty nights, and keep off the coverings at all times excepting those.   By the end of June, the plants begin dying down, and that is the time for taking them up, separating such as you mean to separate, and putting all by for the next autumn.

417. ARCHANGEL, *balm-leaved.*—Lat. *Lamium orvala.*—Fr. *Lamier orvale.*—A hardy perennial plant of Italy, two feet high, and blows a flower of a pale reddish violet colour, in May, June, and July. Readily increased from suckers, and likes a good rich garden soil.

418. ARNICA, *Corsican.*—Lat. *Arnica corsica.*—Fr.

Arnique de corse.—A hardy perennial plant which grows in the mountains of Corsica, and blows a yellow flower in May and June. Propagated by seed and separating the roots. Likes a light loamy soil. Is rather large and coarse.

419. ASPHODEL, *yellow.*—Lat. *Asphodelus Luteus.* —Fr. *Asphodèle jaune.*—A perennial plant, originally from Sicily. It is four feet high, blows in May, June, and July, a brilliant yellow flower. It is multiplied by seed, sown in a hot-bed in pots, and is easily propagated by separating its roots. It likes a good moist soil, and is very ornamental when in flower.

420. ASTER, *Chinese.*—Lat. *Aster chinensis.* — Fr. *Reine Marguerite.* — An annual plant, the height of which is from one to two feet. A native of China. It blows in August and September. The flowers are variegated with red, purple, violet, &c. and it is the great autumnal ornament of every garden, flowering till the coming of frosts. Propagated by seed, sowed in a hot-bed in the spring; and, when the plants have five or six leaves, plant them where they are to remain. The species that are perennial are propagated by separating their roots.

421. AVENS, *the water.*—Lat. *Geum rivale.*—Fr. *Benoite des ruisseaux.*—An annual plant from the Pyrenees and the Alps, which is one foot high, and blows a yellow flower in June. Propagated by sowing the seed in open ground in the shade, or by separating the roots

SHRUBBERIES AND FLOWER-GARDENS. CHAP.

in September or February. It does in any soil, but likes a moist and shady situation best.

422. AURICULA.— Lat. *Primula Auricula.* — Fr. *Oreille d'ours.*—A florist's flower, propagated by seed, rooted slips, and offsets. It is a native of Switzerland, but has been long a favourite plant with English, Dutch, and French florists. It is hardy, but, like the anemone and ranunculus, blows the better for care and protection in severe winters, and in the heat of summer. If you propagate from seed, sow in earthen pans or in boxes in December, or in March, and cover very lightly ; give an eastern aspect, and water gently now and then. When the plants have five or six leaves, transplant them into other boxes or pans, and let them have the same management ; and, when they become strong, put them out in your borders, where, when they flower, you can choose the most fitting for the purpose of potting. Slips you pull off with your hands, and offsets cut off with a sharp knife; both in the end of July, or beginning of August. The *soil* most suitable to this plant is a cool vegetable one ; and the artificial mixtures are very numerous, but the one in most general use is half fresh garden mould and half well-rotted cow-dung. A little sea sand thrown in amongst it keeps it free. Auricula pots should be six inches deep, and as large in circumference at the bottom as at the top ; water only in dry times ; and, in continued wet, lie the pots on their sides, unless you have a covered stage for them. Wooden bars to stand the pots on are very useful. They prevent too great a moisture getting at the roots of the plant, which is the case when the pots

stand on the ground, and they also prevent the worms getting in. A slight covering during the frosts of winter is necessary for a fine blow. Those plants which are planted out in the border should be taken up and parted every three years, or they become weak, blow but little, and shortly die.

423. BALSAM.—Lat. *Impatiens balsamina.*—Fr. *Balsamine des Jardins.*—From the East Indies. A most beautiful, but rather tender, annual plant. Well known to almost every body, and almost universally cultivated, and is very ornamental in the flower borders, in the greenhouse and in the parlour. It blows in July, August, and September, double and single flowers, red, pink, white, or variegated. The best way of propagating is by sowing the seed early in March in a moderate hot-bed. By April, the plants must be potted off singly, and then struck in the hot-bed again; then accustom them by degrees to the open air, and early in May put them out into the borders, or put them into large pots; according as you design them to blow. In a fine warm summer they will be finer in the open air than in the green-house or stove; less drawn up, and bearing flowers larger and far more abundant, and, towards the fall they will ripen seed in abundance, which should be carefully gathered every evening. The pods should be very cautiously approached for this purpose, as, if ripe, they fly in pieces instantly, on being touched, and scatter the seed in all directions. See that the pod be a little yellow before you gather it, and then fold your hand round it, and let it fly open within your fingers. But, to return to the plants, these will never want water after they are once well rooted in the open ground; but a little stirring of the ground round them has a great effect on their growth. Those that you keep in pots will, of course, want some water, but not a great deal; and they should be kept from the scorching sun. Good garden soil suits them best.

424. BARREN-WORT.—Lat. *Epimedium Alpinum.* Fr. *Epimède des Alpes.*—A perennial plant, and an inhabitant of the mountains of the south of Europe. It is a foot high, and in April and May blows a flower, the exterior of which is red, and the interior yellow. It is easily propagated by separating the roots, and it likes good moist earth and a shady situation.

425. BEAR'S EAR.— Lat. *Cortusa matthioli.*— Fr. *Cortuse de matthiole.*—A perennial frame plant of the Alps, five or six inches high, and blows a pink flower, partaking of the violet, in May. Propagated by dividing the roots, and should be cultivated in heath-mould.

426. BIRTHWORT, *the common.*—Lat. *Aristolochia clematitis.*—Fr. *Aristoloche.* — A perennial plant very common in England. It is about two feet high, the flower of a pale yellow, and blows in May and July. Propagated by separating the roots.——BIRTHWORT, *the long.*—Lat. *Aristolochia longa.*—Fr. *Aristoloche longua.* A perennial plant which blows from June till October. The flower is of a red brown at the top, and a bluish violet at the bottom. It is a native of the south of France. Propagated by separating the roots, which have a strong aromatic odour.

427. BULBOCODIUM.—Lat. *Bulbocodium vernum.*—Fr. *Mérendère bulbocode.*—A bulbous rooted plant from the Pyrenees, that blows a light purple flower in March. Should be moved in July. Likes heath-mould, and rather a shady situation.

428. CACALIA, *sow-thistle leaved.* — Lat. *Cacalia sanctifolia.*—Fr. *Cacalia à feuilles de laiteron.* — An annual stove plant from the East Indies, growing one foot high, and blowing a flower of an orange red colour in July. Propagated from seed sowed in a frame in March. Requires very little water, and should be kept out of the house during the summer.

429. ——————. Lat. *Cactus spiciosus.*—Fr. *Cactier élégant.*—A perennial succulent plant from Carthagena ; throws up many long fleshy leaves festooned at the sides, and, in June and July, blows an exceedingly beautiful rose-coloured flower, about three inches long, and double. This plant likes a mixture of light mould and brick rubbish. Requires very little water except when in flower, and must be brought forward in the greenhouse, or frame ; though, in a very warm room to the south, it will blow. Force it into flower by bruising the ends of the leaves ; and propagate by cuttings, which, being left in a dry place for a day or two till the cut end become dry, and then stuck in a pot of mould, will strike quickly ; but these will not flower for a couple of years.

430. CALTROPS, *small.*—Lat. *Tribulus terrestris.*—Fr. *Tribulus hérissé.*—A hardy annual plant from the south of Europe, and blows a yellow flower in June and July. Propagated by sowing seed in a hot-bed, and, when they are fit, transplanting them where they are to remain.

431. CAMPANULA, *the pyramid.* — Lat. *Campanula pyramidalis.*—Fr. *Campanule pyramidale.*—From Savoy. A perennial plant of great beauty, which grows to about four or five feet in height, with several minor branches, the main one blowing a long spike, or pyramid, of delicate sky-blue flowers, in the months of July and August. Propagated by seed, and by parting the root. The seed should be sowed in the spring in a bed of fine earth, under a hand-glass, shaded from the strong heat of the sun, and watered now and then with a fine-rosed watering pot. The seed comes up readily if not covered deeply, and, by the fall, the plants will be fit to transplant into a nursery bed, where they should remain until the following spring, when some of them may be thinned out to be planted in the flower-borders, where they *may* blow the same year; and the rest, being carefully tilled between, will be fine strong plants by the third year, and may all be put out in the same manner, or potted in large wide-topped pots to be brought into the house, where they make a very fine show. By parting the roots after the first year of blowing, you multiply your plants, and each plant that you take off is the stronger for being severed ; but the plants thus used decline every year ; therefore, keep up a succession of plants from the seed, by all means. As to soil, this plant is not very particular, though it likes a good mould ; but it is very particular in its aversion to *manure,* which is destruction to it. It is one of the most ornamental plants that can be conceived, and

suits any situation well.——— CAMPANULA or CANTERBURY BELL.—Lat. *Campanula medium.*—Fr. *Campanule a grosses fleurs,* or *violette marine.*—A very pretty German plant; throws up numerous branches in April and May, garnished thickly with long and hairy leaves, and in June and July, blows abundance of very handsome pendulous flowers, either white or light blue; larger than a common thimble, but somewhat resembling one in shape. It is *biennial,* and should be sowed every spring either in a hot-bed or not, according to convenience, and then pricked out when it comes into rough leaf. So let it remain till the autumn, when you will plant it either in the borders or in the pots where you intend it to blow.——— CAMPANULA, *peach-leaved.*—Lat. *Campanula persicifolia.*— Fr. *Campanule à feuilles de pêcher.*—The last of the Campanulas that I shall mention. It is a native of the northern parts of Europe; a perennial plant that also sends up a great many shoots in the spring of the year, and bears flowers of the same colours as the last, but some are double and some single, and all are much broader at the orifice than those of the last-mentioned plant, but are shorter in length. Propagate by dividing the roots; or, more tediously, by sowing the seeds as soon as ripe. All these plants are handsome, and should form a part of the collection of every one who aims at having an attractive flower-garden; and no one of them, but the first, is particular as to soil.

432. CAMPION, *the rose.*—Lat. *Agrostema coronaria.*— Fr. *Coquelourde des jardins.* —— A plant originally from Lyons and Italy, one or two feet high, and blowing a bright red flower from June to September. Other

varieties have white and double flowers. Propagated by sowing the seed as soon as ripe, in light earth exposed to the sun, and planting out the following March. Also by sowing in a hot-bed or in borders in the spring. Is hardy, and will sow itself when in a warm and dryish soil.

433. CANDY-TUFT, *the purple.*—Lat. *Iberis umbellata.*—Fr. *Ibéride eu ombelle.*—An annual plant from the south of France. About two feet high, and blows, in June and July, a great abundance of purplish flowers. Propagated by seed sown in beds, where it is to blow. Any soil suits it, and it is very ornamental.

434. CARNATION.—Lat. *Dianthus caryophyllus.*—Fr. *L'Oeillet des fleuristes.*—An indigenous plant ; a perennial, but one that has been improved by the great care that florists have bestowed upon it for many years. It is, indeed, by many esteemed the finest of flowers, next after the tulip; which it surpasses in one respect, that of adding great fragrance to great beauty. It is cultivated either in beds, borders, or pots: in the latter for the parlour chiefly; and it is propagated by layers, pipings, or seed. It blows from July to August, flowers of from two to three, or even four inches diameter, of divers colours, and either single, semi-double, or double. But there are three distinct varieties ; which are, the *Flake,* the *Bizarre,* the *Picotée.* The flake has two colours only, and their stripes are large ; the bizarre is variegated with spots and stripes irregularly, and has not less than three colours ; the picotée has mostly a white ground spotted with scarlet, red, purple, pink, or some variety of these colours. The

stalk of the carnation should rise to near three feet, and the bud should be long and uniform, not bursting but at its top to let out the flower, or, if appearing likely to burst at the side, it is as well to open corresponding apertures at two other places, so as to let out the flower evenly all round. The plant is hardy, but to blow well, it should be defended from excess of wet, especially the wet of the beginning of winter, as it renders it more susceptible of frost; and yet it is necessary to avoid stifling it. It cannot do without a free circulation of air, therefore whatever covering of mats or otherwise you use, be careful to keep it off at all times but in constant rain. To propagate *by layers,* take some compost of one of the two kinds that I mention below as proper for this plant; stir the ground with a small hoe round the plant from which you are going to make your layers, and place the compost round on the newly-moved earth; then take as many of the stalks as you mean to lay (let it be about the time of their being in full bloom); fix your knife (a sharp narrow-bladed one) in at an inch below the third joint from the blossom, and bring it up the middle of the stalk until you enter the joint, which you must scarcely divide in two: there stop, then, and pull out your knife. Bend down the stalk to the earth, and make a little drill with your two fore-fingers of one hand, sufficient to hide the whole of the split and a little more at each end of it; put a little wooden peg with a hook to it into the side of the drill, and push it into the ground so far as for it to come down and fix the stalk at the bottom of the drill where you are holding it, and then cover over with compost, pressing it gently down with the flat of your hand. *By pipings,* about the first of July, take the two top joints of a branch, which are the fittest for this purpose ; cut off immediately below the second joint, and with a sharp instrument ; peel off the outer loose skin from the joint, and make a little split up it for about two eighths of an inch ; shorten the leaves a little way above the upper joint, and this will leave your piping about two inches long. Having procured the number of pipings that you mean to plant, throw them into a basin of rain water to soften them. You will now have to plant them, either in the open ground, or on a hot-bed ; but, in either case, you must cover them with a hand-glass, or a striking-glass, which is a small hand-glass, not more than eight or ten inches square. On a gentle hot-bed is best, the mould being one third maiden earth, one third leaf-mould, one third well rotted horse-dung, and with a sprinkling of sharp sand amongst it. Place your glass down where you are going to put the pipings, and thus mark out the space ; then take your pipings out of the basin and force them, one by one, into the mould to about three parts of an inch of their length, and let them be an inch apart from one another. Do not put on the glass till all the leaves and stalks are dry, for they would inevitably rot if you were to do this. When they are dry, however, put on the glass, making its edges fit exactly into the mark that you made by its means before you began planting, and thus you will not disturb or crush any of the outer pipings. Thrust the edges of the glass down a little way into the earth, so that no air can get in. This is what the French call *stifling*. Shade by means of netting or matting from the sun, but yet do not exclude its rays *completely*. It is in giving air, light, and moisture, at this time, and for the following three weeks, that the greatest skill is required. If the pipings appear to be doing well, that is, looking of a good colour and not contracting mould, let the glass stand for about ten days without being moved; but, unless the weather be wet, water over the glass every morning. At the end of ten days, take it off; let it be early in the morning if the weather be dry and hot; and turn the glass upside down that it may become aired. If you perceive any pipings beginning to mould, pull them up instantly; give a little water through a fine rose; let the plants dry again perfectly, and then again put on the glass. The weather being favourable, give air every morning for half an hour or an hour; but never shut up whilst the pipings are wet; and, if you have showery weather, give air between showers, if it be but for five minutes of a morning. In about six weeks they will be fit to transplant into small pots; make use of the same sort of mould; plunge the pots, or simply stand them, in another gentle bed, and put frames or hand-glasses over them till your plants have struck again; and here they may remain till September, when you pot them or plant them out. If you perform this work in the open ground, choose a spot under a wall facing the east, where none but the morning sun comes; use the same preparation of mould, and use a hand-glass, acting in all respects as prescribed in case of a hot-bed. Pot off your plants in the month of March following; using pots of about twelve inches wide at top, and eight inches wide at bottom; these should have good clean circular holes at the bottoms, and, beside, two or three smaller holes in their sides at about two inches from the bottom; and these effectually prevent water remaining about the roots of the plants. The same soil that you struck your plants in will do to blow them in. I will here give MILLER's direction for a mixture, and then proceed to the propagating by seed : "take mould from a good upland pasture, or a common that is of a hazel earth ; dig out earth from the first eight inches from the surface ; let this be laid in a heap to mellow for one year ; then mix a third part of rotten neat's dung, or dung of an old cucumber bed ; mix them well together, turn the heap every month for eight months, and it will be fit for use." *By seed.* The seed of the carnation does not every summer ripen in England ; but seed is procured from the continent in abundance. Sow in pots of light earth, or on a cool bed with a frame over it, in the month of April; and cover in in the slightest possible manner. Shade the young plants from hot sun ; and, when they have six leaves, prick them out two or three inches asunder, in a well-prepared bed of the garden. The next year they will flower, and, therefore, should be planted out, or potted for blowing, in the fall of their first year's growth. Lastly, the carnation is greatly the prey of ear-wigs, so much so, that precautions the most careful are always resorted to to prevent the plants falling a sacrifice to these mischievous vermin. See paragraph 306.

435. CATCHFLY, *pink.*—Lat. *Silene armeria.*—Fr. *Silène à bouquets.*—A hardy annual plant, common in Provence, about a foot high, and blows a pink or white flower throughout the summer. Propagated by sowing the seed where it is to grow. Likes a light, sandy, and warm soil.

436. CENTAURY, *or sweet sultan*.— Lat. *Centaurea moschata*.—Fr. *Centaurée musqué*.——A hardy annual plant from the Levant, about two feet high, and blows a purple flower in July and August.——CENTAURY, *or yellow sweet sultan*.—Lat. *Centaurea suaveolens*.—Fr. *Centaurée odorante*.——A hardy annual plant from the Levant, one or two feet high, and blowing a yellow flower in July and August. Propagated by sowing in pots or in a bed, and planting out when the young plants are large enough.

437. CHRYSANTHEMUM, *Indian*.—Lat. *Chrysanthemum indicum*.—Fr. *Chrysanthème d'automne*.——A perennial plant of China and India, which grows three feet high, and blows beautiful deep purple, white, and yellow flowers in November and December. Propagated by dividing the roots in spring, or by cuttings in summer, and requires moving every two years, and good rich land. ——CHRYSANTHEMUM, *corn marygold*.—Lat. *Chrysanthemum segetum*.—Fr. *Chrysanthème des blés*.——An annual plant, common amongst wheat, which grows one foot high, and blows a yellow flower in July. Propagated by sowing. ——CHRYSANTHEMUM, *garden*.—Lat. *Chrysanthemum coronarium*.—Fr. *Chrysanthème des jardins*.——An annual plant from the south of France, which grows two or three feet high, and blows a yellow or white flower in July, August, and September. Propagated by sowing the seed where it is to blow.

438. CHELONE.—Lat. *Chelone barbata*.—Fr. *Galane barbue*.——A perennial plant, originally from Mexico, which blows a beautiful red flower in July and August. Rather tender. About three feet high.——CHELONE, *the bell-flowered.*—Lat. *Chelone campanulata.*—Fr. *Galane campanulée.*—A perennial plant from Mexico, which blows, in July and August, a red flower. About a foot high.—— CHELONE, *the downy.* — Lat. *Chelone pensthemon.* — Fr. *Galane à fleurs paniculées.*—A perennial plant from Virginia. It is about a foot high, and blows, in July and August, a flower which is yellow in the inside and a light purple on the outside. They are all three multiplied by seed, as well as by separating their roots, in the autumn. They are not very delicate, but it is best to give them moist earth and shady situation.

439. CINERARIA, *or rag-wort.*—Lat. *Cineraria maritima.*—Fr. *Cinéraire maritime.*—A perennial plant from the sea-coasts of Provence and Languedoc. Grows two feet high, and blows a shaded yellow flower from June to September. Propagated by suckers and by seed; if the latter, it blows the second year. It should have a rich soil.

440. CISTUS, *common dwarf, or little sun-flower.*—Lat. *Cistus helianthemum.*—Fr. *Hélianthème commun.*—A perennial plant from the south of France, blows a yellow flower from May till September. There are varieties; white and rose-coloured, and all hardy, and are easily increased from the seed, which should be brought forward in pots.

441. COLCHICUM, *or meadow-saffron.*—Lat. *Colchicum autumnale.*—Fr. *Colchique d' automne.* — A bulbous plant common in Europe, about three or four inches

high, and blows a reddish purple flower in September and October. Propagated from offsets, taken off when the leaves are quite dead, and planted in July or the beginning of August. It is common in the upland meadows of Herefordshire, and other counties of England.

442. COLUMBINE.—Lat. *Aquilegia vulgaris.*—Fr. *Ancolie des Jardins.*—A perennial plant, commonly found in gardens, two or three feet high, and blows a blue, red, or variegated flower in June and July. It likes shade and stiff earth, and is propagated by dividing the roots in the autumn. The single flower may be obtained by sowing the seeds ; but, if sown in the spring, they seldom come up, and never till the next year.

443. COMFREY-LEAVED HOUND'S-TONGUE.— Lat. *Cynoglossum omphalodes.*—Fr. *Cynoglosse printannière.* —A perennial plant, originally from Piedmont and Portugal, about three or four inches high, and blowing a blue flower in March. Propagated by dividing the tufts, in which it grows, after it has flowered. Likes a fresh soil, and requires water in very dry weather.

444. CONVOLVULUS MINOR.—Lat. *Convolvulus tricolor.*—Fr. *Liseron tricolor.*—A hardy trailing annual plant from Sicily, which blows a shaded blue and white flower in June, July, and August. Propagated by sowing the seed in light and rather warm earth.——CONVOLVULUS MAJOR.—Lat. *Convolvulus purpureus.*—Fr. *Ipomée pourpre.* —An annual climber, of great beauty. Grows eight or nine feet high, if it have sticks of that height given it to run up, and blows, from July to September, a beautiful

bell-shaped purple or white flower, in great abundance, but open only in the mornings and evenings of the hot months of July and August. Sow in April where it is to stand, or in March in pots to transplant. Sow some in pots to bring into the house ; but in no case have more than two plants in one spot, as they branch out and become so heavy that winds and rains tear them about and endanger other neighbouring plants by their means. Stake them as soon as they are beginning to run, and cut away straggling branches that they will send out from the bottom. Their height sufficiently proclaims them a plant to be placed in the back part of the flower-border.

445. COREOPSIS, *ear-leaved.*—Lat. *Coreopsis auriculata.*—Fr. *Coréopsis auriculée.*—A hardy perennial of North America, three or four feet in height, and blows a yellow flower from August to September.——COREOPSIS, *alternate-leaved.*—Lat. *Coreopsis delphinifolia.*—Fr. *Coréopsis à feuilles de dauphinelle.*—A perennial plant of North America, eighteen inches high, and blows a yellow flower from July till October. Both sorts propagated by dividing their roots. Any soil suits them, but they like an open situation.

446. CORIS, *Montpellier.*—Lat. *Coris monspeliensis.*—Fr. *Coris de montpellier.*—A biennial frame plant of the coast of the south of France, seven or eight inches high, and blows a pretty red flower in May and June. Propagated by seed sowed in pots in the spring, and likes a light and sandy soil, and but little water.

447. CORN-FLAG. — Lat. *Gladiolus communis.*—Fr. *Glayeul commun.*—A perennial plant from the south of France, one or two feet high, and blows, in July, a purplish flower. It likes a good and rather light soil, and a warm situation. Propagated by offsets. It is prudent to cover the roots in hard winters.

448. COWSLIP. — Lat. *Primula veris.* — Fr. *Primevère officinale.*— A hardy perennial plant, common in meadows all over England. It blows a pale yellow flower in April and May. Propagated by separating the roots, also by seed, sown in November and December, in shallow pots full of good light earth. The seed sown on the surface of this earth should be lightly covered with sandy, or heath-mould, and the pots exposed to the east. Should remain a year in the pots, and be planted out in the spring. ——— COWSLIP, VIRGINIAN.—— Lat. *Dodecatheon meadia.*—Fr. *Gyroselle cultivée.*—A perennial plant from Virginia, which is about eight or nine inches high, and blows in April or May. It does very well in the open ground, and when kept in a house in pots, it should be exposed to the air in mild weather. It likes good earth, mixed with rotten dung. Propagated by separating the roots every three or four years.

449. CREPIS, *or Hawk's beard, purple.*—Lat. *Crepis rubra.*—Fr. *Crépide rouge.*—A hardy annual plant of the south of France, about eight or ten inches high, and blows a purple flower in June and July. Propagated by sowing in borders in the spring, and planting out when the plants have a few leaves.

T

450. CROCUS.—Lat. *C. vernus*.—Fr. *Safran Printanier*.—Indigenous bulb ; and one of the earliest ornaments of our flower-gardens. There are several varieties ; yellow, pale yellow, blue, striped, and white. All are handsome, but none make so great a show in the border as the deep yellow, which should always be planted in clumps of ten or a dozen plants in a clump, the bulbs at three inches from one another, and the clumps should be in the front of borders in which there are shrubs, or between the shrubs so as not to be out of sight. Planting them in long rows spoils the effect ; but having alternate clumps of yellow and blue gives an additional variety, and adds somewhat to the gaiety always produced by this handsome little plant. Do not cut off the leaves of your crocuses when they are overblown ; as this only weakens the plant. Move them when their leaves are dying down in autumn, but not more than once in three years. Separate the offsets then, which you will find abundant, and thus, with little trouble, you propagate them. The crocus likes a good, rather light, and not wet, garden soil ; and it should be planted two inches deep in the ground.

451. CYCLAMEN, *or sow-bread*.—Lat. *Cyclamen Europæum*.—Fr. *Cyclamen d'Europe*.—A perennial frame plant from Austria. Blows, in April, a flower that is white, shaded with pink. Propagated by seed, sowed as soon as gathered. Likes a sheltered situation, and a south-east aspect. Does best in heath-mould. Blows the third or fourth year after sowing.

452. DAFFODIL, *the onion-leaved*.—Lat. *Asphodelus fistulosus*.—Fr. *Asphodèle fistuleuse*.—A perennial plant, and a native of the south of France. Its height is about two feet; it blows from June till September ; the flower is white with a red stripe. It is multiplied by the seed, sown in pots, and put into a hot-bed ; and it is easily propagated by separating its roots. It likes a good moist soil.

453. DAHLIA.—Lat. and Fr. *Dahlia.*—A hardy tuberous perennial plant, originally from Mexico. It grows to the height of ten or twelve feet in rich land, and blows a large handsome flower, red, yellow, white, primrose, purple or scarlet, in September, continuing till the setting in of frosts. The height to which it grows renders it unfit for almost any garden, but the beauty of some of the double varieties, such as the primrose for instance, causes it to be often found even in the smallest flower-gardens. For extensive parterres, the outer rows of shrubberies, and for corners that want hiding, this is a magnificent plant ; and it is also to be kept to a moderate height, but only by putting it in unmanured and poor soil. The poorer the soil, the lower it will be ; and yet it will blow well in such. Always keep it, when in a growing state, tied to good high and stout stakes. Propagate by parting the root ; for from seed, though you procure fresh varieties, you lose the sort that you saved your seed from. When the stems begin to be nipped by the frosts, dig up the plants carefully, separate the offsets from the mother-roots, place them all in a dry place, and as much apart as is convenient. Take care that frosts do not get at them, and plant again in April.

454. DAISY.—Lat. *Bellis perennis.*—Fr. *Paquerette.*—

Indigenous and perennial. Varieties are pale red, deep red, green hearted, variegated, and white, and it is used for edgings, but is a very poor thing for the purpose. It is a pretty little plant, nevertheless, and, in little clumps, parted every year in order not to degenerate, it adds to the beauty of the front rows of the flower-border. Propagated only by parting the roots, in February or March.

455. DEVIL-IN-A-BUSH.—Lat. *Nigella Damascena.*—Fr. *Nigelle de Dames.*—is about two feet high ; blows a sky-blue flower from June till September. Propagated by seed, sown where it is to remain. Likes a warm situation. Native of the south of France, and an annual.

456. DOG'S-BANE.—Lat. *Cynachum monspeliachum.*—Fr. *Cynaque de Montpellier.*—A plant originally from Montpellier, which blows a pale pink, or whitish flower, in July and August. Propagated by suckers : should have a light and warm soil, a good situation, and its roots covered in hard frosts.

457. DRAGON'S-HEAD.—Lat. *Dracocephalum Austriacum.*—Fr. *Dracocéphale d' Autriche.*—From the south of Europe, perennial, from eight inches to a foot high, sending up numerous stems, and blowing tufts of blue or red flowers in July and August. Likes good rich earth, and is easily multiplied by parting the roots, or by sowing in beds. Should be separated at least every three years.

458. ————. Lat. *Dolichos purpureus.*—Fr. *Dolique.*—A pretty climber of the East Indies ; grows ten or

twelve feet high if trained up a frame or a string ; and blows a beautiful pale lilac pendulous flower in June and July. Propagated by cuttings planted under a hand-glass, or by seed, which ripens freely.

459. EGG-PLANT. — Lat. *Solanum melongena.*—Fr. *Morelle mélongène.* — An annual plant, originally from Asia and America. About fifteen inches in height, and blows white or violet flowers in June and July. Bears a fruit which is eaten, but it is raised here only for the curiosity of the egg-shaped fruit which it bears. It likes a light rich soil, and is readily procured by sowing the seeds.

460. FIG, *the common Indian.*—Lat. *Cactus opuntia.*—Fr. *Cactier Raquette.*—From America, where it grows on rocky places, and dry hills, and, in the month of July, blows a yellow flower. This is a green-house plant in England. It is very succulent, and should not be much watered except during the time that it is flowering, and then it may have more water. Cuttings root readily in pots. Perennial.

461. FOX-GLOVE, *lesser yellow.*—Lat. *Digitalis parviflora.*—Fr. *Digitale à petites fleurs.*—A perennial plant from Italy, two or three feet high, and blows a yellow flower in June and July. Propagated from seed, and sows itself.——Common Fox-glove.—Lat. *Digitalis purpurea.*—Fr. *Digitale pourpre.*—A biennial plant, found commonly in England, two or three feet high, and blows a purplish red flower in June, July, August and September. There is a white variety of this species ; both are very

ornamental, and are propagated by seeds, sown and otherwise managed, just as you do the Canterbury bell, which see.

462. FRAXINELLA, *or white Dittany.*—Lat. *Dictamnus albus.*—Fr. *Dictamne fraxinelle.* — A perennial plant originally from the south of France, about two feet high, and blows a white or purple, flower, in June and July. Propagated by sowing the seed in borders, or in pots, as soon as it is ripe. If not sowed till the spring, it does not come up till the second year. When the plants can be moved, they must be put in a nursery to stay two or three years before being planted where they are to stay. When the roots are strong enough, parts may be taken off, but they seldom allow of it. The fraxinella affords scarcely any flower till the fifth year after sowing; but its flowers are so abundant and so handsome, its leaves so rich in colour and in odour, and the whole plant is so elegant, that, where you can procure roots, it well deserves the pains and the patience necessary to procure it from seed. It likes a good soil, and, in the winter, requires a covering of litter after the stalk has died down.

463. FRITILLARY, *crown imperial.*—Lat. *Fritillaria imperialis.*—Fr. *Couronne imperiale.*—A large plant from Persia, near three feet high, proceeding from a large, nearly round, scaly bulb of nauseous smell. It blows in April, a red flower hanging downwards, like a tulip turned down. Another variety blows a yellow flower; and this latter is by far the handsomest. Propagate by parting the offsets every two or three years; take up the

plants in July, long before which time the stalks will have died down; take off what offsets may appear at the sides of the mother bulbs, and then keep them all in a dry place till the middle of August, when you will do well to plant them again, as this bulb will not do so well if it remain long out of ground. Plant at three or four inches depth in land not too much manured, and not too stiff or wet, as it likes rather a sandy loam.

464. FUMATORY, *bulbous.*—Lat. *Fumaria bulbosa.*—Fr. *Fumeterre bulbeuse.*—A perennial plant, a native of Europe, five or six inches high, and blows a purplish flower in February, March, and April. Propagated by separating the roots in autumn, or by sowing the seed in beds exposed to the sun.——YELLOW FUMATORY.—Lat. *Fumaria lutea.*—Fr. *Fumeterre jaune.*—A perennial plant, from mountainous places in England, growing one or two feet high, and blowing a yellow flower from April to November. Propagated like the bulbous fumatory.

465. GAURA, *biennial.* — Lat. *Gaura biennis.* — Fr. *Gaura bisannuelle.*—A hardy plant of Virginia, five or six feet high, and blows a very pretty flower, of a pale red colour, from August to September. Propagated by sowing the seed, which may be done as soon as it is ripe; it will then come up in the spring, and blow the following year.

466. GERMANDER, *the shining.*—Lat. *Teucrium lucidum.*—Fr. *Germandrée luisante.*—A plant that inhabits Provence, Piémont, and St. Bernard. Blows in June and July, a reddish purple flower, and is from one to two

feet high. Propagated by seed, sown in a hot-bed and in borders, as well as by separating the roots in Autumn. Any soil will suit it.

467. GLOBE-FLOWER.—Lat. *Trollius Europæus.*—Fr. *Trolle d'Europe.*—A hardy perennial plant of England, about one foot high, and blows a yellow flower in May, and sometimes again in September. Propagated by dividing the roots in the autumn, and it should have a moist, but not too shady, situation.

468. GLOBULARIA, *wedge-leaved.*— Lat. *Globularia cordifolia.*—Fr. *Globulaire à feuilles en cœur.*—A perennial frame plant of Provence, blowing a blue flower at the latter end of April. Propagated by sowing in pots or in a hot-bed. When once obtained they are easily perpetuated by dividing the roots. They like a light soil.——GLOBULARIA, *blue daisy.*—Lat. *Globularia vulgaris.*—Fr. *Globulaire commun.*—A perennial frame plant, common in France, about five inches high, and blows a blue flower in June and July.——GLOBULARIA, *three tooth-leaved.*—Lat. *Alypum.*—Fr. *Turbith.*—A green-house shrub from Montpellier, one or two feet high, and blows a blue flower in March and April. Propagated like the wedge-leaved globularia.

469. GOLDEN ROD.—Lat. *Solidago sempervirens.*—Fr. *Verge d'or.*—A hardy perennial from North America. About four feet high, and blows, towards the end of autumn, a yellow flower. Propagated by separating their roots in the autumn and in February : also by sowing seed in the autumn.

470. GOLDY LOCKS, *the flax-leaved.*—Lat. *Chryso-coma lynosiris.*—Fr. *Chrysocome à feuilles de lin.*—A perennial plant common in France, which grows to the height of eighteen inches, and blows a yellow flower in September and October. Propagated by sowing in a hot-bed, or a bed prepared for that purpose, and transplanting when fit. It likes light soil and a sunny situation.

471. HAWK-WEED, *wood.*—Lat. *Hieracum sylvati-cum.*—Fr. *Epervière des bois.*—A hardy perennial plant, common in England, about a foot high, and blows a yellow flower in June and July.—HAWK-WEED, *endive-leaved.*—Lat *Hieracium intybaceum.*—Fr. *Epervière tubulée.*—A hardy perennial plant from the Alps, about two feet high, and blows a yellow flower in July and August. Propagated by the seed as well as by suckers. It will do well in any soil, but prefers a dry one.——HAWK-WEED, *the clammy.*—Lat. *Hieracium glutinosum.*—Fr. *Eper-vière glutineux.*—An annual of the south of Europe. Should be sown in the open ground, and it blows a yellow flower in June and July. Is not particular as to soil.

472. HELLEBORE, *black, or Christmas rose.*— Lat. *Helleborus niger.*—Fr. *Hellébore à fleurs rose.*—A native of the mountainous parts of Italy. Blows a pale blush flower in January and February, and is perennial.—— HELLEBORE, *the winter aconite.*—Lat. *Helleborus hyemalis.* Fr. *Hellébore d'hiver.*—A perennial plant, and native of France. Blows a yellow sweet-scented flower in March. Propagated by separating their roots in autumn, and, also, by seed.

473. HOLLYHOCK, Chinese.—Lat. *Althæa rosea.*—Fr. *Alcée rose.*—A hardy biennial plant from China, about six or eight feet high, and blows, from July till September, a flower that is red, pink, white, or a yellowish colour. Propagated by sowing seed in the open earth, about the end of June or July. They may be transplanted in a month after they come up. Do not, generally, blow the first year. Like good substantial mould, and a warm situation.—The common hollyhock of the gardens, and which is ranked amongst biennial plants, will last much longer than two years; but, after the fourth, is not so fine. It requires good rich mould, and will then come to the height of ten or twelve feet; is of almost all colours, blows abundantly, and is easily raised from the seed, but its great height and robustness mark it out for a shrubbery, rather than a border, plant. Keep it staked, or towards autumn, the high winds, assisting its own weight, will tear it about sadly, and it does much mischief often in its fall.

474. HONEY-SUCKLE, French.—Lat. *Hedysarum coronarium.*— Fr. *Sainfoin d'Espagne.* — A hardy biennial plant, originally from Spain and the south of France, about two feet high, and has a red flower in July and August. Propagated by sowing seed in the spring, in light garden mould, and transplanting the plants into the place where they are to grow, in the autumn.

475. HONESTY, or moon-wort.—Lat. *Lunaria annua.* Fr. *Lunaire annuelle.*—A hardy annual plant of Provence, growing two or three feet high, and blowing a flower of a reddish violet, or blue colour, in June and July. When in bloom it adds to the ornament of gardens, and in winter its bunches of fruit produce a singular effect in parlours, where it is often kept. Propagated by seed sowed in open earth, as soon as ripe, and in a sunny situation. It does not blow till the second year, but afterwards sows itself.

476. HOP, *common.*—Lat. *Humulus cupulus.*—Fr. *Houblon commun.*—A hardy perennial plant, common in England. Blows a green flower from June till August. Propagated by seed or separating the roots. Likes a deep loamy soil. Its flower does not recommend it to the florist ; but its large and handsome clusters of fruit, and its general handsome and luxuriant growth fit it well for an ornamental climber, either to run up single stakes given it for the purpose, or to climb over arbors, or such like places. As to its other uses see Hop, in Chap. V.

477. HOUSE-LEEK, *mountain.*—Lat. *Sempervivum.*—Fr. *Joubarbe de montagne.*—A hardy perennial from Switzerland. Five or eight inches high, and blows a purple flower in June and July. Propagated by its suckers. As it grows naturally in dry and rocky places, and on the tops of houses, it is necessary, when planting it in pots, to put at the bottom a good deal of dry rubbish and old plaster.

478. HYACINTH.— Lat. *Hyacinthus orientalis.* Fr. *Jacinthe.*—There are now two thousand varieties of this beautiful bulb distinguished by the Dutch florists. It was originally from the Levant, but, by the care and cultiva-

tion bestowed on it by the florists of Haarlam, and other places of Holland, the oriental plant is infinitely surpassed by those of the north. To procure fresh varieties, it is necessary to sow the seed; and to propagate from roots already produced, you take the offsets and bring these forward to flower; but, of the sowing I shall speak fully at the end of this article. I will now relate how to proceed with bulbs already obtained and old enough to flower. Begin by marking out the sized bed that you wish to have, placing stoutish pegs at each corner, and in two or three places along the sides and ends; dig out the earth to twelve inches deep, then put in one of the three composts that I shall enumerate below, enough to fill the square up to within two inches of the rest of the ground; make the surface as even as a die; mark out with a small line a set of lines lengthways of your bed, and not more than six inches apart; do the same then across the bed, observing to let the lines be at the same distance from one another as the last are; then plant a bulb at every place where the lines intersect each other, taking especial care to let the top of the bulb be even with the earth, and order them so as to have no two of the same colour coming next one another. Then bring more compost, and fill up the two inches that you have yet to make good to bring the bed up to be even with the rest of the ground; and go on filling till you have brought it to be two inches *above the rest of the ground.* But, I should here observe, that, as this ground will settle down, and, perhaps, bury the bulbs too deep, it is proper to dig out the bed and put in the mould in which the bulbs are set, a week or ten days previous to setting them; and this gives time for that settling which always takes place. Do nothing after you have planted (except rake a little now-and-then) till winter, and then, when you expect frosts such as would penetrate two or three inches, or so, bring forth your straw, or whatever else you have, and cover over the whole bed effectually, excepting at times when you are pretty certain of no frost. When the season for frosts be over, of course you remove all paraphernalia for guarding against that element; but you then have others: cold winds, snows, and even quickly after these, the sun itself. Therefore, as soon as you have removed the straw, place hoops across the bed, or a frame of wood consisting of upright stakes driven into the ground, with bending cross-pieces going over from one to the other, in the fashion of a bedstead; and on these throw canvass, or other light stuff, when either cold winds or snows prevail, or, (when the plants are in blossom) when the sun shines out too much on them. The flowers will appear in March and April, and, though the plant is hardy, and even its flowers care not for snow or frost, yet, if you permit the sun to come and thaw this on them, they will not last half the time that they would otherwise do. When the plants are in blossom, such as have not strong stalks should have small sticks put in on the side of them, to which these stalks should be tied. Such plants as are destined to bear seed should be left to have the full influence of the sun, and should remain in the bed till the seed-pod turns quite yellow, and begins to split; but those that are not to bear seed, should be taken up as soon as their leaves turn yellow. Choose a dry day, and take them up cautiously, so as not to damage their offsets; then lay them pretty close to one another on the bed, and cover them over with earth to an inch thick, and in a fortnight they will be in a fit state to be cleared of dirt, dead leaves and offsets, and to be put by in a dry but airy place, where they remain till the autumn. The composts used in flowering bulbous roots are, either, 1 *One half heath mould, a fourth part river sand, and a fourth part well-rotted cow-dung ; or, 2. Two thirds sand; and one third well-consumed leaves ; or, 3. One third river sand, one third fresh earth, one fourth rotten cow-dung, and the rest leaf-mould.* These must be prepared a twelvemonth before they are used ; kept in the air, and frequently turned, or it is impossible that the different materials should be properly incorporated one with the other. *To procure fresh varieties,* sow well-ripened seed from a strong, handsome, and semi-double plant. Choose a well-protected place, make a nice bed of good compost, and sow in drills five inches apart, in the month of September. In the severe frosts, cover over the young plants, and keep grass and weeds from growing amongst them. Cover with clean straw, or thatch. When, in the following summer, the plants die down, hoe between them and give them an inch or so thick of covering of your compost ; and protect them again the next winter. Same treatment for the following summer, and then, in the fourth, they may be taken up and treated as plants for flowering. —In water-glasses, the hyacinth makes a very agreeable show in the house during the most dismal part of the winter. Get blue glasses, as more congenial to the roots than white ones, fill them with rain-water, with a few grains of salt in each, and put in enough water to come up the bulb about the fourth part of an inch. Change the water carefully every week, and place the plants in the lightest and most airy part of the room, or green-house, in which you keep them.   Plant hyacinths in the flower-borders in the manner directed for tulips.

479. HEPATICA, *anemone, or noble liver-wort.*—Lat. *Anemone hepatica.*—Fr. *Anémone hépatique.*—A perennial plant, which is found in great abundance near Castelane and de Grasse, and in shady places in the southern provinces of France. The flower is blue, violet, red, or white, and appears in February and March, and, sometimes, in January. Propagated by dividing the roots and by sowing the seeds. It likes earth that is light, rich, and warm, and rather dry than moist.

480. IPOMEA, *scarlet-flowered.*—Lat. *Ipomea coccinea.*—Fr. *Ipomée écarlate.*—A West India plant ; annual, and a climber. It grows to the height of seven or eight feet, and in July, and on to September, blows a beautiful little bell-shaped scarlet flower. Give it a good, but rather light, soil ; and propagate by sowing in pots in a hot-bed, not many seeds in a pot, so that each plant may be taken out with a ball of earth to its roots. It is considered a green-house plant ; but, if brought on in a hot-bed of moderate heat, and planted out near the end of May in a good situation, will do very well in the open air in England.

481. IXIA.—Lat. *Ixia bulbocodium.*—Fr. *L'Ixia bulbocode.*—A frame plant of Narbonne and the island of Corsica ; a small bulbous root, and blows a violet, purple, or white flower, in March and April. Propagated from offsets. A mixture of peat and sand is the favourite soil of the ixia.

482. IRIS, *small bulbous.*—Lat *Iris xiphium.*—Fr. *Iris bulbeuse.* — A bulbous plant from Portugal, which blows in June; its flowers are *blue, violet, yellow,* or *white.* It likes a light but rich soil, and requires to be moved and its roots separated every three years.—— IRIS, *yellow.*—Lat. *Iris pseudoacorus.*—Fr. *Iris des marais.*— Common in England at the sides of marshy places, growing at the edge of the water, and blowing in June; I never observed these but where the land was stiff clay. Very handsome plant, rising two feet or more in height, and proper for the sides of ponds, or rivulets, in gardens or pleasure-grounds. Move them in August or September.——IRIS, *Persian.*—Lat. *Iris Persica.*—Fr. *Iris de Perse.*—A little bulbous plant of great delicacy; grows seven or eight inches high, and blows a pretty, regularly-formed, and singularly sweet-scented flower, in March and April. If in the open ground, protect it a little during severe frosts by a covering of litter; but its chief use is as a potted plant to bring into the house. Plant the bulbs in the month of October, in pots filled with a mixture of one half sand and one half fine mould; or put some in water-glasses, and treat them as directed for hyacinths.——IRIS, *Chalcedonian.*—Lat. *Iris susiana.*—Fr. *Iris de suze.*—From the Levant. That large and hand-some plant so common in our gardens, flowering so abundantly in June, and having varieties of *deep blue, pale blue,* and *white* tinged with blue. It grows to about the same height as the *marsh iris,* mentioned above, is tuberous-rooted, should have good garden soil to grow in, and should be removed every three years. It is, like most of the others, quite hardy, and makes an elegant show in the gardens while in flower. This last is the

Fleur de lis, which figures in the arms of France; corrupted by us to *Flower-de-luce*, which name it bears commonly in some counties of England to this day.

483. LARKSPUR, *the dwarf.*—Lat. *Delphinum.*—Fr. *Pied d' alouette.*—A hardy annual from Switzerland. Sow where it is to blow, either in beds, in tufts, or in rows ; it looks best in the latter way, and, as it grows not higher than from twelve to eighteen inches in height, its brilliant colours of deep and light blue, pink, and white, make a great show in the front of the flower-border. To have a succession throughout the summer, sow every fortnight or three weeks, from the time of beginning your spring sowings, till the beginning of June.——— LARKSPUR, *tall.* — Lat. *Delphinum elatum.* — Fr. *Dauphinelle élevée.*—Also a hardy annual from the mountains of Switzerland and the Alps. Grows from four to five feet high, and blows a light blue, or deep blue, flower in August. Propagate by sowing the seeds, either in the spring or autumn. Not so handsome a plant as the last, by a good deal.

484. LAVATERA, *common.*—Lat. *Lavatera trimestris.*— Fr. *Lavatére à opercule.*—A hardy annual plant of the south of Europe, three or four feet high, and blows a pink or white flower from July to September. Propagated by sowing in the open earth. Its flower is, of itself, very handsome, and it would be a most showy border-flower, but for the great irregularity, and the rambling disposition, of the branches, which are numerous, and placed wide of one another. It flowers abundantly, is very hardy, continues a long while in blossom,

and ripens its seed in abundance ; and the richer the soil,
the finer the plant. Sow early in the spring where the
plant is to remain.

485. LEOPARDS-BANE.— Lat. *Doronicum plantagi-
neum.*—Fr. *Doronic.*—A perennial plant from the south
of Europe. It is about two feet high, and, in April it
blows a yellow flower. Propagated by cuttings and
suckers. The autumn is the time for removing it.

486. LILY, *the copper-coloured day.*—Lat. *Hemerocallis
fulva.*—Fr. *Hémérocalle à fleurs rouges.*—A hardy bulbous-
rooted plant, and a native of the Levant. Blows, in
July and August, a reddish yellow flower. Any soil suits
it ; but most of all a light loam. Propagated by separating the roots when the leaves dry up ; but should be
replanted again directly.——LILY, *scarlet martagon.*—Lat.
Lilium Chalcedonium.—Fr. *Lis de Chalcédoine.*—A hardy
bulbous-rooted plant from the Levant ; it grows three
or four feet high, and blows a bright scarlet flower in
June and July. Propagated from offsets taken soon
after flowering, which should be planted again shortly.
They like a good soil and good situation.——LILY,
purple martagon.—Lat. *Lilium martagon.*—Fr. *Lis martagon.*
A hardy perennial plant of Germany, which grows three
or four feet high, and blows, in July, a flower which is
reddish or white, spotted with purple or blackish spots.
Often called the Turk's cap. Cultivated like the scarlet
——LILY, *common white.*—Lat. *Lilium candidum.*—Fr. *Lis
blanc.*—This is sometimes called the *lily of France,* from
the circumstance of its being grealy used in France
on festival days and in processions ; but this is only

because of its being a handsome and purely *white* flower, corresponding with the national colour. It grows three or four feet high, sending up a straight stalk, garnished all the way up by narrow leaves, and terminated by several large white flowers hanging in clusters, and which appear in July. It is hardy, cares little as to what soil or situation is given to it, and multiplies rapidly by an increase of its large scaly bulbous roots, which should be separated every two or three years, and planted again directly. If not thus often separated, the offsets become so numerous, that, each sending up their stalk, the plant is over-large and unsightly. It is always handsome, however, in shrubberies, and is also handsome in the back part of borders or in the middle of beds, when kept parted often, as recommended above.——LILY, *white water.*—Lat. *Nymphea alba.*—Fr. *Nymphéa blanc*—A hardy perennial water-plant, common in England; growing in muddy ponds, but never, as far as I have observed it, coming spontaneously in any but stiff clay soils. I never saw it so generally as in Lanchashire, in the neighbourhood of Preston, where there is scarcely a little pond that is not covered over in the month of June with this very beautiful large flower. In garden ponds it is common to see them, and a great ornament they are to such places; but they must be procured first, and planted next: two operations of a most difficult nature; for you have to dig up the root from the bottom of a pond, perhaps two or three feet deep, and then you have to plant it under a similar difficulty. To dig it up you must actually go into the pond, feel for the stem of the plant, pursue it with your hand to the ground, and then dig up as good a ball as you can round the roots. Suffer it to remain out of water as short a time as possible. Some recommend the placing it in a vase, and sinking that to the bottom of your pond ; but I think a better way, is, to place your plant in an old fish-basket, full of suitable mould, and sink that ; if you can, sinking it a little way into the earth at the bottom of the pond, as well as sinking it to the bottom of the water. In this way, the plant is not necessarily confined to so small a space as in the vase; for, when its roots have extended to the edge of the basket, there will be room for them to go through, and as the basket rots away, the plant becomes fixed in the bed of the pond.——LILY, *yellow water.*——Lat. *Nymphea lutea.*——Fr. *Nymphéa jaune.* — Like the former in all respects, excepting that it bears a yellow flower, which is rather smaller than that of the white. Cultivate in just the same manner.

487. LILY OF THE VALLEY. — See SOLOMON'S **SEAL.**

438. LOBELIA, *acrid.*——Lat. *Lobelia urens.*——Fr. *Lobelie brûlante.*——A hardy perennial plant of England, about one foot high, and blows a blue flower in July and August. Propagated by sowing in a good earth, rather consistent than light, and should be watered often.—— LOBELIA, *or cardinal's flower.*——Lat. *Lobelia cardinalis.*—Fr. *Lobélie cardinale.*——A very handsome perennial plant from Virginia. It blows a most beautiful rich scarlet flower in July and October, and rises to two or three feet high. It thrives best planted out in summer in a rich friable soil; but is tender enough to require some protection in winter. It is easily increased by suckers or by seeds;

and the suckers of the old plant should be taken off every autumn or they damage it.

489. LOOSE-STRIFE, *yellow.*—Lat. *Lysimachia vulgaris.*—Fr. *Lysimaque commune.*—A hardy perennial plant, common in Europe, which grows about two feet high, and blows a yellow flower in July, August, and September. Propagated easily by suckers or shoots, and likes moist soil.

490. LUPINE, *dwarf.*—Lat. *Lupinus varius.*—Fr. *Lupin à fleurs variées.*—A hardy annual plant from Narbonne and Montpellier, which grows fifteen or eighteen inches high, and blows a blue or red flower in July and August. ——LUPIN, *common yellow.* — Lat. *Lupinus luteus.*—Fr. *Lupin jaune.* — Nearly resembling the last, only that it blows a yellow flower in June, July, and August.—— LUPIN, *blue.*—Lat. *Lupin hirsutus.*— Fr. *Lupin bleu.*— Grows taller than either of the others. There is a rose-coloured variety. In other respects resembling the yellow. All of them are proper border-flowers, and make a pretty show. Require no uncommon care ; and should be sown where they are to blow.

491. LYCHNIS, *scarlet.*—Lat. *Lychnis Chalcedonica.*— Fr. *Lycnide de Chalcédoine.* — A hardy perennial plant from the south of Russia, three feet high, and blowing a scarlet flower in July and August. Propagated by parting the roots. They like a good light soil, rather moist than dry.——LYCHNIS, *red-flowered.*—Lat. *Lychnis dioica.*—Fr. *Lycnide à fleurs roses.*—A hardy perennial plant, common in Europe, which is two or three feet

high, and blows a red flower in June and July. Propagated like the scarlet. The former of these plants is a very handsome ornament of either the border or the shrubbery. All the species are handsome, but particularly this. It should be parted early in the spring; and, by rights, ought to be covered with litter during the winter, for severe frost will injure it.

492. MAD-WORT, *the rock.*—Lat. *Alyssum saxatile.*—Fr. *Alysson.*—A perennial plant of the East, but common in gardens; grows to the height of one foot, and always keeps its leaves. It blows a beautiful yellow flower in April and May, and often blows afresh in August. Propagated by sowing the seeds in a pot, and putting it under a frame until March or April, when the plants may be transplanted. It is proper for the fronts of borders, or for rock-work.

493. MARSH-TREFOIL, *common buck-bean.*—Lat. *Menyanthes trifoliata.* — Fr. *Menyanthe trifolié.*—A hardy aquatic plant, common in some parts of Europe, is a creeper, and blows a reddish flower in May, June, and July. It has a pretty effect on the borders of ponds, where it will multiply itself.

494. MARVEL OF PERU.—Lat. *Mirabilis Jalappa.*—Fr. *Nyctage faux-Jalap,* or *belle de nuit.*—Large bushy plant, with a rough, black root, growing forked or long, according as the soil is rich and deeply-moved. This root will, in very rich gardens, deeply trenched, get to the size of a very large parsnip in the first year, and, by keeping it in sand in winter, housed, it may be made a

perennial, which it is not in our gardens, unless thus carefully managed. The stalks rise (with good digging and good manuring) to near four feet high, becoming a very branching and large plant. The colours are, red, yellow and white, with mixtures, red and yellow, red and white, yellow and white; and there are some purple sorts. The pie-balled sorts are most esteemed, and, therefore, the gardeners are careful to save seed from none but such plants as have yielded mixed flowers. This is taste, however, and as long as tastes differ it is proper to have all the sorts that can be procured. The yellow makes the greatest show. The flower is borne at the end of every shoot; and the blowing begins in the first week in July, and continues until the frosts set in. The only reason for the most fastidious to quarrel with this plant, is, that it blows but little in the heat of the sun, reserving all its *beauties* for those who rise early enough to see it at from five to seven o'clock in the morning. It is properly a hardy annual, though, as said above, may be rendered perennial, and may be sown in the open air as soon as all chance of injury to the young plants by frost is over. April is the best time for sowing. One plant is enough in a spot, and that not near to any minor plant or shrub, as it effectually sucks all moisture from it, and by its spreading branches, overlays it. The seed is a black fleshy substance coming in a little cup that the flower falls out of when overblown. In pots it makes a pretty show, but it requires so much more sustenance than is to be contained in a small vessel of this kind, that, even in the largest, it will not blow such large flowers as the plants in the open air; and unless the flower be a very large one, that is, about the size of a half crown, it is a pitiful, mean-looking thing, whereas, in full vigour and size, nothing is more showy at a distance, or more delicate when minutely examined, than the flower of this plant. It is a native of the West Indies.

495. MARYGOLD, *common.*—Lat.—*Calendula officinalis.*—Fr. *Souci.*—A hardy perennial plant, common in many parts of Europe, two feet high, and blows a light yellow flower in June, July, and August.——Marigold, *Small Cape.*—Lat. *Plurialis.*—Fr. *plurial.*—A hardy annual plant, originally from the Cape of Good Hope, one or two feet high, blows a white flower in June, July, and August. Propagated by seed sown where they are to grow. Likes a light soil and sunny situation.——Marigold, *African.*—Lat. *Fagetes patula.*—Fr. *Fagétès des jardins.* A hardy annual plant of Mexico which blows a reddish yellow flower from July to October. Propagated by sowing in a hot-bed, or in open earth, if it be good and exposed to the sun, and there is no longer fear of frosts. The plants must be planted in pots, and afterwards in the open earth, taking care to water them frequently when newly planted. They grow to two feet high, and often higher, and should be kept tied to sticks or they will fall about and look ugly. It is rather a staring flower when in blossom, and much more fit for the front of shrubberies, and round lawns, than for borders. It is not particular as to soil.

496. MASTER-WORT, *Great black.*—Lat. *Astrantia Major.*—Fr. *Astrance à grandes fleurs.*—A plant of which the root is perennial, from the mountains of Voges and the Pyrenees. It is two feet high, and its flower is of a radiated reddish or whitish colour, and blows from June to

September. Any soil and any situation except shade, will do for it. Propagated by sowing the seed or by dividing the roots in the autumn, and it often sows itself. It is a hardy plant.

497. MONARDA, *Oswego tea.*—Lat. *Monarda didyma.*—Fr. *Monarda écarlate.*—A hardy perennial from North America, growing two feet high and blowing a red flower in June, July and August. Propagated from suckers, or by sowing the seed in a hot-bed in the spring, and planting out the young plants when they are five or six inches high. They like a soil light, warm, and rich, and should be moved every two or three years.——Monarda, *Canadian.*—Lat. *Monarda fistulosa.*—Fr. *Monarda ...*——A hardy perennial of Canada, three or four feet high, blowing a pale purple flower in July and August. Propagated like the Oswego tea.

498. MULLEIN, *white.*—Lat. *Verbascum Lychnitis.*—Fr. *Moléne Lycnite.*—A hardy annual plant, common in Europe, growing three or four feet high and blowing a white or yellow flower in June, July and August. Propagated by sowing the seed as soon as ripe, and does best in a light, dry and sandy soil. It often sows itself.——MULLEIN, *rusty.*—Lat. *Verbascum ferrugineum.*—Fr. *Moléne à fleurs rousses.*—A hardy perennial plant of the south of France. Blows late in the spring, a flower of a reddish brown and purple in the middle. Propagated by sowing or by dividing the roots, and it will sometimes sow itself. Any soil suits, so that it be not too wet or too shady.

499. NARCISSUS.—Fr. *Narcisse.*—There are many

U

sorts of narcissus, of which our common daffodil is one,
and, I believe, the only one that is not a native of the
south of Europe. I shall enumerate only three sorts, and
shall give instructions relative to the procuring of these
by offsets, and relative to the blowing of them in beds, in
pots and in glasses.—The PAPER WHITE.—Lat. *Narcissus
papyraceus.*—the JONQUIL.—Lat. *Narcissus Jonquilla.*—Fr.
Jonquille.—the POLYANTHUS NARCISSUS.—Lat. *Narcissus
polyanthus.*—Fr. *Narcissus multiflore.*—These are all beautiful flowers, and all sweet-scented ; but particularly the
Jonquil. The first sort is reputed for its delicate and pure
white. It grows to a foot and a half high, bearing two
or three very handsome and paper-white flowers. The
second for its peculiarly sweet scent, which is enough
from only one plant, to perfume a whole room. It blows
a yellow flower, proceeding from a slender and elegant
stalk of from ten to twelve inches in height. The last
sort, of which there are three varieties, the *white*, the *white
with yellow cup in the middle*, and the *all yellow*, for its
abundance of flowers, which are frequently ten or twelve
in number upon each of two, three or four stems, according as the plant is a thriving and well-managed one.
The first has a bulb about the size of a bantam hen's
egg, the second a bulb not bigger than a very small
walnut, and the third a bulb larger than a turkey's egg.
They are all to be had of the seedsmen who import them
yearly from Holland ; but they may be propagated here :
or, at least, those who wish to go to the trouble of it,
by parting the offsets from the mother plants in July, and
planting them in a bed by themselves for a year ;
by themselves, because they do not flower the first
year after being parted ; or they may also be had

from the seed, by proceeding in the same manner as
for the hyacinth. The most common way, however, is
to buy of the seedsmen such bulbs as are wanted; blow
them the first year in pots or in glasses for the house,
and, the next year, plant them out in the borders, or in
beds by themselves; this latter being the best way, because then, by making use of the proper soil, which should
be a good light hazel mould, mixed with a little perfectly
rotten cow-dung, you preserve your bulbs from degene-
rating so fast as they will if turned out into the borders.
Take them up every third year, to take off the offsets,
and bring these on in a bed composed of the same mixture as that recommended for the flowering bulb. In
pots, use the same mixture, or put a little sand with it;
and, in glasses, do the very same as for the Hyacinth.
There are common varieties sold by the florists for the
open borders, which manage as you do the tulip and other
bulbs so planted.

500. NASTURTIUM, *the tall.*—Lat. *Tropæolum majus.*—
Fr. *Capucine des jardins.*—A plant from Peru which may
be trained to the height of ten or twelve feet, and blows
an orange coloured flower during the summer and part of
the autumn. The single flowered sort is annual, and,
being sowed in the spring, in a light soil and exposed to
the sun, will afterwards sow itself. The double flowered is
perennial, propagated by cuttings, and kept in a house.
In the winter exposed to the sun as much as possible,
and watered but little. There is a dwarf kind which
makes a pretty show in the front part of borders or in
pots.

501. NETTLE, *the red dead.*—Lat. *Galeopsis ladanum.*—Fr. *Chanbreuile commune.*—An annual plant common in Europe, which grows one foot high, and blows a pretty pink flower from July to October. Propagated by sowing the seed in any soil. A very handsome plant.

502. ŒNOTHERA, *great flowered.*—Lat. *Œnothera grandiflora.*—Fr. *Enothère à grandes fleurs.*—A biennial plant originally from Virginia. It is generally three or four feet high and blows in July, August and September, a beautiful yellow flower. Any soil suits it, but it likes a moist one and a sunny situation. Propagated by sowing the seed in a bed, but it also sows itself.——ŒNOTHERA, *evening primrose.*—Lat. *Œnothera biennis.*—Fr. *Enothère bisannuelle.*—From North America; biennial; blows a fine yellow flower from July to September. Likes a good garden mould, but is not very nice as to soil; and it should be sown in the spring in the place where it is to blow the following year.——ŒNOTHERA, *purple.*—Lat. *Œnothera purpurea.*—Fr. *Enothère pourpre.*—An American annual, growing eighteen inches or two feet high, and blowing, from June to August, abundance of purple flowers at the ends of its numerous stalks. Sow in the open ground early in Spring, in the place where it is to blow.

503. ONOSMA, *hairy.*—Lat. *Onosma echioides.*—Fr. *Onosma à feuilles de vipérine.*—A hardy perennial plant from the south of Europe, about a foot high, and blows a yellow flower in May. Propagated by seed sown in the open earth. Likes a dry soil; and, though hardy, likes a little covering in very severe weather.

504. PALMA CHRISTI, Lat. *Ricinus communis.*—Fr. *Ricin commun.*—A tender biennial plant from India, from five to seven feet high. Blows in July and August. Propagated by seed sown in a hot bed. When the plants are five or six inches high they should be planted where they are to grow. This plant is annual in the open ground, but, when put into a green-house, it lasts four or five years.

505. PANSY, or *heart's-ease.*—Lat. *Viola hispida.*—Fr. *Violette d' automne.*—A hardy perennial plant, very common in Europe, which blows a blue flower almost the whole of the year.——PANSY.—Lat. *Viola grandiflora.*—Fr. *Violette pensée.*—A hardy perennial, common in most parts of Europe, eight or ten inches high, and blows all the summer, a yellow and violet flower. These are propagated by seed, which ripens abundantly, as well as by separating their roots. Like rich earth and partial shade.

506. PEA, *the everlasting.*—Lat. *Lathyrus Latifolius.*—Fr. *Gesse à large feuilles.*—A perennial plant from Provence. It is four or five feet high, and in July and August, blows very beautiful bunches of rose-coloured flowers. Sow in beds and transplant to where the plants are to blow, or sow where they are to remain, but take care to have sticks, or lattice-work high enough to train them upon.——SWEET PEA.—Lat. *Lathyrus odoratus.*—Fr. *Gesse odorante.*—An annual plant from Sicily. About four or five feet high, and blows a rose coloured flower of various hues in June, July and August. Propagated by the seed sown where it is to remain. There is another ever-

lasting pea, the *grandiflora*, which blows the largest flowers of any, and which is as handsome as any, excepting that its foliage is not so luxuriant. The *crown pea, or painted lady* is very luxuriant in its growth, and, in rich soils, blows very handsome clusters of flowers of a pale blush colour. Propagate all these in the same manner.

507. —————————. Lat. *Petunia Nyctaginiflora.*—Fr.————— A very handsome perennial plant, bearing abundance of beautiful white flowers from May till October. It is a very fine border flower, but, in severe winters must be covered. It does extremely well in pots, and some should, by all means be potted and housed every autumn to redouble the chance of preserving the stock. Propagate by cuttings placed under a hand-glass, where they will soon strike ; or make it an annual by sowing seeds in the spring of the year.

508. PHLOX, *smooth, or bastard lychnis.*—Lat. *Phlox glabenima.*—Fr. *Phlox glabre.*—A hardy perennial plant, originally from North America. Grows about two feet high, and blows a pretty purple flower in June, July and August. Propagated by dividing the roots in the autumn and in February.

509. PINK, *China or Indian.*—Lat. *Dianthus chinensis.*— Fr. *L' œillet de la Chine.*—A hardy biennial plant of China, one foot high, blowing a bright red flower in July. Propagated from seed, from layers, and by dividing the roots, which like a light but good soil, dry rather than wet, and a sunny situation. It is generally cultivated in our gardens as an annual ; as it blows the first year, and

will not survive the winter unless protected from frost. A very pretty border flower ; but should be grown in beds, or largish clumps.———PINK, *the garden.*—Lat. *Dianthus Hortensis.*—Fr. *Œillet Lacinié.*—This is supposed to be a variety of the carnation. Its origin is common in England and all over Europe. There are many pretty varieties, and these are on the increase every year in England, the manufacturing people of the north bestowing vast pains in propagating and cultivating them. The plant is smaller in every particular than the carnation, but is its *miniature.* There are varieties double and single, red, white, and laced. It grows in tufts and sends up many stalks, each bearing a flower ; but these tufts should not be suffered to remain unparted more than one year. Propagate by *layers, pipings* or *seed,* just as with the carnation, only that, the pink being much the hardier of the two, you need not bestow the same pains upon it that you must on the carnation. Pipings will strike in the open ground, without any hand-glass over them, but you are surer to succeed by using the glass, and in the manner directed for propagating carnations in the open ground. No plant of this kind should be suffered to blow more than twelve flowers. All above that number should be cut off as they appear in the bud. Any soil almost suits it.

510. POLYANTHUS.—Lat. *Primula elatior.*—Fr. *Primevère.*—An indigenous plant which has been brought to great perfection by the florists. It blows, in March and April, flowers of various colours, red, brown, yellow, purple, and variegated ; the flower stem should rise above the foliage, should be perfectly erect, and send out from

five to seven small foot-stalks each to be terminated by a flower. Propagate by seed, or by parting the roots, which latter should be done every year, or the plants are sure to dwindle away and ultimately die. The Polyanthus likes a shady situation, moist ground, and manuring of neats' dung; but the soil mentioned under the head "*Auricula*" suits it well. It is well to have some always in pots the same as those for the Auricula, and by these means you procure an early show in the green-house and can the more readily and surely save the seeds of such plants as you most admire. In the seed-bed, you have only to follow the instructions given for the management of the Auricula bed.

511. POPPY, *red, or corn rose.*—Lat. *Papaver rhœas.*— Fr. *Pavot coquelicot.*—A hardy annual plant about two feet high, and its flower red. Blows in June and July, and is propagated by sowing the seed in a light and rich earth; afterwards they sow themselves.——POPPY, *garden.*— Lat. *Papaver somniferum.*—Fr. *Pavot des jardins.*——This sort grows larger than the last, has several varieties, double and single, of most colours excepting blue. It is easy to propagate from the seed, but, unless great variety be required, hardly worthy of a place in the flower border. This sort it is that yields *opium.* Prefer good deep soil; but they are not particular in this matter.

512. PŒONY, *hairy leaved.*—Lat. *Pæonia hirsuta.*—Fr. *Pivoine à feuilles velues*—is a hardy perennial plant from the south of France, which blows a purple flower in June.——PŒONY, *common red.*—Lat. *Pæonia roseo Officinalis.*—Fr. *Pivoine à fleurs roses.*—A hardy perennial from

Spain and the south of France, and blows early in the spring. Propagated by separating the roots in the autumn and the spring. Not particular as to soil or situation. Two or three feet in height, and makes a very fine show when planted in borders bounded by green-sward.

513. PRIMROSE.—Lat. *Primula vulgaris.*—Fr. *Primevère.*—That very pretty early-flowering native plant which we find all over England by the side of shady lanes, and in coppices of the winter-cutting, bearing numerous bright yellow flowers, each upon a foot stalk of two or three inches in length. By taking the pains, you may procure abundance of its seed, and propagate it as you would the *Auricula,* which see. Or you may transplant into your garden, at Michaelmas, any number of the plants, which will make a beautiful show in the early spring months. The situation and soil should be those for the *Polyanthus ;* that is, shady as to situation, and moist, as to soil.

514. RANUNCULUS.—Lat. *Ranunculus asiaticus.*—Fr. *Renoncule.*—A native of the Levant. It is a tuberous rooted plant, greatly ornamental, and deservedly a choice florist's flower. It blows, early in the spring, flowers single, semi-double or double, and of almost every colour ; but the scarlet, being the most admired, is the most usual. It is propagated either by offsets from the tubers, or by seed ; and both very much in the same way as in the case of the *anemone. By seed,* sow in January, under a frame and light, but take care to have the earth, to a foot and a half deep, taken out previously and well frosted, and, when thawed again, put it back into the frame. This destroys all vermin. Make it fine, and sow your

v 5

seeds in very shallow drills four inches apart, covering the seed in the slightest possible manner. I should, perhaps, have first said, that the seed should be saved from a semi-double plant the stem of which is strong and high, the flowers large, thick and round, and of brilliant colour; and also that it should be gathered in a dry time, scraped off from the stalk by patiently using your finger-nails for the work, and kept in a dry, though airy, place till the time for sowing. Let your seed-bed be in an eastern aspect, the one best suited to the *ranunculus* whether a seedling or a flowering plant; water with a fine-rosed watering-pot, so as to keep up a continual moisture, and, when the plants are up, give plenty of air; remove the light from the frame, and cover over with hurdles or a thick covering of netting. Do not move these young plants till their leaves are perfectly dead, and then do as with young *anemones*. *By offsets.* The time of planting out your old root is precisely that directed as the proper time for planting out the anemone; and, it is at the time of planting that you part the offsets from the mother-roots. They are easily discerned, each complete root having a bud enveloped, as it were, in a greyish down; the under part being composed of several dark brown claws, for the most part tending inwards at their points. These look as if perfectly dead, but, a few days under ground plumps them up to a considerable size; and it is even, with some, the practice to put the roots into a basin of water a few hours previous to planting them, a practice of very doubtful utility. The offsets that you take off are just as fit for blowers as the mother-roots; they do not, like the hyacinth and tulip, require nursery beds to bring them into flowering in a

course of years; therefore, there are no instructions
further necessary as to the propagating by offsets. But,
as to general cultivation, something must be said. The
florists invariably plant them in beds in the manner described under the head *Hyacinth*, except that they are
not to be planted at any more or less than an inch and a
half under ground; but they flourish also either in
clumps in the border, or in pots in the green-house. In
either of these cases, the soil that the ranunculus likes is
a good fresh, strong, rich loamy one; or, if you prepare
soil, let it be fresh loam with a manuring of well-rotted
horse or cow-dung. The *scarlet-turban* is the most
showy variety, and produces a most brilliant effect in a
bed; and, when thus planted, it is well worth the while
to take all the precautions necessary to bring forward the
plants well through the winter, and to guard their blossoms against too much wet or sun in the spring. To do
this, cover in winter, and shade and water in the spring,
as you do in the *hyacinth* bed. When you plant in pots,
take care that the pots be good deep ones; such as are
used commonly for the auricula, drain them well with pot-
sherds, but give frequent waterings in dry weather, or,
in such small masses, the earth soon burns, and you loose
your blossom-buds, if not the plant. About the end of
June your plants will be dying down, and then is the
time to take them up, cut off the fibres of the roots and
pull off the leaf-stalks; and put away the roots, well
freed from dirt. This root and the anemone take no
harm from remaining twelve months out of ground.

515. ROCKET, or *dame's violet*.—Lat. *Hesperis matro-
nalis*.—Fr. *Julienne cultivée*.—A biennial plant from Italy

which grows a foot and a half high, sending up many stalks crowned by double fragrant flowers. Varieties red and white; and blows from May to August. Propagated by parting the roots in autumn; or by cutting of the stalks of the flowers, which, being cut into convenient lengths, you make three splits in the end of each of about half an inch up; force the split end into the ground, and they will readily take root if you put a hand-glass over them, and place them where none but the morning sun can get to them. Better still to strike them under a propagation glass in a gentle hot-bed. There are very few prettier, and still fewer sweeter flowers than the double rocket; but it is said by theorists not to thrive near large cities I think that the smoke of London or Manchester is incompatible with the health of anything animal or vegetable; but I do not think smoke prejudicial to this plant in particular, for I have seen it remarkably fine in the neighbourhood of London, but never have I seen it so fine as in the vicinity of the smoky towns of the North of England, where it grows most freely in a strong clayey soil.

516. RING FLOWER.—Lat. *Anacyclus valentinus.*— Fr. *Anacycle de Valence.*—An annual plant from the south of France, about one foot high and the flower of a yellow colour, which appears in June and July. It is raised from seed sowed where it is to bloom, and does well in good earth that is warm and light.

517. ROSE CAMPION, *smooth-leaved.*—Lat. *Agrostemma cælirosa.*—Fr. *Coquelourde rose.*—A hardy annual plant of the South of France, eight or nine inches high, and blows a pink flower in July and August.

**518. RUSH, *the flowering.*—Lat. *Butomus umbellatus.*—Fr. *Butome en ombelle.*—A perennial, found in the borders of rivers and in the marshes in England and other parts of Europe. Grows three feet high, blowing in July a bunch of pretty large red flowers. It is a handsome plant, and well suited to damp or swampy places, or to the sides of ponds or rivers. Propagated by dividing the roots.

519. SAFFRON. See COLCHICUM.

520. SAND-WORT, *majorca.*—Lat. *Orenaria balearica.*—Fr. *Sabline de Mahon.*—A hardy perennial plant from Corsica, about two inches high, and blows a white flower in May and June. Propagated by seed, or separating the roots. Likes a sandy and warm soil, and a southern aspect.

**521. SAXIFRAGE, *the golden.*—Lat. *Chrysosplenium alternifolium.*—Fr. *Dorine.*—An inhabitant of France and many other parts of Europe. It is five or six inches high, and blows a yellow flower in April. Propagated by dividing the roots in October, and likes a shaded and moist situation, and is well suited to ornament the edges of water. A perennial plant.——SAXIFRAGE, *thick-leaved.*—Lat. *Saxifraga crassifolia.*—Fr. *Saxifrage à feuilles épaisses.*—A hardy perennnial plant originally from Siberia, which blows a pink flower in March and April.——SAXIFRAGE *palmate.*—Lat. *Saxifraga palmata.*—Fr. *Saxifrage palmaïe.*—A perennial plant common in France and England, blows a white flower in April and May. A foot high.—— SAXIFRAGE, *hairy.*—Lat. *Saxifraga hirsuta.*—Fr. *S. velue.*—A perennial frame plant, about eight or ten inches high, blows a white flower spotted with red in May.   From France and the Pyrenees.   Propagated by separating the roots.   Not particular as to soil, but likes a shady situation.

522. SCABIOUS, *sweet.*—Lat. *Scabiosa atropurpurea.*—Fr. *Scabieuse fleur de veuve.*—A hardy biennial plant, originally from India.   About two feet high, and blows, in August and September, a deep violet-coloured flower.————SCABIOUS, *devil's bit.*—Lat. *Scabiosa succisa.*——Fr. *Scabieuse tronquée.*—A hardy native perennial plant, which blows from August till September.   Propagated by seed sown in any border.   Varieties, deep purple, flesh-coloured, and white.

523. SIDA, *broad-leaved.*—Lat. *Sida abutilon.* — Fr. *Sida abutilon.*—An annual stove plant, from India.   Four feet high, and blows a yellow flower in June, July, and August.   Propagated by seed sowed in a hot-bed, and afterwards transplanting the young plants where they are to remain.

524. SILPHIUM, *jagged-leaved.*—Lat. *Silphium laciniatum.*—Fr. *Silphium lacinié.*—A hardy perennial, three or four feet high, originally from North America, and blows a yellow flower in July, August and September.——SILPHIUM, *three-leaved.*— Lat. *Silphium trifoliatum.*—Fr. *Silphium à feuilles ternées.*—A hardy perennial plant of North America, about eight feet high, and blows a yellow flower in August and September.   Propagated by seed sown in the open earth, or by separating the roots in the autumn.

525. SNAP-DRAGON, *common.* — Lat. *Antirrhinum majus.*—Fr. *Muflier des jardins.*—A perennial plant, common in uncultivated places, and on walls, in England. Blows in June, July, and August, its flowers are purple, red, or white.——SNAP-DRAGON, *small.*—Lat. *Antirrhinum orenticum.*—Fr. *Muflier rubicond.*——An annual plant, common in Europe, growing about a foot and a half high, and blowing a reddish, or white, flower, with spots of yellow, in July. Propagated by seed, sown in a border, and the plants afterwards planted, where they are to remain. Both of these are handsome border flowers, but the latter is rather too small to make any *show.* The former, on the contrary, is very showy, very hardy, and remains a long time in flower. Sowed on the tops of old buildings, old walls, or heaps of dry rubbish, it thrives almost as well, and blows quite as well, as in the best-prepared borders.

526. SNOW-DROP.—Lat. *Galanthus nivalis.* — Fr. *Galantine, perce-neige.* — A native bulbous-rooted plant, which, in January and February, blows a white flower, and is seven or eight inches high. There is, also, a double sort. —— SNOW-DROP, *summer.* — Lat. *Leucoium æstivum.* — Fr. *Nivéole d'été.* — A native plant, which blows a white flower in the beginning of summer. Bulbous, and propagated by offsets. Likes a moist soil.

527. SOAPWORT, *common.*—Lat. *Saponaria officinalis.*—Fr. *Saponaire officinale.*—A hardy perennial plant, about two feet high, and very common in England. Blows, in July, red or white flowers, and there are some double. Propagated by the runners. Likes any soil or situation.

528. SOLOMON'S-SEAL, *angular.*—Lat. *Convallaria polygonatum.*—Fr. *Sceau de Salomon.*—A hardy perennial common in England and many parts of Europe, which blows a whitish flower in May and June, and rises to about eighteen inches high. Propagated by dividing the roots in the fall. Not particular as to soil, but it likes a shady situation, and will even succeed under trees.—— SOLOMON'-SEAL, *or Lily of the Valley.*—Lat. *Convallaria maïlis.*—Fr. *Muguet de Mai.*—Like the former, it will succeed under the drip of trees. A native perennial plant, with large oblong leaves rising from the root; sending up a stalk eight inches high, which bears from six to twelve white pendant sweet-smelling flowers in May and June. Propagated by dividing the roots in the fall. It likes a moist situation; and will grow under the drip of high trees.

529. SOLDANELLA, *Alpine.*—Lat. *Soldanella.*—Fr. *Soldanelle des Alpes.*—A perennial plant from Switzerland, three or four inches high, and blows, in March and April, a blue, reddish, or, sometimes, white flower. Propagated by separating the roots. Likes good heath mould, with a fourth part of maiden earth. Should be protected from hard frosts.

530. SPIDER-WORT, *Virginian.*—Lat. *Tradescantia Virginiana.* — Fr. *Ephémérine de Virginie.*—A perennial plant, originally from Virginia. It is about a foot high, and blows, from June till October, a bluish violet-coloured flower. There are some, also, with white flowers. It flourishes in any soil or situation. Propagated by separating the roots in March and October.

531. SQUILL, *Italian.* — Lat. *Scilla Italica.* — Fr. *Scille d' Italie.* — A hardy bulbous-rooted plant, common about the environs of Nice. It is about eight or ten inches high, and blows a blue flower in March and April. Propagated by its offsets. Likes fresh sandy earth, or a mixture of light soil and sea sand.

532. STAR OF BETHLEHEM, *yellow.* — Lat. *Ornithogalum luteum.* — Fr. *Ornithogale jaune.* — A bulbous-rooted plant, common in England, and blows a yellow flower in March, and is three or four inches high. Propagated by separating the offsets in the autumn. Likes rather moist earth and shaded situation.——STAR OF BETHLEHEM, *spiked.* — Lat. *Ornithogalum Pyrenaicum.* — Fr. *Ornithogale des Pyrenées.* — A hardy perennial plant, originally from the Pyrenees, one or two feet high, and blows a yellow flower in May and June.——STAR OF BETHLEHEM, *common.* — Lat. *Ornithogalum umbellatum.* — Fr. *Ornithogale en ombelle.* — A hardy perennial plant of England. From six to nine inches high, and blows a white flower in May and June. Both sorts propagated by the offsets, taken from the plants in the autumn, and planted directly.

533. STOCK, *the Brompton.* — Lat. *Cheiranthus coccineus.* — Fr. *Giroflée cocardeau.* — The stock, if not a native of England, is completely naturalized, and has been cultivated here with greater success, perhaps, than in any other country. There are four distinct sorts that I shall mention, because these are all of them most deserving of being cultivated in the flower-garden, where they produce show, odour, and durability, surpassed by none.

The Brompton stock grows to about two feet high when flourishing, has long hoary leaves, narrow, and rather waved at the edges, and, above the foliage, there rises a stalk studded round thickly with scarlet double flowers as large each as a small rose, and which appear in May and June.   This plant is a biennial, and should, therefore, be sown in the spring or summer, and treated accordingly ; but as it suffers from the frosts of winter, when brought on too forward the first summer, it is best not to sow till the middle or latter end of June. Raise the plants in a frame, and keep them thinned out in order that, though not large when winter comes on, they may still not be weak. Plant out the young plants in the fall, and, if the winter be very severe, and you have the means of doing it, cover them with litter during such severity ; as, though frosts must be very hard, indeed, to kill them, yet a severe winter will spoil their blossom-buds and cause them to blow but little, and single.——STOCK, *Queen's.*—Lat. *Cheiranthus incanus.*—Fr. *Giroflée des jardins.*—This is also a biennial ; grows a foot or more high, producing white, red, or purple double flowers in May and June ; but these come on innumerable branches which this stock sends out from its main stalk on each side.   Leaf like the former ; and it is cultivated like the former.——STOCK, *ten-week.*—Lat. *Cheiranthus annus.*—Fr. *Giroflée annuelle* (or, *quarantain, forty-day*) ; is a very handsome and sweet little annual plant, blowing from May to September or October. It grows from twelve to eighteen inches high, with greyish coloured leaves, branches out a little, and, if from good seed, bears double flowers, red, white, or purple ; equal to either of the preceding in odour, and not far surpassed by either in appearance. Sow early in March, or in February, on a hot-bed and under a frame or hand-glass. Take care to keep the plants thinned out so as not to let them get weak, and give plenty of air, especially in the middle of the day. Early in April plant them out where they are to blow, and let this be in the front part of the flower-borders ; put in four or five plants in a clump, or more, so that, when you find their flower-buds appearing, you can pull up those plants that are showing for single flowers, except one, which you should always leave for seed. The red is by far the most showy variety. Sow again in May, and the plants of this sowing will, when planted out, keep up a succession of flowering till October.——STOCK, *wall-flower leaved.*—Lat. *Cheiranthus interregimis.*—Fr. *Giroflée grecque.*——Also an annual, rising to ten or twelve inches high, having leaves unlike all the former, of a darkish shining green, and being perfectly smooth. Blows, in May and June, double or single flowers, white, red, or violet. To be treated like the *ten-week stock.* All these plants bear their seed on plants that blow single flowers, and, to make sure of saving seed that shall produce double flowers, the seed plant should stand amidst those that are blowing double. The double-flowering ones show themselves very early ; their buds are much larger and rounder than the single, and appear to be bursting when the single have no such appearance.

534. STRAWBERRY-BLITE, *slender-branched.*—Lat. *Blitum virgatum.*—Fr. *Blitte effilée.*—An annual plant of France and the greater part of Europe, which grows one or two feet high, and blows from May to August. When

once raised in a soil which it likes, it sows itself without further trouble.

535. SUN-FLOWER.— Lat. *Helianthus multiflora.*— Fr. *Soleil multiflore.*—A hardy perennial plant, originally from North America, about four feet high, and blows yellow flower in July and August. Propagated by seed sowed in a border in July, and the young plants planted when they are fit, in the places where they are to remain; also by separating the roots in the autumn or spring.——SUN-FLOWER, annual.—Lat. *Helianthus annuus.* —Fr. *Soleil à grandes fleurs.*—An annual, which came originally from Peru; grows from four to six feet high, having the coarsest stem, leaf and flower of any culti- vated plant. The flower is yellow, and appears in July and August. Is sometimes double, and is from six inches to a foot in diameter; bears abundance of oily seed which is much liked by poultry of every sort. Pro- pagated by its seed, sowed early in spring, and the plant when in their sixth leaf removed to where they are to blow. Fit for nothing but very extensive shrubberies, where, when seen from a distance, the sight may en- dure it.

536. THISTLE, *the globe.*—Lat. *Echinops ritro.*—Fr. *L'échinope ritro.*—A hardy perennial of the south of France, growing three or four feet in height, and blows a light blue flower in August. Propagated by sowing or by separating the roots. Any soil suits it.

537. THRIFT.—Lat. *Statice Armeria.*—Fr. *Statice à bordures.*—A native of the Alps; the roots are perennial

and fibrous ; it rises three inches high or more, and spreads very fast. The variety with bright scarlet flower, which comes in May and lasts throughout the month of June, should find a place in small borders, but it should be regularly parted every year to prevent its spreading too widely.

538. TIGER-FLOWER.— Lat. *Tigridia pavonia*—Fr. *Tigridie panachée.*—A very beautiful bulbous plant from Mexico. Grows from one to two feet high ; with narrow sword-shaped leaves, and a stalk longer than these, which, in the month of July, blows many flowers of a yellow or scarlet colour beautifully spotted with purple. The flowers never come out more than one or two at a time, and they last but six hours, when they drop, and are, the next day, succeeded by others. This plant is not quite hardy ; therefore, the best way to cultivate it in the open ground is as you do your superior hyacinths, taking it up when its leaves decay, and keeping it out of ground and in a dry place, till spring, when you replant it in the bed or in the border. In pots, in the green-house, it does very well, but not better than in the open air when treated as above, and in a suitable soil ; namely, a fine and somewhat light and deep garden mould. Propagate by separating the offsets from the mother bulbs, and treating them as you do tulips.

539. TOAD-FLAX, *ivy-leaved.* —Lat. *Linaria cymbalaria.*—Fr. *Linaire cymbalaire.*— A hardy annual plant, found on old walls ; which, hanging over the sides of a pot, will blow a pale purple flower during the whole of the summer. Propagated by seed.

540. TUBEROSE, *common*.—Lat. *Polyanthes tuberosa*.—Fr. *Tubéreuse cultivée*.—A green-house perennial plant, about three feet high, and a native of the East Indies. Blows a white flower in August and September, and has a very powerful scent. Propagated by the offsets, which are separated from the principal root every year, as it blows generally, but once. The offsets should be planted in a hot-bed, and they blow in about two years. Like substantial though light earth. The bulbs of this plant are imported annually, by the florists and seedsmen, from Italy, as are those of the Amaryllis, from Guernsey; and it is better to buy these and only force them into flower by means of the stove, or hot-bed to begin with, and then the green-house, than to attempt to propagate them from offsets, which are long in coming to perfection.

541. TULIP.—Lat. *Tulipa sylvestris*.—Fr. *Tulipe Sauvage*.—This is the native tulip, but is so completely eclipsed by the eastern plant of the same name that it is scarcely known, though one variety, the double yellow, is a most desirable border flower, producing handsome large and very double flowers in May. It is multiplied by parting its offsets every year from the mother bulb, and likes a lightish soil.———Tulip, the florist's— Lat. *Tulipa Gesnariana*—Fr. *Tulipe des fleuristes*.—From the Levant. A hardy bulb that has occupied the attention of Florists more than any other plant. There are early blowing and late blowing varieties, the former appearing in April, and the latter in May and June; and as to colours, they match the rainbow. I will mention the names of two or three of the *early* and the *double* varieties: Early blowers, *Duc van Thol, Clarimond, Duc ras*

Orange.   Double, *Marriage de ma Fille, double red, double yellow.* Of single late-blowers there are upwards of six hundred named varieties, so I give none of these.   For borders, they are sold by the Florists at five shillings the hundred.   All are propagated in the same way : by offsets or by seed ; but most commonly by offsets, because to do it by seed is expensive and most tedious, as the seedling plants do not come into flowering till the fifth or sixth year.   *By offsets :* When you take out your old bulbs to plant, break off the largest offsets from the sides, and plant them at two or three inches apart in a bed of sandy loam with a sub-stratum of rotted cow-dung at about eight inches beneath the surface.   Let the bed be raised a few inches above the adjoining ground and rounded so as to turn off rains, and have it hooped over so that, in severe frosts or long-continued rains, you may throw over a covering to guard against either.   *By seed :* Procure the seed from those plants that have the tallest and straightest stems, the flowers the most even, the most clear in the cup, and of the purest colours : and let the seed remain on the plant till the pod in which it is contained becomes of a brown colour, and begins to burst.   Sow and manage in the manner directed for the *Hyacinth,* which see. For bulbs that are already blowers, most Florists choose square beds, in which they plant them in rows at seven inches asunder ; the beds being first prepared in this way : they are marked out according as the dimensions are determined on ; then the earth is digged out completely to the depth of twenty inches or more ; a layer, ten inches thick, of good fresh earth from a rather sandy pasture is put in, and upon it a thin coat of well-rotted cow-dung ; on that, another layer of the fresh pasture-mould is laid in, to about four inches above the surface of the ground, in the middle; and sloping down at the sides, where also it should be a little higher than the adjacent ground, to which it will settle. It is left so for ten days, and then, about the end of October, being intersected by lines across and athwart in such way as for every intersection to be seven inches from the neighbouring ones, holes about four inches deep are made at every one of these, a little drift sand deposited in each hole, and the bulbs are put in and covered over carefully. Beds of this kind are generally hooped over, so as to admit of covering during the winter; but some have a high frame to cover them, so high as to admit of ones' walking under; and these are covered with canvas awnings and are intended to keep off the fierce rays of the sun while the plants are in blossom. When planted in the flower-border, tulips should be put in clusters of from six to twelve, and the bulbs not nearer to one another than six or seven inches. They should be planted, in very light soils, at six inches beneath the surface; and, in heavy soils, at four inches beneath the surface, and should have a little sand put into the holes that they are planted in. Lightish pasture-ground is most suitable to them, and the manure for them is always rotted cow-dung. When the leaves begin to turn brown, and the upper part of the flower stem also begins to turn, take up the bulbs and place them in a dry but airy situation, where they will remain till September or October, when you separate their offsets from them and replant both offsets and mother bulbs in their respective beds. I must again observe, that, in the flower borders, they look best in clusters; the early ones particularly are ornamental in

this way, being very short in the flower-stalk and blend-
ing well with the yellow and blue crocuses.

542. VALERIAN, *blue flowered greek.*—Lat. *Polem-
onium cæruleum.*—Fr. *Polémoine bleue;* is a hardy perennial plant, common in many parts of England, blowing
in May, June and July, a bright blue, or a white flower.
Propagated by seed or by separating the roots. Any soil
suits it, but not a shady situation. About two or three
feet high.———VALERIAN, *red.*—Lat. *Valeriana rubra.*—Fr.
Valériane rouge.—A perennial plant of the south of
France, three or four feet high, and blows a red flower
from June to October. There are other sorts with white,
pink and lilac flowers. They come handsomest in a light,
warm and rich soil, and are propagated by sowing the
seed, and by dividing the roots. When once obtained
they sow themselves.

543. VERNONIA, *long leaved.*—Lat. *Vernonia novebo-
racensis.*—Fr. *Vernonia de New Yorck.*—A perennial plant
from North America, three or four feet in height, and
blows a blue, or light purple, flower, from September
till November.—VERNONIA, *tall.*—Lat. *Vernonia præalta.*
—Fr. *Vernonia gigantesque.*—A hardy perennial plant from
North America, five or six feet high, and blows a purple
flower from September till November. These plants are
very ornamental in Shrubberies, as they blow when all
other things have done. Propagated by separating their
roots : also by seed, sown in the open earth. Like a
rich loamy soil.———VERVAIN, *cluster flowered.*—Lat. *Verbena multifida.*—Fr. *Verveine multifide.*—A hardy biennial
plant from Buenos Ayres. Blows a deep purple flower

from July till October.——VERVAIN, *rose*.—Lat. *Verbena aubeltia*.—Fr. *Verveine d' aublet*.—A biennial frame plant from North America. About six inches high, and blows a red flower from June till August. Propagated by seed or by dividing the roots. Will do in any soil.

544. VETCH, *bitter spring*.—Lat. *Orobus vernus*.—Fr. *Orobe printanier*.—A perennial plant common in France and other parts of Europe, about a foot high and blows in March and April. Propagated by seed, sown in the open earth, as soon as it is ripe. When the roots are strong enough, plant them where they are to grow. It is sometimes necessary to let them wait till the spring of the following Autumn before they are removed. Likes any soil. —— VETCH-MILK (*Goat's rue leaved*). — Lat. *Astragalus galegiformis*.—Fr. *Astragale galégiforme*.—A perennial plant originally from Siberia. Its height, four feet, blows, in July and August, yellow flowers. It is multiplied by seed sowed in a bed of light earth which is exposed to the south east. When the young plants are five or six inches high, plant them where they are destined to grow.

545. VIOLET.—Lat. *Viola odorata*.—Fr. *Violette odorante*.—A hardy perennial plant, common in England and most parts of Europe, and blows a deep blue flower in March and April. Varieties white, and rose-coloured; double blue, white, and rose-coloured; they all like a moist and shady situation, and the single varieties are easily propagated by seed sowed in a shady place as soon as it is ripe, that is, about the beginning of August; they do not come up till spring, and when of a pretty good

size, the young plants should be transplanted into a shady bed there to remain until autumn, when you may plant them where they are to remain.   The double sort bears no seed, therefore is propagated only by dividing the roots, which is the easiest and, perhaps, best way of progating either.   Do this as soon as the plant has done flowering, keep it moist till it have taken root; water, if the weather be very dry; and do not part the roots more than once in three years, as the tufts must be pretty thick to flower well.

546. WALLFLOWER.—Lat. *Cheiranthus cheiri.*—Fr. *Giroflée jaune ;* or *Violier.*—A biennial plant of the South of Europe. Grows from one to two feet high, and blows a fine yellow flower from April till June. Propagated by seed, sowed in a hot-bed of moderate heat, or, in beds out of doors in March. When they are four or five inches high, they are planted where they are to remain. They want little watering and a soil rather dry than moist. The double ones are propagated by cuttings planted in good earth and rather shaded. This plant is called hardy, but in very severe frosts it should have protection, or it blows late and sparingly, and not so double as otherwise it would. It may be made the hardier by being sowed in poor ground, which causes the plant to be less succulent and consequently less susceptible of frost. It grows well on old walls, or any walls, indeed ; or on rubbish of any kind, and makes a pretty show wherever it is found.

547. WOOD-SORREL, *violet coloured.* — Lat. *Oxalis violacea.*—Fr. *L'oxalide violette.*—A perennial bulb origi-

nally from North America, and blows a violet coloured flower in May and June. It grows three or four inches high, and likes a light soil and is propagated by parting the offsets, or seed which should be managed like the tulip only that it requires less pains.

548. WILLOW-HERB, *the rose bay*.— Lat. *Epilobium augustifolium.*—Fr. *Ephilobe à épi.*—A native perennial plant, owing its vulgar name to the resemblance of its leaf to that of the common willow. It grows three or four feet high, sends up innumerable branches, which are decked thinly all the way up by narrow pointed leaves, and, towards the tops of these branches, it bears a peach blossom flower in July and August. It is a troublesome thing in a flower border, on account of the great quantity of stems that it sends up from its very wide-spreading root, and, on this account (as well as on account of its height not suiting a border) it is not cultivated in it, but is generally amongst the front rows of the shrubbery. The soil that it likes best is a moist one, but it does not refuse a pretty dry one. There is a white variety; both propagated by dividing the roots in the fall.

549. XERANTHEMUM *annual, or immortal herb.*— Lat. *Xeranthemum annuum.*—Fr. *Immortelle des jardins.*— A plant from the South of Europe. About a foot high, and blows in July and August, a purplish flower. Propagated from seed sowed in the open ground where it is to grow. When it is in a warm situation it propagates itself.

550. ZINNIA.—Lat. *Zinnia multiflora.*—Fr. *Zinnia mul-*

liflore.—An annual plant originally from North America. Sends up many flower stalks about a foot and a half high, and, at the end of each, bears a brownish red flower, in the months of July, August and September. Propagated by sowing the seed in April where the plants are to blow, or in February in a hot bed, to be planted out in April, not particular as to soil or situation ; will do well in rock-work, and makes a pretty show in the border.

551. ZIZIPHORA, *oval-leaved.*—Lat. *Ziziphora capitatum.*—Fr. *Ziziphora.*—A hardy annual plant from Syria, about six inches high, and blows a purplish flower in June and July.—*Ziziphora spear-leaved.*—Lat. *Ziziphora tenuior.*—Fr. *Ziziphora lancéolée.*—A hardy annual plant from the Levant, about a foot high, and blows in June and July. Both are propagated by seed sown in the autumn or in the spring where they are to remain.

KALENDAR.

January.

KITCHEN-GARDEN.— *Sow* radishes in a southern aspect, and protect them. *Pot* young cucumber plants, and put them in the bearing-bed at the end of this month.

February.

KITCHEN-GARDEN.—*Sow* masagan and Windsor beans, melons, radishes, spinage, basil. *Line* cucumber-beds.—— FRUIT-GARDEN.—*Strike* cuttings of currants, gooseberries, vines, and make layers of the latter; prune fruit-trees, begin grafting towards the close of the month, and sow walnuts.

March.

KITCHEN-GARDEN.—*Sow* artichokes, masagan beans, Windsor beans, capsicums on hot-beds, cauliflowers to come in in the autumn, celery on gentle hot-beds, cress, cucumbers on beds, lettuce, marjoram, marygold, melons, nasturtium, onions, parsley, peas, radishes, sage, borage. *Plant out* cauliflowers, hops in clumps for their tops, small onions of last May's sowing. Old onions for seed. *Pot out* melons of last sowing. *Divide offsets* of garlick, cives, shalots. *Make* asparagus beds, and *dig* old asparagus ground and throw up earth on the surface, and the same with clumps of artichokes, and dig between cabbage-stumps planted in the autumn to bear seed this year. *Clip* box-edging.——FRUIT-GARDEN. *Graft* all sorts of trees, prune, protect blossoms of peach and other fruit-trees, look after vermin narrowly, and transplant trees.——FLOWER-BORDERS. *Sow* adonis, alysson, prince's feather, snap-dragon, yellow balsam, candy-tuft, catchfly, convolvulus minor, devil-in-a-bush, hawkweed, Indian pink, ketmina, larkspurs, lavetera, linaria, mignonette, moon-wort, nasturtiums, nigella, palma Christi, pansey, sweet-pea, per-sicaria, scabious, sun-flowers, strawberry spinage, stocks two ten weeks, sweet sultan, Venus' navel-wort. *On hot-bed, sow* con-volvulus major, amaranthus tricolor and globe, balsams, china aster, china hollyhock, chrysanthemums, colutea, capsicums, jaco-bea (French grounsel), ten-week stock, zinnia, marvel of Peru. *Plant* autumnal flowering-bulbs, such as the tiger flower.

April.

KITCHEN-GARDEN.——*Sow* Windsor, long-pod, and kidney beans, beets, broccoli, for autumnal use, Brussels'-sprouts, sugar-loaf cabbage; savoys and dwarf green cabbage for winter use, kale for winter use; carraway, carrots, chervil, coriander, corn-salad, cress, cucumbers in beds, dill, fennel, hyssop, lettuce, mint, parsnip, peas, radishes, rampion, rape, samphire, savory, scorzenera, sorrel, squashes in hot-bed, tarragon, thyme, tomatums in hot-bed, worm-wood.——*Move* capsicums, cauliflowers of last month, melons and cucumbers to their bearing beds.——*Plant* potatoes, slips of thyme, lavender, mint, rosemary, rue, sage, tansey, sorrel, wormwood.—— FRUIT-GARDEN. Propagate by layers; head down young trees, and cut stocks' down close to the ground; finish grafting; prune young fruit-trees, and watch and destroy vermin.——FLOWER-BORDERS. *Sow* the same as last month, or sow at the very end of April, for succession, the same things; but those then sowed in a hot-bed may now be sowed in the open ground.——*Propagate* by layers, slips, and cuttings, and by separating roots.——*Put out* the less tender of your green-house plants.

May.

KITCHEN-GARDEN.—*Sow* succession crops of Windsor, long-pod, and kidney beans; broccoli for spring use, cauliflowers for December, Indian corn, cress, cucumbers under hand-glass, onions to plant out next spring, peas, pumpkins, radishes, salsafy, skirret, spinage, squash. *Prick out* celery, and *move* cucumbers sowed last month. *Plant* potatoes, and squashes sowed last month.——FRUIT-GARDEN. Look to your grafts, and loosen or take off the bandages; disbud fruit-trees.——FLOWER-BORDERS. Weed, and set out plants just coming up, to their proper distances from one another. At about the middle of the month, or the end, sow again for succession, larkspurs, mignonette, ten-week stock and wall-flower-leaved stock, minor convolvulus, and Virginia stock. *Propagate* by cuttings, slips, and layers. *Pot out* geraniums, fuchsias, and other green-house plants.

June.

KITCHEN-GARDEN.—*Sow* Windsor and long-pod, and kidney beans, pumpkins, and tomatums. Thin out young asparagus plants. *Weed* all the garden over. *Clip* box-edgings, and quick-set also.——FRUIT-GARDEN. Tie up young grafted trees, water newly-planted ones if dry weather, net up morello cherries and currants.——FLOWER-BORDERS. Take up bulbous-rooted plants and put them by. Tie tall-growing flowers up to sticks.

July.

KITCHEN-GARDEN. *Sow* kidney-beans, early dwarf cabbages, cress, endive, squashes for a late crop, turnips. *Plant out* celery in trenches, leeks.——FRUIT-GARDEN. Begin budding. Water newly planted trees, nail fruit-trees that want it, head down young espaliers, stop fruit-bearing shoots of vines.—— FLOWER-GARDEN. *Pipe* carnations and pinks; *divide* roots of Auricula and plant them.

August.

KITCHEN-GARDEN. *Sow* kidney beans, early dwarf cabbage, cauliflowers for spring use, cress, lettuce, spinage, turnips, borage. *Break down* the leaves of Brussells'-sprouts. *Plant out* endive for winter. *Dig up* mushroom spawn. *Gather* onion, and other seed. ——FRUIT-GARDEN. Finish budding, and loosen the bandages round buds put in earlier, or take them entirely off; *plant out* strawberry-plants that struck in the fore-part of this spring.—— FLOWER-GARDEN. *Divide* and *plant* roots of auricula and colchicum.

September.

KITCHEN-GARDEN. *Sow* cress, lettuce. —— FRUIT-GARDEN. *Propagate* by layers, and cuttings. Plant fences of quick, &c.—— FLOWER-BORDERS. *Take up* tiger-flowers, and other tender bulbs; and pot and enter the green-house plants that were put out in April. *Put in pots*, Guernsey and belladonna lilies.

October.

KITCHEN-GARDEN.—*Sow* masagan beans and cresses.—*Plant* artichokes, asparagus, horse-radish, lettuce under hoops so as to be covered in winter. *Cut down* sea-kale leaves. *Lay down* turf. *Earth up* celery, *Divide* offsets of cives, garlick, shalots. *Put by* endive for winter use.——FRUIT-GARDEN. Transplant young trees and stocks of all kinds.——FLOWER-GARDEN. Very hardy flowers, such as larkspurs, may be sowed to stand the winter. *Plant* hyacinths, tulips, anemones, ranunculuses, &c. *Separate* layers of pink, carnation, &c. and put hyacinths, narcissuses, and jonquils in glasses.

November.

KITCHEN-GARDEN.—*Sow* leeks, early peas, and masagan beans. *Cover* asparagus beds with wood-ashes. *Take up* beets and carrots, and turnips, and put them away for winter use. *Plant* cabbage-stumps for seed, cauliflower-plants to come in in the spring, lettuces in hot-beds for winter use, rhubarb in rows after parting old beds, and dig between and manure this last.——— Fruit-garden. Sow the fruit-stones that have been kept till now in sand, cut down old stocks of raspberries, and dig about the roots. Sow hawthorn berries, and plash young hedges.

December.

Kitchen-garden.——*Sow*, cucumbers about the middle of the month, radishes in hot-beds; and *earth up* peas well. *Make* cucumber-beds.

CLASSIFICATION OF SHRUBS.

Flowering trees and shrubs of from twenty to forty feet high, and proper for the back part of shrubberies.—Catalpa, Cedar, Lime, Locust, Loblolly-bay, Oleaster, Pawpaw, Pistachio-tree, Service-tree, true and bastard, Snow-drop-tree, Tulip-tree.

Shrubs of from ten to twenty feet high; proper for the middle of shrubberies.—Cashiobury-thorn, Lilac, Magnolias, grandiflora, tripetella, acuminata, Ziziphus, Rose-acacia, Bladder-nut, Cypress-tree, Laburnam, several sorts; Dogwood, two sorts; Gordonia pubescens, Georgia bark, Guelder-rose.

Shrubs of from five to ten feet high; and proper for the outer rows of shrubberies; for lawns and parterres. — Indigo, the shrubby bastard; Jasmin, Kœbreuteria, Magnolia Glauca, Privet, Sea Buckthorn, Spindle-tree, St. John's Wort, the hairy; Arbutus, Sumac, Syringa, Tamarisk, Trefoil, shrubby; Laurel, Silver-leaved Almond, Double-flowering Almond, Carolina Allspice, Althea Frutex, Barberry, Bladder-senna, three sorts; Broom, white and yellow; Buckthorn, Box, Bird-cherry, Double-flowering Cherry, Fontanesia, Rhododendron, Oleander, the small-flowering; Laurestine, Roses, standard; Gum-cistus.

Shrubs of from one foot to five feet high; and proper for the edges of shrubberies; for small grass-plats, and to mix with herbaceous flowers in borders.—Alexandrian Laurel, Symphoricarpos, Mezereon, Rest Harrow, Jerusalem Sage, Scorpion Senna, Spiræa, several sorts; Widow Wail, Dwarf Almond, Fruitful Calycanthus, Marsh Andromeda, Silvery Anthyllis, Azaleas, white, red, and yellow; Candle-berry Myrtle, Dwarf American Cherry,

Shrubby Diotis, Fuchsia, Geranium, Roses, Kalmia, Large-flowering St. John's Wort.

Trailing and climbing shrubs, proper to hide walls, or other naked places. — Clematis, Caper bush, Honeysuckle, Flowering Bramble, Large flowering St. John's Wort, Ivy Irish and Common; Periwinkle, Jasmin, Passion-flower, Trumpet-flower.

Evergreen shrubs; proper to mix in the shrubbery, or to form winter pleasure-grounds. — Arbutus, Hare's-ear, Red Cedar, Laurel, common, Portugal, and Alexandrian; Oleander, Privet, Evergreen Thorn, Live Oak, Thuja, Rhododendron, Laurestine, Rose Chinese; Magnolia Grandiflora, Box, Cistus, Mezereon, St. John's Wort, Cypress.

Green-house shrubs.—Myrtle, Olive-tree, Orange-tree, Oleander, Large-flowering Pomegranate, Psorolea, Vervaine, Widow-wail, Geranium, Bread-tree, Camellia Japonica, Climbing Cobea.

CLASSIFICATION OF FLOWERS.

Tall-growing flowers; proper for the back part of flower-borders.—Convolvulus Major, Dahlia, Gaura, Golden-rod, Hollyhock, Honeysuckle, Hop, Mullein, Nasturtium, Palma Christi, Pea, Sun-flower.

Flowers of middling stature; proper for the middle of flower-borders, and to mix with low-growing shrubs.—Aconite, Asphodel, Campanula pyramidal; Carnation, Chrysanthemum, Chelone, Coreopsis, Columbine, Fritillary, Hellebore, Honesty, Iris, Lavatera, Leopard's Bane, Lily, Lobelia, Loose-strife, Lupine, Lychnis, Marvel of Peru, Marygold, Master-wort, Pea, Phlox, Poppy, Silphium, Soapwort, Sun-flower, Thistle, Valerian, Vernonia, Willow herb.

Flowers of from two inches to two feet high ; proper border-flowers.—Adonis, Amyrallis, yellow ; Anemone, Archangel, Aster, Auricula, Balsam, Barren-wort, Birth-wort, Bulbocadium, Caltrops, Campanula, Canterbury-bell, Campion, Candy-tuft, Catchfly, Centaury, Cineraria, Cistus, Colchicum, Hound's-tongue, Convolvulus Minor, Cowslip, Corn-flag, Crepis, Crocus, Cyclamen, Daffodil, Dragon's head, Daisy, Devil-in-a-bush, Fox-glove, Fraxinella, Fumatory, Germander, Globe-flower, Goldy locks, Hawkweed, Hellebore, Hyacinth, Hepatice, Larkspur, Lily of the Valley, Lobelia, Mad-wort, Marygold, Monarda, Narcissus, Nasturtium, Red Nettle, Œnothera, Onosma, Pansey, Petunia, Pink, Polyanthus, Pœony, Primrose, Ranunculus, Rocket, Ringflower, Rose Campion, Sand Wort, Saxifrage, Scabious, Snap-dragon, Solomon's seal, Soldanella, Spider Wort, Stock, Strawberry-blite, Thrift, Tiger-flower, Tulip, Vetch, Violet, Wall-flower, Wood-sorrel, Xeranthemum, Zinnia, Ziziphora.

Flowers that like moist or swampy situations ; proper for the edges of ponds or rivulets.—Avens, Marsh Trefoil, Flowering Rush.

Water-flowers.—Lily, white and yellow.

Green-house and Frame-flowers.—Amaryllis, Bear's Ear, Cacalia, Cactus, Coris, Cyclamen, Dolichos purpureus, Egg-plant, Indian Fig, Globularia, Ipomea, Ixia, Sida, Squill, Tuberose, Rose, Vervain.

INDEX.

INDEX.

B. BENSLEY, PRINTER, ANDOVER.

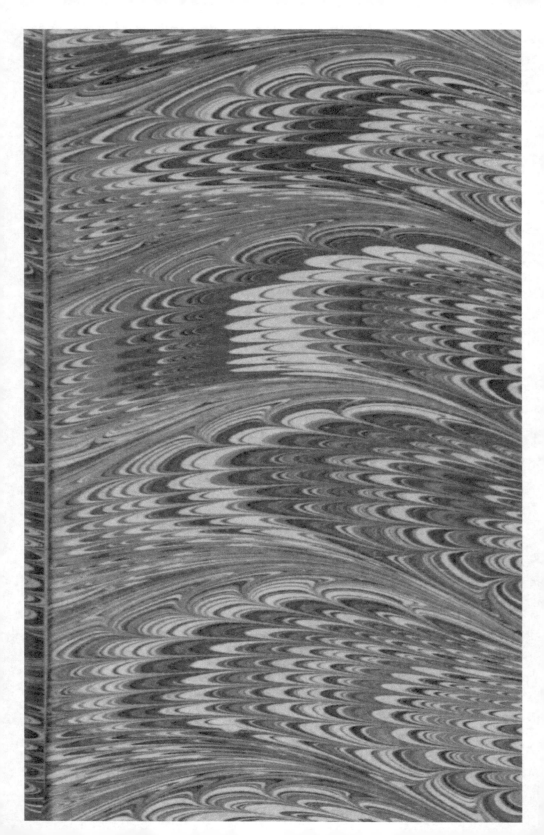

Check Out More Titles From HardPress Classics Series In this collection we are offering thousands of classic and hard to find books. This series spans a vast array of subjects — so you are bound to find something of interest to enjoy reading and learning about.

Subjects:
Architecture
Art
Biography & Autobiography
Body, Mind &Spirit
Children & Young Adult
Dramas
Education
Fiction
History
Language Arts & Disciplines
Law
Literary Collections
Music
Poetry
Psychology
Science
…and many more.

Visit us at www.hardpress.net

CPSIA information can be obtained
at www.ICGtesting.com
Printed in the USA
BVHW041445200819
556330BV00012B/639/P

9 780371 019467